CLARIFYING PUBLIC CONTROVERSY

An Approach to Teaching Social Studies

CLARIFYING PUBLIC CONTROVERSY

An Approach to Teaching Social Studies

FRED M. NEWMANN *University of Wisconsin*

with the assistance of DONALD W. OLIVER *Harvard University*

Little, Brown and Company *Boston*

PREFACE

Although this book is addressed most specifically to teachers of high school social studies, we trust it will be useful to other audiences concerned with the clarification of public controversy: citizens who wish to assert and defend their views on public issues; officials directly responsible for public decisions; high school and college students enrolled in courses on social problems; and scholars and teachers attempting to create and organize knowledge on the subject. There are obvious hazards in trying to accommodate such diverse audiences in one book. We hope that in the attempt to offer a resource for general use we have not sacrificed depth of analysis.

The functions of each chapter are described in the introductions to Parts I, II, and III. Because individual chapters do not build cumulatively upon each other into a comprehensive theoretical structure, the reader should feel free to begin at any point and to read eclectically without regard to chronological sequence. Those inexperienced in discussing public issues might begin with the cases and questions following Chapters 4 through 8, then turn to the content of those chapters, next to the analytic framework of Chapters 2 and 3, and finally to pedagogical issues raised in Chapters 1, 9, 10, and 11. Pre- and in-service teachers can extract the separate sections on rationale (Chapter 1), analytic framework (Part I), substantive issues (Part II), and implementation (Part III), depending upon their particular concerns. Those familiar with Donald W. Oliver and James Shaver, *Teaching Public Issues in the High Schools* (Boston, 1966) will find new material in Chapters 1, 3, 4 through 8, and 11. Teachers can use the book as a reference source for lesson and unit planning by finding in the index key concepts or problems and referring to the treatment of these in Chapters 4 through 8.

v

This text evolved out of association with the Harvard Social Studies Project which began in 1956 under the direction of Donald W. Oliver. The most recent phase of the project was co-sponsored by Harvard University and the Cooperative Research Branch of the United States Office of Education, from June, 1963 to June, 1968. During that period, in collaboration with Donald W. Oliver, several graduate students, and teachers at Newton High School in Newton, Massachusetts, I conceptualized, developed materials for, taught experimentally, and conducted research on a three-year curriculum focusing on the analysis of public controversy. The official report of this work appears in Malcolm Levin, Fred M. Newmann, and Donald W. Oliver, *A Law and Social Science Curriculum Based on the Analysis of Public Issues*, Report to U.S. Office of Education, Bureau of Research, 1969. From the multitude of cases and instructional materials developed for that project, many were selected, revised and re-organized in a format appropriate for widespread dissemination and use in secondary schools. The American Education Publications (AEP) *Public Issues Series* was born from this editorial effort. Although materials from the federally funded phase of the Harvard Social Studies Project have been exhausted, we are continuing to expand the *Public Issues Series*.

The purpose of the Harvard project has been not merely the creation of a curriculum or product. Perhaps more important has been the improved training of graduate students in social studies through intensive clinical experience in writing, teaching, and evaluating curriculum. The project has worked closely with talented teachers in Newton, Concord, and Arlington, Massachusetts; with graduate students at Harvard University; and with faculty members at other colleges and universities. Although it is impossible to mention all the students, teachers, and staff members who have assisted the project, we wish to acknowledge contributions of the following: Susanna Adams, Wayne Altree, David Archibald, Phyllis Bachelor, Mary Jo Bane, Harold Berlak, Arthur Blackman, Jules Cohn, Nancy Dellmuth, Allen Dobbins, Todd Endo, Saul Engelbourg, Peter Filene, Jerry Fletcher, Mal Gallagher, Alan Gartner, Len Godfrey, William Hollman, Harriet Kern, Malcolm Levin, Douglas Macey, Edward Martin, Susan Matthewman, Charles Miller, Fritz Mulhauser, Gordon Neisser, Sharlene Pearlman, Phil Schrag, Ernest V. Seasholes, Morton Seavey, James Shaver, David Swanger, and Saul Yanofsky.

Seven years of exciting interaction with such persons in the social studies shop at the Harvard Graduate School of Education generated many of the ideas in this book. Following completion of the project, a year and a half at the University of Wisconsin provided me with an opportunity to take inventory on insights gleaned from the graduate seminars, lesson planning for students at Newton, critiques of the lessons over coffee, endless debates on the nature of rational verbal behavior, and hours of listening to and analyzing students' taped discussions.

To Donald W. Oliver I owe nothing less than the inspiration to pursue problems of social theory, educational rationale, materials development, teaching strategies, and evaluation. He has established an intellectual framework (which we assume to be dispensable) capable of guiding the profession in these areas, and he is an inexhaustable source of creative ideas. His influence is especially apparent in Chapters 1, 2, 3, 9, and 10, much of which attempts to refine the original work by Oliver and Shaver. At many points in these chapters we quote, without explicit citation, material jointly authored in the AEP *Public Issues Series* booklets, *Taking a Stand* and *Cases and Controversy* (the teacher's guide). Chapter 11, which places the teaching of public issues in a broader context, is also based on a jointly authored article, "Education and Community" in *Harvard Educational Review*, 37 (1967), 61–106. In expressing appreciation for Donald Oliver's profound contributions to this book, however, I do not wish to implicate him in its shortcomings, all of which are my responsibility.

I wish to acknowledge the assistance of others who read and critiqued portions of the manuscript: Mr. David D. Marsh, Dr. John R. Palmer, Dr. Gary G. Wehlage, all of the University of Wisconsin, Madison; Dr. Alan Tom, Washington University, St. Louis; Dr. James P. Shaver, Utah State University; and my wife Joy who, showing no mercy for her husband's prose, offered continually fresh observations on matters of style and substance.

Fred M. Newmann

CONTENTS

ix

Chapter 1

Discussion of Public Issues as Citizenship Education

We intend in this book to describe an approach to the discussion of public issues and to provide an analytic framework and a series of substantive concepts useful for implementing the approach in the classroom, legislature, living room, or coffee house. We can illustrate at the outset what the approach aims to accomplish by considering the following "before" and "after" conversations of Joe and Clarence. We shall then attempt to justify the importance of helping people move from Discussion 1 to Discussion 2 as a central focus of citizenship education in the United States.

I. Clarifying One's Position in Discussion: An Illustration

Joe French lived with his wife and two children in the second-floor five-room flat of a two-family house in suburban Glendale, fifteen minutes by bus from the outskirts of a large city. On the first floor lived the landlord, Clarence Summerton, and his wife. Clarence had run a small independent grocery for several years, but now in his early sixties was about to retire. Joe, after living in the Summertons' house for three years, had just finished his studies at a nearby medical school and was about to move to a new area for his internship. Just this year he had become friendly with Larry Burson, a first-year medical student who wished to move out of the city. Joe suggested that Larry might be able to get his apartment. Accordingly when Larry and his wife came to visit, Joe introduced the couple to Mr. Summerton. After the Bursons left, Joe offered Clarence a second cup of coffee and the conversation began.

DISCUSSION 1[1]

Clarence: I don't have anything against them personally, Joe, but the folks in the neighborhood wouldn't stand for it.

Joe: You mean just because the Bursons are black you'd refuse them a place to live? You have no right to discriminate against a person just because of his race.

Clarence: I'm not discriminating against anyone. Just exercising my right to lease my property to tenants of my choice. I have to think of the property values in this neighborhood, and I wouldn't want to put the Negro family or folks in the neighborhood in danger.

Joe: How can blacks ever get an equal chance in this country if people like you keep refusing them housing?

Clarence: They *do* have an equal chance. Just like the Italians, Jews, the Irish — they've all made it without these riots, hate, and violence. Negroes have plenty of rights — education, voting, welfare, — but they don't have the right just to move in wherever they want and to burn down our cities.

Joe: They're only asking for basic human rights. That's what the American Revolution was all about — violence to get self-government and equality. Studies show that the white man discriminates against Negroes — in education, business, labor, housing, etc.

Clarence: Well, what kind of a sacrifice am I supposed to make just to help them? Suppose my friends turn against me, move out of the neighborhood, and it becomes all black. What will I have left? I don't see where I have any obligation to help the black man. What has he ever done for me?

Joe: I help lots of patients at the hospital even though they've never done anything for me.

Clarence: Well, that's different. Anyway I can't help the fact that my neighbors are so prejudiced — they can't either. It's the way they were brought up.

Joe: Clarence, although I'd hate to do it, if you deny housing to this couple, I may report you to the Equal Opportunities Commission.

Clarence: Don't get me wrong, Joe. It's not because of skin color. The main reason is the size of the family. They said they had three kids, and you did notice that Mrs. Burson was pregnant with a fourth. I don't think we could stand the noise. Mrs. Summerton and I are getting on in years, you know. Well, thanks for the coffee, I've got to go.

What purpose did this discussion serve or what did it accomplish? Some

[1] The book contains many discussions, mainly in Chapters 1–3, 9, and 10. Many are not exact quotations from actual conversations, but illustrations contrived by the authors. Language in real discussions, in or out of the classroom, would be messier, less efficient; the intellectual operations we note would be less apparent, less likely to occur in a short segment of dialogue. Thus, many dialogues may seem unrealistic or atypical. The constructed dialogues are, nevertheless, authentic in that they represent distillations of arguments and discussion strategies actually observed in several years of classroom and "real world" discourse on public controversy. To rely primarily upon direct quotes would require the reader to search through numerous pages for the concepts and dynamics of discourse that concern us. These can be presented more quickly and clearly through fictional examples in somewhat truncated, idealized form.

might consider it useful, because each participant learned the other's opinions. Although neither party was persuaded to change his mind, at least different kinds of reasons were given for each side, and perhaps it stimulated more careful thought. On the other hand, it might be criticized as a waste of time, because the discussants failed to resolve their disagreement and failed even to improve the reasoning behind their own positions. Among youth and adults we find a rather pervasive pessimism that cautions us not to expect much from discussions by folks like Joe and Clarence. This pessimism manifests itself in four common criticisms of discussion on public issues.

A. "People are stubborn and afraid to change their minds." Although it is true that people resist change, maintaining one's position on an issue does not necessarily prevent or inhibit a useful discussion. A discussion in which adversaries maintain their positions (e.g., being for or against a given medicare plan) but create more complicated and elaborate rationales for them would be beneficial. At the same time, it is important to assure discussants that changing one's mind is by no means a mark of inferiority. When confronted with a more reasonable position, one has an obligation to concede and should be respected for being sensitive to new evidence or valid arguments. We must try to teach that stubborn adherence to a position just for the sake of winning or saving face is irrational. We can and should reward people for conceding and qualifying their positions, instead of ridiculing them for losing or giving in.

B. "It's just a matter of opinion, so what's the use of talking. Issues in religion or politics have no 'right' answers, cannot be resolved through rational discussion." This assumption, strengthened by frustration in encounters with people of forceful opinion, leads to wide acceptance of the tolerant notion that each person is entitled to his opinion, that in a sense all opinions are equally valid. We strongly disagree. "Opinion" issues can be clarified and, at times, resolved through rational discourse. Moreover, reasonably objective standards for evaluating the rationality and validity of positions indicate that some opinions are "better" than others. A position or opinion that is supported by reliable evidence, that contains consistent claims, that takes into account a range of analogous situations, and that defines vague terms is more valid than a position that is unsupported by evidence, inconsistent, insensitive to analogies, and uses ambiguous language. (Some of these "standards" for rational opinions are developed in detail in Chapters 2, 3, and 9.)

C. "The average person doesn't have enough facts to discuss complicated public issues intelligently, and if he did have access to enough facts, the solution would be obvious so there would be nothing to discuss." Given the human impossibility of gathering all information relevant to many issues, we must also face the moral necessity to decide even with incomplete evidence. Discussion need not be a "pooling of ignorance." On the contrary, it is an important vehicle for communicating factual information, for deciding how incomplete our evidence is and what sort of information is urgently needed (see Chapter 9). Even assuming that it would be possible to settle factual disagreements through accumulating evidence, value dilemmas and definitional issues remain. Disagreements in these areas cannot usually be resolved simply by gathering information. What we consider to be valid evidence for factual claims is itself largely determined by our beliefs on nonfactual issues.

D. "Even if discussion helps you arrive at a better position, what's the point when the average person doesn't have the power to affect public policy anyway?" Undoubtedly, the layman seems powerless to determine his destiny in several senses (e.g., see Newmann, 1964), and we would agree that discussion unrelated to consequences in the world of action can become a sterile academic exercise (see Chapter 11). While the average person lacks the power to fundamentally change his society or the world, he does make personal choices relevant to larger controversies, choices that do have public consequences. To support or oppose a public candidate, to comply with or resist the draft, to become involved in reform or reaction in the ghetto or university, to engage in social discrimination, to agree or disagree with one's neighbor on the value of United States participation in foreign conflicts — such choices vary in the extent to which they redress individual grievances or generate social change. But they do have considerable personal impact, and they do arouse public concern and debate. These are sufficient grounds for trying to arrive at such choices through reasoned deliberation. Even the decision to withdraw and to remain apathetic on public issues involves questions of social responsibility and interpretations of the political-legal system that should be seriously discussed before one makes that choice.

Let us consider different settings involving discussion of public issues and ask more generally what tends to be accomplished through talk or dialogue. Imagine a class listening to a teacher lecture on race relations; an informal cocktail party where guests make small talk about the need for racial harmony; a smoke-filled committee room in which two politicians try to convince their colleagues to vote for an open-housing bill; a seminar or coffee-house roundtable in which each participant tries to develop a justifiable position on an open-housing law currently before the city council. Without imagining mutually exclusive types, we notice differences in the apparent objectives of such conversations. That is, what a person expects to "get out of a discussion" may vary as follows.

A. Transmitting Information or "Truth"   The class listening to a lecture (and/or the teacher delivering it) may be primarily concerned with transferring information from one source to another. This is really not a discussion, but one-way communication of messages. Messages might contain social science theory, data, historical interpretation, or religious sermons. Tellers and listeners are found not only in the formal school setting, but at social affairs, football games, television interviews, in the doctor's office, or in legislative halls. Generally the transmitter is considered (or considers himself to be) an authority qualified to deliver information to a less knowledgeable audience.

B. Social Opining or Unloading

Discussing public issues may also provide opportunities to unload one's feelings or get something off one's chest. In the backyard, on the bus, in the clubhouse, or at a leisurely social affair, the conversation can be light and friendly or profound and serious with mutual tolerance that allows each person to express strong opinions. However, the tension of ideological disagreement is deliberately avoided. People look for sympathetic listeners and an audience receptive to opinion giving, rather than rigorous intellectual probing or adversarial tactics. The implied purpose is more personal catharsis than communicating information or resolving conflict between parties.

C. Adversarial Combat and Persuasion

Some people develop a position before they begin conversation, and see the conversation as a device to persuade others to adopt the previously decided view. Courtroom discourse between legal adversaries, academic debates in which opponents try to score points, and arguments in business or politics or between friends when each side is trying to "win" are combative conversations where the primary objective is to persuade. Discussants desiring only to win are likely to stress only those points favorable to their position and to use a number of argumentative strategies (e.g., ad hominem attacks, loaded language, humor, sarcasm) irrelevant to the substance of the issue at hand. This is not to condemn all adversarial dialogue, for certainly the attempt to persuade someone of the merits of a position is valid and desirable. However, when discussions become so combative that discussants are unwilling to modify their views in response to valid argument, then irrational, irrelevant, and repetitive strategies may dominate the conversation.

D. Problem-Solving and Clarification

Instead of bringing preconceived solutions to discussion, participants may look upon discussion as a means of figuring out or developing their beliefs and justifications. It is assumed that mutual exploration with others will contribute to the sophistication of one's own position, and that even though at the end of discussion no definitive solution has been reached, the effort will have been productive if it brings increased complexity in justifying opposing positions. Such discussions reveal honest inquiry without regard to personality conflicts, the need to win, or to preserve status as an authority.

In contrast to social opining, clarification discussions do present direct challenges and pursue issues in depth.

The example of Joe and Clarence does not fit exclusively into any of these categories; it contains varying degrees of several, as is the case with most discussions on public issues. Yet it is often possible to describe a prevailing tone in terms of one category. Transmitting information, social opining, and persuasion serve important functions in daily life, and we do not wish to minimize their utility. This study, however, is devoted primarily to the need for more conversation oriented toward clarification.

Clarification may well arise from discussion that begins in a relaxed atmosphere of unloading feelings, evolves into high-pitched combat, and employs at certain points truth-giving techniques. But these discussion postures are likely to be productive only if participants consciously strive to develop positions that are more complete and complex (by including distinctions, qualifications, stipulations, concessions, summaries) than when the discussion began. Successful clarification discussions combine the tension of serious intellectual challenge with cooperative inquiry. One must be willing to examine the most unquestioned assumptions and to modify one's position in response to persuasive combat rather than accepting the more relaxed posture of tranquil interpersonal chat. One must also show restraint (or magnanimity), avoiding a more hostile posture that aims primarily at defeating an adversary. Given these objectives, the conversation between Joe and Clarence leaves much to be desired.

In addition to certain attitudes or predispositions toward the purpose and function of dialogue, productive discourse also requires applying specific concepts and strategies. Discussants are often unaware of complexities and ambiguities in the concepts and values they use to justify their views. A few of these concepts — equality, welfare, moral responsibility, and property rights — were referred to by Clarence and Joe. In asking whether a property owner has the "right" to discriminate on the basis of race, we might wish to explore the distinction between legal and moral rights. It might also help if we were to explain the difference between equality construed as same treatment for all, versus equitable treatment for all. If one assumes a moral obligation not to discriminate, what is the basis of such a duty and what kind of personal sacrifice can be demanded in its behalf? Shortcomings in the positions of Joe and Clarence are due largely to their failure to deal with such substantive problems in ethical reasoning, the subject of Chapters 4–8.

Discussions may also be unproductive because skills in discussion process are lacking. A person may not know how to use an analogy to examine a general value judgment; he may neglect to raise questions of relevance; he may be unfamiliar with various strategies for resolving definitional disputes; he may not know how to question the reliability of sources for factual evidence; he may be lax in stating explicitly the issue under dispute. These skills or strategies are necessary to move the discussion along. They could be called critical or reflective thinking strategies appropriate for conversational situations (as contrasted with library study or essay writing). Chapters 2 and 3 deal primarily with discussion process problems.

Were Joe and Clarence to incorporate such substantive and procedural insights, excerpts of their revised discussion might look like this:

DISCUSSION 2

> Clarence: I have nothing against Negroes, Joe, but it wouldn't be good for the welfare of the neighborhood. The folks wouldn't stand for it.
>
> Joe: "Welfare of the neighborhood"? What do you mean? Can you give any evidence of harm that is likely to occur just because you rent to the Bursons?
>
> Clarence: Well, perhaps I should concede that renting to the Bursons would not cause considerable harm to them or the neighborhood. However, I still maintain the right to select my own tenants as part of my legal and moral property rights. Do you think, for example, that a landlord should be compelled to invite Negroes to his private social affairs simply to give them "equal opportunity"?
>
> Joe: No. Although I believe in equality, I also believe in certain rights of property and privacy. I just think that equal opportunity to housing is a more important value than the property owner's right to exclude tenants on the basis of race. I agree with you, however, that your right to privacy and property is more important than giving everyone an equal opportunity to attend your parties.
>
> Clarence: I think in general Negroes do have equal opportunity, even if I refuse to rent to the Bursons. They can find housing elsewhere, they do get an education, have the right to vote, can get jobs, and even welfare checks. Many are prosperous and in positions of leadership. Your analogy to the American Revolution is wrong, because the patriots were clearly denied self-government and equality, but Negroes have these rights and have achieved them peacefully.
>
> Joe: We still haven't defined what we mean by equal opportunity or self-government. We need to arrive at some definitions and also examine more evidence, such as commission reports. I think, in a sense, the Negro's plight today is even worse than that of the patriots years ago.

Discussion continues to compare both situations. Different criteria are suggested for equal opportunity (e.g., guaranteed affluence, subsistence, the right to compete) and for self-government (e.g., right to vote; rights to control economic resources, weapons; minority-majority rule). The importance of relative expectations and the need for some standard measure to determine the extent to which such rights are available is also discussed.

Joe: Because we can't seem to reach agreement on these issues of equal opportunity and self-government, could we just assume or stipulate for a moment
that the Negro is denied these rights and then ask what should be our duties
or obligations to correct the situation? Is it true that you believe you may
help if you wish, but should not be expected to make any personal sacrifice?

Clarence: Yes, Joe. Life is pretty much a struggle where each person has to
watch out for himself. It's a competitive situation where if I start giving to
others, I could be left behind. Of course if someone did a good turn for me,
I would have a moral obligation to repay the favor. Yet the Bursons haven't
helped me, so I shouldn't have to make any sacrifice.

Discussion continues focusing on situations involving different kinds of moral
responsibility — doctor-patient, good samaritan-helpless victim, parent-
child, citizen-country. Distinction is made between moral *duty* versus the
"opportunity" to act benevolently. They agree that one has no obligation
to a person who voluntarily, deliberately causes his own misfortune, but
that victims of accidents or misfortune beyond their control deserve help.

Clarence: Well, we seem to agree that people should not have to suffer for
events beyond their control, but this doesn't solve the problem. The Negro
can't help being black, but neither can folks in the neighborhood help being
prejudiced. They were taught that way.

Joe: But the major issue is whether you should take a chance with your personal happiness to help the Bursons. We agreed earlier that this would not
cause considerable trouble in the neighborhood, so how could you refuse
them?

Clarence: Yes, but we also agreed, through the analogy of private parties, that
in some situations property rights are more important than equal opportunity.
Then we got involved in the factual and definitional problems of how much
equality and self-government Negroes actually have today, compared with
the patriots. We had trouble agreeing on that, so we assumed Negroes were
disadvantaged and went on to discuss moral obligations to make a sacrifice
to help others. Because the Bursons couldn't choose their skin color, I agree
that I should not deny them housing on that basis. But they do have control
over their family size. At our age it would be terribly disturbing to live
beneath four young children in that five-room apartment; the house is just
not adequate for both families. To deny them housing on this basis would
be a more legitimate use of my property rights. I wouldn't be denying them
equality or self-government that I agree they have a right to.

In the revised discussion Joe and Clarence explored substantive issues
dealing with interpretations of welfare; equal opportunity, property rights,
and self-government; and alternative bases for moral obligation. Discussion
skills included examining evidence relevant to the support of factual claims,
using analogy (private social parties and American Revolution) to test posi-

tions, conceding and modifying views, explicitly stating the issue at hand, and summarizing points of agreement and disagreement. Revealing an effort to use discussion as an aid in developing one's views, Clarence constructed his final opinion through a recapitulation of the conversation. Although his position may not be changed (i.e., he still opposed renting to the Bursons), the justification for his view became more defensible and considerably more complicated. (Whether it is the *most* defensible position can be debated at much greater length.)

The willingness to engage in oral dialogues as a method of clarifying one's committments and the ability to use certain intellectual strategies (e.g., as illustrated in Discussion 2) for challenging and justifying public policies are critical in our image or vision of the ideal citizen. The thrust of citizenship education should not be educators transmitting to students specific views of reality that educators have found to be correct, but rather supplying the student with an analytic scheme and diverse viewpoints that he may use to clarify conflicting commitments in ways that make sense to him and can be defended in public.[2] Before discussing specifics in the analytic framework and substantive problem areas, we will present a rationale for this proposed concept of citizenship education.

II. Rationale

Advocates of curriculum designed for use in a system of compulsory public education have a special obligation to justify their proposals. As long as our society continues to compel most people to spend at least twelve years of their lives in school, we must regard compulsory mass public education as a significant limitation on human freedom. This interpretation alone does

---

[2] In focusing primarily on the creation of an intellectual framework, we have not directed enough attention to the person unmotivated or unwilling to rationally examine his views. Our approach is useful primarily to those who already have some interest in dealing seriously with policy dilemmas. It provides little assistance in inspiring or engendering receptivity to rational clarification in those uninterested in or opposed to such inquiry. In emphasizing clarifying student views we do not intend to suggest that any position held by a student is automatically considered valid and that the teacher's task is merely to help the student state better reasons for it, expressed in comprehensible form. Quite the contrary. No position should be considered valid until it meets the test of rigorous rational inquiry. Developing a position that meets this test often involves the agonizing rejection (or modification) of opinions long cherished but rarely examined. Thus the objectives of clarification and justification do not entail reinforcing the status quo. Even though one's yea or nay stance on a given issue may not change, the evolution of his rationale from a single, fuzzy-minded reason to an elaborate argument that rebuts intelligent challenges signifies important change. This is not to say that we as individuals would endorse a fascist position that happened to be argued more systematically than a democratic one. We subscribe to libertarian values more fundamental than sophisticated rational argument. In Chapter 9 we consider the problem of whether (and when) a teacher should consciously attempt to persuade students to adopt specific positions consistent with values, other than rational discourse, held by the teacher.

In addition to developing views that can be justified on an intellectual level, the citizen must be able to act and implement or strive for fulfilling policies he supports. This latter concern for social action skills has heretofore not been the focus of our curriculum effort, but we affirm its importance, with suggestions for implementation, in Chapter 11.

not repudiate the notion of compulsory education, though in Chapter 11 we bring serious charges against the present system. Because of its restriction of freedom, all that becomes part of compulsory education must be justified rather carefully. The grounds for studying a subject when the state compels you to study it, or when a teacher employed by the state requires it, must be clarified. Providing a rationale for curriculum recommendations is, therefore, more than an intellectual ritual for the amusement of academics; it becomes a social duty owed to the citizenry at large.

Because of public support and public enforcement of our system of compulsory education, arguments on the legitimacy of the system or specific policies within it must take account of community interests that are presumably served (or violated). One's rationale for curriculum recommendations should, therefore, be grounded in an explicitly stated social theory (Shaver and Berlak, 1968, p. 63). This is not to require each proponent to create an original, comprehensive interpretation of society, but only clarification of the major assumptions one makes regarding social dynamics and how they relate to the educational needs of individuals in the community.

One way to uncover assumptions in one's social theory is to ask why Clarence and Joe had an argument, why disputes of this nature occur in America, and also why it is so difficult to arrive at some "true" and final solution that both adversaries would accept. Consider these hypothetical answers:

A. Their argument is a manifestation of racism in American society. The whites' feelings — superiority, guilt, and fear — about blacks have produced institutions that deny black people equal recognition as human beings. Because it is not acceptable to admit one's racism publicly, Clarence thought of a rationalization for discriminating against the black family. Controversies of this sort will continue until blacks gain independent political and economic power and until whites learn a method of resolving their own psychological insecurities that does not depend upon oppression of blacks.

B. Their argument is largely the result of a social-economic system in America that allows owners of private property to exploit others. Property has become the key to attainment of human rights, and capitalism distributes property unequally. To ensure high property values and profit, real estate interests limit housing — thus the Bursons' difficulty in finding a place to live. Until the capitalist institution of private property is fundamentally modified, there will always be conflict between those who have property and those who do not.

C. The argument reflects an inevitable problem in the life cycle of citizens in America. The system requires that individuals prepare themselves to be income-producing adults. Students do not receive income because they do not contribute to the economy; they are preparing themselves to do so later. Thus each person must struggle through a few years of hard times. After he earns his degree, however, Dr. Burson will be able to live comfortably on the income from his medical practice. More adequate housing and prosperity will be his reward for temporary struggle and sacrifice.

These short, oversimplified explanations illustrate the range of issues a comprehensive social theory could face: What leads people to hold certain feelings and attitudes toward others? How does the economic system work? Does everyone in the society have the opportunity to pull himself up by his bootstraps? Where does political power lie and how can it be acquired? What forces are responsible for maintaining the status quo and for changing certain institutions? Does the legal, economic, and political system discriminate against certain groups of people? Are some processes (e.g., urbanization, industrialization, automation) beyond human control? An apparently modest request for clarification on the social assumptions behind one's educational recommendations could lead to a multivolume treatise on the dynamics of society and the nature of man. In this book we address ourselves to just a few dimensions in an incomplete description of American society. We shall explain the nature of disagreement over public policy with reference to a model of value conflict,[3] and shall suggest tendencies in American society that threaten two values we hold most important — freedom of choice and rational consent.

A. American Creed: Source of Consensus and Conflict

We construe public controversies as manifestations of conflicts among several values ingrained in an American Creed (Myrdal, 1944). The creed is a set of values phrased in general, abstract language to which most Americans would proclaim allegiance and commitment, including:

> the worth and dignity of the individual
> equality
> inalienable rights to life, liberty, property, and pursuit of happiness
> consent of the governed
> majority rule
> rule of law
> due process of law
> community and national welfare
> rights to freedom of speech, press, religion, assembly, and private association

---

[3] A detailed rationale for our approach is provided by Oliver and Shaver (1966, Chapters 1–5). Here we shall summarize, rephrase, and slightly modify that interpretation of society and citizenship education.

Such values are fundamental to the American political system. They are continually reaffirmed in justifications of public policy, forming the nucleus of what may be considered America's constitutional morality. Other, less constitutionally oriented values include:

brotherhood
charity
mercy
nonviolence
perseverance, hard work
efficiency
competence and expertise
competition, rugged individualism
compromise
cooperation
honesty
loyalty
integrity of personal conscience

Mydral (1944, p. 4) describes the impact of such values in American life:

America is continuously struggling for its soul. These principles of social ethics have been hammered into easily remembered formulas. All means of intellectual communication are utilized to stamp them into everybody's mind. The schools teach them, the churches preach them. The courts pronounce their judicial decisions in their terms. They permeate editorials with a pattern of idealism so ingrained that the writers could scarcely free themselves from it even if they tried. They have fixed a custom of indulging in high sounding generalities so splendidly gifted for the matter of fact approach to things and problems. Even the stranger, when he has to appear before an American audience, feels this, if he is sensitive at all, and finds himself espousing the national Creed, as this is the only means by which a speaker can obtain human response from the people to whom he talks.

The emergence of such diverse values is attributed to such historical phenomena as the Judeo-Christian tradition, the Enlightenment, English law, Puritanism, the frontier, American capitalism.[4] Because of its complex

---

[4] We do not intend to suggest that most values in the Creed are actually enforced or followed consistently in America. The values are worshipped as ideals, and the "youth rebellion" may be explained in large measure as protest against the failure of previous generations to live up to their Creed. The actual behavior of many Americans might display a greater committment to such values as materialism, conformity, sensationalism, hedonism, aggression and violence, and hypocrisy. But these values are not usually accepted as justifications for actions. The Creed consists of only those values that are publicly praised as part of the moral, legal, and constitutional tradition. The extent to which the Creed values serve primarily as rhetoric, rather than as genuine guidelines for policy, is problematic.

origins, the Creed contains conflicting commitments that foreign observers have cited as paradoxes in American culture; for example, on one hand an emphasis on competition and rugged individualism, but on the other a profound concern for community cooperation and compromise; the belief in the sanctity of higher law, natural law, or personal conscience is used to justify violating duty to obey governmental law. Myrdal claims that the Creed is embedded in an intense American nationalism; a conception of America as a land of exceptional promise for the downtrodden and the persecuted; a notion that Americans (as a chosen people) have a special obligation to create an exemplar of democracy for the world; and the optimism that America's problems can be solved (progress and the perfectability of man). This unbounded faith in the American experience may mitigate the possibility of value conflicts within the Creed leading to serious social rupture.

It is customary and often persuasive for a person to justify his position by showing it to be consistent with a value in the Creed. Clarence, by stating his commitment to rights of private property, justified his refusal to rent to a black family. An opponent to that policy, however, can hold a contrary position, also consistent with the Creed, albeit a different value within the Creed: Joe, who is committed to equal opportunity, insists that Clarence has no right to deny housing to the Bursons. The discussion reveals that adversaries agree to both values in general, but this consensus breaks down when applied to a specific social choice. On the question of renting to blacks, Clarence values private property rights over equality, whereas Joe's priorities are reversed. As another illustration, Jack and Marion have been discussing whether a religious minority like the Amish should be exempt from compulsory school attendance and social security laws.

> Jack: In this country we believe in majority rule and the majority of the people in Pennsylvania think the Amish should go to public school. Therefore, they should not be excused.
> Marion: No, they *should* be excused. The Amish are a religious minority and our country was founded on a belief in preserving the rights of religious minorities, even though the majority have different views.

Once discussants have identified the Creed values that seem to be in conflict, they can move on to consider whether one value should be given higher priority in the situation at hand.

Our discussion in this section focuses primarily upon value conflict as a basis for public controversy. But disputes on public policy do not result simply from conflicting value choices (see Chapter 2). Disputes over definitions and factual claims are equally significant in fomenting and prolonging controversy. Both the hawk and the dove can affirm primary devotion to national security for the United States (i.e., agree on the basic value), yet in discussing Vietnam, can disagree on factual predictions concerning the consequences of alternative policies for implementing the agreed-upon value. We emphasize value conflict not because it is the only stimulus or reason for controversy, but because when public policy must be defended as good or bad, proper or improper — when a position must be justified with reference to some ethical framework — then (even when factual or definitional issues are resolved) conflicting values often remain continuing sources of disagreement.

In weighing the priorities of different values in the Creed, one inquires whether it is possible to construct a hierarchy of the diverse values. If we could show that some values are more fundamental than others, this could guide us in choosing among those in conflict. It can be argued, for example, that equality should be considered the basic value from which many others (e.g., impartiality or due process of law) can be derived. One could view majority rule as requisite to a more fundamental value: consent of the governed. Although we assert the fundamental value of human dignity, we have been unable to organize the diverse values into any logical hierarchy or scheme that clearly facilitates making and justifying choices among apparently conflicting values. Perhaps someone in the future will arrive at a conceptualization of human affairs that leads to a universally accepted method for choosing among conflicting priorities or that demonstrates the apparent value conflicts to be illusory. This would reduce or even eliminate social controversy rooted in conflicting value commitments. Until that time, however, we can construe the argument between Joe and Clarence as one manifestation of ambiguity and conflict within ideals to which Americans are generally committed.

Objections have been raised to basing this conception of public controversy on the value system of one society at a given point in time. It is argued that the American Creed presents too narrow a range of choices, and that teaching the Creed values is brainwashing if it excludes other value frameworks such as revolutionary Marxism or some form of existentialism. We believe that the Creed contains values sufficiently diverse to embrace ideals of many cultures and to be responsive to changing times. But not all values in the Creed have always been supported by all people with equal enthusiasm. In the history of race relations, property rights have long prevailed over equal opportunity. Capitalist emphasis on private profit and free enterprise has clearly dominated socialist yearning for more equal distribution of wealth. Yet equality is part of the Creed, regardless of what has happened in practice, and a socialist could reasonably defend a proposal for equal distribution of wealth or even a classless society as consistent with values in the American heritage. Similarly, a fascist emphasis on national security and unity, a black militant's claim to political-economic power, a radical's plans for revolution to establish participatory democracy, a South Sea islander's emphasis on tranquility, an African's loyalty to tribe, a Buddhist's desire for contemplation, a hippie's concern for personal freedom and love — each diverse orientation can find values within the American tradition to support its position.

In examining events and social organization at any point in time, some values take precedence over others. Witness the resources devoted by the United States to waging war versus ending poverty in the 1960's. One is thereby tempted to conclude that the subordinate values (e.g., equal economic opportunity) are not really part of the American value system. Values dormant at a given point in time, however, may later emerge as dominant. Witness the long struggle to establish separation of church and state, or the apparent waning concern among youth for the Protestant work ethic and increased emphasis on fulfillment in interpersonal, rather than material, terms. To acknowledge considerable diversity in American values, however, is not to suggest that any human choice can be justified simply by finding the appropriate verse in an all-encompassing American Creed. Quite the contrary. Some choices and values clearly violate the Creed: for example, a person who sees no need to justify the use of violence, or one who sees no harm in punishing the innocent. In Chapters 2 and 9 we discuss dealing with persons who hold value frameworks incompatible with the Creed. In the conclusion to Part II we comment on how social and environmental changes will require us to rethink and possibly redefine major values in the Creed itself.

B. Individual Human Dignity

Although Creed values cannot be ordered into a coherent hierarchy, some values are considered more fundamental than others. Such Creed values as national security, separation of powers, property rights, or due process of law should be supported, not because they possess intrinsic goodness unto themselves, but because their implementation can relate to the fulfillment of a more basic value: *individual human dignity.* As Oliver and Shaver (1966) point out, values in the Creed help both to define human dignity and to suggest means for achieving it. This value emphasizes the intrinsic worth of each person because he is a person (see Harris, 1966). A sense of individual worth might be defined as a composite of several criteria: the ability to make choices that affect one's life (e.g., in career, religion, politics, or family relations); guarantees of physical protection of life and property; equal treatment under the law; ability to defend oneself against prosecution by the state; and others. Such defining characteristics also can be translated into public policies instrumental to achieving individual human dignity. Arguments over the priorities of equal opportunity versus property rights, for example, can be construed as debates over conditions most crucial to attaining human dignity.

As Oliver and Shaver (1966) argue, individual human dignity must be accepted *on faith* as a root value. To attempt a rational justification of the goodness, rightness, or sanctity of this ideal will result either in an infinite regress, circular argument or both. One could claim that a society that practices high regard for all individuals *as persons* will avoid civil strife or revolutions, so that peace is more likely in societies that value human dignity. Yet, one can ask, why should peace be valued? Because it allows more individuals to develop their innermost potential. The argument justifies the original value with an aspect or defining characteristic of the value itself. Instead of justifying human dignity in this rather utilitarian form, by suggesting that adherence to such a value results in desirable consequences, one could try to justify it through appeal to tradition or authority: "Individual human dignity is good, because it has been continuously taught by major religious, philosophical, ethical, and legal authorities." One can challenge this by pointing to a long historical tradition in which human dignity seems continuously denied by authorities and institutions. Why should we accept the views of some authorities rather than others? Because some are divinely inspired? Why should divine wisdom be preferred to nondivine? The persistent demand for reasons to support value judgments leads ultimately either to an infinite (unending) series of "why's" or a proposition for which no further reasons can be furnished (that is, an act of faith — in this case perhaps in God, natural law, or the inherent worth of human beings).

Human dignity is a vague ideal that continually begs for clarity in specific controversies. Human dignity might reasonably be defined by two, among several, facets: the right of each person to pursue a business or career of his choice, and the right of each person to have a voice in determining public policy. To maximize the latter (i.e., allow the greatest number of people to have a say), the procedure of majority rule is adopted. Suppose, however, that a majority in a small community decides to revoke the license of the town's only liquor store. The ensuing controversy between the owner and the majority of town meeting members could be construed as a decision on whether the owner's right to free enterprise is more or less crucial, as a defining criterion of human dignity, than the right of majority consent. Although the vagueness of individual human dignity presents troublesome definitional problems, we see the consequences of such ambiguity on balance to be more useful than harmful, both for teaching purposes in the classroom and for conflict resolution in the society at large. Our observations on pluralism in American society will help to explain this position.

1. Pluralism and Freedom of Choice

We assume that although it may never be made explicit, each person harbors some vision of fulfillment, some vague definition of human dignity for himself. Alternative visions or definitions can be induced from different life styles, careers, and commitments, and we could speculate on the nature of these definitions for a career soldier, a ghetto dweller affirming his African identity, a personnel director in a large corporation, a priest who has left the church, a study group leader in the League of Women Voters, a hippie artist in an experimental community, a forest ranger, a bartender, a physicist, or a community organizer. For individuals to pursue diverse and unique interests, the society must allocate public resources among a wide range of human activity, and the government must guarantee group or personal autonomy, secure from intrusions by those who wish to impose their conceptions on others. For a person or group to gain public, legitimate recognition of his definition of dignity, he must translate his purposes into language consistent with Creed values. Thus, the career soldier pleads for attention to national security, the black separatist equal opportunity and cultural autonomy, the forest ranger conservation of resources, the bartender free enterprise, the priest brotherhood and social conscience, the community organizer participatory democracy. Conflicts between North and South, city dweller and farmer (or suburbanite), hippies and squares, or hawks and doves reflect diverse views and life styles, a pluralism of conceptions of human dignity.

Because the plurality of approaches to human dignity signifies a confusion and a lack of precision, some would claim that the value offers no help in explaining public controversy in America. Yet we see considerable merit in this sort of "confusion." We believe that a critical (but not sufficient) aspect of human dignity is the freedom of the individual to choose among alternative conceptions of dignity itself. For this reason preserving and encouraging diverse alternatives is a requisite for human fulfillment. To define human dignity with precision would be to dismiss alternative conceptions which, according to our assumption, would deprive it of the critical freedom to struggle among conflicting interpretations of the concept itself. Whatever else dignity may be, it must certainly embrace the high degree of ambiguity required to allow freedom of choice among diverse alternatives.

To choose among diverse conceptions of human dignity requires the existence or availability of genuine options — alternative occupations, ideologies, political-economic systems, and life styles — as well as opportunities for individuals to examine, experience, and judge the alternatives. We believe, however, that significant individual choice is highly limited in America, and we have a dim prognosis for the future of pluralism. Although we cannot provide a thorough treatment of this problem here, we can suggest how an increasingly interdependent mass society inhibits the pursuit of options that diverge from the norm.

Although technology and bureaucratic forms of organization have freed us from physical toil for subsistence, our affluence itself reflects the standardization and homogeneity necessary for efficient assembly-line production and mass marketing. Throughout the country, autos, schools, hotels, offices, homes, even the tents we camp in, look the same. The proliferation of standard size lots in the suburban sprawl (and even for cottages at the lake), the synchronized roar of lawn mowers on Saturday morning, charcoal broiling of hamburgers on the patio, and departures to and from work represent a uniform, predictable social routine. Ideally the media could be a powerful source in communicating alternative, diverse patterns of work, methods of social organization, and conceptions of the good life. Even though the mass media includes presumably competing networks, newspapers, and magazines, their dependence on mass merchandising, along with economic incentives to form conglomerates, results in programming based on the lowest common denominator rather than attempts to reach unique audiences or create new ones. The presentation of news, entertainment, and advertising does little to inform us of those few divergent options that do exist, much less to inspire a reevaluation of the status quo.

Despite our pride in "local control" of education, all Americans are in effect required to attend school from age 6 to 16, and those who want decent jobs must take additional years in college. Curriculum and the style of teaching-learning are relatively uniform across the land. Although individual differences in the *pace* of learning may be respected in some instances, content is virtually identical (see Chapter 11 for additional comments on how schooling stifles diversity).

There is wide diversity in careers and occupations, but the style or ethos of work within the prevailing bureaucratic structure is the same, regardless of specialty or field: desk sitting, paper pushing, conference holding, the 9 to 5 day, pleasing supervisors, and the influence of past records and formal credentials on one's sense of self-worth. There is little opportunity to experiment with more than one "career" during a lifetime. Erikson (1968) speaks of the developmental importance of a psychosocial moratorium during which a person should have opportunity to try on various styles, roles, and commitments without having to make a life-long, irrevocable choice in any one direction. Pluralism may exist in the world of work, but our system of work and our conception of the life cycle does not encourage us to partake of whatever options might exist.

The position that diverse life styles (and conceptions of dignity) are requisite to freedom of choice must be qualified, because certain life styles and social conditions are detrimental to expanded choice. Farmers may aesthetically prefer life on the land, but they do not wish poverty upon themselves as a distinctive cultural trait of rural life. Although blacks may wish to create institutions separate and different from white middle-class America, they may not wish to perpetuate as part of their family style an unemployed, absent father. On the other hand the mobile junior-executive organization man, the artist, the Unitarian, and the student revolutionary may consciously value much in their distinctive styles. Human conditions that arise from exploitation, cruelty, and economic deprivation must be distinguished from those that can be more clearly attributed to voluntary free choice. The diversity that results from the former is not to be encouraged. We realize the difficulty in distinguishing among "healthy" and "unhealthy" sources of human diversity. Should we support slavery or economic depression because they produce unique art or styles of life?

Green's (1966, 1969) examination of pluralism recognizes an important problem in the value itself. Pluralism assumes the right of different groups (e.g., a religious sect, an Afro-American center, a sportsman's club) to exist, protected from intrusion or domination by outsiders considered to have alien values. But if such pluralism is to invigorate the larger society by expanding alternative paths to dignity, group members and outsiders must have enough contact to become aware of each others' options. Yet the infusion and mingling between group members and outsiders brings the very real danger of destroying the distinctive nature of the group itself. There is a fine line between allowing enough contact so that each segment can be aware of, and possibly adopt, the other's approach, but also allowing each group to protect itself against infiltration and assimilation that would erase the distinctiveness of its particular vision of human fulfillment.

Cognizant of considerable social (and some theoretical) obstacles to implementing pluralism and free choice, we can consider another possible benefit of ambiguity in the underlying value of human dignity. In a sense its vagueness serves a unifying function conducive to societal cohesion. When pluralism in the society develops into public conflict, the citizen is often forced to choose one Creed value as more important than another (states rights versus freedom and equality in the slavery issue; national security versus protection of the innocent in the McCarthy era; worker security versus free enterprise during the rise of organized labor; property versus human life in riots). If groups in society are continually at each others' throats over priorities given to separate Creed values, what is to bind the larger community together so that conflicts can be managed in such a way as to preserve pluralism? Myrdal (1944) finds in American nationalism a source of societal cohesion. Because nationalism can turn into destructive chauvinism, we seek additional grounds for consensus. Human dignity, because of its generality and vagueness, can serve as a root or basic value to which all can claim allegiance. Accepting that it may be defined in various ways creates a definitional problem for all to share. Though people may differ in their formulas, there is some degree of security or sense of community in knowing that most people share an emotional commitment to the "general idea." Such ambiguous platitudes seem to serve the important social function of creating enough psychic bonds among adversaries so they are willing to try to resolve their conflicts without destroying the society around them.

2. Rational Consent

Loyalty to the vague ideal of human dignity is not sufficient to prevent conflicting interests from destroying each other. In addition, we believe men must develop a process for arriving at collective decisions, a process that affirms the right of each person to have voice in the public decisions that affect him and favors a method of reasoned discussion and free exchange of views through which each person decides what his position will be. We combine these ideas in the value *rational consent,* which we consider equal in significance to freedom of choice (pluralism) as a requisite to individual human dignity.

Exerting some control over one's destiny is another way of acknowledging the importance of freedom of choice. (A wide range of issues relevant to this value are discussed in Chapter 7.) The ideal of consent of the governed has been interpreted to stand for three general levels of citizen involvement in forming public policy: consent to specific policy decisions (e.g., as in town meetings or referenda on fluoridation or bond issues); consent to delegate decision-making power to elected representatives and their appointees (e.g., as in elections to legislative and executive offices along with rights of impeachment and recall); consent to procedures or institutions that define the consent process itself (e.g., constitutional conventions that establish separate branches of government, define nature of governmental power, criteria for selection of public officials, etc.). The consent ideal usually implies that decisions at all three levels will be made through some form of majority rule and that the losing minority consents to abide by majority decisions. The moral right of minorities to resist the decision of a majority is granted in certain cases: for example, if the majority denies certain unalienable rights like "life, liberty, or the pursuit of happiness" without due process of law. Denial of certain rights is construed as violating the consent process itself, which thereby cancels the consent contract and the obligation of the minority to acquiesce. Individuals who feel they have never consented to be governed according to a given system will also assert the moral right to resist policies of the ruling body.

The following circumstances lead us to believe that opportunities for meaningful consent in America are diminishing at all three levels (Newmann, 1963).

1. Increasing complexity and interdependence of the outcomes of social decisions make it almost impossible for the average citizen to have sufficient knowledge to take defensible positions on major issues. Whether the United States should build an ABM defense system, which drugs or foods should be banned from public consumption, can a better education be provided by decentralized school administration, is a guaranteed income the most efficient solution to poverty — these are problems on which experts and professionals spend years of full-time study. Unable to investigate such issues independently, the layman must rely on experts, yet because of the technical, specialized nature of the experts' decisions, the citizen has trouble understanding justifications of experts who disagree. To deal with some issues, such as crime, poverty, or disarmament, one must have knowledge, not only on scientific matters, but on how different policies affect an increasingly complex network of economic, political, and social institutions. With so many sources of input into a given decision it seems impossible for one man to comprehend the entire process and tremendously difficult to assess the consequences of one's actions on the system at large. The citizen (or public official) who takes a stand is confronted by interlocking, overlapping departments and jurisdictions, a maze of agencies in which it is difficult or impossible to locate any person with the power to act responsibly.

2. Vast bureaucracies, in both the public and private sector, often are unresponsive to constituencies they serve. Hierarchical organizations in which decisions flow from top to bottom deny consumers of the goods and services effective control over the bureaucracies. These organizations are as diverse as the Department of Health, Education and Welfare; Internal Revenue Service; large automotive manufacturing corporations; major television networks and other news media; drug companies; urban school systems; private hospitals; and labor unions. This is not to suggest that those who make decisions in such organizations are part of a conspiracy by a power elite, nor that individual bureaucrats intentionally deny the citizen his rights. Rather, the nature of corporate bureaucracy, and its operation in our current political-legal-economic system, has few guarantees that citizens' interests will be served.

3. There are considerable inequalities in the abilities of different groups to influence public policy. Those who control the media are able to shape public opinion. Wealthy industrialists can afford to hire full-time lobbyists to pursue special interests in legislatures. Companies who hire retired military personnel can attract lucrative defense contracts. The well-educated and

affluent can exert more efficient influence than the poor and uneducated. The poor, women, consumers, children, and disadvantaged minorities, because of lack of education, economic resources, or legal rights, are less able to participate in the consent process.

4. Emphasis on public and private long-range planning allows decision-makers in one generation to close off options for their successors in the next. The next generation may find its air and water irreversibly polluted, its green land converted to pavement, its economy committed to war rather than peace. We may be losing the ability to affect our immediate environment during our own lifetime, though perhaps gaining increasing power to determine the lives of future generations.

Counterarguments to this dismal picture are familiar. We still have a representative system in which people choose their leaders periodically in free elections. To keep their jobs the elected representatives must heed the will of the people. At the very least, this consent to delegate decision-making power continues to operate in America. Important decisions made outside of the public arena — e.g., the decision by a television network to produce a given show, or by an auto manufacturer to produce a given model — come under consumer power through the free market mechanism in which the consumer's dollar is his vote. Large corporations and government bureaucracies, therefore, must give the public what they want. Finally, successful grass roots protests by citizens have forced action in their interest: civil rights demonstrations resulting in progressive legislation; repudiating the Johnson administration on Vietnam; Ralph Nader's crusade against the auto industry; increasing student participation in university policies. Those who choose to become involved *can* have some influence.

By way of rebuttal, we should bear in mind at least these points. The very representatives to whom power is delegated face considerable obstacles in determining public policy. Each representative to Congress must somehow speak for over four hundred thousand citizens. Simply identifying what his constituency believes is enough of a problem, much less the next step of implementing it (should he wish to). Congressmen have commented on their own powerlessness to affect national policy, their inability to gather enough reliable information to make a reasonable judgment, their impotency in the face of established interests — whether it be the Defense Department, a wealthy campaign contributor, or a powerful lobby. Secondly, citizen control over the private sector through participation in a free market economy has been persuasively attacked by those who argue how the market economy has been replaced by a planned economy (e.g., Lichtman, 1966, or Galbraith, 1967). Control is said to rest neither with stockholders nor consumers, but with a "technostructure," the managerial strata, or the few wealthy stockholders who own substantial portions of stock. The ability of the corporations, through advertising, to shape public demand also casts some doubt on the degree of "consent" assumed to be a logical consequence of a free market economy. Finally, how successful have visible grass roots efforts at reform been in the struggle for peace, civil rights, or consumer protection? Even if we grant that the more dramatic protest efforts have achieved considerable success, how many martyrs must die and how much human energy must be expended to prove that the consent process "works," if only one tries hard enough? The fact that certain atrocities *eventually* diminish or end is not persuasive evidence that citizens can control their lives or that the consent process is working.

What sort of consent do we seek as an alternative to the present state of affairs? First, we do not advocate the extreme of direct democracy in which all citizens debate and vote on all public decisions; considerable power must necessarily remain delegated to the peoples' representatives. Second, we are not claiming that a group that has pressed its case and lost has, because of the loss, necessarily been denied full participation in the consent process. Recurring losses by some groups on some issues, however, do constitute denial of consent rights: for example, Negroes being intimidated and prevented from registering to vote or being denied membership in a major political party. We do see the need for public policies that will provide more equal opportunity for all groups to participate in present channels of consent and that also create new channels and legal rights to increase popular control in areas where it has not yet been established.

Because of limited education, lack of free time, lack of economic resources, and intimidation, many people are unable to participate in existing channels of political expression. Laws that deny the right to vote or hold public office because of age, residency, criminal record, or history of mental illness should be reexamined. Methods of equalizing economic and educational resources should be developed so that a wider variety of interests can exert persuasive influence on centers of power (e.g., the military-industrial complex). Public laws providing for released time from the job for involvement in community affairs, tax incentives for community newspapers, subsidies to the poor, and limits on political contributions of the rich should be considered. Increasing leisure time for some segments of the population may allow greater levels of citizen participation than in the past (many youths, less concerned with economic security than their parents, find time to become politically involved).

Even those who pursue normal channels in the system are easily discouraged because of vast forces and decisions apparently beyond their control. Demands for citizen review boards of police departments, community control of schools, student participation in governing universities, local community control of urban renewal and highway projects, welfare mothers' organizations, and tenants' unions are manifestations of the desire to bring decisions made by large or distant powers under the control of those significantly affected. We need to examine various areas of public life and ask whether institutions based on new constituencies with new legal powers should be developed. We have no solutions at this point, only the belief that human dignity cannot be preserved unless consent of the governed becomes more meaningful in many areas. After further study one might conclude that the social system itself is out of control, beyond the influence of even a power elite. If this is true, then the consent ideal, along with human dignity, would have to be abandoned, but we see no need for such despair at this point.

One aspect of rational consent is the citizen's ability to influence policies that affect him. The "rational" aspect of this value emphasizes reasoned discussion as a way of developing one's personal positions on public issues and of resolving issues among disputing parties. One might distinguish between the citizen in his living room trying to decide whether the nation should adopt a guaranteed minimum income versus a Congressional committee trying to decide whether to recommend its passage. Both the conflict of ideas in a person's mind and the conflict that erupts between persons of differing views should be handled through rational discussion rather than brute force, random choice, or subtle forms of coercion — e.g., blackmail, or thought control. (In Chapters 2 and 3 we shall define in detail what we mean by rational positions and discussions.) A rational position takes account of its factual consequences, supports its factual claims with reliable evidence, contains logically consistent propositions, offers useful definitions of key terms, states qualifications of value judgments so as not to risk unsupportable implications, and rebuts counterarguments. Rational discussion allows consideration of diverse viewpoints, regardless of their source. It encourages mutual inquiry into problem-solving rather than trickery, combat, or deceit to win a point. It values development of unique personal positions rather than dogmatic consensus to a party line.

We need to clarify our commitment both to rationality and to the importance of discussion in developing rational positions. These commitments are not based on the belief that rational discourse will solve public controversy by ending it. Hawks and doves, militants and Uncle Toms, liberals and conservatives all can develop rational justifications of their views and continue to oppose each other. Supreme Court Justices, paradigms of our concern for rational discourse, write conflicting opinions. If rational discourse offers no guarantees of conflict resolution, no insurance that through sifting and winnowing we shall reach consensus, what is its value? The canons by which one identifies one opinion as more rational than another establish a universal language of proof or justification, without which it would be impossible for men to discuss and debate the good and the just, impossible to have confidence in their moral judgments or explanations of the world. In addition, rules of rationality provide some assurance that a variety of views can be examined, which is, of course, crucial to our conception of choice and human dignity.

To plead for rational discourse in handling disputes is not necessarily to rule out the use of violence. We can and must have discussions on whether violence or force is a justifiable means for protecting certain human rights and institutions. Rational arguments for using violence can be made: for example, in cases of personal self-defense against unjustified aggression, or to protect a citadel of rational discourse (university or legislature) from those attempting to destroy it. Because violence tends to eliminate rational discourse, there is a prima facie duty to avoid violence as a means of settling disputes. To identify those situations in which a rational man can justify using violence (that is, denying rational discourse as a problem-solving method) is itself a dilemma that should be analyzed through rational discussion.

Our emphasis on rationality has come under attack through the claim that it ignores irrational or nonrational bases of human behavior. It can be argued that positions on public issues, even the learned opinions of court justices, are merely rationalizations for irrational value commitments, or contrived reasons to support vested economic and political interest. One can posit various instincts, such as aggression, sex, thirst for power, and the need to be loved, and claim that such unconscious drives determine opinions, that rational proof and argument are simply devices to make inner needs more socially respectable. We fully acknowledge the significance of this general view. To be rational, however, is not to neglect this interpretation of human nature, but, on the contrary, to deal with it. This means at least searching for hidden reasons behind our views. It involves holding a critical attitude toward argument, a suspicion that motives and feelings unrevealed in the public intellectual defense of one's position may lie at its base. The limits of rationality are discussed at greater length in Chapter 3.

Given our position on the importance of rationality, one may still question our concern for oral discussion as a means for developing rational positions. Instead of viewing the citizen in an informal discussion, one could propose a concept of reflective inquiry or critical thinking in the solitude of a study or library, a personal mental dialogue with books or newspapers, as opposed to oral dialogue with peers and adversaries. It can be argued that oral discussion among peers can divert people from studying basic substantive issues into irrelevancies, exchange of mutual ignorance, and attempts to preserve interpersonal harmony or win personal duels, In contrast, reflective library research allows one to search objectively for truth with the help of authors who have given considerable study to public problems. Thus, it is argued, we should teach people how to read critically, how to write logical briefs on issues, not necessarily how to talk with their peers.

Our emphasis on discussion skills is not intended to minimize the value of solitary study and reflective examination of printed material. On the contrary, such skills are vital for productive discussions. One can improve discussion by referring to relevant literature, and once the findings or positions of authors have been introduced, discussants can evaluate them. Two general reasons support our belief that isolated book study on public issues must be supplemented by oral dialogue. First, it is difficult to develop a sophisticated position in the absence of challenges to one's views. The layman has no real opportunity to test his views on the authors he reads. He can imagine challenges and arguments, but these fantasies are often a poor substitute for the points that live adversaries can raise. Oral dialogue and debate give immediate stimuli to test the particulars of a person's position; "canned" messages like newspapers or books cannot produce challenges to meet spontaneous, idiosyncratic concerns of their readers. Though the risks of human interaction are clear, it can, when disciplined, contribute greatly to the sharpening of personal positions. Second, effective participation in the consent process requires oral skills. To put one's views into effect, he must learn to persuade others, not only in print, but in face-to-face situations. In political canvassing, in meetings of voluntary associations, legislative halls, bull sessions, on the coffee break, or at cocktail parties, and whether one happens to be actively working for some public cause or not, discussion on public issues are an inevitable part of our lives. When compared with the influence of media passively absorbed (e.g., television, books, newspapers), our experience in face-to-face interpersonal conversation (in home, office, school, or bar) has profound influence on our views of people and the issues as well. On these grounds it seems reasonable to stress the importance of developing skills to make oral discussion of public issues more productive.

C. Problems in Value Education.

To further clarify our approach to citizenship education, we can respond to familiar objections, most of which relate to controversies on the place of values in education. We propose teaching both a method to analyze positions on value issues and techniques that encourage students to take a stand on controversial, value-laden problems. A value, defined in more detail in Chapter 2, is a claim or belief that something (an act, an object, an event, a policy, a person) is good, right, should, or ought to be — or the negative opposites of such judgments. Objections to dealing with value issues as a central focus of public schooling fall into two broad categories:

competence — those that question our intellectual or academic ability to resolve value issues; and indoctrination — those that suggest that, even if we had competence, it should not be the function of the school (i.e., the state) to shape young minds on these matters.

1. Competence Problem

Many high school teachers, college students, history and social science professors, and parents have suggested that value judgments, because they are matters of "opinion" rather than "fact," cannot be proved or supported with much certainty. We can say with confidence that Lincoln was the sixteenth President of the United States, or that Japan attacked the United States on December 7, 1941, but we are not nearly so certain that the North was justified in forcing the South to remain in the Union or whether the United States was justified in dropping the atomic bomb on Japan. Because we have not developed sophisticated intellectual disciplines for resolving value-opinion problems, we are not really competent to teach about such issues. Instead we should confine inquiry to those matters on which scholars have developed respected bodies of knowledge. Learning the findings (or methods of inquiry) of established disciplines such as history, economics, sociology, psychology, or anthropology would be a more responsible objective of curriculum than to speculate on controversial, unsolved questions of value and opinion.

Although value judgments on public issues cannot usually be answered with the certainty represented in the Abraham Lincoln and Pearl Harbor statements, it is not true that questions studied by historians, psychologists, or economists are easier to resolve than problems studied by moral philosophers, jurists, or editorial journalists. Many *factual* questions of crucial historical importance are studied by scholars in established disciplines but remain controversial and unresolved: What part of intelligence is genetically (as opposed to environmentally) determined, and do races differ in their genetic makeup on this variable? What combination of resources devoted to harsher law enforcement, preventive education, and rehabilitation will produce the least costly method of reducing crime? Why do certain youth become radicals? How could the Korean war have been prevented? These are issues of "fact" and explanation (rather than value problems), but history, economics, psychology, sociology, political science, and biology have given us few reliable findings. History and social science have discovered unequivocal "truth" only about highly specific issues in relatively few areas. Because controversial issues are as prevalent and important in the "knowledge" provided by history and social sciences as they are in the ethical-political-legal analysis we espouse, the mandate to confine curriculum to such disciplines is no protection against raising problems for which even scholars have no final solutions.[5] The fundamental curriculum decision is not really a choice between teaching fact versus opinion or between history–social science versus value analysis. Rather it is whether we wish to teach only about those questions to which we have found widespread consensus on the answers or whether we wish to teach about questions (be they fact, value, or any other type) on which considerable controversy exists.[6] We believe that issues and questions for which controversy abounds are not only worthy of study, but are often much more important to the individual and society than those for which final answers have been discovered.

To argue that other disciplines have as much difficulty in seeking the truth as we do is not a sufficient response to the competence problem. We must demonstrate that our scheme *does* offer clarification and a useful framework for thinking about public issues. Yet it would be folly to argue in a few paragraphs that we are competent in this regard. The reader will have to reach his own judgment on this issue by examining our rationale and conceptual scheme (presented here, or the earlier version in Oliver and Shaver, 1966), teachers' guides and curriculum materials for students (the American Education Publications [AEP] Public Issues Series), films illustrating aspects of the approach (available through AEP), and empirical evidence on classroom outcomes (see Oliver and Shaver, 1966, for initial research; Levin, 1968; or Levin, Newmann, and Oliver, 1969, for most recent data). The reader's own attempt to teach the approach is perhaps the best test of its utility.

Another claim in the competence argument is that although we may be able to make, with some sophistication, a dispassionate analysis of what values people hold and why, this is quite different from teaching people how to go about refining their own personal value choices. We have neither the right nor the skills to engage in the latter. This objection signifies a concern for the distinction between teaching people how to think and analyze versus teaching them how to feel, and relates to the indoctrination problem.

Suppose that students have studied various cultures, using the vantage points of several disciplines (such as psychology, political science, sociology, anthropology, and economics) to identify what values individuals and groups

[5] See Newmann (1967) for a more extended commentary on the problem of using social science disciplines as a basis for curriculum development. Our point here on the controversial and indeterminate nature of knowledge is not to suggest that because the disciplines and our curriculum both contain unresolved issues that the teaching of either would accomplish the same objectives.

[6] The choice is not between mutually exclusive alternatives, but mainly a question of the proportion of time we spend dealing with controversial problems as opposed to those for which the "correct" answers can be widely agreed upon.

held, why they held them, and how different types of value-laden behavior were related. One day students begin to ask such questions as: Is it right for Eskimos to send their elderly out on the ice to die? Should cannibals be allowed to devour their fellowmen? Should adultery be outlawed in the United States? Is the property tax in Center City fair? Should children be separated from parents as on the kibbutz? Teacher replies: "I am not competent to tell you what is right. Cultures and individuals within them, as we have seen, hold different values for different reasons. Who are we to judge another's values? It is not us, but the Eskimo, the cannibal, the suburbanite, the Israeli who must live with his choices. Thus, if we must judge them, we should judge them not as right or wrong, superior or inferior compared to us, but as holding values similar to or different from ours. We are concerned only with how societies behave. An auto mechanic who tells you how your car runs is not really competent to tell you where to drive it."

Under the guise of dispassionate, objective, scientific analysis such a teacher *is*, we believe, teaching students how to feel as well as how to explain the feelings of others. He is teaching students to govern or temper their desire to make moral judgments. He is suggesting that a relativistic attitude about human value choices is the fairest way to judge people, and that moral reservations should be replaced by feelings of "scientific" neutrality. But the distinction between thought and feeling or the cognitive versus the affective is difficult to make. Describing value orientations different from the student's can lead the student to question the validity of his own values, which may lead to feelings of insecurity and anxiety. Therefore, we are deluding ourselves if we believe that "objective" description and explanation of value-oriented behavior does not influence students' feelings about their own value choices. Because the most dispassionate teacher cannot avoid influencing how students feel about value problems, we believe teachers have an obligation to consider explicit strategies for dealing with this aspect of curriculum.

A final manifestation of the competence problem is the concern that once students begin to analyze the justification for deeply held beliefs, the teacher may open a Pandora's box of emotional issues that he is unable to resolve. Questioning student beliefs that heretofore were taken for granted may lead to psychological trauma, insecurity, cynicism, or loss of faith in democracy or the authority of parents. Tough-minded challenges of value choices may destroy a person's former belief system without reconstructing a new one. We shouldn't risk the trauma unless we have proven techniques for dealing with it.

We agree that one must take care to avoid such consequences, and would not condone destroying a student psychologically in an effort to have him develop more rationally defensible views on public policy. Because of its willingness to deal explicitly with personal positions, our approach does indicate a need for teachers to be sensitive to the world views, philosophies, and cherished values of students. But nothing advocated in the approach logically leads to hurting persons along lines mentioned above. On the contrary, because a major point of the approach is to help people develop convictions based on firmer grounds than were formerly available, we think such citizenship education will in the long run increase a person's confidence in the positions he advocates. The responsible teaching of any subject — art, physical education, or history — demands teachers who strive to maintain the individual dignity and sense of worth of each student. We are unable to offer detailed pedagogical techniques that ensure that teachers would treat students accordingly. But our experience indicates that teachers are able to explore policy and value judgments in depth without inducing the skepticism, cynicism, insecurity, or lack of patriotism that some may fear to be a likely consequence of this approach.

2. Indoctrination Problem

A healthy respect for the integrity and worth of each person's mind leads many pre- and in-service teachers to deny an intent to shape or mold the student's thinking. In stating his objectives the teacher explains that he does not wish to teach a student *what* to think, because that would be brainwashing or indoctrination. Instead he aims to teach the student *how* to think, how to reach his own independent conclusions. Teaching a method of thought (i.e., how to think) is, however, no less an attempt to shape or influence or manipulate one's mind than teaching one to believe in specific content or truths. Commitments to the value of critical thinking should not disguise that educators, almost by definition, intend to shape and influence people's thoughts. The basic issue is the extent to which our influence tends to liberate or enslave the student's thought.

We admit that our approach to citizenship education attempts to influence people in certain ways. It is not completely open-ended or value-free. We wish people to develop justifications for their positions that reflect specific intellectual strategies discussed in Chapters 2, 3, and 9. We hope they will employ some ideas discussed in Chapters 4 through 8. We hope they will hold attitudes conducive to using such strategies: a desire to examine their own beliefs in dialogue with others; a willingness to concede or modify their views in the face of challenging evidence; a commitment to the values of clarity, logical consistency, and attention to empirical findings; and, of course, valuing human dignity, pluralism, and rational consent. Because we believe that fulfilling such objectives would lead to freer minds, we do not see this sort of mind-shaping as indoctrination.

Indoctrination is persuasion aimed at restricting rather than expanding a person's area of choice. Suppose we wished to persuade people to believe that "the individual should always sacrifice his personal interests for those of the state." To indoctrinate would be to use such techniques as coercion and fear (punishing people who did not affirm this belief and act accordingly); emotional identification (creating popular heroes in novels, television, or movies whose self-sacrifice always results in great social achievement); repetition (constantly placing the message before the public); censorship (refusing to allow for the discussion of opposing views). In contrast, one could also try to persuade people through rational analysis. We would search for historical evidence that supports and contradicts the claim, examining different philosophical positions. Our debate would explicitly label and prohibit techniques of indoctrination and would encourage individuals to develop unique positions on the problem. In asking whether evidence is being stacked, whether advocates engage in nonrational strategies (e.g., ad hominem remarks, sarcasm, or winning points on irrelevant issues), whether proponents have considered and rebutted alternative views, rational analysis has a liberating effect.

Having admitted our attempt to influence students in particular ways and having claimed this influence to be more liberating than restrictive, at least three objections to indoctrination remain: It is suggested that a person's beliefs on public policy are essentially private matters, personal convictions not too different from religious commitments. Teachers in public schools who probe an individual's beliefs represent an infringement by the state on a person's privacy or his right to free exercise of speech and political association. Discussing public issues in school involves dangers of political partisanship. The school has a special place in society, isolated from partisan conflicts of the world beyond. Injecting political discussion into the classroom would deprive the school of its unique ability to study the world in an objective manner. If all sides of public issues could be presented in an unbiased fashion then such issues might be fruitfully considered, but because true impartiality is impossible to achieve, we should not risk changing the school milieu from an ivory tower to a partisan, smoke-filled room. Students influenced by the particular political attitudes of their teachers may arrive at convictions in conflict with those of their parents; taxpaying parents should not have to allow their children to be indoctrinated according to the teacher's bias. Furthermore, because young people are so impressionable and susceptible to influence, conclusions reached during childhood and adolescence can become irreversible, determining much of their future views. For this reason one should not teach anything that cannot be shown to have lasting truth. Teaching controversial issues, because of the lack of right answers, presents great risks that strong opinions would be formed that later would have to be revised.

Responding to these points separately, we first reject the notion that an individual's views on public policy are solely his personal, private concern. If John intends to oppose a school bond issue, to encourage opposition to the draft, or to support a friend who refuses to rent to Negroes, John's beliefs have consequences beyond himself, and they are, therefore, a legitimate subject for community debate. Views on public policy are, by definition, of concern to the community. This is not to argue that the secret ballot should be abolished or that each citizen be required to proclaim his beliefs on the town commons. To urge students to take a stand is in no way to suggest that the classroom become a witch-hunt, trial, or public confessional; this would violate our notion of individual dignity and integrity of each student. To avoid intrusions into those private dimensions of positions on public policy, it is important to distinguish between the merits of an argument or intellectual position and virtues of the person who holds it. Because the distinction can be difficult to make in practice, the teacher must be careful not to injure the student in probing for clarification.

On the issue of bias and partisanship, we feel that in general the teacher should not try to persuade students to take particular views on issues, but to help them develop a style of justification.[7] Although this instruction offers no protection against political partisanship in the classroom, prohibiting discussion of controversial issues is no greater a safeguard against the same danger. Studies of the content of textbooks have shown that even those that claim to give an impartial objective view of history contain very clear political attitudes: for example, interpretations that neglect racist influences in provoking civil disturbance or those that portray American foreign policy and militarism as flawless concern for democracy the world over. We agree that partisanship should be avoided, but suggest that this can best be achieved through open discussion of public issues, which exposes partisanship, making it thereby easier to challenge; and pluralism in the teaching staff, which, by exposing students to people of differing political persuasions, reduces the chance that any one view will dominate.

What about teacher bias that opposes a parent's policy preference or value judgment? If the views of the parents are rationally justifiable, this approach to curriculum would strengthen and affirm, not challenge their views. If parents' beliefs are untenable, children should be taught to disband them and try to reeducate their parents to hold more defensible views. That is, the teacher as professional has no obligation to be a mouthpiece for the views of parents. Although he should be aware of parents' views and could probably learn something from them, he must protect his role

---

[7] In Chapter 9 we discuss alternative roles of the teacher as neutral summarizer, devil's advocate, and committed advocate — the last recognizing circumstances in which it would be legitimate for a teacher to try to teach students to accept his own personal view on an issue.

as an independent intellectual. According to our present system of education, parents who wish to hire as teachers mouthpieces of their own ideologies are free to do so.

Finally (on the issue of the impressionability of adolescents), we question whether adolescents are any more susceptible to influence (especially by school teachers) than older folks. Little evidence supports this claim. If they are as impressionable as some would believe, this is all the more reason to practice at this point in their lives the critical analysis of public issues. Such analysis does not doom the child to irreversible beliefs, but if done competently would free him to constantly evaluate and reassess his position.

III. Summary

Construing public controversy in America as manifestations of conflict among several values in a large and diverse American Creed, we postulate individual human dignity as the most fundamental value of all. We assume considerable disagreement and ambiguity in the definition of human dignity, but suggest two phenomena as requisite to its fulfillment: freedom of choice among diverse alternatives, and rational consent as a process by which to deal with conflicts arising out of the pluralism we advocate. The conception of citizenship education advanced in this book attempts to define and implement, for the most part, one value: rational consent. Exercising rational consent requires persons to clarify and justify their views on public issues in conversations with peers.

The ability to put forth rational justifications of one's views is certainly no guarantee of effective participation in the consent process. In addition, one needs tactical skills for influencing human groups and those who exercise power (methods of winning elections, of pressing grievances to bureaucracies, or of organizing popular and financial support). In this sense, developing rational discourse should be seen as a necessary, but not sufficient, condition for effective participation in the consent process.[8] However, the value of rational analysis of controversy does not rest solely on its possible contribution in increasing citizen political activism. Its value lies less, perhaps, in enhancing participatory power, and more in developing intellectual power for comprehending the controversies that impinge upon us.

---

[8] To achieve influence in the consent process one might at times resort to non-rational processes — demagoguery, deceit, violence. If one's objective is to exploit others or to avoid being exploited such strategies may prove more effective, in the short run, than rational inquiry. We must be careful to note whether techniques in the acquisition of power or the manipulation of people conflict with the ideal of rational consent and then decide whether the value can be legitimately violated. See Chapter 3, "Limitations of Rational Discourse," pp. 79–84.

PART I   # Discussion Process

Introduction   If a concern for productive discussion is critical to rational consent, we must ask more specifically: What is productive discussion? What particular competencies and conditions seem requisite to its fulfillment? To clarify our conception of rational discourse, we propose: (1) an analytic scheme to differentiate between the types of issues raised in discussion and appropriate strategies for supporting and challenging different types of claims (Chapter 2); (2) discussion process moves or techniques to relate claims so that discussion as a whole is cohesive, clarified, and coherent (Chapter 3); (3) substantive concepts, theories, and distinctions to qualify and make more complex positions that would otherwise remain as undifferentiated, simple-minded, or "gut-level" reactions (Chapters 4–8); and (4) changing the school environment so that deliberation on public issues can be related to social-political action relevant to personal positions (Chapter 11).

For the approach to be effective people must also share a certain attitude or disposition toward discussion of public issues. They must see discussion as a vehicle for developing, clarifying, and justifying their views, not primarily as a device for dominating others or for parading one's knowledge, rhetorical skills, or charismatic charm. We believe that the dynamics of interpersonal conflict and adjustment, differentiation of status among discussants, the common image of discussion as intellectual sparring, and other realities prevent most citizens from valuing discussion as an opportunity for clarification. Our research and development efforts unfortunately have not focused on developing "healthy attitudes" toward discussion, but we comment on problems raised by this deficiency in the conclusion to Chapter 3.

35

The case, "The Mutiny Act," provides details of a specific controversy to which we apply the analytic scheme and discussion process concepts developed in Chapters 2 and 3.

THE MUTINY ACT

The fate of Billy Budd raises a sharp question for discussion: What should be done when martial law demands the execution of an apparently innocent man?

The British Warship *Indomitable* swept proudly across the sea in the naval war against France in 1798. Yet a sense of rebellion lay beneath the ship's staunch pose. The dark hint was made more ominous by the memory of the wild mutinies that had struck two ships of the fleet a year earlier.

Mr. Claggart, the master-at-arms of the *Indomitable,* tried to run a tight ship. He enforced a discipline so strict that many of the crew despised him. There was the day, for example, when Jackson, the maintopman, felt weak and ill. He begged Claggart not to send him aloft, saying he did not have strength to hold onto the lines and spars. But Claggart ordered him aloft, and Jackson feebly climbed to his post. Half an hour later, Jackson's body crashed to the deck. Several men rushed to the scene of the fall and carried the limp body to the ship's surgeon. A few men knew that Claggart was at fault. They moved toward him cursing, with knives drawn. "After him, mates," one yelled. "Cut into him."

Suddenly the Captain came upon the wild scene.

"Stand fast! Master-at-Arms, what is the matter here?"

The men stopped in their tracks.

"These dogs are in bad temper, sir," Claggart replied.

"You will come to attention when I address you!" commanded Captain Vere. "Let me remind you that this ship is at war. This is a wartime cruise, and this vessel sails under the Articles of War. Volunteer or 'pressed man,[1] veteran seaman or recruit, you are no longer citizens, but sailors: a crew that I shall work into a weapon. One lawless act, one spurt of rebel temper from any man in this ship, high or low, I will pay out in coin you know of. You have but two duties: to fight and to obey, and I will bend each contumacious spirit, each stiff-necked prideful soul of you, or crush the spirit in you if I must. Abide by the Articles of War and my commands, or they will cut you down. Now choose."

[1] A *'pressed man,* or *impressed man,* was a sailor forced into service, often after being kidnapped from the docks to help fill out a warship's crew.

This case is based on a story in *Billy Budd and Other Tales* by Herman Melville. Sections of dialogue are taken from the play *Billy Budd* by Louis O. Coxe and Robert Chapman. Copyright 1951 by Louis O. Coxe and Robert Chapman. Excerpts reprinted by permission of Hill and Wang, Inc., New York.

We deliberately have not chosen a contemporary major issue (e.g., Vietnam, black power, or university rebellion), or one that is historically significant — we learn of Billy Budd through literature, not journalism or history. Although classic, persisting issues are often framed in the context of sensational historical conflicts involving "casts of thousands," less publicized and even hypothetical events also bring agonizing choices to individuals who seek to justify their views.

The men stood silently. Captain Vere asked if anyone knew the cause of the accident, but no one offered information. The meeting was dismissed when the surgeon reported to the Captain that Jackson had just died.

On the day of this "accident" a new member of the crew came aboard, a young, fair-haired lad called Billy Budd. Budd had been impressed from a merchant ship to serve on the *Indomitable*. He looked immature and inexperienced to the older seaworn men. Yet Budd had served as a common seaman 10 years in the merchant service, though never on a navy ship. He felt he had much to learn from the toughened, experienced crew, many of whom looked in amazement upon the innocent appearance of their new mate.

Billy had a speech handicap that caused him, during moments of excitement and emotional stress, to stammer — to fight helplessly for words he desperately wanted to pronounce. But the speech impediment was the only defect in a character that seemed almost angelic.

Budd had been on board barely an hour when Jenkins, the Captain of the Maintop, began to needle him:

"How old are you, kid?"

"I don't know, maybe . . . twenty," Billy replied.

Jenkins concluded that Billy was an illegitimate child, because he knew nothing of his parents or where he was born. "Mama taught you some pretty manners, eh? Oh. Ain't got no mama, you say? Well you know what that makes you."

Billy was puzzled: "What do you mean, Mr. Jenkins?" A few crew members interrupted and asked Jenkins to leave Billy alone, but Jenkins snapped, "You're forgetting who's boss here. Come now, you scared to talk back?"

"N-no. Why would I be scared, Mr. Jenkins?"

"He stammers! The little bastard's so scared that he's stammering."

"Don't call me that again, Mr. Jenkins."

"Sounds fine to me. I like the way it rolls out of your mouth. Bastard Billy Budd. . . ."

Without another word Billy struck a blow that knocked Jenkins to the deck. Jenkins pulled a knife and got up, lunging at Billy. Three crew members crowded protectively around the boy.

"Would you shake hands, or would you rather fight?" asked Billy.

"Why you little. . . ." Jenkins lunged forward again. Billy grabbed his arm, bent and twisted it into a paralyzing hold. Jenkins howled to be let go. Billy released him.

"Now will you shake hands?" asked Billy.

"Shake hands? . . . Well, you beat me fair. You got more guts than I figured."

Having shown his strength, Billy soon gained the reputation of peacemaker among the quarreling, rowdy crew.

One quiet evening Billy met Claggart walking on deck. Billy remarked on the calmness and peaceful look of the sea. Claggart frowned: "The sea's deceitful, boy. Calm above, but underneath a world of monsters and murderers. Only the sharpest teeth survive. . . . Tell me, Budd, how have you the nerve to stand and talk to me? You know that half the crew would knife me in the back if they had the chance. Aren't you smart enough to hate me as the others do?"

Billy answered that he had no reason to hate Claggart; the men must be wrong in their feelings.

"You're a fool, fellow. In time you'll learn to fear me like the rest. Now get on with you."

That same evening Claggart took aside Mr. Squeak, a crewman, and ordered him to see that Budd was put on report: "Disarrange his gear; make him look sloppy."

Captain Vere had closely observed Billy Budd, not always directly, but by listening to remarks of the crew. Budd was clearly an energetic, able seaman. When the time came to replace the Captain of the Foretop with a more youthful sailor, Vere had Billy in mind. Billy accepted the promotion modestly and most of the crew offered congratulations.

While making his rounds the next day, Claggart met Dansker, one of the most experienced and wisest members of the crew. Dansker was a sensitive observer of people's emotions. He noticed that Billy Budd's presence had seemed to make a difference in the attitude of the crew toward Claggart. He also sensed that Claggart felt this difference.

Dansker remarked, "You are afraid of Billy Budd."

"Afraid of Budd? What nonsense is that?" challenged Claggart.

Dansker continued, "He commands the respect of the crew; they turn from hating you to loving him, and this leaves you powerless."

That night Billy was awakened by an unfamiliar crewman who invited him to a private meeting. Billy, drowsy but curious, followed along. The man had a plan: "You was impressed, Budd, and so was many of us. Could you help? Here's two gold guineas for you if you put in with us. Most of the men are only waiting for the word. If you join us, there's not a man on board who won't follow. The ship'll be ours when we're ready to take it."

At first Billy could not understand the proposal, but on a moment's reflection he jumped to his feet, "I don't know what you're driving at, but you had better get out of here now, before I toss you over the rail." As the unrecognized mate departed, Billy met Claggart (who had overheard part of the conversation) and Dansker. Billy covered up, saying that he had just told an afterguardsman (whom he was unable to recognize) to get back to his post.

The next day Claggart went to the Captain's cabin.

"Captain Vere, I deeply regret having to make a report of movements secretly afoot, but I have some indistinct suspicion about a man, and God forbid, sir, that this ship should suffer mutiny."

"Never mind the apology. Name the dangerous man," commanded Vere.

"William Budd, sir, captain of the foretop."

"Budd?" The Captain instructed an aide to find Budd and to bring him to the cabin immediately, without creating any stir among the crew.

"Now, Mr. Claggart, cite me a specific act or spoken word that confirms your general charge

and suspicion, and remember that in a case of this sort there is hanging for false witness."

"I understand. Last night on my rounds I discovered that Budd's hammock was unused. Later I found him in a conclave among several men, who, like himself, spread unrest and rebellion in the crew. They met near the lee forechains. When I ordered them below, young Budd and others threatened me and swore they'd drop me and some other officers overboard some night. If you desire further proof, it is not far."

At that moment Vere's aide and Billy came to the cabin. "Now," said Vere, "tell this man to his face what you told me of him." Claggart moved toward Billy, looked him squarely in the eye, and began, "Certainly, sir. I said this man, this William Budd, acting so out of angry resentment against impressment and his officers, against this ship, this Service, and the King, breeds in the crew a spirit of rebellion against the officers, the mates, and me, urging some outrage like the late revolt. I myself have seen and heard him speak with manifest malingerers and men who growl of mistreatment, harshness, unfair pay, and similar complaints. I say this man threatened his officers with murder, and was bent tonight on urging other men to act concertedly in mutiny. I have nothing further to say, sir."

At first Billy did not understand. When he did, he turned pale, with a pained and tortured look on his face, as he tried to speak.

"Speak, man," ordered Captain Vere. But Billy stood as if paralyzed, except for a dumb gesturing and choking — the signs of a convulsed tongue-tie. Captain Vere knew of Billy's speech impediment. He put a soothing hand on Billy's shoulder: "There is no hurry, my boy. Take your time."

But Vere's kindness only further frustrated Billy's attempts at speech. With a look of pained exasperation, in his last attempt at self-control, Billy shot his right arm out like a lash and struck Claggart full upon the forehead. Claggart dropped to the deck and lay motionless.

Captain Vere lifted Claggart's body to a sitting

position and called for the ship's surgeon. He ordered Billy to retire to a stateroom and to say nothing until he was called.

The surgeon came and confirmed Claggart's death. "Go now," said Captain Vere. "I must presently call a court to try the man who, out of God's own instinct, dropped the man who lies before us. Tell the lieutenants that a sailor, in an accidental fury, has killed this man. But charge them all to keep the matter to themselves."

Mr. Seymour, the first officer; Mr. Ratcliffe, the first lieutenant; and Mr. Wyatt, the sailing master, hurried to the Captain's cabin. They pondered the problem: Should the trial be held immediately, or should it be postponed until the ship joined the rest of its squadron? There was some feeling that the unusual incident should be referred to the Admiral. Vere seemed convinced that Claggart had lied to Budd's face. The other officers, having little regard for Claggart, shared much sympathy for Billy.

"What are you going to do, Captain," asked Seymour, "wasn't this last act of the Master-at-Arms the very act you had waited for to let the law itself destroy him? For it was certainly a lie, which would have brought him hanging if Billy hadn't killed him."

"Yes," agreed Vere, "but by a fair process of authority. Budd has prevented that; in fact, turned the law against himself."

Seymour persisted, "But you can't condemn the boy for answering with his arm, for lack of words. The motive was justified." Other officers criticized Claggart as an evil, unjust man, and asked mercy for Billy Budd.

The court, however, was called to order. Billy was summoned to appear. Captain Vere, the sole witness in the case, concisely narrated all that had led up to the incident. He omitted nothing about Claggart's accusation and the manner in which Billy had received it. Mr. Seymour turned toward Budd, "Captain Vere has spoken. Is it or is it not as Captain Vere says?"

"Captain Vere tells the truth," Billy replied.

"It is just as he says, but it is not as the Master-at-Arms said. I have eaten the King's bread and I am true to the King."

"I believe you, my man," said Vere, with suppressed emotion.

Seymour continued the questioning: "Mr. Budd, was there any malice between you and the Master-at-Arms?"

"I bore no malice toward the Master-at-Arms. I am sorry that he is dead. Could I have used my tongue I would not have struck him. But he foully lied to my face, in the presence of the Captain. I had to say something . . . and I could only say it . . . with a blow. God help me."

They asked Billy if he had known or suspected any trouble on board among any section of the ship's company. Looking confused and slightly guilty, Budd lingered on the question. It recalled to his mind the meeting that night in the forechains. He believed there had been no possibility of mutiny. He did not want to play the informer, perhaps falsely, against his shipmates. He finally answered that he knew of no trouble.

"One question more," said Mr. Seymour. "You tell us that what the Master-at-Arms said against you was a lie. Now why should he have lied so maliciously, if there was no malice between you?"

Billy looked bewildered and upset. Unable to answer, he turned an appealing glance toward Captain Vere. Vere rose to his feet. "The question you put to him comes naturally enough. But how can he rightly answer it? Or anybody else? Except for the corpse who lies within this ship? Yet the point you make is hardly important. Aside from any motives by the Master-at-Arms, and regardless of how the blow was provoked, this court must confine its attention to the blow's consequence."

A sentry led Billy back to his cell. Captain Vere and the three officers faced the necessity of reaching a verdict.

They exchanged looks of troubled indecision. They felt that they must decide, and without long delay. Captain Vere stood with his back toward them, gazing through a porthole at the sea. The court's silence continued, broken slightly by low-toned deliberations among the officers. Vere paced to and fro.

Finally Captain Vere spoke. "Up to now I have been but the witness, little more; and I should hardly think now to take another tone. But I am obligated also as a fellow officer to express my moral concerns.

"If, regardless of the circumstances, we are bound to conclude that Claggart died as a result of Billy's blow, then does that deed of his constitute a capital crime punishable by death? . . . How can we send to death a fellow creature, innocent before God, whom we also feel to be innocent? Nature itself causes us to be moved by such questions.

"But do these uniforms signify our allegiance to Nature? No, to the King. We move through the ocean, an element of Nature, but as the King's officers, is our duty similarly natural? In receiving our commissions, we in a most important way ceased to be free and natural agents. When war is declared are we, the commissioned fighters, first consulted? We fight at command. If, in our own judgment, we happen to approve the war, that is but coincidence. So in other matters and so now. If Budd is put to death because of our proceedings, would it be so much we ourselves who do the condemning, as it would be martial law operating through us? We are not responsible for the law and its rigor. Our vowed responsibility is in this alone: that however pitilessly that law may operate, we nevertheless adhere to it and administer it.

"Clearly, the unusual circumstances in this matter move the hearts within you. So too is mine moved. But let not warm hearts betray heads that should be cool. The heart stands for the feminine in man, and hard though it be, it must be ruled out here."

The three listeners, disturbed by the new course of the argument, shifted in their seats. Vere paused for a moment, then abruptly changed his tone and went on:

"To steady us a bit, let us recall the facts. In wartime at sea, a man-of-war's sailor strikes his superior officer, and the blow kills. Just the blow itself, apart from its effect, is a capital crime according to the Articles of War. Furthermore. . . ."

"Aye, sir," broke in Wyatt emotionally, "in one sense it was. But surely Budd intended neither mutiny nor homicide."

"Surely not, my good man. And before a court less arbitrary and more merciful than a martial one that plea would hold weight. But we proceed under the law of the Mutiny Act, and that act derives from *war*. In His Majesty's service — in this ship — there are Englishmen forced to fight for the King against their will — against their conscience, for all we know. Thus, the danger of mutiny is real. History bears me out. In war, the impressed men are cut down in the same swath with our volunteers. Budd's intent or non-intent in this case has nothing to do with our duty to uphold the law."

Ratcliffe, the junior lieutenant, spoke for the first time: "Can we not convict and yet lessen the penalty?"

"Lieutenant, even if that were lawful for us under the circumstances, consider the consequences. The ship's company have natural feelings. Most of them are familiar with our naval custom and tradition. How would they take it? Even if you could explain it to them — which our official position forbids — they would not understand. They have been too long molded by arbitrary discipline and are not accustomed to intelligent thought. No, to the crew Billy Budd's deed, however it is explained, will be plain homicide committed in a flagrant act of mutiny. They know this should be followed by the death penalty. If not so followed, the crew will ask why. They will think our sentence weak-minded. They would think that we flinch, that we fear an uprising, that we are afraid of enforcing the letter of the law, lest it provoke new troubles. Such thoughts on their part would be a shame to us and deadly to discipline."

Captain Vere crossed the deck, resuming his place by the porthole. Mr. Wyatt jumped out of his seat and declared, "I can't bear to hang a man I know is innocent. My blood's not cold enough. I cannot give the judgment you are forcing upon us. I ask to be excused from this court."

Seymour ordered Wyatt to sit down. Vere turned and addressed the excited officer:

"Before you can escape the issue here, you must strip off your uniform, and after that, your flesh. Decide you must. Oh, you may be excused and wash your hands of it, but someone must decide. The law orders us to act and shows us how. God knows I wish I could acquit Budd. But tell us, show us how to save him without putting aside our duty. Speak, man, help us save him!"

Wyatt gazed into space without a reply. Then Vere concluded: "I hope there is a grace of soul within him that shall forgive the law we bind him with, and pity us."

After a few moments, Mr. Seymour broke the silence: "Well, gentlemen, will you decide?" He handed paper and pen to each man.

Billy Budd was convicted and sentenced to be hanged at the yardarm the following dawn.

At 4 o'clock in the morning all hands were summoned on deck to witness punishment. Captain Vere stood above with his officers. Below them on the quarterdeck the marines were stationed in full equipment. Billy Budd faced aft, as a few mates prepared him with the line and noose.

The crewmen, filing up through the hatchways, had no idea what was about to happen. When they saw Billy for the first time in the fatal position below the mainyard, they began to murmur, to ask perplexed questions. A harsh announcement cut them short: "No talking in the ranks! You men are at attention! You hear me? Silence in the ranks!"

Mr. Seymour stepped forward and read:

Proceedings of the court-martial held aboard H.M.S. Indomitable *on the eighth August, 1798. Convened under the authority of Edward Fairfax Vere, Senior Captain, Royal Navy, and composed of the First Officer, the Sailing Master, and the First Lieutenant of said vessel. In the case of William Budd, foretopman, Royal Navy. While attached and so serving in the aforesaid vessel, he did, on the 8th day of August, 1798, strike and kill his superior officer, one John Claggart, Master-at-Arms, Royal Navy.*

With that, the crew broke into shouts and cheers — hurrahs for Billy Budd. Then the cold realization of what was about to happen turned the cheers to sullen threats. Lieutenant Wyatt commanded, "Stand back! Sentries, guard the prisoner. Fire if you must."

The ranks of men settled slowly down to grim-lipped silence, staring with angry eyes at the ritual going on before them.

Seymour asked Billy if he had anything to say. Without faltering or stammering, he uttered his last words: "God bless Captain Vere."

Then, as the ship's company looked on, Billy Budd was hanged.

| Chapter 2 | # Approaches to Different Types of Issues |

Several questions bring out controversial responses to the Mutiny Act case. Was Billy guilty of mutiny? Did he have a fair trial? How would the crew react to lenient punishment? What were Captain Vere's legal and moral obligations? Is killing ever morally justified? But the issue that seems to raise all these problems is a decision on a specific policy or proposed action: Should Captain Vere sentence Billy to hang? If this or a similar policy judgment did not need to be made, the significance of other questions would fade. Social controversy arises in response to the advocacy or implementation of specific action or policy choices by citizens or officials in affairs that concern a community with diverse interests. Such issues can be phrased in broad social policy terms: Should the United States withdraw from Southeast Asia? Should students have a voice in university hiring practices? Should the federal government guarantee jobs for the poor? Policy issues can also be phrased as choices for personal action: Should I resist the draft? Should I contribute funds to an organization of student radicals? Should I join a poor peoples' demonstration?

By phrasing issues in questions that invite "yes" or "no" replies, we do not suggest that taking a stand involves merely making categorical choices. Defensible positions must demonstrate more complicated interpretations of policy judgments. Yet social action forces upon us many choices that can be construed primarily as yea or nay commitments: voting for Johnson represents categorical rejection of Goldwater; signing a petition (however qualified its plea) endorses its position; serving in the Armed Forces rejects resistance; supporting a particular law, bond issue, or court decision says "no" to its alternative.

42

The policy judgment itself, however, does not establish its validity. A judgment derives its reasonableness, wisdom, or defensibility from arguments used in its justification. Thus we distinguish between a judgment or position on an issue (the acceptance or rejection of a given policy) versus the rationale in support of that position. This distinction is made in the familiar claim, "You have the right position, but the wrong reasons." Rational discussion involves questioning, examining, and building rationales or justifications behind positions or policy judgments. Arguments over the justification of policy judgments usually involve three broad types of issues: moral or value issues; issues of definition; and issues of fact and explanation. These issues are closely related, but can be discussed separately. Figure 2.1 illustrates how the different types of issues might arise in discussing "The Mutiny Act."

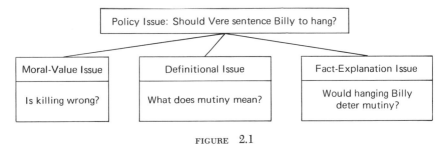

FIGURE 2.1

I. Moral-Value Issues

Moral statements or value judgments suggest that some objects, persons, or actions are good or bad, right or wrong, and that the "goodness" or "badness" is based on general moral principles (as opposed, for example, to particular laws, customs, or personal taste). Joe argues that Billy Budd should *not* be hanged, "because it is morally wrong to take a man's life." Alex says that, though it is regrettable, Billy *should* be hanged, "because it would be morally wrong for Captain Vere not to administer the law impartially." These opposing positions disagree about the priority that each person is willing to give to the value of human life versus the value of impartial administration of the law. Generally the values on which people base their positions are taken for granted rather than explicitly announced. We believe that impasses in controversial discussion could be considerably clarified if discussants tried to identify and label the values in conflict.

In the most general sense, values could be defined as ideals that people favor and strive to achieve. Such choices can be expressed in several ways: general moral principles and imperatives (the previous examples; also "do unto others . . ." or "all men should be treated equally"); constitutions and laws ("no one may be tried twice for the same crime," "the sale of narcotics is forbidden"); unwritten customs or patterns of behavior (for example, the high value that Americans place on material possessions or formal education); actions indicating disagreement in matters of personal taste (the quality of art, literature, food, personal virtue). Disputes of public significance involve all these modes of expressing value choice, but rational discourse over policy judgments involves a rhetoric in which values are justified primarily by general moral or legal principles.

In Chapter 1 we identified values (the Creed) customarily invoked to justify policy choices, and we saw that in many specific controversies, some values in the Creed must be violated if others are to be upheld. Should a landlord be able to discriminate by race? The value "equal opportunity" would apparently bar racial discrimination. Yet the value "right of private property" seems to allow the landlord enough autonomy to discriminate. The values of self-determination and national security come into conflict in debates on foreign policy: If the United States isolates itself from the affairs of foreign countries, it supports their self-determination, yet those nations may act in ways that threaten the peace and security of the United States. To preserve national security, the United States must intervene, but this violates the principle of self-determination. Other value conflicts are relevant to policy choices:

POLICY CHOICES	VALUE CONFLICT
Should federal aid be given to parochial schools?	freedom of religion versus separation of church and state
Should police have the right to interrogate suspects without a lawyer?	protection of the innocent versus public safety
Should books and movies be censored?	freedom of speech versus morals of the majority
Should the government regulate businessmen's rate of profit?	private property and enterprise versus general welfare
Should capital punishment be abolished?	retributive justice versus "thou shalt not kill"

A. Supporting and Challenging Value Judgments

Given a discussion in which policies have been justified by general values, we can ask how values themselves might be justified or challenged. There are several possible strategies.

1. Using Value-laden Language

Moral or value statements can be phrased in "loaded" words that give rise to strong personal feelings. Such terms as "killing," "upholding the law," "impartial," "democratic," and "communistic" tend to arouse positive or negative feelings. According to Irving Lee (1956, p. 18):

> It is one of the commonplaces of studies in semantics that a number of words may refer to the same thing though each may imply strikingly different atti-

tudes to it. As Sam Weller said, "When a poor fellow takes a piece of goods from a shop, it is called theft, but if a wealthy lady does the same thing, it is called monomania." It has been recently observed that "the rich are alcoholics and the poor are drunks." We learn rather quickly to reserve some words for use when things are considered pleasant and desirable and others for the contrary. If you wished to express approval of someone, would you not be likely to choose the former of the following pairs? Strength of purpose — pigheadedness, generous — spendthrift, zealot — fanatic, patriot — chauvinist, progressive — new-fangled, supporter of free enterprise — capitalist.

If one's feelings or commitments depend largely upon how a given event or policy is labeled, and if any given event or policy could be labeled in several ways, then we must scrutinize the appropriateness of value-laden terms used to arouse feelings for a given situation. Labeling problems will be discussed more fully in the section on definition.

2. Using a Respected or Venerable Source

Value statements may be justified by showing that they are prescribed by a source that most people consider sacred or authoritative: the Bible, the Constitution, the Declaration of Independence, or the words of a highly respected public figure. The reasoning could proceed: "Billy Budd should not be hanged (policy stand), because it is wrong to kill (value-laden terms), because the Bible says, 'Thou shalt not kill' (venerable source)." Yet sacred sources themselves often contain contradictory values. In the Bible we find "thou shalt not kill" on the one hand, and "an eye for an eye, tooth for a tooth" on the other. In the Constitution, we have the value of states' rights, but also prohibitions on state actions. For this reason, using venerable sources is often insufficient for justifying the priority of some values over others, and also because disputants may disagree as to which sources are more authoritative (in the Budd case, should the laws of England or God's command to have mercy take priority?).

3. Predicting a Valued Consequence

Suppose Alex argues that Billy should be hanged, because he feels that the value of impartial administration of the law is important. Joe asks, "Why is it so important that Captain Vere abide by the law?" "Because," replies Alex, "abiding by the law will lead to hanging Billy, which will provide an example for other members of the crew who are contemplating violence; this will teach them a lesson and result in a more orderly and effective ship."

When a policy or value statement is justified through predicting consequences, two problems arise. First, one must be able to show that the predicted consequence is highly probable, a factual issue. Second, even assuming that the prediction is correct, we may continue to ask the value question: "Are these consequences good?" (Is social order on the ship more valuable than the life of an innocent person?) If, however, one can reach agreement that predicted consequences of a value choice are likely to occur and that the consequences should be valued, this offers persuasive justification for the original value choices.

B. Relationships Between Specific and Higher Order General Values

Alex, in addition to predicting the consequences of a value choice (obeying the law), suggested that this specific value choice was related to another more general value: social order. One might argue that specific values — equal economic opportunity, due process of law, majority rule, efficiency, privacy, etc. — are *logically* necessary to attaining more basic, overriding values. One might assume, for example, that *equality* is the root of all morality, and then try to show that such values as brotherhood, impartiality, majority rule, or due process of law are specific ingredients, without which equality is impossible. Or one might cite the *pleasure principle* as the foundation of all values and attempt to show that private property, religious freedom, and physical safety are intrinsically related, while others, such as anarchy or inequality, are logically incompatible. Other possible root values could be *human dignity* or *individual freedom*. Most often the root or higher order values are phrased so vaguely that it is difficult to demonstrate that specific values are unequivocally consistent or inconsistent with them. Is majority rule necessary to attain equality, maximum pleasure, and individual freedom? Is private property consistent or inconsistent with any of these? In searching for logical connections between specific and general or higher order values, we must be alert to problems of ambiguity in abstract, analytic value hierarchies.

C. Value Conflicts as Inconsistencies in Personal Positions

Justification for policy and value choices can be improved by finding inconsistencies and contradictions in value commitments. Using analogy is an effective way to probe for value conflicts.

> Alan: It was right for Captain Vere to hang Billy because he had to obey the law. He had no choice.
>
> Barbara: What if your kid sister were seriously injured, and your father was arrested for speeding while he was taking her to the hospital. Do you think he should be convicted and fined?
>
> Alan: No.
>
> Barbara: Then you're allowing your father to break the law.
>
> Alan: Of course, but that's different. My father was trying to save my sister's life.
>
> Barbara: Billy Budd was trying to save his own integrity and honor. Perhaps for him that was worth striking an officer — breaking the law.
>
> Alan: I guess in my father's case I think the value of my sister's life is more important than the value of my father's obeying the law. But I think obeying

the law on the ship is more important than the value of Billy Budd's keeping his honor or integrity.

The analogy is an authentic or hypothetical situation involving principles similar to the original case, but which elicits a *denial* of a value or policy initially supported. To avoid appearing inconsistent in the face of this denial, the typical response is "That's different," which is intended to imply: "I am not being as inconsistent as I may appear to be, because the new or analogous situation you used to trap me is not comparable to the original case. Thus I should not be expected to support the same value in both cases." Discussants should then explore the principles or criteria on which the analogy is considered fundamentally different or congruent with the original situation. This can lead to an explicit explanation of why one would uphold a value in one situation and reject it in a similar situation, which helps to clarify the nature of the value conflict and one's justification for his policy choice.[1]

D. Dealing with Incompatible Value Frameworks

These strategies for clarifying value statements are helpful only if participants in the dialogue share a commitment to values in the Creed. Such values are psychologically internalized and serve as ground rules or morality for public policy. Without common agreement at this general level, effective communication on value conflict is unlikely. Suppose, for example, that in the discussion of the Mutiny Act, Alan totally rejects the value "killing is wrong," and has no objections to killing innocent people. In the absence of any commitment to human life or protection of the innocent, Captain Vere's choice will not raise any important questions for Alan. Unless his value framework included those commonly accepted as part of the Creed (e.g., majority rule, human life, peace, equality, due process, honesty, brotherhood, law abidance, property, etc.), the problem of choosing one value over another would not arise.

Another roadblock to discussion of value priorities is the relativist: the person who claims there are no absolute standards by which to judge men's actions; that one man's values are as good as another's; that although one may have been taught that X is wrong, it is not wrong for Harry unless Harry believes it to be wrong. The extreme relativist refuses to apply norms or morality to anyone beyond himself. This position can be characterized by such statements as: "If Harry believes equality is good, then equality is good for Harry." "If I think that criminals should receive a fair trial, that value is okay for me, but no one else must accept it." "Although I thought it was wrong for the Nazis to slaughter the Jews, the Nazis thought it was

---

[1] Detailed discussion on the use of analogy appears in Chapter 9.

right, so it was right for them and wrong for me. But there's no reason to argue about it because each person has his own values." Unless one's adversary believes it is appropriate to judge others on the basis of values he holds and that men should adhere to some generally desirable absolutes, then it is impossible to carry on a reasoned conversation about which values are preferable to others in a given situation.[2]

A final obstacle to productive consideration of value issues is the denial of rational discussion and argument as an appropriate vehicle for resolving disputes. We assume that clarifying and justifying value choices can be achieved through rational dialogue and debate. This assumption can be challenged by those who deny the value of rational thought itself. For example, the spiritualist might maintain that solutions to value issues should be sought only through divine inspiration, command, or revelation; the Machiavellian would claim that values become justified only by exercising power and manipulation, not by developing a logical argument. Both positions dismiss the relevance and effectiveness of rationality. Findings in contemporary psychology lend support to viewing man as irrational by nature and motivated primarily by unconscious emotional drives. His choices do not result from deliberate rational thought, but from impulses and environmental conditioning. Those who accept this view of man may deny the value of rational consideration of value issues. Although we are deeply aware of irrational or nonrational bases of human behavior, our position assumes a commitment to rationality as an effective way to deal with human choice. We shall deal with the limits of rationality at the conclusion of Chapter 3.

II. Issues of Definition

Important disagreements often revolve around how key words or phrases are used in discussion. Two people might disagree on whether Billy was "responsible" for the death of Claggart. For one person "responsible" might mean "acting with deliberate intent." For the other it might mean simply "acting so as to bring about a result, regardless of intent." Before discussants could decide whether Billy was responsible, they must discover the separate definitions or interpretations that each has given to the concept "responsible," and then arrive at a mutually satisfactory interpretation. Another definitional problem in the Billy Budd case is whether Billy's behavior should be considered an act of mutiny (whether it constitutes "mutiny" determines whether it becomes subject to penalties in the Mutiny Act). This issue illustrates various approaches to definitional problems.

---

[2] A more extended consideration of the relativism issue appears in Chapter 4.

A. Types of Definitions	We could offer three definitions of mutiny:

1. Mutiny is a revolt against military authority (definition by translation or synonym).

2. Mutiny is what happened on the ships in stories like *Mutiny on the Bounty* or the *Caine Mutiny* (definition by example).

3. Mutiny is a willful, planned attempt by subordinates to overthrow or disobey their superior officers on a ship (definition by criteria).

1. Definition by Translation or Synonym	Some definitional problems can be solved by providing synonymous words that translate the concept into terms understood by the discussant. The doctor, when asked to clarify what he means by "fractured tibia," replies "broken leg." In such situations, discussants do not disagree over the nature of the thing being labeled. They wish merely to substitute labels that are mutually understood for those that are unfamiliar or have a narrow technical meaning. Definition 1 defines mutiny in this fashion. Although definition by synonym can facilitate communication (as in learning a foreign language), arguments on public issues often cannot be solved in this way. Instead of being ignorant or uninformed of labels, discussants who argue the definitional issues of policy judgments tend to disagree on the nature of the phenomenon being described. *Which* label to apply becomes a problem.

2. Definition by Example	Another approach points out a specific instance or example of the concept in question, as in Definition 2. To explain "fractured tibia," the doctor simply might point to an X-ray or to the patient's leg. To define "civil disorder" someone might refer to "what happened in Watts, Detroit, and Washington, D.C., on the dates. . . ." Definitional issues can be solved if discussants reach agreement that various suggested examples do or do not belong in the given class "mutiny," "civil disorder," etc. In such cases additional labeling or describing general defining properties is unnecessary. Often, however, examples do not resolve definitional issues so easily; the search continues for more general defining characteristics. Scrutinizing examples aids in verbalizing and testing the general properties that examples share and that differentiate some from others. If, by considering *Mutiny on the Bounty* and the *Caine Mutiny*, discussants agree that Billy Budd's actions are *not* in the same class as the former two, and that the former are clearly mutiny, the definitional issue is resolved.

3. Definition by Criteria	As disagreement arises over which label is most appropriate or whether Billy's actions fall in the same category as other "mutinies," it becomes necessary to describe in more detail the general properties or criteria one

wishes to assign to the concept in question. Does "mutiny" mean "conspiring" to take over the ship, or only performing acts involved in the actual takeover? Does it include knowledge of the conspiracy? Does it include impulsively striking an officer when there is no intention of disobedience?

The importance of using several criteria can be illustrated in the problem of defining "communist." We might define a communist as: (1) someone who believes in the teachings of Karl Marx; (2) someone who goes to communist party meetings; and (3) someone who works for world domination by countries whose leaders believe in Marxist teachings. By this definition a person would have to meet all three criteria to be classified a communist. That a person believed in the teachings of Marx would not be enough. We might call him a Marxist, but not a communist. The fact that someone had gone to communist party meetings would not give us sufficient information to classify him as a communist, because a curious student or an FBI agent might go to party meetings.

Definition 3 cites some criteria by which to define mutiny. We can challenge the criteria. Should the idea of mutiny be restricted to ships — suppose airplane passengers forcefully overthrew the pilot and crew? Suppose also that as a token of appreciation to the ship's captain, crew members disregarded his orders for rest and recreation and instead spent their time repairing the ship and planning a surprise party for the captain. Criterial definitions can be tested when we pose situations where the criteria are not met, yet we feel mutiny does exist (the airplane); or situations where the criteria do apply, but we feel mutiny does not occur (tribute to the captain). Examples serve to test the criteria, and the criteria serve to clarify similarities and differences between examples and the concept we wish to define.[3]

Apart from reaching agreement on the criteria that define a term, discussants must also decide whether a given instance *in fact* meets the criteria. Was Billy's action "willful"? It seems unlikely that he wished to kill Claggart, but did he not desire to hurt him? As another example, suppose Milton argues that the United States should give foreign aid only to democratic countries. Louie presses for a definition of democratic.

Milton: A democratic country holds elections for its leaders and has a written constitution.

Louie: The Soviet Union holds elections and has a written constitution but it's not democratic, is it?

Milton: No.

Louie: I think we should add that in a democratic country, individuals are

---

[3] An "operational" definition contains criteria that can be more easily observed as specific behaviors or quantities: for example, "mutiny has occurred when subordinate officers hold meetings or exchange messages indicating their intent to take command of the vessel or when persons other than the captain begin giving orders without the captain's consent."

guaranteed freedom of religion, press, assembly, the right to vote, the right to fair trial, the right to own their businesses. . . .

Milton: Okay. So we agree on the criteria. Now is the Soviet Union democratic?

Louie: I don't think it guarantees all these rights to its citizens.

Milton: Can you prove that it doesn't?

Louie: I can't prove it, but I have the feeling that these rights are denied in Russia.

The boys first reached agreement on the criteria for their definition of democratic, but they still must decide whether Russia in fact meets their criteria.

B. Classification   Moving between general criteria and specific examples is, in essence, the process of classification: developing categories or classes to organize specific data. The key terms we argue about may be viewed as important general classes whose boundaries have not been clearly defined; or perhaps each discussant can clearly define the classes in his mind, but all discussants hold different views of what constitutes the definitional properties of a given class. In two criterial definitions of "subversion," it is assumed that any or all criteria under each are sufficient defining properties.

A	B
Criticizing the policies of duly constituted government.	Participation in acts of violence intended to overthrow duly constituted government.
Giving aid in any form to enemies of the government.	Giving military aid to enemies of the government.
Seeking to change the structure of duly constituted government.	
Inciting violence.	

Consider whether specific actions constitute subversion under either or both classes. (Assume all actions are instigated by an American citizen living in the United States.)

SUBVERSION?

Example	A	B
1. Editorial that opposes United States involvement in Vietnam.	yes	no
2. Speech arguing that Constitution should be changed to abolish the Supreme Court.	yes	no
3. Giving blood to Germans during World War II.	yes	no
4. Starting a riot over race relations.	yes	no
5. Sending ammunition and weapons to Germans during War II.	yes	yes

<table>
<tbody>
<tr><td></td><td colspan="2" align="center">SUBVERSION?</td></tr>
<tr><td>*Example*</td><td align="center">*A*</td><td align="center">*B*</td></tr>
<tr><td>6. Training guerilla troops to march on Washington and occupy all government agencies.</td><td align="center">yes</td><td align="center">yes</td></tr>
<tr><td>7. Trying to persuade people to vote on election day.</td><td align="center">no</td><td align="center">no</td></tr>
<tr><td>8. Contributing funds to the cancer drive.</td><td align="center">no</td><td align="center">no</td></tr>
</tbody>
</table>

In Figure 2.2, class A represents a much broader concept of subversion than class B. All class B subversion (i.e., examples 5 and 6) would fall under class A, but many activities considered subversive by A are not so considered by the criteria of B.

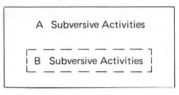

FIGURE 2.2

Definitional arguments can be clarified by distinguishing general or more inclusive from specific or narrower meanings of a concept, and by making explicit the differences in meaning among alternative interpretations of a term. In discussing "what to do about violence in American society" a classification scheme could not only clarify various meanings in an academic sense, but would suggest many problems toward which the vague concern for policy on violence could be directed:

"VIOLENCE" AGAINST

I. objects
    A. constructive
    B. destructive
II. animals
    A. self-defense
    B. subsistence
    C. sport
    D. cruelty
III. humans
    A. self-defense
    B. revenge
    C. personal gain
        1. monetary
        2. status
        3. love

IV. governments
   A. self-defense
   B. revenge
   C. conquest
   D. revolution
      1. for democracy
      2. for dictatorship

C. Attributes of Useful Definitions   Three attributes can be used to judge whether a given definition is adequate.

1. Noncircularity   A definition fails to clarify the meaning of a term when the term is used to define itself. For example, the dictionary defines subversion as "the act of subverting;" a statistician might be defined as "someone who works with statistics"; a democracy as "a country with a democratic government." In all cases, the word to be defined is repeated, rather than explained, in the definition. To enhance the meaning of a term it is necessary to use in the definition language different from the term to be defined.

2. Convertibility   A definition can be thought of as an equation in which the term to be defined "equals" the definition:

slave = human who is legal property of another
human who is legal property of another = slave

Suppose the definition: "a slave is a man." To convert the equation we arrive at "a man is a slave," which is false because not all men are slaves. This definition is not convertible because the size of the class denoted by slave is smaller, rather than equal to the size of the class denoted by man. A term to be defined might also be a class *larger* than the proposed definition:

violence = armed conflict between two nations

Although the definition seems reasonable, it is too narrow, thus not convertible. Armed conflict between two nations is only one of several subclasses of violence: civil war, personal assault, race riots, etc. This problem is illustrated when we use the term and its definition interchangeably in common discourse: "Violence often occurs on the streets of Harlem." "Armed conflict between two nations often occurs on the streets of Harlem."

In a convertible definition the size or domain of the term to be defined equals the size or domain of the definition. Thus the definition must be large or exhaustive enough to encompass all subclasses of the term (which the previous definition of violence failed to do); yet the definition must not be too large — it should not include any subclasses that are not part of the term (a fault of the definition slave = man). Substituting a proposed definition for the term in a variety of sentences tests whether the term and definition represent classes of equal size.

3. Discriminating Power

Definitions should be sufficiently precise to distinguish among actions or events that appear to belong in a single class but, because of subtle differences, should be classified separately. In defining "mutiny" perhaps we should distinguish between planned conspiracy to overthrow and replace established authority versus impulsive violence against a superior officer or nonmalicious forms of disobedience. The classification scheme for violence above is a definition that attempts to discriminate among several possible meanings. As a final example, suppose a group is discussing "What has been the most civilized society in history?" Sam chooses Renaissance Florence; Joe, Periclean Athens; Ron, the island of Samoa; and Bob, twentieth-century United States. After considerable argument they learn that each has a different definition for "civilized." Sam stresses aesthetic and artistic achievements; Joe, citizen participation in public affairs; Ron, peace and tranquility; and Bob, technological and economic development. As the different criteria are made explicit, the vague concept "civilized" might even be discarded and discussants could judge each society by the narrower, more differentiated definitions. The discriminating power of definitions can be increased by stating what is *not* intended or included as well as what is.

D. Steps in Reaching Agreement
1. Definition as Convention or Usage

The first step in resolving definitional disputes is to recognize different interpretations that discussants may give a term: for example, construing mutiny as *any* act of disobedience in a military setting versus only willful conspiracy. Once the differences in definition are identified, discussants must either decide which is more appropriate or build a new definition combining important features of the differing interpretations. To achieve consensus it is often important to bear in mind that definitions are arbitrary conventions agreed upon by people, conventions that represent no logical, scientific, or absolute "truth." Water falling from the sky could be labeled "paint" instead of "rain"; violent international conflict could be called "peace" instead of "war." The utility of a definition depends not merely on its meeting these attributes, but also upon whether it is *accepted* by discussants or a population at large.

2. Authoritative Source

Dictionaries and scholarly works can supply varied uses and commonly accepted definitions. Frequently, however, these sources are not available in informal, nonacademic settings. Even if they can be consulted, authoritative sources often fail to resolve disagreement. A dictionary defines mutiny as "insurrection against, or refusal to obey constituted authority, esp. military or naval authority; insubordination." Does this include all disobedience? Does insurrection include planning, knowledge, and execution of an uprising? Is someone who is *coerced* into a conspiracy a participant in mutiny? Sources can leave much to be clarified. Those that provide several alternative interpretations of a term — a dictionary defines "responsible" with five different meanings — fail to tell us which is the most appropriate in the context of a specific discussion.

3. Stipulation
When discussants cannot agree and authoritative sources are either unavailable or unhelpful, a temporary solution can be reached by arbitrarily assuming a given definition for the sake of moving the discussion along. Discussants must agree for the moment to use a word in a specific way, even though reservations remain whether the term is properly defined. In discussing the treatment of Billy Budd, someone might suggest: "Whenever we use the term 'responsible' it means causing an event to occur and does not imply intending the event to happen." Stipulation involves a willingness by dicussants to forestall extensive argument of a term's "true essence" and to accept aribtrary conventions to proceed to considering other issues.

E. Persuasion Through Ambiguity and Loaded Language
To persuade, a speaker may use words that communicate and arouse strong feelings rather than clearly defined ideas. Communist, conservative, reactionary, radical, left-wing, right-wing, and racist exemplify emotionally loaded terms used in political discourse. We have mentioned various criteria for defining "communist." Liberal is another common term ambiguously used. Some are called liberal because they believe the federal government should take greater leadership and spend more money to improve the general welfare of the people in all states through better education, more dams for public power, or public aid to people for medical care. Others derive their "liberal" label from strong commitment to civil liberties: freedom of speech and assembly for students, communists, and others, and voting rights for Negroes. When the label might express two quite different meanings, how do we classify a person who believes in greater federal leadership in welfare spending but who expresses no concern about the loss of civil liberties by minority groups?

A speaker may try to impress his audience by using terms that sound scholarly or scientific, but which remain vague and undefined for the listener. X complains, "Kids are saucy and wild today because their parents are afraid to hit them." Y replies, "This is an unsophisticated view of child rearing. Broad cultural, economic, and social factors make your explanation much too simplistic." The retort, with all its abstract language, says little more than "I think your view of the problem is too simple," which is not substantiated without further support and specification.

Advertising emphasizes "scientifically proven ingredients" (hexachlorophene or silentium) that, though impressive sounding, are often unexplained. Technical or specialized jargon, though useful in approaching certain problems, can be used primarily to make a listener feel ignorant rather than to clarify issues. Justifying personal behavior as "natural manifestation of Oedipal anxiety" or supporting national monetary policy for its consistency with "Keynesian economic analysis" may be reasonable and illuminating in conversations where discussants implicitly share clear definitions, but the danger is that scholarly and authoritative appearance will deter the "untutored" from requesting systematic definitions of ambiguous words. The challenge of productive discourse is not to avoid definitional issues, but to raise them and then work toward resolution. This can be facilitated if one is alert to ambiguous loaded language and specialized jargon, and willing to question their usage without fear of appearing ignorant.

III. Issues of Fact and Explanation

Discussion of the appropriate policy toward Billy Budd raises such issues as: Did Billy actually intend to kill Claggart? Did Claggart deliberately provoke Billy's attack? Would hanging Billy tend to deter the crew from mutiny? As distinguished from issues of value or definition, these are problems of determining what actually happened or will happen. Factual claims are attempts not to prescribe what ought to be or what is "good," nor to clarify the meaning of specific words, but attempts to say what the world is like, was, or will be. Are riots caused by communist agitators? Did United States foreign policy help or hinder the movement for national independence for African nations? Will blacks and whites be able to reconcile their differences within the next fifty years? Are rebellious students sincere or just looking for publicity? Will a United States setback in Southeast Asia seriously threaten our national security? Disagreement over factual claims is so widespread that some observers believe it to be the major source of public controversy.

A. Broad Scope and Variety of Factual Disputes

Controversies arise over whether particular events occurred in the past, are occurring at present, or are likely to occur in the future: "Did police rough up the accused at the station house?" "Is the administration making plans to crack down on student disrupters?" "Will the whites accept the blacks coming into the school?" Numerous controversial claims imply lawlike generalizations, describing systematic relationships among phenomena: "Whites are more intelligent than blacks." "The higher one's income, the less likely he is to be prejudiced." Some controversial generalizations imply *cause:* "Capital punishment deters crime." "Appeasement leads to aggression." "Racial segregation leads to low self-esteem for blacks." "Exploitation and injustice are the result of a capitalistic economy." Causal claims are particularly critical in justifying policy judgments, because we are usually obliged to predict consequences attendant to or caused by the policy we recommend: "Is withdrawal of United States troops from Vietnam likely to lead to peace and self-determination for the Vietnamese?" "Will establishing black studies departments provide equal educational opportunity and maintain high academic standards?" "Will cutting off funds to student disrupters bring peace to United States campuses?" Making predictions in the form "policy X results in events Y and/or conditions Z" is perhaps one of the most difficult kinds of factual claims to verify, yet this is the type of claim used so frequently to persuade persons that some policies are preferable to others.

Many much broader generalizations can be offered to explain specific events and justify the desirability of policies: "Allowing people to stick with their own kind gives them a sense of security and belonging." "The structure of United States government prevents any one branch from gaining control over the others." "Primitive ceremonies and rituals mark transitions from childhood to adulthood." "A society cannot function unless its members abide by basic rules and share common values." "The black power movement helps to give Negroes a sense of identity and control over their destiny." These claims attempt to establish the nature or essence of things, to ascribe purpose, function, pattern, or design to a set of events. They imply lawlike causal relationships, but at times also seem to represent attempts at definition.

Factual-explanatory issues differ from value and definitional issues not only in a logical-analytic sense (the difference between "should" questions, "meaning" questions, and "nature of reality" questions), but also, we think, in the attitudes people hold toward resolving disagreement in the different categories. Although people may accept differences on value and definitional issues as subjective opinions that cannot be proven absolutely, they seem less tolerant of ambiguity in the factual-explanatory area. A heritage of scientific investigation has conveyed the assumption that factual claims can be objectively confirmed or denied, with varying certainty, regardless of one's feelings. This position assumes that a world of reality exists "out there," separate and detached from our perceptions and conclusions about that world. Scientific investigation "discovers" the nature of that reality, constructing descriptive statements that are accurate or true.

To illustrate the distinction between observing and drawing conclusions about reality versus the reality itself, consider the widespread belief in the claim: "President Kennedy was assassinated in Dallas on November 22, 1963." Though no one actually saw a bullet in transit from the rifle owned by Oswald, though no one saw Oswald pull the trigger, though only a few doctors observed the wounds, thousands believe that: "Oswald, acting alone, killed Kennedy" is true beyond reasonable doubt. Others, examining the same evidence, believe the claim is highly doubtful, if not clearly false.

B. Supporting Factual Claims

The example indicates the need for procedures by which to verify claims or handle disagreement among conflicting claims. Facts do not "speak for themselves" in the sense of eliminating disagreement. In discourse, there really are no facts, but only factual claims or conclusions that humans reach through observing and reasoning. Because we are not able to observe historical or contemporary events directly, our judgments about what the facts are must be judgments about the accuracy of others' factual claims, most of whom have not been direct observers either. We tend to verify factual claims or establish their accuracy by (1) supplying supporting evidence and (2) following a process of reasoning that creates logical relationships among claims.

1. Sources of Evidence

Joe argues that Billy Budd should be hanged to prevent mutiny or further violence on the ship. Frank questions whether hanging Budd would in fact deter future violence. Joe replies, "If people know that harsh punishment is in store for them, they won't break the law as readily as if you treat them leniently." "How do you know," persists Frank, "that capital punishment deters crime?" This request for support of the factual claims could be answered in several ways.

Rather than building a detailed verification of the claim, Joe might answer: "I just know that people won't do things they know they'll be punished for. It's common sense." Or: "Once I wanted to steal a motorbike, but after one of my friends was fined and sent to jail for stealing, I decided it wasn't worth the risk." Or: "Senator Smith, who has spent several years studying crime prevention, says that penalties for crime must become tougher if we are to prevent crime."

Common knowledge or common sense, the first source of evidence just cited, is frequently used, but it is not very helpful in resolving factual disputes. People seem to have different hunches or intuitions about what is common knowledge, and when they disagree, each using common sense or common knowledge as a source to support conflicting claims, what they believe to be true is obviously not so common. When the appeal to common knowledge supports conflicting beliefs then additional sources and kinds of support are necessary to verify a claim.

Personal observation (second source used by Joe) can be more helpful, but, as mentioned earlier, can rarely be applied, since we cannot be eyewitnesses to all events about which we wish to draw conclusions. Even eyewitness observers have difficulty verifying their claims. First is the possibility of personal bias, when observers notice only what they wish to, unconsciously blocking out phenomena undesirable or inconsistent with their expectations. Persons with different personalities and motives will describe the same set of events differently. Historians are known to believe that firsthand observers may be "too close" to a situation to perceive it accurately. The second problem is generalizing from a single observed instance to other similar situations. On what basis can Joe's own experience regarding stealing a motor bike help to prove that hanging Billy would deter mutiny? One would have to explore similarities and differences in the two situations and the reasoning by which Joe's observation is considered support for his claim about Billy.

Authority, the third source used by Joe, is crucial to supporting factual claims. How could we prove that American colonies revolted against England, that the Chinese population exceeds the United States', or that a given defense system is adequate to meet a nuclear challenge, without accepting testimony or claims of others considered to be knowledgeable authorities or experts in the field? Because authorities can disagree on factual-explanatory issues, we must judge whether a given authority should be trusted or believed: that is, the extent to which he should be considered *reliable*. Some criteria for judging reliability are: (1) On what basis can the authority be considered an expert? If he is recognized by other authorities or scholars in a field, if he has had appropriate training and experience for dealing with certain kinds of issues, if he experienced or observed the facts in question — all help to qualify a person as an expert. (2) In what sense can we be sure that the authority is "unbiased"? It is important to learn whether the authority seems to have strong emotions about or a personal stake in the claims he makes. Advertisers make claims not to inform the public but to sell products; politicians seeking reelection may be primarily interested in "winning" rather than communicating "objective" truth; even scientists may have a personal interest in promoting some claims rather than others to sell an invention or push for a particular policy. (3) Do the authority's claims meet tests of logical evaluation? Apart from credentials and the bias issue, we must ask whether the authorities' claims are consistent with conclusions of other reliable authorities, whether he supports general claims with more specific ones, and whether his conclusions are logically consistent.

2. Relationships Between Specific and General Claims

Suppose that Frank had claimed: "Capital punishment does not deter crime," and when asked for evidence, stated:

1. Those states with capital punishment have crime rates higher than states in which capital punishment has been abolished.

2. A survey showed that 80 per cent of convicted murderers in 1938 were aware of the death penalty when they committed the crime.

3. Nine of ten prison wardens believe that capital punishment has no effect in preventing crime.

4. I know a psychiatrist who says that if a person really wants to kill, the threat of capital punishment won't stop him.

A string or series of specific claims that seem to support a more general claim is persuasive evidence. Once specific claims are provided, however, two problems remain: (A) Even if the specific claims are true, do they logically result in the general conclusion? (B) Are the specific claims themselves true? Answering these questions requires attention not only to the sources of claims, but also to problems in collecting data, generalizing from "samples" to larger populations, and the logic or reasoning used to conclude that one claim leads to or follows from another.

Statistics and sampling were used to support Frank's claim. To be even more specific, he might quote statements of each criminal and prison warden surveyed, or list the states and their crime rates. He could accumulate hundreds or even thousands of highly specific claims, but with these claims alone it would be difficult to see whether the general claim is supported or refuted. To summarize numerous specific claims, we use a *statistic*, which is itself a claim, usually expressed numerically, arrived at by counting and arithmetic (e.g., averages or percentages). Statistical claims allow us to observe "trends" in numerous otherwise unrelated specific claims. They help to summarize differences between groups (e.g., crimes in those states that do or do not have capital punishment); and they help to summarize ways in which different things vary together (e.g., as taxes increase, inflation decreases; or the more education one has, the higher his income).

One major reason for questioning statistics is that they are not based on observations of the total population of persons or events we wish to describe. We cannot survey the attitudes of all muderers past, present, and future, so instead we take a *sample*. Predictions about the future and most general claims about past and present are, in this sense, based on incomplete data. The challenge is to establish some basis on which our claim about a *sample* of people or events can be generalized to a larger population, or behavior in a different time and place from the observed sample. Frank got the opinion of only one psychiatrist. Perhaps many others disagree. How many opinions will verify the claim that psychiatrists see capital punishment as no deterrent? Increasing the number of observations in a sample may help to make the sample more representative of the general population, but not necessarily. Quality is also a problem. Suppose that the survey of criminals included only those convicted of armed robbery during the depression, a time when men were more desperate than in the prosperous 1960's. As another example, it is frequently claimed that leisure time has increased in the United States over the last fifty years. For which groups? Certain professionals such as doctors and attorneys are known to work harder than before, but blue collar workers have more free time. In asking how representative a sample is, we must ask not only is it large enough to represent the general population, but does it seem to have characteristics similar to the larger population?[4] When we question whether Joe's fear of harsh punishment can be generalized to the crew on an English warship of the eighteenth century, we are asking essentially whether Joe's "sample" represents a general human reaction to the threat of punishment.

Generalizing between individuals and groups is necessary to discuss public policy. Claims must be made about the needs, problems, and behavior of large groups — blacks, whites, poor people, housewives, farmers, politicians, children, criminals, etc. Although we do not use exact percentages or numbers in common discourse, using such terms as "all," "most," "some," "the more this, the less that," implies statistical claims. Claims that "most whites are racist," or "most blacks wish to become independent," or "politicians are generally interested only in furthering their careers," or "suburbanites are usually politically apathetic" may be accurate or inaccurate at some level of statistical certainty. Because each is based on observation or contact with a relatively small proportion of the members in a general class, we must identify characteristics of the sample (e.g., randomly selected, representative of different categories in the general class) that allow generalizing from it to the larger class. General claims that become fixed images, insensitive to significant variety and differences within a class, are *stereotypes*. Stereotypes are claims based on observations that do not accurately represent the large class. Describing farmers as close-to-the-soil,

---

[4] Apart from the sampling problem, statistics can be misleading in other ways. A business may boast an increase in profits of 100 per cent, yet if it were known that previous profit was only $1, the 100 per cent looks less impressive. A finance company might advertise "only $10 down and $5 per week with two years to pay." Yet this may amount to 30 per cent interest on the sale. The apparently low weekly installment disguises the relatively high interest. Therefore, statistics must be interpreted in both absolute numbers and comparative percentages.

A common error in statistical interpretation is to assume that because two variables are related numerically that, therefore, one causes the other. For example, as the number of ministers in the United States increased, so did liquor consumption. Does this mean that ministers cause alcoholism? Although the size of the clergy and the gallons of liquor rise and fall together, proving a causal relationship would be hard. Both are probably a function of a third variable: increase in the general population. To say there is more crime per capita among Negroes than whites does not establish that Negroes are genetically more prone to crime than whites. Crime could be a function of a third variable: poverty, for which Negroes may have a higher per capita rate, probably because of discrimination by whites. To discover whether any given statistical association also represents a causal relationship, the effects of variables not measured in the given statistical association must be examined.

raw-boned, uneducated, and underpaid ignores the many wealthy white-collared, executive business managers who run large corporate farming enterprises.

Just as we convert observations on specific individuals to claims about groups, we also do the reverse. By virtue of an individual's membership in a class, we ascribe to the individual attributes that have been previously assigned to the class. Knowing, for example, that whites as a group have higher income than blacks, it would be reasonable to predict, on observing two complete strangers, that the white man makes more money than the black. Because such predictions are made without investigating each individual case, people tend to disapprove of this form of judgment as "prejudice." Yet such predictions are necessary and justified in public policy decisions. If an insurance company can prove statistically that people convicted of drunken driving are more likely to have accidents than those with no traffic convictions, and Jones has a record of two drunken driving convictions, then, *in the absence of any other information,* Jones can be expected to be a higher risk than Brown, who has no convictions. Predictions from group attributes to individuals can, of course, be highly questionable. Knowing that Nazis committed war crimes and that X was a Nazi should not by itself persude us that X committed war crimes (though statistically he would be more likely than, say, a Canadian to have done so). To generalize from a class to an individual with questionable or unsubstantiated evidence is *guilt by association,* which can be just as inaccurate as a stereotyped claim. X, for example, may have risked his life to subvert and end Nazi atrocities. Because discussants often do not have enough statistics to build airtight cases for claims about individuals and groups, we should guard against overgeneralizing in either direction.

3. Deductive Reasoning

Supporting and challenging general factual claims requires not only presenting specific claims and citing sources, but also logical argument to demonstrate the validity of conclusions that might otherwise seem unsubstantiated by the evidence offered. Although we cannot present a definitive treatment, we wish to illustrate a few principles and problems in establishing the logical validity of claims verified through deductive reasoning.

> Sam: There probably won't be any riots in Deadwood.
> Pete: What's your evidence?
> Sam: We don't have any slums or college campuses.
> Pete: Sounds reasonable.

Pete might have challenged Sam to demonstrate more clearly how his evidence supports his conclusion. Sam could make this clear with a more formal argument: Riots are most likely to occur in urban slums or on college campuses (major premise). Deadwood has no urban slums or college campuses (minor premise). Therefore, riots are unlikely in Deadwood (conclusion).

Sam's conclusion is reasonable only if his major and minor premises can be verified (or are accepted as "true"), but the evidence given initially did not even make the major premise explicit. Although people do not usually take stands in this formal syllogistic style, we can test the validity of common, more natural arguments by converting them into such formats. This exposes unstated assumptions and focuses on whether conclusions follow logically from the assumptions.

Factual issues (as well as definitional ones) can be approached as problems in logical *classification*. Suppose Sam is trying to demonstrate that J. Robert Oppenheimer sympathized with communists. This is equivalent to saying that Oppenheimer belongs in a class called "communist sympathizers." When asked for evidence, Sam points out that Oppenheimer publicly opposed United States development of the hydrogen bomb. Suppose we press Sam and he converts his argument into deductive form: Communist sympathizers opposed United States development of H-bomb (major premise). Oppenheimer opposed United States development of H-bomb (minor premise). Therefore, Oppenheimer was a communist sympathizer (conclusion).

The minor premise establishes Oppenheimer's membership only in the general class, "H-bomb opponents." What subclasses compose this group? The major premise assumes communist sympathizers do. But is it conceivable that loyal Americans also opposed the bomb? If they too were a subclass, Oppenheimer could belong to either group. Because the major premise does not establish that the *only* people who opposed the bomb were communist sympathizers, the conclusion is not warranted. Construing factual claims as questions of classification focuses attention on possible deductive fallacies (though Deadwood is excluded from the class, "cities with slums and campuses," should it also be excluded from the class, "cities likely to have riots"?).

Major premises can stipulate general conditions that, *if* fulfilled, produce certain results. The minor premise establishes fulfillment in a specific instance: If penalties for looting and arson are increased, rioting will decline. Today the legislature increased the penalties. Therefore, rioting will decline.

If we assume factual truth of the major premise, the conclusion is valid. Such reasoning can be faulty, however: If penalties for looting and arson are increased, rioting will decline. Today the legislature refused to increase the penalties. Therefore, rioting will not decline. The major premise does not establish whether rioting will decline *only if* penalties are increased. Rioting could decline from other conditions as well (e.g., granting of demands, imposition of curfew, presence of national guard, severe rainstorms).

It was claimed in 1964, "If Goldwater is elected, the war in Vietnam will escalate." Opponents of the war who interpreted this as *only if* were disturbed to learn that the war could be escalated by Johnson as well. Many people believe that if a person really wants to work, he can have a reasonably secure and prosperous life. On observing alcoholics, criminals, the unemployed, and unstable families, believers in that premise conclude the only reason or cause for such a plight is lack of desire or motivation to work. Other factors (e.g., the structure of an economic system, one's childhood, discrimination) might also influence one's security and prosperity but have not been recognized in the major premise.

In addition to questioning the factual truth of premises, it is important to be concerned with their *necessity* or inevitability. People might oppose abolishing the death penalty on the "realistic" grounds that our penal institutions are not well enough staffed to change from a punitive to a rehabilitative orientation. On another issue, some will oppose a decrease in defense spending on the grounds that this will put millions out of work. Though this may be true, we can question the necessity of the basic premise: millions of people employed in defense industries. Would it be possible to have an economic system with high employment, but low concentration of money and labor in defense? People who question the necessity of premises or givens in the social world are often criticized and dismissed as utopian or unrealistic. But unless one can demonstrate that the "world-as-it-is" is the *only possible* world, the conclusions from "realistic" premises should be viewed as tentative and contingent, rather than inevitable or logically exhaustive.

IV. Relationships Among Value, Definitional, and Factual Disputes

Distinguishing among three types of issues is not meant to obscure their substantial interdependence in dialogue and justification. To justify the value "international aggression is wrong" in Vietnam, we must define who is the aggressor and specify ways in which given events can constitute international aggression. One might list such defining criteria as (a) foreign troops crossing a border without permission or invitation from the occupied country and (b) the invaders' use or threats of violence. To determine whether the historical situation meets these criteria, we must reach conclusions on factual issues: Did the troops cross the border without invitation from the home country? Solving this factual problem hinges in turn upon further definitional, factual, and value issues: If Vietnam is defined as one unstable nation including both the North and the South, then hostilities might be construed as civil war, not as foreign invasion. If the Viet Cong and NLF have wide popular support in the South, then troops from the North were in a sense "invited." If violence is carried on to oppose illegitimate or undemocratic regimes, then perhaps it should not be considered wrongful aggression. Yet what are the defining characteristics of a democratic regime? Values will influence our definitional conclusions on this issue. Values will also influence our conclusions on factual matters (e.g., which regime has the greatest popular support?) as we choose to value some sources of information over others (e.g., reports from United States Army officers versus those from captured Viet Cong).

A. Legal Issues

Interrelationships among the three types of issues are illustrated in legal issues. A "law" is a rule, based on governmental authority, defining permissible or unpermissible conduct. The definitional phase in a legal question concerns whether a particular action can be classified under an existing law: Does Billy's act in striking Claggart fall within the classes of action specified in the Mutiny Act? To answer this we must delve more deeply into what acutally happened when Claggart was struck: Was Billy's act deliberate and malicious, or involuntary? Did Claggart provoke the act? — factual issues. In applying the law, judges impose certain standards of fairness or justice: How much importance should be given to the spirit as well as the letter of the law? Establishing priorities for protecting the innocent, the welfare of the ship, the need to obey the law, or avoiding cruel and unusual punishment requires value judgments. Thus legal issues, as most policy issues, involve interdependent value, definitional, and factual claims.

B. Disagreement Over Frame of Reference

Disagreement abounds on how best to frame the central issues in a controversial situation. Such disagreements can be explained psychologically as conflicts among frames of reference — the values and beliefs that influence how each person interprets the world. Suppose Sam, Harry, and Mike list what they consider the major issues in the Mutiny Act case.

> Sam: What should Vere do to keep his power over the men? If he doesn't hang Billy, what should Vere do to protect his position against attacks by authorities in the home port?
> Harry: Can Billy's action be classified as mutiny? What provisions does the law make for clemency?
> Mike: Why did Claggart feel so threatened by Billy? When people feel threatened, is it natural for them to try to destroy their perceived enemies?

Sam seems concerned with the problem of Vere maintaining his power or leadership; Harry is interested in legal aspects of the case; and Mike is curious to explain the causes of human behavior. We might label these frames of reference the *power* framework, the *legal* framework, and the *human nature* or *behavior* framework. The differing frames of reference could forestall or even prevent agreement on which issues should be discussed. When a discussion seems to be "going nowhere" it helps to look for disagreements not just in facts, definitions, and values, but in the more basic frames of reference.

The framework that a person brings to discussion often appears grounded in a general ideology, belief system, or world view. Such thought schemes consist of a network of (a) ethical (value) choices that prescribe goals toward which men should strive; (b) concepts that tend to simplify or organize otherwise random experiences and perceptions; (c) factual claims, explanations, and predictions about the nature of men, human behavior, and the course of history. With respect for the complexity and multiple interpretations of historically significant systems of belief, we have tried to illustrate in Table 2.1 prescriptive, analytic, and descriptive components of some influential frames of reference.

The table's brevity obscures many complexities in the religious, philosophical, scientific, economic, psychological, and political traditions that the

TABLE 2.1   SCHEMATIC COMPARISON OF BELIEF SYSTEMS

Ideology or Belief System	Values	Concepts	Factual Assumptions — Explanations
1. Christianity	brotherhood, salvation	sin, good works, faith after-life	story of creation; the Messiah
2. Jeffersonian democracy	liberty, consent of the governed	inalienable rights; separation of powers; individuality	perfectability of man; dangers of political centralization
3. Marxist socialism	economic equality	social class; economic exploitation	history of class struggle; predicted demise of capitalism
4. Nazism	world conquest	race, nation	historical role of racial-national groups
5. Black nationalism	dignity for blacks	black power, black culture, white racism	white mother country ruling black colony; effects of racism on black identity
6. Social Darwinism	survival	self-interest, aggression, natural selection	evolutionary effects of struggle for survival
7. Behaviorist psychology	management of human behavior	stimulus, response, reinforcement	malleability of behavior
8. Freudian psychology	healthy personality	the unconscious; id, ego, superego	Oedipal conflict, mechanisms of defense, influence of early childhood on later development
9. Keynesian economics	full employment, economic abundance	demand, savings, investment	government policy to control demand — employment

ideologies represent. It provides, nevertheless, a scheme for distinguishing one world view from another. Any given individual will probably harbor more complicated beliefs than are accounted for by any single scheme in the table, and we suspect that most people cannot articulate a coherent, logically consistent world view. Yet when people seek to advocate policy consistent with a "philosophy of life," or "value system," it is reasonable to identify critical components or elements in that system, however over-simplified they appear at first.

In Christianity, for example, the major goal, salvation, derives meaning through contrast to the opposite concept, damnation. And both are embodied in the notion of an afterlife. Just as heaven and hell clarify the nature of the major goal or value, the concepts of good works and sin help to specify the basis on which the value is achieved. The goal's validity and its related concepts are said to have been established in particular historical events: The story of creation establishes the existence of God and his relationship to man; the life of Christ further specifies possibilities for salvation, models of behavior, and such virtues as mercy or turning the other cheek. One could proceed down the list of thought systems trying to identify for each the salient components and relationships in prescriptive, analytic, and descriptive domains.

One might add to the list and make each entry more complete. A digest of dominant belief systems would be helpful in construing the day-to-day language of laymen and officials debating policy.[5] Notice that Systems 6–9 are scientific explanations rather than philosophies or ideologies — they are called explanatory models and commonly presumed *not* to imply or advocate values (but explain empirical reality in a "valueless" manner). Despite disclaimers by academic investigators, explanatory models do have value implications, however unintended by the model's advocates. Skinnerian explanations of behavior lead to attempts to control or shape human responses, under the assumption that efficient control is to be desired. Adam Smith's description of the market and Galbraith's account of the new industrial state both imply duties and responsibilities for government and other groups in society. Though Freudian theory may seem valueless, it is logically tied to therapeutic practice in which patients are treated according to specific goals or criteria. Thus a digest of significant belief systems (frames of reference) could include entries containing such obvious value commitments as those articulated in Jeffersonian democracy and Christianity, as well as those that are allegedly "value free," such as systems analysis or pragmatism. In identifying such schemes we learn not only how people

[5] Three quite different and intriguing attempts to discover frames of reference through which people view reality can be found in Kelly, 1955; Smith, Bruner, and White, 1956; and Lane, 1962.

differ in the basic assumptions they hold, but also ways in which value, definitional, and factual issues are intertwined.

V. Role of Academic Disciplines in Clarifying Public Issues

Assuming that one can distinguish among value, definitional, and factual aspects of a dispute, what help are the academic disciplines in resolving the controversies? History, social science, law, and philosophy contribute in two general areas. First they provide information and substantive findings, frames of reference, generalizations, and concepts relevant to public issues (see Berelson and Steiner, 1964). A discussion on United States policy in Vietnam would look to history for information relevant to factual controversies (e.g., testing the applicability of the Munich analogy and the domino theory) and definitional problems (e.g., historical cases used to differentiate between civil war versus foreign aggression). Political science articulates models of government and patterns in delegating power that might clarify alternative policies for nation-building. Arguments on the net economic benefit to be derived from United States "investment" in the struggle could be enlightened by reference to cost-benefit analysis and theories of economic development. Law could clarify the network of international legal obligations and methods for adjudicating disputes peacefully. Philosophy makes explicit alternative value systems used to justify the worth or success of policy (e.g., utilitarianism, existentialism, situation ethics), and anthropology can describe values that groups adhere to in practice. Part II of this book, though not organized according to conventional discipline categories, presents concepts and theories that arise from sources within and beyond the disciplines which provide substantive insight for dealing with social controversy.

A second contribution of the disciplines lies in the models of inquiry and persuasion they employ. Mindful of differing definitions or descriptions of "scientific method" or "disciplined thinking" (see Dewey, 1933; Ennis, 1962; Kaplan, 1964; Schwab, 1964; Berlak, 1965), we make no attempt here to describe a definitive model. We do note, however, certain processes or steps consistently considered necessary to arrive at "the truth." When we create hypotheses and explanations for describing the world, and/or prescriptions for judging and affecting it, we are expected to defend or support our conclusions. "Support" usually means demonstrating the conclusions to be at least consistent with logic and empirical observation. Philosophy illustrates a dialectic model for probing logical implications of one's claims and categories. Science gives us such methods of observation as the survey, experiment, and case study, along with ground rules for evaluating the validity and reliability of empirical claims.

We are particularly impressed with legal (jurisprudential) reasoning as a model of inquiry. In common law tradition, judicial reasoning is general enough to confront the factual, definitional, and value issues inherent in public controversy. Yet it approaches these concerns through a definite pattern or strategy of thought (see Levi, 1948; Zelermyer, 1960). Formal inquiry results from actual, specific controversy between parties. In contrast to the scholar who defines his own questions and creates his own problem, the judge finds himself between disputing parties who demand solution of issues that the judge had little or no influence in creating. Decisions on the concrete controversy at hand must be publicly justified with reference to general principles so that judges in the future can decide all like cases consistently with the present case.

We may say that X should be held responsible for the killing, because he intentionally shot Y, and that, in general, people who intentionally inflict harm on others should be held responsible. Suppose, however, a prosecutor in the future uses this precedent to argue that a knifing victim should be found guilty of manslaughter for shooting his attacker. Though he harmed another intentionally, we would not hold the knifing victim responsible, but would add the qualification that even intentional killing can be justified in self-defense. The interaction between specific cases and articulating qualified general principles, consistent with relevant precedent, are perhaps the most critical features of legal reasoning. Separate steps in this process can be described:

1. Given facts on a controversy between two or more parties, decide precisely what issues are to be resolved. Judicial opinions distinguish between those issues in a case that can and should be handled in the judicial tribunal versus those that should be handled elsewhere.
2. For each issue, search for similar cases in the past and uncover the rules or principles governing past decisions.
3. Ask whether each issue in the present case significantly resembles any in precedent cases.
   a. If the case does not fit any precedent cases, arrive at a rule *de novo* and justify it. (Because of the untiring efforts of judges and adversaries to show relevance of present issues to those of the past this rarely occurs.)
   b. Does the present case resemble cases with conflicting lines of precedents?
      1. If conflicting precedents are not apparent, simply repeat the precedent ruling; *or* justify any departure from precedent if a new ruling is applied.
      2. If conflicting lines of precedent are involved, select one line, justify it and the rejection of alternatives; *or* reject all precedents and justify applying new principle.

The outline is not intended to convey a mechanistic process to be slavishly followed. It is, after all, of no substantive assistance even to jurists. That is, it gives no guidance in determining which issues should be decided in a given case, no criteria for deciding which precedent cases are relevant, no grounds for justifying departures from precedents. Its value to the citizen lies primarily in the intellectual processes it illustrates: defining and limiting the issues to be explored; searching one's experience (past and hypothetical future) for similar cases, and articulating the principles one would apply to these "precedents"; using the concepts and distinctions made from comparing precedent cases to develop a qualified general principle that can solve the case at hand and be consistently applied to like cases in the future.[6]

Although we rely heavily upon academic disciplines for both substantive clarification and methodological guidance, we do not believe they must be taught to children *as disciplines* that must be mastered before taking a rational stand on public issues. Several authors have questioned the social and intellectual utility of basing school curriculum on university-based disciplines (see Oliver, 1957; Bolster, 1962; Newmann, 1967; Roszak, 1968). We will briefly summarize a few of those arguments here: (1) Because the disciplines encompass bodies of knowledge too enormous for anyone to learn, and because they contain diverse and conflicting schools of thought, one must look beyond the disciplines for educational philosophy and criteria to govern selecting content. (2) Disciplined scholarly inquiry represents only one among many styles of life and thought worthy of emulation. (3) Because boundaries and definitions of fields of investigation are rapidly changing, one must take care not to become trained in a discipline that may soon become obsolete. (4) Much wisdom and seminal thought has come from thinkers not engaged in scholarly pursuits (e.g., social activists, artists, etc.). (5) The disciplines have not provided solutions to many of the most significant problems that citizens face. For such reasons, mastery of academic disciplines should not be considered essential either to the resolution of public issues or to the development of an "educated man." We prefer to use the disciplines eclectically, searching for knowledge from many sources. Whether an idea is worth "knowing" depends not on its membership in the structure or heritage of an academic field, but upon its power to clarify persisting dilemmas of ethical-political choice.

---

[6] Legal reasoning has been criticized for a blind adherence to values and principles of the past said to be increasingly obsolete and irrelevant to problems in the modern world. It is also chided for a paralyzing concern for logical consistency, as opposed to freer, less systematic modes of thought (e.g., situation ethics or transcendental insights that cannot be rationally articulated). Observers who probe emotional bases for legal opinions see them as rationalizations for values of the times, political expediency, or irrational personal choices. We think, however, that legal reasoning is not per se restrictive. It offers as much latitude for imagination and new ways of thinking as the humans who make decisions possess. The only important constraint is the principle that like cases should be decided in like manner, a principle we would endorse as requisite for justice and fair play.

Chapter 3

Discussion with Direction

To recognize strategies of clarification for the issues examined in Chapter 1 is a first, but not sufficient, step toward productive discourse on public issues. In addition we must give constant attention to the flow of dialogue: that is, the extent to which discussants listen and respond to each other, the depth with which issues are explored, and the cumulative development of positions and rationales as a result of conversation. It seems necessary to think on two levels at once. We must take a stand and think of reasons to defend it, but we must also ask about the discussion process: Am I sensitive to what other people are saying, or did I miss an important point? Do I know what the central issue is, or should I try to make it more explicit? Are we jumping around from issue to issue? Did someone change the subject without making an explicit transition? Should I challenge whether some comments are relevant to the issue we are discussing?

Discussants who consciously attempt to anticipate and deal with some of the following problems may avoid the extremes of "free association" or disconnected opinion on the one hand and sophistic or emotional combat (shedding more heat than light) on the other.

I. Sensitivity

Conversations often go in circles because individuals do not direct comments to the specifics of each other's statements. Often discussants are talking about different issues, even though they are considering one general topic or problem. Concerned primarily with their own positions, they simply do not *respond* to one another's statements. Such insensitivity frequently is responsible for conversation failing to "get anywhere," as hypothetical dialogues on the Mutiny Act illustrate:

> Harriet: Captain Vere is so dogmatic. He doesn't even want to give Billy a chance.

Beatrice: The real problem is making the distinction between what is morally right and what is legally right.

Zelda: I really don't like sea stories anyway. They're always so rough and bloody.

Beatrice: Obviously Billy had no legal right to hit Claggart. But what other way was there to defend himself?

Zelda: I saw a movie on television Sunday night something like "The Mutiny Act." The good guy got killed because some cruel captain wanted revenge.

Here each girl gives an opinion or states a position without noticing what others are saying.

The next conversation is more sensitive:

Harriet: Captain Vere is so dogmatic. He doesn't even want to give Billy a chance.

Beatrice: I don't think the problem is so much what type of man Vere is, but rather the legal bind in which he is caught.

Zelda: I don't see what difference either position makes: Harriet sees the problem as a flaw in the character of Captain Vere. Beatrice sees the problem as a poor sea captain caught in an unjust legal system. As far as I am concerned the results are the same: An innocent man is hanged.

Beatrice: But it *does* make a difference, because the central problem is to find out whether Captain Vere did the right thing.

Harriet: I agree, and I don't see how you can blame the system when the young officers offered several possibilities for saving Budd's life that the captain all but ignored.

Zelda: I see what you people are saying now. You agree with me that a wrong was committed in hanging Billy. Our problem now is to find out where to put the blame. We can blame Vere or we can blame circumstances that are beyond Vere's control.

Making judgments about a conversation's sensitivity is fairly easy when we listen carefully to others, or when we read what they said. It is much more difficult, however, for a person to be sensitive when he himself is caught up in an argument. Usually a discussant has to make a *conscious effort* to connect the speakers with the issues being expressed.

In the previous argument, a sensitive participant might say, "Harriet is blaming the man, Vere; Beatrice is blaming the system, the law; Zelda at first doesn't see the relevance of this distinction, but later she agrees that it is useful." If another person entered the conversation at this point and wished to move the discussion forward, he should have this kind of summary in mind.

In her last statement Zelda helped to clarify the issue around which the discussion revolved. She also might have made explicit her agreement or disagreement with others in the dialogue. Such summary statements indicate that the members of the group are listening to each other.

One can demonstrate sensitivity to others' comments by summarizing statements of agreement and disagreement, as well as by conceding a point or modifying one's position in light of previous comments. Sensitivity is also demonstrated in specific challenges to previous statements ("If you believe in capital punishment for accidental killing at sea, what about penalties for fatal auto accidents?").

II. Stating the Issue

An argument usually begins when people have different viewpoints about the rightness or wrongness, the legality or illegality, the justice or injustice of an action or policy, or the truth of a claim.

Conversation may begin with people stating their "gut-level" feelings about one aspect of a concrete situation: "Billy was wrong to strike Claggart." "Vere had a right to hang Billy." "Showing Billy mercy would have made the crew more loyal." In a complicated situation such as "The Mutiny Act," many reactions to diverse parts of the case may be immediately thrown into the discussion. One challenge of *disciplined discussion* is first to sort the different things being said about various issues or topics. Another helpful strategy is to identify points of agreement and disagreement. These steps allow the participants to focus on a limited number of issues and pursue them systematically. When participants discuss one issue at a time, it is also easier to be sensitive to each other's statements.

To state issues clearly, it is useful to translate major positions or opinions that elicit disagreement into *questions*. Stating the issue in question form emphatically focuses the discussion on a single topic. Did Beatrice, Harriet, and Zelda come to a clear statement of the issue? To what extent does the following dialogue state issues clearly?

> Henry: Captain Vere really had no choice; the Mutiny Act stated that striking an officer in wartime was a capital offense.
> Dagmar: The captain could have disobeyed the law. He did have that choice.
> Henry: But why should the captain stick his neck out? Why should he do what he knew was wrong, and suffer possible punishment for that later?
> Dagmar: But it wasn't wrong to save Billy's life. The law itself was wrong.
> Henry: You mean obeying the law is wrong?
> Dagmar: Sure, when your conscience tells you that a higher moral law is being violated. The Nazis were obeying the law when they executed innocent civilians in concentration camps. Obeying the law was not right.
> Henry: Well, suppose my conscience tells me that it is wrong to come to school and be brainwashed by English and social studies teachers. Is it right for me to defy the school attendance laws and stay home?
> Dagmar: But that's different. You're not being brainwashed. You're being educated to know more about the world around you.
> Henry: I think you're right, but my example points up the broader issue we're discussing: When is it reasonable or justifiable to obey one's conscience when

it means disobeying the law? To answer this question we've got to explore a number of situations and ask about each: What is there about this situation that makes conscience more important than law, or law more important than conscience?

Henry has suddenly stepped outside the give-and-take of the argument by summarizing the general issue over which he and Dagmar disagree. One advantage of this skill is that it provides *focus* for the discussion. A second major advantage of stating issues explicitly is that it tends to broaden the discussion and show how numerous similar situations can be related, compared, and contrasted. In the previous discussion, for example, it shows how Nazi laws and school attendance laws might clarify dilemmas in "The Mutiny Act."

III. Pursuing Issues With Continuity

Only one or two issues were discussed in the short sample conversations on previous pages. Longer discussions usually raise several issues, expanding the possibility of confusion. Usually each participant tends to raise an issue that supports his stand on the more general topic. He then pursues this issue as long as he is "winning," only to switch the issue when he begins to lose ground.

Changing the issues too quickly tends to disrupt attempts to clarify or resolve basic disagreements. The systematic pursuit of an issue means sticking with it long enough to deal with its problems thoroughly, making sure that the discussion group follows the complexities of different positions on the issue. This may be referred to as *discussion continuity*.

Find the points in the following discussion on the Vietnam war where continuity is broken.

Bernard: Say, Stanley, what do you think of that law Congress passed about burning draft cards?

Stanley: It's a good law. Those guys really bug me. Just a bunch of beatniks trying to dodge the draft. They ought to be in jail.

Bernard: I don't think it's a good law. How are you going to enforce it fairly? Suppose somebody tears up his draft card by mistake?

Stanley: Who'd do that?

Bernard: It's a stupid law. What harm does it do to burn a draft card? Besides, look what they did to David Miller. He's a sincere, cleancut kid, but they put him in jail.

Stanley: Well, he's not so bad, but some of those other guys. . . . Besides they are encouraging others to buck the draft. . . . It's unpatriotic.

Bernard: It's not unpatriotic if you believe that the war is a violation of American principles.

Stanley: You mean the war in Vietnam?

Bernard: Yes, we're killing a lot of people and using gas and napalm and all that just to support an unpopular dictatorship. That's against our principles.

Stanley: Well, it's also against our principles to let the communists take over.

Bernard: The Viet Cong aren't just communists. There are a lot of other people in their movement too. It's the government that calls them all communists. They say they are nationalists.

Stanley: What government? Ours or the one in Saigon?

Bernard; Both.

Stanley: Well, if our government calls someone a communist, he probably is.

Bernard: Is that your definition of a communist?

Stanley: Well, not exactly, but our government must know who they are.

Bernard: If our government called your brother a communist would you agree with that?

Stanley: Oh no! My brother isn't a communist.

Bernard: How do you know?

Stanley: He doesn't belong to the party; he's never even read Marx or talked to a communist.

Bernard: Well, if these Vietnamese peasants hadn't read Marx or didn't belong to the party, they wouldn't be communists either. Right?

Stanley: Well, that's different. Besides, my brother is being drafted to fight while these guys burn draft cards.

Bernard: That's too bad.

Bernard and Stanley raised numerous related issues, but many difficulties and considerations in each position on the issues were not pursued. When so many aspects of an issue such as draft card burning are left unexplored, the discussion is short-circuited.

IV. Explicit Transitions

At some points in discussion it is useful to leave one issue and move on to another. This may happen before or after an issue has been fully clarified; for example, an argument may become so deadlocked that no agreement is likely. Discussants may then agree to disagree, and take up another issue related to the general topic. Or one member may see that there is a prior issue that must be settled before the issue under discussion can be productively explored.

When someone changes the issue under consideration, he should make this known with an *explicit transitional statement*, explaining why changing issues at that point would move the discussion forward.

In the previous discussion on Vietnam, the first change in issue occurs with no warning. The issue shifts abruptly from "Should burning a draft card be unlawful?" to "Is war in general, or the Vietnamese war in particular, consistent with American principles?"

Stanley might have warned Bernard that he was changing issues, and said why:

Stanley: Well, some guys are encouraging others to buck the draft. And I think this brings us to the more important issue on which the draft card burning issue rests. The more basic question might be stated this way: "Is the draft necessary for national defense?" And I say it is necessary.

Bernard: I would agree that it is unpatriotic to hinder our national defense. But is our defense at stake in Vietnam? The real issue then is: "Should we be fighting in Vietnam at all?"

Stanley: All right, let's drop the draft card burning issue for now and get at the issue on which it rests: "Should the United States be in this war?" I say yes. We are, in the long run, defending our own freedom from aggression.

In this exchange Stanley and Bernard have explicitly changed the issue to guide the discussion in a direction they think more appropriate.

V. Relevance

People can disagree about conclusions or positions on specific issues. They can also disagree on whether they should move to a new issue. An even more common problem is determining whether a particular statement is *related* to the issue under consideration:

Hubert: I thought that when a sea captain was on a ship on the high seas he was his own master, a dictator. Why does Vere have to obey the Mutiny Act?

Jasper: Captain Vere has a narrow military mind. He probably likes the idea of pushing people around, just like Claggart did.

Hubert: Vere's personality or character, what you're talking about, is really not relevant to whether or not he is bound by the Mutiny Act. Stick to the issue.

Jasper: Sure, it's relevant. I'm saying Vere sees himself as a military man and therefore thinks he's bound by military law.

Hubert: But I'm asking is he *really* bound by the law, whether he thinks he is or not.

Jasper: Oh, I see your point. You're saying that we ought to establish the legal facts of the case before we determine how Vere interprets these facts.

Challenging the *relevance* of a statement is a way of pressing toward greater continuity — systematically focusing on one issue at a time. It also forces a discussant who has switched issues to provide a transitional statement. In this example, Jasper switches the issue. Then Hubert clarifies for Jasper why it is unwise to move to a new issue so soon. Jasper agrees.

A common argumentative tactic is to elicit agreement or concession from an adversary on an issue that appears relevant. But one can give the impression of winning points through persuasive statements that are actually irrelevant to the major points of contention. Close attention to the relevance of statements is especially necessary when the following three strategies are used.

A. Ad Hominem

One way to dismiss or discredit an argument is to attack the person who states it. *Ad hominem* remarks are aimed at the man rather than the argument. Some discussants question their adversary's motives ("You're just trying to make me look stupid" or "You're just saying that to start an argument"); others indulge in more blatant name-calling: "You're a pigheaded liar" or "What a ridiculous argument" or "I shouldn't even waste my time talking to you." Using humor and sarcasm is particularly persuasive in leading an audience to doubt a man's ability or integrity: "My worthy opponent, as incumbent school committee chairman, certainly has great knowledge of school affairs. His five close relatives whom he appointed to top administrative posts must keep him well informed." Ad hominem remarks generally distract attention from the basic issues being discussed and instead focus on the persons. This is not to say that personal credentials, ability, and integrity should never be discussed.

If a school board is deciding whether to appoint X, his personal ability would quite properly be a major issue for discussion. If we are trying to decide whether to believe Y's statements about the effects of radioactive fallout, then Y's credentials, expertise, and motives may be very relevant. But even when personal credentials are relevant, we must remember that name-calling ("communist" or "ivory tower egghead") does not help to verify claims related to personal competence. Unfortunately, discussants often fail to distinguish between ad hominem remarks and those relevant to the main issue.

B. Metaphor

We can sharpen or accentuate a situation by relating it to a vividly imagined symbol that cannot be literally applied (e.g., "A mighty fortress is our God"). Suppose Harry is arguing that giving money to slum dwellers won't ensure that they spend it correctly to improve themselves. To clinch his point, he reminds Joe, "You can lead a horse to water, but you can't make him drink." The metaphor is impressive, but how relevant is it to the main point if it implies that slum dwellers are no different from horses?

Another metaphor might designate new African nations as "instant nations," to discredit them. Americans associate "instant" with instant coffee. The phrase implies two derisive elements: the Africans think they can build a nation as easily as one can make a cup of coffee, and obviously instant coffee is not as good as brewed coffee — good coffee, like a good nation, takes time to brew. Although making coffee is far afield from nation-building, the metaphor suggests that "if you want quality, some things just take time," which is brought out more vividly by the metaphor than by saying it directly. How coffee-brewing resembles nation-building is highly questionable, however persuasive the metaphor seems at first glance.

C. Analogy

Although we discuss the clarifying function of analogy in Chapter 2 and especially in Chapter 9, we must be alert to problems of relevance they create. Harry and Joe have been arguing about the desirability of guaranteed income to alleviate poverty in the United States. Harry has pointed out that this policy will probably cause increased income tax for the wealthier people, and Harry doesn't see why he should pay higher taxes to support poor people. "Well, suppose X is lost at sea on a lifeboat," suggests Joe. "The boat has five people on it, with a hole in it and it is necessary to bail constantly. X is the only one with food. To keep up the bailing, search for food, etc., he needs at least three other people. Shouldn't he share his food with others?" "Of course," agrees Harry. "Then," reasons Joe, "you should be willing to make a financial sacrifice for the poor people in slums."

Is the lifeboat analogy relevant? Harry may feel that "it's different" from the situation dealing with the income tax, but if he is unable to articulate important differences (e.g., Does Harry's own life depend immediately upon charity to slum dwellers?), he will be unable to argue that the analogy is irrelevant. Even if we conclude that an analogy is irrelevant, distinctions made in reaching this conclusion can clarify issues and positions that had heretofore been confused (see Chapter 9).

VI. Summarizing

Summarizing the course of conversation and the cumulative development of individual positions is helpful for wrapping up or encapsulating discussion, and for increasing sensitivity, issue stating, explicit transitions, continuity, and relevance.

> Dan: We've discussed several issues: Should Vere enforce the law literally? Would a more lenient interpretation invite mutiny by the crew? Should striking an officer under provocation be considered mutiny? I think we should summarize where we've come and where we're going in this discussion.
>
> Jack: We started by agreeing that according to the letter of the law Billy's act was mutiny and illegal. We seem to disagree as to whether Vere has a moral obligation to excuse Billy in spite of this. Once we agreed to stipulate that leniency would not increase likelihood of mutiny, then we seemed to agree that Vere should not hang Billy.
>
> Stan: I started out assuming that Vere had no choice but to hang Billy. But after concluding that Billy was really provoked, that he did not intend to kill, that the crew might well respect the captain even more for showing mercy, I feel Vere has no basis, except for the letter of the law, for hanging Billy. As we've shown, the letter of the law should be subject to a higher moral judgment.
>
> Dan: Now, I think we better consider on what basis we should make such higher moral judgments.

Because it involves thinking on several levels at once, summarizing is a complicated and difficult cognitive task. One must recall substantive arguments and positions, the specific issues on which participants agreed and disagreed, the evolution of one's own personal position, and some gestalt or general pattern of interaction in the group. One's summary statement will not be useful to the group unless it closely approximates how other group members see what has transpired. Contrasting interpretations of the course of discussion can divert disagreement away from substantive issues (Should Billy be hanged?) to the problem of accurately recording the discussion itself (What have we been saying?). Periodic summaries may avoid unnecessary conflict over the latter problem. Summaries tend to interrupt the flow of dialogue, however, and when used too often will be seen as disturbing intrusions. Occasional summaries are necessary not only to record or capture what the conversation achieves, but also to focus attention on agenda questions: what should we discuss next?

VII. Limitations of Rational Discourse

Rational discourse as developed here and in Chapters 1 and 2 is far easier to describe as an ideal model than to observe in actual conversation. Understandably the model can be criticized as unrealistic: people just do not think or argue rationally and systematically; their opinions are formed through irrational or nonrational influences; they are not secure enough to examine their views openly in situations of conflict. Thus, because of human nature or conditions of social structure, it is unrealistic to expect persons to converse according to our rational discussion model.[1] Another criticism is that even if it were possible, rational discourse may not be particularly desirable.

A. Is It Possible?

Much human behavior, especially response to conflict, is commonly assumed to be governed by psychological dynamics beyond an individual's rational control. The beliefs, attitudes, opinions we espouse — the very statements we make — are seen as attempts to meet underlying emotional needs: for example, the need to reduce anxiety. Anxiety may be attributed to feelings of guilt, insecurity, uncertainty, inconsistency, incompetence, etc., and numerous defense mechanisms *unconsciously* are employed to compensate for or cope with such feelings. Through selective perception we notice only those aspects of a problem that confirm previous beliefs, thus eliminating ambiguity and challenges to our views. By projecting our own inadequacy or guilt on our adversaries we dismiss or refuse to take seriously the inconsistencies they might discover in our position. By attempting to dominate others in conversation we bolster our sense of personal competence. We

---

[1] The "model" is composed of analytic distinctions between types of issues, suggested strategies for dealing with the issues (Chapter 2), and skills in discussion process for developing group and individual positions (present chapter). Chapters 9 and 10 (and the "after" conversation between Joe and Clarence in Chapter 1) further illustrate different facets of the model.

avoid uncomfortable disagreement by simply hiding our true feelings on an issue, reaching a cordial, polite consensus that preserves interpersonal harmony. These are just a few ways in which psychological needs and mechanisms can impede rational discourse.

Although we recognize the influence of nonrational emotional drives, we have not seen evidence that they totally determine how we perceive and approach issues (and people). Nor can we assume that emotional phenomena cannot be controlled to enhance our ability to deliberate rationally. By explicitly recognizing psychological processes, we have taken the first step toward bringing our judgments under more rational control. A major reason for consciously analyzing biases and defense mechanisms, whether through psychotherapy, sensitivity training, or academic courses in psychology, is the assumption that analysis itself will bring greater control over the impulses and emotions that would otherwise be seen as inevitable or unmanageable. We can guard against selective and distorted perceptions, for example, by including in discussion groups people with diverse frames of reference, where conflicting views of reality presumably check and balance each other. We can learn to recognize in others the use of various "defenses" (e.g., aggression, projection, conflict avoidance) and thereby distinguish between rational and nonrational components in an argument. We can encourage informal social rewards that deemphasize the value of "winning" an argument, placing greater value on mutual clarification. We greatly need research on how emotional and psychological phenomena can be harnessed to develop more rational discourse, and although our own work has not focused directly on this problem, we would seriously encourage the application of findings in psychology and social psychology, along with training skills in group work, to this end.[2]

Certain political, sociological, and economic views use a different basis for doubting the possibility of rational dialogue. According to a prevailing argument, the major obstacle to rational dialogue lies in the way power is distributed in society and the fact that preservation of economic-political self-interest is the primary consideration for determining individual positions on issues. Each person seeks to maintain or increase his power, but in a world of scarcity (and especially under a capitalistic system), this can be accomplished only at the expense of another person's power or self-interest. Therefore, members of different social classes, or individuals possessing unequal power, cannot (and should not be expected to) reason with each other. Because individuals will adopt only those positions that tend to maintain or increase their power, one persuades others and justifies his views by

---

[2] Shaver (1968) is attempting to teach high school students about some psychological processes that influence their opinions on public issues.

appealing to self-interest, power, and force, not dispassionate reason. The university administration will begin to establish a black studies department not when presented with rational arguments, but when confronted with the threat of campus disruption. Management is convinced not by the logic of the union's plea for higher salaries, but by the risk of profit loss pursuant to a strike. A politician's vote is determined less by a rational consideration of what is in the public interest and more by the political support he sees himself likely to win and lose as a result of that vote. Because people cannot escape the influence of political-economic self-interest, it is unrealistic to expect them to consider issues in an open, rational manner.

We agree that in many situations power or material threat to self-interest is so paramount that whatever discourse might occur would focus exclusively on the issue, "What course of action is most in my self-interest?" To assume that self-interest or enhancing one's power is the primary consideration in social controversy does not, however, make rational discourse impossible. This assumption merely delineates the major value on which rational arguments will be considered persuasive or unpersuasive; it by no means eliminates controversy or the use of rational inquiry to deal with controversy. Generals, Congressmen, and citizens may agree that the United States should act to preserve and enhance its power as a world leader, but they will disagree whether intervention in Vietnam or the construction of ABM systems would achieve this goal. Low-income blacks may agree they must fight for economic power, but they will disagree whether this should be done through black capitalism or socialistic cooperatives. Upper middle-class professionals may agree that higher taxes threaten their economic interest, but they will disagree which items in the city budget should be cut. Thus reaching conclusions on how to get power or how to keep it involves dilemmas that rational discourse can clarify. To persuade others to adopt your views (so that you will have more power) also requires some reliance on rational argument. Even the hard-core radical, who often equates rationality with hypocritical or do-nothing liberalism, must depend on rational inquiry — for his research on the power structure, for debates on tactics he has with comrades, for presenting his ideology to those he hopes to convert. A self-interest or power interpretation of social dynamics does not in this sense rule out using rational methods.

The absence of rational deliberation and our disenchantment with it do not necessarily indicate that rational discourse is impossible. More probably these signify a glaring deficiency in our approach to education. Schwab (1969) claims that when models of rational inquiry are presented in school, it is in the context of abstract problem-solving relevant to academic disciplines. Students rarely have the opportunity to observe rational decision-making applied to practical problems or questions of specific policy in the real world. If in school one learns a mode of rational inquiry that is applied only in science and formal scholarship, he could readily assume that practical decisions of necessity must be based on whim, personal taste, or other nonrational grounds. In failing to concentrate on rational thinking applied to the making of actual social choices, schools have ill-prepared us to cope with the irrationality we see in so many public policies. Because we have not observed or experienced complexities involved in making public policy, we are unable to distinguish between decisions that are clearly in error versus those that appear nonsensical only because we are ignorant of conflicting interests and valid reasons that stand behind them. The challenge for education, therefore, is to concentrate more directly on using rational deliberation to make public policy. We should not conclude that rational discourse is impossible until more attention has been given to its development. Neither schools nor other institutions (e.g., the family, the media, business, etc.) have devoted sufficient effort in this direction.

B. Is it Desirable?

In Chapter 1 we discussed briefly the justification for rational process. We claimed that the "rules" of rationality establish a language for approaching questions of proof or justification, without which it would be impossible for men to discuss goodness and justice. Discussion on such problems is ignited or stimulated when a policy proposed by one group (or person) is perceived as threatening or harmful to another — either in a material, self-interest sense or in the psychological sense of violating values held to be sacred. We assume that because of the real or perceived harm arising out of policy recommendations, policy advocates (including those who counsel apathy or no policy) are morally obligated to give reasons for their views. Example: the United States Commissioner of Education decides to enforce guidelines that deprive local school districts of federal funds if they refuse to racially integrate their schools. Because of the perceived harm done to local schools by the withdrawal of aid and the perceived harm done to black and white children by delaying integration, each side is obligated to justify its position.

The Commissioner could demonstrate the validity of enforcing federal guidelines through different styles of justification. He could appeal to chance by flipping a coin, deciding arbitrarily in advance that "heads" means enforce, "tails" means delay enforcement. He could call upon such sources as divine revelation, intuition, or common sense and do what he instinctively knows or feels to be right without offering justification on any other grounds. He could assume that might makes right: if any agent has the power to enforce its will, then this alone is sufficient justification for the course it takes. Finally, he could make a rational case, citing a number of different reasons and attempting to rebut counter-arguments. His brief or rationale would include defining key terms, predicting the consequences of alternative policies, citing evidence for controversial factual claims, and explicitly recognizing major assumptions and values.

Using reason is preferred to other styles of justifications, because, by definition, it is requisite to moral deliberation, and also because it seems critical to fulfilling other values — particularly pluralism and freedom of choice. By honoring evidence and opinions from all relevant sources, by debating what is "relevant," and by eternally questioning premises (even the premises of rationality itself!), rational discussion offers the greatest invitation to diverse views: alternative approaches to issues. The rule that any statement, regardless of who makes it, can be open to the scrutiny of independent sources protects against dogmatism or the complacent assumption that final truth has been found. Through its emphasis on consistency, rationality reinforces one keystone of justice: that like cases should be decided in like manner and that citizens should have stable expectations as to what behaviors will be treated as lawful and unlawful. The rule that reasons within an argument must be consistent and that public policies should be consistent with each other helps to prevent the injustice that would ensue if policy could be made on such nonrational grounds as whim or fancy. Finally, we believe that without the criteria for justification and verification that rationality provides, it would be virtually impossible for men to debate community issues. We would have no basis for deciding what constitutes a reason, a piece of evidence, a truth, a falsehood, an irrelevancy. Pluralism and consent of the governed cannot be achieved without public debate on community issues, and such debate is inconceivable without reliance upon a language of this sort.

Yet what can rational discourse accomplish? Critics note that even those adversaries behaving most rationally (e.g., Supreme Court justices) often will not resolve disagreements. "Old-fashioned liberalism" with its emphasis on reason is berated for having failed to solve the world's most pressing problems, allegedly because of too much discussion and not enough action. Although we believe that rational dialogue has rarely prevailed in our approaches to public controversy (except perhaps in judicial tribunals), we agree in spirit with both criticisms. They are, however, misdirected. While rationality has by no means ended controversy, it has provided bases for conciliation among antagonists and in some instances, through the accumulation of impressive evidence, seems to have "settled" issues (perhaps temporarily) — the safety of fluoridated water, the health hazards of cigarette smoking, the right to counsel for indigents accused of felonies. The desirability of rational discourse, however, lies not in its power to terminate controversy or solve problems, but in its potential to provide evidence and reasons for positions, to discover alternative approaches to issues, and to distinguish crucial issues of disagreement from superficial and irrelevant ones.

"Solving" public problems or maximizing the justice and good that flow from public policies rests perhaps upon a combination of will or commitment and intelligence. Both seem necessary, but certainly neither is sufficient to eliminate misery and injustice. We see rational discourse as critical to intelligent consideration of public issues, but it alone cannot inspire people to hold "good" values, nor can it instill the willpower and commitment necessary for effective action.[3]

We noted in Chapter 1 that reliance upon rational justification does not preclude the use of violence. Neither does it prohibit nonrational techniques for attaining power or attracting followers. A political candidate could, through rational deliberation, conclude that he will gain more votes if he appeals to voters' fears, if he discredits his opponent through smear and innuendo, if in some situations he refuses to discuss the issues but instead flirts with the ladies. When one is faced with questions of power, action, and tactics of persuasion, one could rationally conclude to adopt devices that appeal to men's nonrational motivations.

The rational model can be justly criticized as a limited or parochial approach to the quest for truth. As will be reiterated in Chapter 9, it would be frightful for curriculum to focus exclusively on developing tight logical justifications for every preference or claim we express. Because the meaning of existence cannot be explored exclusively through a scientific, rational mode, it is important to look upon rational deliberation as only one among several paths to truth and meaning. The search for beauty, for interpersonal intimacy and honesty, for the spontaneity of play, for the depth of religious conviction, and for a sense of craftsmanship represent only a few alternative dimensions of experience, none of which should be stifled by excessive zeal to develop a rational man. By concentrating here on rational discourse in making decisions on public issues, we do not mean to deny the value of contrasting orientations appropriate for other facets of the good life.

---

[3] The argument has been made that a person totally committed to rationality would never cease inquiring into the complexities of a problem. So intrigued would he be by verifying all assumptions and claims and by searching for all conceivable approaches to an issue that he would not be capable of making a decision or taking action in support of or against a policy. The university academic who never signs a political petition because he is perennially uncertain of the correct answer illustrates the paralyzing effect that allegiance to inquiry can have. We believe that a commitment to rationality entails no such course. To act on the basis of incomplete evidence is an existential and moral necessity that is also consistent with canons of rationality.

PART II

Substantive Problem Areas

In addition to analyzing intellectual disagreement, rational persuasion, and the flow of dialogue, we must explore some specific ideas, values, or concepts on which social controversy persistently focuses. Whether we discuss the justification for Roman persecution of the Christians, disobedience of the Fugitive Slave Law, United States support of counterrevolutionary regimes, or police actions at the Democratic convention in 1968, we find recurring problems in ethical reasoning, recurring appeals to certain values, distinctions, generalizations, and arguments. In this section we identify and discuss the complexities in numerous concepts frequently mentioned or alluded to in conventional discourse. Chapters 4–8 do not build upon each other into an elaborate cumulative theory. Rather they provide a variety of separate issues and complexities that, if taken into account, would increase the thoroughness or depth of arguments on specific policies. Hence this section should be seen not as a self-contained treatise on the nature of controversy, but as a reference source that raises substantive problems.

Because public controversy can be construed in a variety of categories or dimensions, it might be helpful to describe some schemes that were considered prior to adopting five areas: morality-responsibility, equality, consent, welfare-security, and property. Although we cannot demonstrate these as the most efficient or useful categories, we can relate how alternative rubrics were considered and either discarded or subsumed under the present headings.

Persisting issues could be grouped under such topics as war, race relations, labor movements, crime, sex, religion, pollution, commerce, education, housing, health, etc.[1] Although these may be appropriate headings for study units (many are included in Problems of Democracy texts and in the AEP Public Issues Series), we sought categories that would transcend the specific subjects of controversy and would raise issues common to a variety of conflicts. Considerable journalistic and academic attention has already been given to topics above, and we hoped to find new perspectives.[2] Initially we wished to introduce students to a wide range of controversy in different cultures at different times. To aid in selecting cases, we identified five domains of social decisions common to most societies, about which Westerners will have conflicting points of view:

The Use and Control of Violence
Maintaining a Standard of Living
Establishing Priorities and Privileges
Providing for Dissent and Change
Defining Boundaries between Public and Private Concerns

Cases were selected to illustrate each area (see Chapter 9, p. 255 for examples), and the areas were eventually subsumed under the present Chapters 4–8.

While continually questioning this scheme for classifying controversy, we asked whether men tend to use certain pervasive or prototypical perspectives in approaching social conflict. The thought schemes or ideologies presented in Table 2.1 (p. 66) offered one set of perspectives. In examining intellectual traditions, we derived still other categories. Each of the following perspectives tries to explain or improve certain domains of human experience; each implies a general purpose or goal.

PERSPECTIVE	DEALS WITH	IMPLICIT GOAL
Legal-ethical	procedures for determining values and for judging the distribution of power	Justice
Personality	individual motivation and styles of choice	Emotional maturity
Political	methods of attaining and retaining control	Accommodation of conflicting interests

[1] For example, see the "problematic areas of culture" described by Hunt and Metcalf (1968).

[2] Discovering, modifying, and discarding categories were stimulated primarily by the daily challenge of teaching controversial issues to high school students for three years. The categories were developed for a framework that we teachers could use to select content, a framework that would help us ask critical questions and that would steer us to significant controversies and scholarship. Once we developed an intellectual framework, then we could debate which aspects of the framework should be taught explicitly to students.

PERSPECTIVE	DEALS WITH	IMPLICIT GOAL
Economic	production, distribution, and exchange of goods and services	Material well-being
Religious	ultimate meaning of life and death	Salvation
Proof process	verification and explanation	Truth
Rhetoric	persuasion and clarification	Communication

The first five perspectives have roots in the academic disciplines of jurisprudence, ethics, philosophy, political science, psychology, economics, and the study of religion. Proof process and Rhetoric, on which Chapters 2 and 3 are based, can be applied more generally to evaluating discourse from any perspective. Sociology, anthropology, and such newly emerging fields as futurology or ecology conceivably could provide even broader, "meta" perspectives that examine community issues through an integrated combination, or restructuring, of all perspectives. Clashing perspectives in many instances can cause controversy (a citizen pleading for justice berates the politician who knowingly compromises his principles to accommodate conflicting interests). Given a particular controversy, the perspectives may help to identify alternative issues for discussion (in considering welfare policy, how much attention should be given to quantitative economic costs and benefits versus psychological effects on sense of self-worth).

Because the perspectives are parallel to and reflected in scholarship in the disciplines, we sought specific contributions of the disciplines. In controversial cases (e.g., Stamp Act crisis of 1765, Brown versus Board of Education decision of 1954), we tried to list several issues relevant to the controversy that the separate disciplines might illuminate. A grid or matrix was devised to help map out for each case issues relevant to the fields of ethics — law, political science, economics, sociology-anthropology, psychology, history. The grid indicates possible agendas for discussion. Not all grid cells could be appropriately filled in for any given controversy. The most pregnant controversy might be that for which the greatest number of cells had entries. (See the grid for the Mutiny Act.)

The grid raises several issues but provides few resources for solving or dealing with them. To find explanations, concepts, models, and reliable generalizations we studied the separate social science disciplines (including history, ethics, and philosophy) and compiled for each a set of ideas useful to justify positions and to explain conflict. Our intent was to create separate chapters on the contributions of each discipline, but with additional experi-

GRID (Case: The Mutiny Act)

Discipline Perspective	Policy-Value Questions	Fact-Explanation Questions	Concepts, Definitions, Distinctions	Theories, Models
Ethical-Legal	Was it right to hang Billy? Who was responsible for Claggart's death? Did Billy have a fair trial?	Did Billy violate the Mutiny Act? What legal authority did Vere have to try and sentence Billy?	moral vs. legal rights and duties; responsibility; provocation; spirit vs. letter of law; due process	retributive vs. rehabilitative justice; greatest good for greatest number; judge as executor or interpreter of law
Political	What should be done to maintain political stability on ship? Should Vere act to keep his power?	What was the likelihood of mutiny by the crew?	power; conflicting interests; authority vs. power; self-interest	conflict and compromise among conflicting interests
Sociological-Anthropological	What conditions are necessary to preserve cohesion and loyalty in the crew?	What values did crew hold regarding obedience and lenient punishment?	group norms; expectations; authority; roles	cultural norms and deviance
Psychological	Should Vere act to relieve tension and frustration of crew?	Why did Billy and Claggart act hostile to each other? Did Billy have control of his actions?	sanity; normality; aggression; psychic security; anxiety	influence of the unconscious; defenses for handling anxiety
Historical	What should Vere have done to avoid the problem earlier?	Was Billy part of a conspiracy? How had previous analogous situations been handled	evidence; multiple causation; precedent; hindsight	influence of men vs. broad forces in historical events
Economic	no major issues here	no major issues here	no major issues here	no major issues here

ence in teaching and in debating controversial issues among colleagues, we concluded that the criteria and boundaries of traditional academic disciplines imposed unnecessary and artificial constraints. That is, the arguments, claims, or ideas expressed by the citizen groping for a defensible position are grounded in experience far less structured than the domains of formal scholarship suggest. The most powerful ideas used by laymen, policy-makers, and even scholars have been studied and argued within many intellectual traditions or perspectives. Aiming toward a more holistic and organic view of social controversy than chapters titled "economics" or "political science" would imply, we tried to incorporate insights from many fields into topics that we consider more indigenous to or at the nucleus of controversy itself.

The values or concepts to which citizens actually refer and depend on to justify their opinions are fraught with ambiguity that the citizen has rarely discovered. Henry argues that the war is "immoral" and that people have a "moral responsibility" to disobey authority when the authority orders immoral acts. Harry argues for guaranteed minimum income for "equality of opportunity." Jim pleads for black community control of schools, referring to traditional rights of "self-government or consent." Joe advocates persecution of American communists as necessary to protect "national security." Chester opposes open-housing legislation as a violation of his "property rights." Based on actual dialogue on widely ranging controversies, we have clustered or arranged the ambiguities and complexities into problem areas indicated in these examples. Any significant controversy (e.g., the Civil War or ABM) will probably involve issues relevant to all areas, but each has its own unique philosophical, definitional, and empirical problems.

The topics in Chapters 4–8 represent a bold interdisciplinary excursion into the intellectual traditions of philosophy, ethics, jurisprudence, history, economics, sociology, psychology, political science, and anthropology. In eclectically relating contributions of these fields to persisting social issues as we see them, we have undoubtedly oversimplified and misrepresented some authors and schools of thought. We believe this is unavoidable in any attempt to synthesize and integrate wisdom from diverse sources. We hope that scholars in the separate fields will not construe our effort as a pretense of expertise in any of the many disciplines we call upon.

Cases follow each chapter, with questions that summon the reader to apply analysis in a portion of the chapter to a concrete social issue. Most cases will be relevant to the content of more than one chapter, and no case will illustrate more than a slight fraction of issues raised in a chapter. In the conclusion to Part II we comment on the possible irrelevance and obsolescence of the chapters themselves.

Chapter 4   # Morality-Responsibility

A passenger is cast overboard from a sinking lifeboat to lighten its load so that women and children may live. A pilot bombs innocent villagers to root out the enemy. A governor pardons a convicted murderer. A judge awards damages because of a broken contract. A real estate broker, honoring wishes of clients, refuses to show property to Negroes. Discussions on these issues evoke such statements as: "He had a responsibility to the group." "Though legally justified, it was morally wrong." "He didn't deserve such punishment." "You must keep your promises." "My only responsibility is to myself or my client." Efforts to establish one's duties or obligations by considering the interests and rights of others are by definition efforts in moral deliberation. Because most public issues involve conflicting duties, obligations, and responsibilities, discussing public issues is essentially a venture in moral reasoning.[1] Although argument on public controversy involves issues that go beyond moral questions, we intend, drawing largely on the field of ethics, to discuss problems related primarily to the question, "What would be morally right or what is one's moral responsibility?"[2]

I. Types of Obligations and Duties

From the diverse contexts in which morality becomes an explicit issue, obligations are debated on three levels:

1. *Commutative* obligations, in one-to-one personal relationships. (Is X bound by his promise to Y? Does Joe "owe" his father anything?)

---

[1] Blanshard (1966) argues that political issues are in the final analysis ethical issues.

[2] We have cotitled the chapter "responsibility," because responsible action is commonly interpreted as that in which a person meets his moral obligations. This chapter relies considerably on the works of Edel (1955), Frankena (1963) and Baier (1965) and on collections by Olafson (1961) and Brandt (1962).

90

2. *Contributive* individual obligations to sacrifice for the good of the group. (Should the man on the lifeboat give his life for the survivors? Should the youth be forced to serve his country?)

3. *Distributive* group obligations to individuals. (Should the majority give equal privileges to a dissenter? Should the government grant special financial assistance to disadvantaged persons?)

Commutative obligations may seem least related to public policy, more personal or private in scope. In fact, however, person-to-person obligations are prescribed and enforced by the community through laws and customs. Such personal relationships as between husband-wife, parent-child, employer-employee, professional-client are continuing topics for public debate as laws on adultery, child neglect, collective bargaining, or mercy killing illustrate. Most public issues might appear to raise distributive obligations: What should the government do for poor people? How much should be allocated to defense versus education? But arguments about what the government should do can also be translated into commutative or contributive obligations: What obligation do I have to raise the salary of the teacher who lives across the street? Why should I pay higher taxes to help poor people? Although the three categories of obligations certainly do not answer such questions, they help to construe cases through diverse interpretations of obligations and duties.

II. Alternative Meanings of Responsibility and Obligation

A. Causal Versus Moral

The claim that "Jack was responsible for the accident and so he should pay," usually implies that Jack caused the mishap to occur and that, because he caused the event, he has incurred certain obligations. Middle-class whites commonly react to the plight of poor blacks by saying, "Because I've never done anything to them, I have no responsibility for the problem — thus no obligations to help solve it." This position assumes that obligations arise only when some direct causal link connects a person to an event or state of affairs. There are some difficulties with this position. First, it is often difficult to pinpoint and isolate clear causes of complex social events (e.g., wars or riots), because of multiple causes and the infinite regress that traces all causes back to Adam and Eve. Second, we can find numerous cases in which it is widely agreed that one does have some moral obligation, even though one had no participation in the actual events. An unsuspecting bystander witnesses an auto accident in which all passengers are seriously injured and unable to summon help. Although aiding the injured will cause the bystander inconvenience, and possibly considerable loss of time, it would be generally agreed that although he did not cause the accident, he has an obligation to help the injured. Conversely, in some situations a person directly causes an event, yet should not be held morally responsible: harm inflicted by the mentally insane, or the young child lacking self-control.

When individuals or groups are said to be "responsible" for a state of affairs, we must ask whether a causal or moral responsibility is intended. As suggested, moral responsibility may arise on grounds other than direct cause: for example, the ability that one has to relieve suffering; contractual and legal obligations; tacit consent to perform duties, etc. One challenge of moral reasoning is to define more specifically criteria by which one incurs moral responsiblity.

B. Prima Facie Versus Actual Obligations

If Mary promises to babysit for Mrs. Jones on Wednesday, we could agree in general that she had an obligation to keep her promise. If, however, on Wednesday evening Mary's mother became seriously ill and Mary had to take her to the hospital, we could agree that Mary's actual obligation was to care for her sick mother rather than keep her babysitting promise. We could list many such obligations — keeping promises, obeying the law, caring for one's children, honesty, refraining from violence — that help to define one's moral duties in general. That is, one should fulfill such obligations unless one can find a special reason or exception for violating them. Such obligations are *prima facie* guidelines for moral behavior. In the actual course of events, extenuating circumstances often make it impossible to follow prima facie duties. Mary cannot both keep her promise and care for her sick mother. She must choose what her *actual* obligation is in those circumstances. Although we have a prima facie duty to obey the law, a protestor with strong moral objections to the Selective Service System and the Vietnam war may burn his draft card, feeling an obligation to act out a dramatic form of civil disobedience; likewise, the northern abolitionist who violated the fugitive slave law to help runaway slaves or the Jewish sympathizer in Nazi Germany who helped Jews escape Nazi law. Heated public controversies are often disagreements over whether a person's or group's prima facie obligations should actually be followed.

III. Bases of Moral Judgments

Although the values and the sources of values which people hold sacred are not often sufficient to resolve dilemmas of moral choice, they are often adhered to with such passion that the beholder perceives a solution. We can identify and point out complexities in numerous principles or values that people use to prescribe their prima facie obligations.

A. Principles or Values as Bases for Moral Judgments

1. Prudence

Basing one's obligations on prudence alone is often said to be immoral, because prudence places highest value on self-interest or self-satisfaction: one maximizes one's own individual objectives, without regard for the needs and rights of others (unless such regard is useful in attaining one's self-interest). If morality assumes a serious concern for others' rights, then prudence seems to be an immoral basis for deciding on one's obligations. A real estate broker can refuse to show property to Negroes, "Not because I dislike them or because I think they don't deserve equal opportunity, but only because I risk economic losses to my business if they move into the neighborhood." This represents reasoning based on self-interest or prudence alone. A more sophisticated type of self-interest, often called enlightened self-interest, does consider the rights and interests of others, but only as a means to further selfish goals: "I will sell property to Negroes, because if I refuse, they might picket my business and prosecute me for violating the fair-housing ordinance, which would damage my image as a respectable businessman." Although this broker would in effect be helping to guarantee equal rights to others, his basic justification for such action is prudence — the success of his own business. The politician or university administrator who advocates reforms, not because he considers them intrinsically justified, but mainly to "avoid trouble or protest" acts on the basis of "expediency," another form of prudence. Although some will argue that prudence or expediency are not truly moral considerations, we believe that such issues cannot be avoided and that the essence of moral deliberation lies in balancing and testing the significance of the prudent course of action in contrast to action based on other principles.

2. Law

In a society professing great respect for the authority of statutory law or regulations, the law often becomes synonymous with morality itself, and there are those who believe that the essence of morality is obedience to the law of the times. This belief can extend to the point where, if no law can be found to cover a given decision, it would be claimed that any possible actions (within the law) would be morally right. This position in extreme would hold that Mary, the babysitter, could either help her mother or babysit for Mrs. Jones because no law told her what to do, but neither action is morally preferable. Similarly, the legalist approach could uphold Eichmann's action in arranging for extermination of the Jews because he was obligated to follow orders from his superiors; or the morality of slave-owners obeying laws that buttressed the institution of slavery and its atrocities.

There are problems in basing one's moral code totally on obeying the law. First, types of law differ: statutory; local, state, and federal; constitutional; common law; and even "natural law." Precedents or rules may conflict, depending upon what type or level of law is respected. Although local ordinances have banned certain types of speech and demonstrations, protestors have violated these laws in the name of upholding their constitutional rights to free speech. Amish religious laws have conflicted with laws on education; state law has differed from federal law on the public's responsibility to provide counsel for defense of the indigent. Second, within a given source of law precedents can conflict. In constitutional law, the Plessy v.

Ferguson decision conflicts with the Brown decision; decisions upholding the police power of states conflict with decisions that authorize Congressional regulation of state affairs. To argue that the "most recent" law should be followed does not solve the problem. United States action in Vietnam is held consistent with that part of the United Nations Charter that gives nations the right to resist aggression, but is said to violate the provision that outlaws intervention by one country in another's affairs.

Finally, in certain situations distinctions are apparent between one's legal and moral obligations. We search for "higher" principles when laws do not compel any particular action, either because the laws contain conflicting guidelines or because they do not address themselves to the problem (Should Mary care for her sick mother or babysit for Mrs. Jones?). We raise moral questions about one's obligations when a person obeys what most would consider to be an unjust law (e.g., the Nazi commandant operating an extermination camp), or when deliberately violating the law is justified by appeal to a higher moral principle (e.g., patriots fighting the American Revolution or Negroes sitting at lunch counters).

To decide which moral values or principles can justify violating the law is, of course, a persisting issue, and some more general ideals (beneficence, utility, justice, freedom) have been used to define the "higher" moral values. Given the assertion that one is not morally bound to obey immoral laws, we may try to define morality by these general values or by more specific criteria. Lon Fuller (1964) suggests that for a law to be moral, it must (1) apply equally to everyone who comes within its scope; (2) be publicly promulgated so that people can be expected to be aware of it; (3) be clearly enough expressed so that people understand what it requires; (4) not contradict other laws also in effect; (5) not require what is humanly impossible; (6) remain relatively constant through time; (7) be enforced by official action consistent with the formal rule; and (8) not punish people retroactively for behavior presumed to be legal before new laws were made. These criteria may be necessary but not sufficient conditions for judging the morality of law; in addition, one might wish to impose such other values as "passed by majority rule" and "not infringing on personal privacy."

Having accepted a prima facie duty to obey the law, we must be prepared to face situations that require additional principles to justify one's moral obligations.

3. Utility

One additional principle stresses "the greatest good for the greatest number," and although the concept was originally suggested as a criterion for making legislative decisions, it has served as a more general basis of morality. The man who abandons the lifeboat so that several others may live could justify such an obligation on this utilitarian ground. The principle also justifies using majority rule to make social decisions, on the assumption that majority rule maximizes the number of people likely to be satisfied.

The utility principle raises the problems of defining what is meant by "the greatest good," and calculating the extent to which "good" is achieved by various actions or policies. The good has been defined as a situation in which the total amount of pleasure is maximized and the total amount of pain is minimized. This has also been called maximizing "happiness." Yet how can we weigh the relative pleasure or happiness resulting from sensual pleasure, material comfort, or psychic peace of mind? Utilitarians proposed developing a "calculus" that accorded positive and negative values to different human conditions, experiences, states of mind, and the legislator was to use such a calculus to mathematically maximize total happiness. The plausible hypothesis that one man's pleasure might be another's pain creates severe problems of application. Nevertheless, the general principle is commonly invoked when we speak of the soldier's duty to give his life for his country, the wealthy's duty to pay taxes for the benefit of the poor, the dissenting minority's duty to follow rules or decisions laid down by the majority, taking private property through eminent domain, or punishing criminals by the larger society. Yet the utility principle can be questioned because of other standards of morality: when the majority persecutes a religious minority, when vigilante justice by a majority denies due process of law, or when a strong populous nation occupies a small weak neighbor. In such cases, such principles as equality, justice, freedom, or charity may be considered morally superior or perhaps as prerequisites to the happiness of the greatest number.

4. Freedom

It is argued that the freedom or autonomy to choose one course of action among several is the most fundamental requirement of moral behavior, that without such freedom it is impossible for man to be moral. This view taken to its extreme suggests that any coercion denies man the opportunity to be moral. That is, formal laws enforced through sanctions in effect deny men the opportunity to be moral by prescribing, instead of allowing individuals to choose, acceptable social activity. Using individual autonomy as the sole basis for morality, however, raises the perplexing contradiction that X's exercise of complete freedom may result in his restricting the autonomy of others. If X is highly moral, he would voluntarily restrict his own actions so as not to interfere with others' freedom. But because not all men agree with this standard of morality, and because even those who do may be unable to calculate the effects of their actions on others' freedom of choice, men have restricted individual choice, through laws and social institutions, to preserve freedom.

Liberty, autonomy, and individuality are often procalimed as man's most sacred rights. ("Give me liberty or give me death.") It is said that man's very humanness depends upon preserving his freedom. Our commitments to free choice and rational consent are consistent with this position. With this in mind, it may seem odd that none of our chapters is entitled "liberty" or one of its synonyms. Because conflicts between individual freedom and social obligations pervade so many social issues, we chose not to isolate freedom as a separate problem, but to deal with it as it arises in different forms throughout the substantive problem areas. Chapter 7 on consent deals with freedom, most specifically in considering rights of individuals to freely control their lives.

5. Beneficence

Love and charity, expressed for centuries, though not universally followed, in teachings of Christianity, serve as another powerful value in moral reasoning. We shall combine them here into one principle, "beneficence," and emphasize doing good to others, which may involve forgiveness, "turning the other cheek," giving alms and charity, offering emotional comfort and kindness, and generally making personal sacrifice to benefit others. Beneficence has also been cited as the ultimate criterion for judging whether any given action is morally right. A persistent difficulty in applying the principle is distinguishing between a person's will, intent, and motivation versus actual consequences arising from his actions and deeds. Is it consistent with the principle of beneficence for a political leader to advocate war, based on a sincere intention to preserve peace and goodwill on earth? Or suppose a selfish motive leads to "good deeds": the mammoth business corporation contributes millions for philanthropic projects, but the basic motivation behind the charity is self-interest — tax deductions preserve profit, and advertising preserves a respectable image. The distinction between beneficent *motives* and *deeds* suggests that appealing to beneficence alone will not necessarily solve one's moral dilemmas. Even assuming the most beneficent motive, should we forgive children or fanatics who unknowingly injure others? Even if we could afford it, for example, would it be right to donate money to the poor whenever they beg? Should we turn the other cheek to aggressors (foreign invaders, student radicals)? Actions apparently consistent with beneficence may lead to violating other values (and perhaps perverting beneficent intent).

6. Justice

We may be told that it was immoral for Stalin to persecute the Kulaks; immoral for Britain to exploit India; immoral for the United States to bomb civilians in Vietnam; immoral for a storekeeper to deceive customers about the quality of his products. If we ask for reasons behind such moral judgments, we may be told such actions are unjust or unfair. Because "justice" often is used synonymously with morality, analyzing its meanings should include most of the values already discussed: i.e., the previous actions may be judged unjust or unfair (or immoral) because they violate values of *beneficence, freedom, utility,* or *law.* But justice also implies more specific principles. Three themes most salient to more specific connotations are:

Justice as Fairplay. The principles or values behind fairness in the sense of fairplay are those discussed under morality of the law; rules of the game must be clear and publicized, they must apply to all equally, (again, see Fuller, 1964): they cannot require what is humanly impossible, they cannot punish retroactively, official enforcement must be consistent with the rules, they cannot be changed capriciously. A hippie or a southern segregationist both may protest injustice when law enforcement officers suddenly enforce a long forgotten statute; a school committee may protest a racial imbalance law that seems impossible to obey; or a citizen may protest that whites receive harsher treatment than Negroes for minor violations, because police are afraid of inciting a riot. All such protests could claim injustice because one or more specific rules of fairplay had been violated.

Justice as Just Desert. Injustice arises when we feel a person does not get "what he deserves," implying that there should be some equivalency between the rewards or punishments a person receives and his actual behavior or deeds: a self-made businessman, who through years of hard work builds a fortune, justly deserves his income; the person who actually committed the crime is the only one who really deserves the prison term; the derelict, because he lacks ambition, deserves his poverty; and the plagiarist, because he did not create the work, does *not* deserve credit. Retributive justice emphasizes the equivalency between deeds and deserts: "eye for an eye, tooth for a tooth," as does the biblical maxim, "as ye sow, so shall ye reap."

A major problem with this concept is deciding which deeds are worthy of rewards (money, property, status, responsibility, or salvation) and which deeds should be punished (through loss of above rewards, imprisonment, banishment, or death). Deciding whether given deeds are worthy of rewards or punishments inevitably introduces other values into the conversation, e.g., love, freedom, utility, equality. Another problem arising from emphasis on deeds is determining whether a person should always be held responsible for his actions. Generally, we excuse people from responsibility for those deeds which the individual does not voluntarily choose to do (because of loss of emotional control, duress and coercion, or provocation).

Basing deserts on deeds alone might lead to a meritocracy, with great inequalities between possessions and privileges of those more able and willing to do good works versus those less able or motivated in directions that deviate from the norm. Advocates of an alternative to the "bootstraps theory" of deserts based on deeds can point to the importance of basic human *needs* (food, clothing, shelter, education, self-government). They suggest that regardless of deeds, persons have human rights that entitle them to humane considerations, and that it would be unjust to require people to "earn" some deserts by particular deeds. Thus we feel it is just for a breadwinner with six dependents to have more tax exemptions than a person with only one dependent; it would be just to help criminals toward rehabilitation, rather than inflict only punishment upon them. A modern dispute illustrates the two possible bases of just desert: does justice consist primarily in punishing participants in urban riots for their misdeeds, or providing social services appropriate to their needs?

Justice Based on Equality. We have noticed the importance of rewards and punishments *equivalent* to deeds or needs. Perhaps in deciding whether justice has been done, the equivalency is more critical than evaluating the merit of the deeds or needs. That is, our sense of injustice is aroused most when we feel the *equivalence* between rewards and efforts or needs is violated — when a person gets more or less than he deserves. A commitment to equality is evident in criteria for due process in criminal law: rules should apply equally to everyone; similar crimes should be treated equally regardless of status or fortune; defendants should have equal opportunity before the law (rights to counsel, to call witnesses); jurors and judges should be impartial to both sides.

7. Equality

Equality is one of the most central values on which moral obligations may be justified (see Chapter 5). One of its political manifestations is the guarantee that each citizen should have an equal voice (i.e., one man, one vote) in his government. It is allegedly immoral to deny the franchise because of race, religion, wealth, or political views, because "all men are created equal." Opposition to unequal treatment extends to opportunities for education, employment, and such public services as recreation, transportation, police protection, and health. The equality ethic also applies to the individual's obligations to society: all citizens should have such equal duties in military service, paying taxes, prudent and reasonable actions under common law, and tolerating religious and ideological differences. Equality is frequently raised in economic controversies (free competition, labor-management, taxation), and more recently in the drive for equal educational opportunities for disadvantaged groups. We might argue that the "golden rule" should serve as a basis for all morality: do unto others as you would have them do unto you. Here, reciprocity is rooted in the concept of equivalent deeds, and to act under this mandate is to value equality. Our behavior toward others must be equal to that we wish upon ourselves. Whether in criminal court, the marketplace, the classroom, the home, the church, or the army, firm adherence to equality presents difficulties: first, in distinguishing equal treatment or deserts from *identical* treatment; second, in measuring or assessing the extent to which equality is achieved; and third, in resolving inevitable conflicts when, in order to guarantee equality, it may be necessary to deprive a person of previously held freedom. These problems are discussed in Chapter 5.

8. Honesty

Although dishonesty may be condoned by political expediency, we generally find moral objection to public officials who deceive their constituents by deliberately making campaign promises they cannot keep or by refusing to tell the whole truth on given issues. Similarly, we can feel moral outrage at merchants, manufacturers, and professionals who misrepresent their products and services. The child's concern when a father breaks his promise to bring ice cream and the nation's concern when its neighbor breaks a treaty both can be traced to the value of honesty. Here we construe honesty broadly to include obligation to "tell the truth"; the duty to "keep one's word," which extends honesty to actually doing what one says; and acting in accordance with the convictions of one's conscience. The last type of honesty is illustrated by the person who believes something to be clearly wrong, yet refuses to act or protest because of an inconvenience or conflicting self-interest: bystanders who, though morally outraged by the crime they observe and able to stop it at no danger to themselves, refuse even to report the crime because they do not want the inconveniences of "becoming involved." A person who knows he has acted in violation of his conscience has not been honest with himself.

This is not to suggest that to be moral one must always tell the truth, keep one's promises, or act consistently with conscience, although indeed, the value of honesty suggests these to be prima facie duties. If the value of honesty conflicts with such other values as freedom, utility, and beneficence, it may be necessary to sacrifice honesty to be more moral. A captured American pilot, when interrogated by enemy forces, could make a reasonable moral argument for deliberately lying to his captors about United States military plans and resources. So might the friend who allows a mother to believe her missing son is still alive, although he firmly believes all evidence indicates he is dead.

B. Sources of Moral Principles

Suppose two people argue whether it is morally right to burn draft cards as a form of civil disobedience. One emphasizes a moral obligation to obey the law, feels that laws concerning the draft are moral and that civil disobedience is harmful to society because it is likely to lead to anarchy. The other claims each person has a right to freedom of expression, one must be honest with one's conscience, and draft-card burning is a legitimate expression of moral outrage. The discussants recognize a conflict between the values of law and order versus free expression of conscience. Once the differing values are identified, the next question might be: Where do you get your values and how do we know that your source of values is more acceptable than mine? This question implies that the validity of one's values somehow depends upon where the values come from. Four possible sources or ways to arrive at the values one uses to support his moral judgments include:

1. Intuition

If asked, "How do you know that love, justice, or freedom are the right values?" one can respond, "I just know it, it's part of me in my heart, it's obvious, it's common sense." This suggests that further inquiry into the source of the values will not serve any useful purpose, because the values are *intuitively* self-evident, having no rational basis necessarily, yet they are acceptable, mainly because of strong unexplainable individual feelings.

2. Revelation

Another possible response is "God told me," or "it's in the Bible," or "I have received the word through mystical experience." Although it may suggest a Judeo-Christian orientation, revelation could presumably occur in other mystical contexts — yoga, hallucinogenic drugs, or secular contemplation. In any case, revelation signifies the communication of values by a transcendental power, and the recipient concludes that his values not only seem intuitively right, but they actually have been revealed to him by some nonhuman agent or force.

3. Introjection

A third response: "My values are right, because they are the values of the society I live in and I believe in them, because this is what I have been taught. Other societies may have different values, but each society trains the young to support its own values." Introjection assumes a deliberate attempt at social learning by members of the society who through child rearing inculcate the society's priorities. The value is "correct" because the society believes in it and has taught it to the child.

4. Moral Reasoning

Consider the answer: "The values I hold are right, because I have tested their validity by reasoning, observation, and discussion. Value commitments are entitled to legitimacy only to the extent that they have been arrived at through critical rational examination and argument." This position suggests that, although one might begin with intuitive feelings, revealed insights, and social learnings, no single source is sufficient to establish the worth or truth of a value choice. Only through moral reasoning can one build a case that a given value is right or good.

Intuition, revelation, and introjection, while they contribute to a moral debate, cannot serve alone as ultimate sources. If one relies only upon intuition, revelation, or introjection, he can do nothing except follow the dictates of his mind, God, or society. Though he may argue extensively about what these sources really say to man, his only obligation is to obey commands issuing from sources beyond his control. We find two problems with this orientation: (1) History shows that people have differing and conflicting intuitions and revelations and that societies teach different values. If people merely follow lessons or values from these sources, they have no method for resolving conflicts among the differing values that present themselves. Additional direction must be sought. (2) Accepting intuition, revelation, or society's rules without debate denies man the opportunity to make choices of his own. We believe, however, that the essence of morality, and possibly even of humanity itself, lies in man's autonomy for conscious deliberation about one's values and obligations. In Chapter 1 we tried to demonstrate the validity of individual choice, and rational deliberation. The section on free will and determinism further explains the importance of individual choice as a definitional requisite of moral behavior. Although intuition, revelation, or introjection may have unavoidably (and perhaps appropriately) influenced the development of this very position, it cannot be sufficiently substantiated without also engaging in moral reasoning.

IV. Some Underlying Issues in Moral Reasoning

When discussants use moral reasoning to justify principles or values, they will not necessarily agree on solutions to moral issues. Inability to resolve specific issues can be attributed partly to persisting disagreement on more fundamental philosophical problems.

A. Universalism Versus Relativism

Joe and Pete are discussing whether the Romans were morally justified in persecuting the Christians.

> Joe: No, it was definitely wrong. People are entitled to worship as they please, as long as they do not interfere with others. Even though the Christians might have been causing some trouble, the Romans had no right to treat them so brutally with such violence.

> Pete: Well, you and I happen to believe in religious freedom, but it's obvious that the Romans didn't share this value. The Romans thought Christians a danger to their empire. Who are we to tell the Romans that they should respect Christianity? People in those days just believed in different values, so persecution was morally right from the Roman point of view.

> Joe: I don't care who does the persecuting or when and where it happens. Persecuting a person for his religious belief is just wrong.

> Pete: I don't think you have any right to tell other people what they should believe in. Each person or culture is entitled to hold whatever values they want.

Joe and Pete appear to be deadlocked over whether they should generalize a commitment to a particular value (religious freedom) to a group (Romans) that evidently placed lower priority upon it. Do we have a moral right to apply our values universally to actions of others? Instead perhaps we should learn what values another group holds (or held) and then judge that group on its own terms — did it fulfill the values it held as important? If we adopt the universalist approach, we sometimes feel a bit guilty for "imposing our values on others." Evidently certain values we believe in — individual freedom or toleration — tell us not to judge others, except by their own standards. Yet, if we adopt a completely relativist position, we should not allow ourselves to make any moral judgments except about our own actions. This could lead to such statements as, "If the Nazis thought it was right to exterminate the Jews, then it was right for them; if my neighbor believes it is right to kill her child, then it is right for her. In neither case should I interfere, because that would be imposing my values on someone else."

Most people are neither extreme universalists nor extreme relativists. Joe seems to believe it is always wrong to persecute people because of religion, but we could further test his tendency to apply his values universally. We learn that he also places high value on capitalism and free enterprise, yet he contends that socialist countries have a moral right to develop their own economic system. Joe will not, therefore, always wish to impose his values on others. Conversely, though Pete tolerated values different from his in the case of Roman persecution of Christians, we learn he would not tolerate genocide in modern times. While generally taking a relativistic approach, in some situations Pete is willing to impose certain of his values on other groups. Discussion of moral issues can be clarified if persons are challenged to specify the extent of their commitment to either a universalist or relativist orientation. Without testing the philosophical framework underlying one's specific value choices, a discussion like the preceding could easily become deadlocked with Joe repeating, "Religious persecution is always wrong," and Pete answering, "It may be wrong for us, but it was right for the Romans because they thought it was."

As stated in Chapter 2, it is impossible to resolve a social controversy with the extreme relativist who consistently refuses to apply the values he holds to a community at large. As Oliver and Shaver (1966, p. 32) point out, relativism

> ignores the fundamental ethical basis of societal controversy: the desire of one individual or group to persuade the community that one decision is more consistent with the general values of the group than another. To ignore or refuse to deal with the problem of justifying decisions *vis-à-vis* the general values simply avoids the issue; it does not resolve it.

For this reason we cannot accept a subjective relativist position. In addition, we believe men widely share values that seem to transcend historical and cultural differences. Although men of different cultures would dispute the morality of a sizable range of behavior, there is also a realm of behavior that is almost universally believed to be brutish and uncivilized, and another realm widely considered to be essentially human. But to suggest that some values may be legitimately applied beyond oneself (or one's immediate community) is not to say that all should be. The latter interpretation would obviously violate our commitment to pluralism and free choice. One approach to the relativism-universalism dilemma is for each person to define the point that separates his commitment to personal and cultural autonomy from his allegiance to those universal norms essential for the minimal realization of human dignity.[3]

B. Consistent Principles and Situational Judgment

The following conversation illustrates a problem somewhat related to the universalist-relativist issue.

> Dick: I think the patriots had a right to revolt against England, because the British were denying them basic rights of self-government and equal economic opportunity and because the patriots had tried to plead their cause peacefully, but Britain wouldn't respond.
>
> Jane: Well, if that's your main reason, then you would probably support the violent rebellion of the Negroes in Detroit last summer. Even if they have the right to vote, they don't really have self-government or equal economic opportunity, and their many peaceful protests haven't gotten results.
>
> Dick: No. The two situations are completely different, and it's silly to try to make my reasons for justifying the American revolution apply to modern problems of the Negro. The issues are so different you can't even use the same reasons or principles.
>
> Jane: Well, you can't just say each situation is completely new. You must have some general reasons and be consistent. If judges on courts acted that way, always saying each situation is completely new, then the law would change with every case and we would never be able to predict what law or principle we should follow.

Dick and Jane disagree on the importance or necessity of basing one's moral judgments on general principles applied consistently over several cases.

Extreme situationists (e.g., as described by Fletcher, 1966) would claim that general rules simply becloud and confuse our thinking, preventing us from openly examining each situation on its merit. For example, as medicine first develops artificial kidneys and hearts, these are scarce and expensive, not available to everyone who needs them. A doctor or official who decides which patients shall have the devices is essentially deciding that some people will live and others die. Do we call him a murderer? Do biblical command-

---

[3] In choosing which norms to apply to the actions of others, the citizen should distinguish between those norms appropriate primarily for his private evaluation and those that he would feel justified in imposing, through argumentative persuasion or coercion on others.

ments or principles of common law or state constitutions help us make this new moral choice? Because our tradition of principles and laws grew out of such completely different situations, perhaps they are irrelevant for present and future moral choices. This position in extreme would advocate eradicating from memory principles of justice and morality that have been invoked in the past, so that each situation could be decided anew. The situationist approach warns us not to think about guerilla war in Vietnam as analogous to Nazi aggression, or to think about results of international nuclear war as victory and defeat as in "conventional" warfare. Such examples might be cited to show that applying rules and principles used to govern past behavior not only confuses new situations, but leads to erroneous conclusions.

However, important reasons exist for not abandoning the search for consistent application of general principles. First, principles used to justify action may be impossible to eradicate from memory. Whether we like it or not, principles of justice seem to remain in our nervous systems. The question becomes "How should such principles be used?" We could also argue that many situations do *not* differ in the most relevant or salient aspect of moral choice — both the American Revolution and Negro rebellion concern basic human rights and how best to attain them. Making explicit such commonalities among issues helps to clarify the issue over which people disagree. Comparing situations and testing whether principles of the past can be applied consistently does not necessarily make one a slave to accepting past principles. On the contrary, comparing and distinguishing among situations stimulates rejecting some principles as irrelevant, qualifying others as not sufficiently complete to deal with the new situation, and accepting others as adequate in some instances, no matter how "old" the rules or principles might be. We agree with Jane that to abandon a concern for principles and consistency would lessen the chances for stability and predictability in law and social mores, without which a society could not hold together. Finally our commitment to rationality, by definition, inevitably leads us to be concerned with consistency and general principles, but it also commits us to making qualifications and fine distinctions that often in effect totally reject many "general principles" that the situationist would evidently prefer not to consider at all.

C. Intrinsic Versus Pragmatic Reasoning

Another perennial ethical debate is whether a given act should be judged right or wrong because it brings good or evil *consequences,* or whether, regardless of consequences, the act itself is intrinsically moral (or immoral). The former position, called the pragmatic (or teleological) approach, is illustrated by: "It is wrong to steal, because if everyone acted as if it were right to steal, then the stability of family and society would be threatened.

No one would feel secure; people could not accumulate fortunes or build identity, because one could never claim anything as truly his own." The pragmatic approach looks for consequences of actions, then judges the goodness or badness of such results, which determines the rightness or wrongness of the original act.

In contrast, consider a situation where the servant to a wealthy family frequently steals food, alcoholic beverages, and other abundant items. Although it might be difficult to demonstrate that this sort of theft has serious or evil consequences, such thievery would commonly be called "wrong," simply because stealing in any situation may be considered evil or immoral. This is the "intrinsic" argument. Although one might point to desirable effects of killing, stealing, lying, or exploiting, some people believe something in the nature of the act makes them essentially wrong.[4] Similarly some *rules* are considered to be inherently moral; for example, the golden rule or a commandment such as "honor thy father and mother," or a commitment to abide by majority rule even if part of a dissenting minority. Finally, although one might judge the effects of a particular act to be bad, one might conclude the act to be morally right, because the person had moral *intentions* or *motives*. Misjudgment or accident cases illustrate: a military commander sincerely trying to save lives mistakenly orders the bombing of a civilian village instead of a munitions factory; a good samaritan applying first aid causes additional injury; a teacher trying in earnest "to do what's best for the child" humiliates him before the class. A concern for motivation and intention is thus another dimension of the tendency to judge the morality of an act by what is intrinsic or internal to the act, as well as by its effects or consequences.

Pete and Mike argue whether it is morally right to burn one's draft card to protest the Vietnam war.

> Pete: There's no point in doing it because look at the effect it would have. You'd turn a lot of people against you. You might be convicted, and if so, you would be prohibited from holding public jobs for the rest of your life. So you really couldn't persuade anyone to stop the war. And it's a bad influence on the young who, from your lesson, will learn disrespect for the law.
> Mike: Even though it may have bad effects, or possibly even defeat some of my purposes, there are some things you have to do just because they are right. I feel that I must protest and make a sacrifice. To be silent on this issue or to work through the normal channels of an evil system is simply immoral. I must take a stand, regardless of the consequences.

Pete, concerned mainly with the effects or consequences of the action, op-

---

[4] The view that certain acts are intrinsically moral or immoral is equivalent to the assumption that persons have certain prima facie duties.

erates on a different philosophical level from Mike, who bases his morality in the intrinsic nature of an act. (One might argue that Mike is really concerned with effects *on his conscience,* and thus a pragmatist, but this could be held true of all moral reasoning. We assume pragmatists are concerned primarily with the realities of the social world, not mainly inner states of conscience.)

Each orientation presents problems. The intrinsic approach presents difficulties in building a case or giving additional reasons to justify attributing inherent moral worth to some acts or rules and denying this to others. It is also quite difficult to discover the actual motivation behind particular acts.

The pragmatist, on the other hand, must show some causal connection between the acts in question and the consequences he predicts, which can lead into controversial factual claims. In addition, the pragmatist needs a method for ascribing positive or negative values to the consequences he foresees (e.g., on what grounds should he assume that teaching the young to disrespect the law is bad, evil, or undesirable?).

Although we see no way of resolving or eliminating the disagreement that might result from these two frameworks, it would be a considerable accomplishment if discussants could recognize points at which this type of issue causes their disagreements. Recognizing and explicitly stating the nature of their moral dilemma may lead them to modify their positions, possibly to agree that they disagree at this fundamental level or even, perhaps, to dismiss this level of disagreement as irrelevant to the basic question they are considering.

D. Free Will and Determinism

A two-year-old child, in a moment of anger, pushes her six-month-old sister down the stairs, and the infant dies. A hippie, while under the influence of drugs, knifes a boyfriend. A professional gangster plans and carries out the murder of a rival. Should all three be held morally responsible for their acts? The most common answers are that the child is not morally responsible, the gangster is, and the hippie is probably the most questionable case. One obvious distinction between the child and the gangster is that one knows the difference between right and wrong. Because the child is assumed unable to distinguish between right and wrong, and because he is viewed more as a creature of impulse rather than rational choice and self-control, we excuse him from moral responsibility. We do not excuse the gangster who deliberately planned and carried out his actions under his own free will, fully aware of right and wrong alternatives. What about the hippie? Did she freely choose to do wrong or was her behavior really out of her own control? One might argue that she could be expected to know the dangers of drug taking, and that her conscious decision to take drugs was a free choice. Or one might even object that perhaps she could not control the circumstances that determined her decision to take drugs: the way her parents raised her, or hostile influences in the environment. If we accept a deterministic conclusion, moral blame or responsibility seems less justifiable, but once we assume the ability and opportunity to make a free choice, then moral responsibility is readily assigned (those who believe jobless urban Negroes to be morally responsible for their plight argue that they have chosen to be indolent and poor rather than to work and to strive for mobility).

Advocates of extreme determinism seriously threaten the concept of moral judgment. A religious theory of predestination claiming that God long ago determined the course of our actions, or does so currently day-by-day; a historical theory that claims some inevitable design in which all actions are governed by precedent causes; a psychoanalytic theory that says that human behavior results from unconscious forces arising from early childhood — such frameworks imply that man cannot freely choose or self-determine his actions. Because making moral judgments, by definition, largely rests on the ability of men to choose among alternatives, extreme determinism denies the possibility of morality itself.

Debates over the extent to which an Eichmann or an urban Negro could freely choose his actions illustrate various meanings of the claim "he had no choice." *Fatalism*, the most extreme sense of determinism, holds that men have no power to influence events voluntarily, because the course of history is controlled by forces beyond individual control, whether through some transcendental design or randomly. Accepting this sense of determinism makes it logically quite difficult to hold anyone morally responsible for his actions. *Causation* is a more limited sense of determinism, suggesting only that some events actually bring about other events, or the events we observe have occurred only as a result of other events. This does not necessarily imply that all events are unavoidable or that man has no choice in shaping events as he wishes. Public policy debates illustrate that one can believe both in causation and free choice. Military leaders may have assumed that a United States withdrawal from Vietnam would cause communist aggressors to take over Southeast Asia. We are still free, however, to decide whether we wish to defend Southeast Asia by fighting in Vietnam, or to withdraw from that commitment.

The more extreme determinist will argue that our decision on Vietnam was not as free as it seemed, because our very thoughts were caused or determined by much previous experience over which we had no control: the history of foreign affairs that gave birth to both the current situation and our own ways of thinking about it. One problem with this position is the difficulty of demonstrating causal relationships between previous events and current options or ways of thinking. Although historians, psychologists, and lay citizens frequently offer causal explanations, human behavior seems sufficiently complex so that most causal claims have not been proven conclusively. We may discover regularities that allow us to make predictions: for example, people who smoke have a much higher cancer and coronary rate than nonsmokers, so eventually we conclude that smoking causes cancer and heart disease. But for a more fundamental cause, we might then ask, "What causes smoking?" Further investigation may show that such variables as life-styles, personality dynamics, environmental conditions, and genetically determined traits all contribute in varying degrees to the smoking habit. What then would be the "real" cause of cancer and heart disease? Because of multiple causation and the problem of regress from immediate back to original or "fundamental" causes, we are usually unable to identify any exclusive cause or causes. Even though we may have discovered impressive statistical regularities, we are hard pressed to demonstrate with finality the causes of war, prejudice, poverty, or political success. Until we can identify with certainty the direct causes of human thoughts and actions, we need not conclude that thoughts and actions are totally determined, or that voluntary choice is impossible.

Neither must we assume that all human actions are the result of conscious, voluntary choice. Several criteria can be used to assess how much action should be attributed to free choice. A given action may be considered voluntary to the extent that it meets such criteria as the following: Alternative courses of action must in fact be available to the person. The person, prior to the action, must be aware of the alternatives. He must be able to predict the consequences of his actions. He must be able to distinguish between what would be conventionally accepted as right and wrong behavior. He must be emotionally and physically capable of acting in the manner he considers right.

Psychological and biological forces can violate these criteria. The angered child, an adult who goes beserk, a prisoner injected with truth serum, a drug that unpredictably stimulates aggressive behavior, abnormal sexual appetites, physical disabilities—all these reduce opportunities for rational voluntary choice. Certain social forces also inhibit choice by restricting alternatives available and by making systematic deliberation on choices impossible.

Policemen who are provoked by protestors have been excused from responsibility for brutality on the ground that a reasonable man could not avoid acting impulsively when provoked. A person is not morally obligated to obey the provisions of a contract if he was ordered at gunpoint to sign it, or forced under other forms of duress. A classic argument that defends those accused of war crimes is that social coercion can destroy real options, thereby making it impossible for the individual to exercise voluntary choice.

Because Eichmann could have been shot for violating orders, he had no choice (any reasonable man would be expected to obey orders rather than risk his life). A counterargument holds that it was possible for Eichmann to debate with himself whether it would be more morally correct to obey his superiors or to defy them and sacrifice his life for innocent Jews. In this sense, coercion and duress do not necessarily eliminate free choice. Rather, they imply a situation in which one must make a great personal sacrifice to choose that action that many would consider the most moral alternative. Although Eichmann might have to pay a serious (or the ultimate) personal penalty, nevertheless he was still free to decide the moral question.

Some have attempted to escape a deadlock on the free will-determinism issue by arguing: "We can assume that an individual either acted voluntarily or that he did not, just so we agree that our attempt to locate moral responsibility is itself a moral act." Holding a person morally responsible means essentially that he deserves praise or blame, and *ascribing* praise or blame is morally correct. Ascribing praise or blame serves desirable social goals: creating conscience necessary for social cohesion, deterrence of crime, and providing a mechanism for settling disputes. To be sure, there are also arguments against the morality of ascribing responsibility: e.g., it creates false pride and destructive guilt feelings; or, a man has no moral right to pass judgment on another's actions. The free will issue can be held in abeyance if one examines the morality of *ascribing* responsibility.

The free will-determinism question can be overemphasized, and some would consider it merely an unsolvable academic puzzle because of the following apparent contradiction. One assumes that what one voluntarily chooses to do can be meaningful only if it actually affects the environment. But once we assume that our actions will have an effect, our own actions will determine or limit the choices available to others and ourselves in future situations. Thus accepting free will entails accepting a form of determinism. This paradox, along with the many complexities mentioned previously, indicates that deciding whether a person is morally responsible is not simply deciding whether his action was voluntary or determined. In addition to the problems in resolving this issue, one would want to consider motivations (whether the act was intentional, malicious, negligent, or an honest mistake); circumstances that might qualify or modify prima facie duties (e.g., killing in self-defense); moral values that might compete in a particular situation (e.g., one's duty to obey the law versus one's right to self-expression).

V. Public Issues and Moral Dilemmas

The four main issues discussed in the previous section raise the broadest questions of moral responsibility. In this section we identify moral dilemmas particularly salient to public policy.

A. Range and Extent of Personal Obligations

How far beyond immediate self-interest should one's obligations extend? More specifically: (1) Which of my obligations should be the concern of the state or community at large and which should be strictly private? (2) How far beyond immediate personal and family obligations do I have responsibilities to people in other communities? (3) How far backward or forward in time do I have responsibility for the actions and welfare of others?

1. Privacy Versus State Jurisdiction

The state has legislated obligations in several areas that many individuals oppose as intrusions by the state on personal privacy: prohibiting or restricting contraceptives or sexual intercourse (extramarital, interracial); standards for child neglect; compulsory schooling; surveillance, such as searches, electronic eavesdropping, subpoena of personal documents, and censoring films and literature; zoning regulations that determine physical specification for one's home; and even the legal prohibition of suicide. Yet the state has also set up mechanisms to protect rights of privacy: for example, the right against self-incrimination and laws that prohibit trespassing or eavesdropping. In general the democratic rhetoric values individual autonomy and privacy, challenging the state to justify whatever obligations it creates for individuals. (Imagine, for example, the reaction to legislation that would limit the children that each family could have, or that would prohibit individuals from insulting one another.) Burdens or infringements on the individual's right to determine his own obligations can be justified by showing such infringements to be necessary to the well-being of the community. This argument creates at least three problems: first, what do we mean by community welfare or well-being; second, what group of people constitutes the community; and third, whether establishing obligations to the state will actually prevent the kind of harm to community that may be feared. In arguing about the legitimate concerns of the state in personal morality, the boundaries of that "community" to which the individual is most obligated are hard to define.

2. Radius of Individual Responsibility to Different Communities

If a wife suspects her husband of cheating on income tax returns, does she have a moral obligation to report this to the federal government? Should a taxpayer in the suburb of a metropolitan area pay higher taxes to improve education for the disadvantaged in the inner city ghetto? Should Americans make financial sacrifices to help diseased and hungry people in India, in distant parts of the United States, or in their own town or neighborhood or family, and which group deserves highest priority? Should an atomic scientist contribute his skills toward the development of more powerful defense systems for his own country or toward disarmament proposals for world peace? Should Negroes direct their energies and loyalties primarily to equality for black people in general, rather than to individual economic success or the military defense of the United States? To what extent should a labor leader place the interests of his union above "national interest"? Each question involves conflicts among persons' obligations to several different communities whose goals and interests may conflict. The problem is to decide which communities deserve the highest, most steadfast loyalty and which have lower priority should one's obligations between them conflict.

Several different principles or criteria define the communities to which one has obligations. (1) The family is often considered most immediate and important because of the *genetic "blood"* relationship among its members (except for husband and wife — and adopted children — whose obligations to each other are based more upon voluntary devotion and love). A concern for heredity is also extended to the larger racial, national, or religious group, as evidenced by those who place their obligations to fellow Catholics, Jews, Negroes, or Italians above their sense of obligation to the city in which they all may live. (2) The city, state, or nation creates *political* jurisdictional communities, whose boundaries usually encompass several different "blood" communities, imposing standard obligations on all, such as taxpaying, law obedience, voting, and military service. (3) Other communities are *voluntary associations* or organizations that create obligations on members who may belong to various "blood" or political-legal communities: professional associations, labor unions, political parties, social clubs, institutions of employment. The United States has abundant voluntary associations that deal with topics and causes as varied as collecting antique buttons, preventing cruelty to animals, controlling world population, or promoting sky-diving. (4) *Geographical proximity* can determine and limit one's obligations, the assumption being that one has more clearcut obligations closest to home, or, if away from home, to people in his most immediate vicinity. We have a greater obligation to aid our next-door neighbor in distress than a distressed person on the far side of town.

In an ultimate distress situation, more than one person is in danger of losing his life. We then ask whom must we help? All these criteria might be considered in addition to such other principles as familiarity and friendship, and the relative worth or value of the victims (e.g., because of his youth, intelligence, skills, or ideology). People will argue about whether any or all these criteria should be used. Usually, however, the argument fails to identify these considerations explicitly as alternative criteria. Some might argue that the radius of one's obligations should extend, without preference, to all human beings, or that the *type of problem* is more important in determining obligations than the boundaries of one's community (e.g., eliminating disease and starvation in India deserves higher priority than putting one's son through college, regardless of what communities we live in or who our relatives are).

3. Obligations Across Generations

This problem parallels defining community boundaries, but deals with obligations and responsibilities through *time* rather than across space. The problem poses philosophical differences of how much a present or future generation should suffer from the sins or mistakes of a previous generation. A white southerner can argue that he should not have to make concessions or personal sacrifice to help blacks simply because of the injustice done by his ancestral slave holders. A social worker will argue for heavy commitment of public funds to educate disadvantaged children, claiming they should not have to suffer because their parents were unable to provide a decent home life and education. Both arguments assume that children should not be made to "pay" for the errors of their parents. On the other hand, we find the biblical view that it *is* just for the sins of the father to be handed down to his offspring or the view that Germans can never be forgiven for Nazi atrocities. The view that children *deserve* to inherit the wealth of their father says, perhaps more positively, that children should reap their parents' harvest (be it reward or punishment).

A businessman who accumulates a large estate and trust fund for the future enjoyment of his children, at some sacrifice to the parents' enjoying their own lives, illustrates his obligation to future generations. The same person, however, may refuse to make a financial sacrifice for clean air, clean water, or world peace, claiming these to be too long range, with no apparent payoff to his immediate interests. Though he sees some obligation to his immediate blood relations, the welfare of the larger community is beyond his moral duty. This implies that future generations *should* reap the consequences or take responsibility for solving problems that previous generations created: that the white southerner shall thus be expected to pay for the legacy of slavery, because we could not expect his ancestors to dedicate themselves completely to social justice in the future.

Still it is widely assumed that the nation must make a commitment to youth and future generations. Meeting the needs of the elderly takes low priority compared to investments in youth, whether in education, consumer goods, medicine, or recreation. The moral obligation to save the life of the young before that of the aged is commonly taken for granted, but this too can be open to question if one weighs the relative ease with which new youth can be reproduced versus the accumulated experience that is lost to the world forever when the elderly die.

B. Collective Responsibility

We can also ask about responsibility and obligations of groups, rather than of individuals. Corporations, armies, government bureaucracies, and whole societies and nations have been "blamed" for social problems through that moral reasoning which absolves individuals from responsibility by claiming that "systems," far transcending individuals, basically cause social problems.

Who should be held responsible for Nazi extermination of the Jews; for the plight of blacks in the United States; for the nuclear annihilation of thousands of Japanese; for starving masses in India; for monotonous and uncreative television programming in the United States; or for the "rape" of our natural environment. If by "who" we imply that certain guilty individuals must be found, our witch hunt would probably turn up thousands, and we would not be able to identify any obvious leader or organizer of the masses implicated in each crime.

The plight of the Afro-American, for example, has been blamed on Southern slaveholders, or even farther back, on African chiefs who betrayed their own people; on genetic inferiority; on an economic system that requires skilled labor; on the forces of technology that created not only the cotton gin, but also the industrial urban environment to which rural folks must adjust; or on the white man's unresolved problems of sexual identity. No obvious villain emerges, and if we apprehend all those millions who seemingly bear some responsibility, most could deny any conscious or deliberate discrimination or persecution. Well-intentioned individuals could deny responsibility with such statements as: "I can't hire untrained people." "If the cotton isn't picked I'd go broke." "Allowing them into our schools would cause violence and riots." "Selling them real estate would just depress property values." "What would my friends think if I tried to help them." "Don't protest too hard or you're likely to get in trouble with the boss and the landlord." Responsibility can be ascribed to various systems: an economic system that requires competition and increasingly skilled labor; a political system of majority rule in which minorities are at a disadvantage; a religious system placing heavy emphasis on self-help, with only lip service to love and charity; a social-psychological system in which humans need to feel superior status.

The conventional approach to morality assigns blame only when the connection between an individual and some immoral action is reasonably clear and direct. In the previous situations, however, discrete actions of individuals contribute only indirectly and partially to evil-doing: a bureaucrat who simply takes inventory of a poisonous gas supply; a homeowner who merely wants to maximize his profit when selling his house; a Negro who fails to protest, because he wants to keep his job; a professor working at a university that accepts government contracts for development of biological warfare. Yet thousands of apparently harmless individual actions can combine to produce social catastrophy. When this happens, we blame the general system or society at large, which is somewhat artificial because societies and systems do not have consciences — only individuals do. Although a corporation is legally considered a "person," it remains an abstraction without a conscience. Although stockholders may have individual consciences to direct corporate policy, limited financial liability serves in effect also as moral insulation from cumulative evil done by the corporation. Whatever evil the corporation does (e.g., racial discrimination, manufacture of lethal products, unsafe autos or drugs) can be seen as a result of other abstract, intangible forces (consumers, managers, government policy, competitors), also without personal conscience.

Edmond Cahn (1961) addresses the problem of collective responsibility and claims, "the new predicament of democratic man is his moral involvement in the misdeeds of government." Cahn argues that citizens have collective responsibility to try to prevent such misdeeds, to see that reparations and compensation are made for victims, and to protest the wrongdoings when they occur. Individuals can be held responsible not only for committing immoral acts, but for authorizing, inciting, assisting, or ratifying their occurrence. This principle, however, does not solve the problem of locating moral responsibility when an individual commits an act not by itself immoral, and when he cannot be expected to see that his act when combined with many other innocent acts adds up to a cumulative evil. Though responsibility and blame should be placed with the "system" that combined the acts to produce evil, we apparently do not have an ethical framework appropriate for effective control of "systems," i.e., such abstractions as corporations, technology, bureaucracy, and nationalism.

The problem is particularly confusing because spokesmen for systems or for large groups invoke moral values to justify or criticize a system's existence. Governments speak of their nation's responsibilities to spur economic development, end discrimination, or prevent international conflict. Corporations proclaim their responsibility to enrich culture and provide community service. Schools announce their responsibility for educating youth and passing on a cultural heritage. Bureaucracies are responsible for stopping crime, ensuring health standards, or preserving natural resources. Political parties endorse candidates and policy platforms. When large groups or collectives fail to live up to certain moral standards, they can be condemned and scolded, as in the guilt clause directed against Germany at the end of World War I or the United States government criticisms of Red China. On what basis does it make sense to praise or blame collectives? And what moral burden must individuals who belong to the collectives assume? Should we incriminate an individual because of membership or deeds that make apparently insignificant contributions to some cumulative evil?

C. Action Versus Inaction

The classic illustration of the moral issue surrounding the consequences of an individual's relationship to a collective is the person who fails to protest or resist what he considers immoral policy by a group to which he belongs: e.g., "Uncle Toms" in the South; members aware of corruption in their union; soldiers who agree to fight although they consider the war morally wrong. Those who fail to speak out or act against a particular policy implicitly support such policy by their silence. Thus, such "consenting" individuals can be held morally responsible for actions of the collective to which they belong.

The more obvious example of how inaction can be judged morally is the bystander who fails to give aid to the victim of a crime or accident. Inaction or silence is assumed to represent a chosen way to deal with a moral problem, which in some cases may be the "right" moral solution (e.g., refusing to betray personal confidences to irresponsible news reporters). Before we condemn a person for inaction or silence, however, we should be certain not only that action or taking a stand was morally required, but also that the person chose not to act. It is possible that one's silence or inaction represents ignorance that a given problem exists, and once informed of the situation that person would then consciously choose a response. The suggestion that we should not blame people for uninformed non-choices may seem reasonable, but it creates additional problems. One might condemn Mr. Jones, an affluent upper middle-class white suburbanite for failing to speak out for renewal and equality in urban ghettoes. Yet Jones may have a way of life that essentially isolates him from the real impact of ghetto life. We might suggest that Jones consult newspapers and television to become familiar with the problem, but this information may be so foreign to Jones that he actually cannot see a real problem. At what point do we say that Jones is no longer "ignorant" but has actually chosen not to take responsibility for the problem?

D. Redressing Wrongs

If it becomes established that some moral wrong has been done, it is usually assumed that something should be done to correct or rectify the situation. We can distinguish four basic approaches to redressing wrongs.

1. Retribution

Punishing the transgressor, or having him suffer in a way "equal" to his wrongdoing, is the retributive approach. Connoted by "an eye for an eye, tooth for a tooth," it symbolizes reciprocal harm done to the offender. Although criminals may be subjected to less extreme punishment in modern times, the idea that wrongdoers should be made to suffer remains. It is justified by either a theory of revenge or deterrence.

2. Rehabilitation

This approach emphasizes constructively educating, treating, or in some way changing the transgressor so that in the future he will no longer commit moral wrongs. Rehabilitation has been tried with criminals, delinquent children, and even warlike nations (who in defeat have been given economic and political assistance so they could become self-sufficient and democratic, instead of undeveloped, aggressive, or dictatorial). Punishment might be justified as one way of teaching criminals to reform themselves; thus it might also be claimed as a rehabilitative technique.

3. Compensa-
tion

Although the previous two approaches focus primarily on the wrongdoer, compensation stresses the victim, and the need to pay the victim for his losses. Whether in the form of damages in a civil law suit, an injunction requiring one company to abstain from producing something patented by another, deciding the custody of children of divorced couples, or levying fines in criminal cases to help indigent victims, compensation attempts to redress a grievance by meeting the victim's needs.

4. Condemna-
tion

Groups may censure delinquent members; nations may publicly condemn each other for violating treaties, aggression, or exploitation; and teachers may scold pupils. One might infer that speaking out against a given action (by labeling it wrong) helps to correct it, or at least the wrong would be far more serious if it went unnoticed. Although one might believe that scolding a wrongdoer in effect serves to punish or even rehabilitate him in some ways, it would be hard to make this case persuasive. Using moral language to evaluate an act may have important consequences for the conscience of the speaker but may have little or no effect in redressing actual wrongs.

BLACK BOY

A Negro youth tries — with dwindling success — to survive and advance within the codes of Mississippi.

Richard Wright gives credit for his beginnings as an author to his "sheer idleness" as an eighth grader in a rural Mississippi school in the 1920's. He set down a story — a wild tale called *The Voodoo of Hell's Half Acre* — in his composition book. Many townspeople were surprised when the editor of the local Negro newspaper agreed to publish it in three installments. His story continues:

A few days later my classmates came to me with baffled eyes, holding copies of the *Southern Register* in their hands.

"Did you really write the story?" they asked me.

"Yes."

"Why?"

"Because I wanted to."

"Where did you get it from?"

This case is abridged from pp. 127–129, 144–148, 157–160, 162–169, of *Black Boy* by Richard Wright. Copyright 1937, 1942, 1944, 1945, by Richard Wright. By permission of Harper & Row, Publishers. Reprinted in Donald W. Oliver and Fred M. Newmann, *Negro Views of America: The Legacy of Oppression,* American Education Publications, Columbus, Ohio, 1967.

"I made it up."

"You didn't. You copied it out of a book." . . .

They were convinced that I had not told them the truth. We had never had any instruction in literary matters at school; the literature of the nation or the Negro had never been mentioned. My schoolmates could not understand why anyone would want to write a story. . . . They looked at me with new eyes, and a distance, a suspiciousness, came between us. If I had thought anything in writing the story, I had thought that perhaps it would make me more acceptable to them, and now it was cutting me off from them more completely than ever.

At home the effects were no less disturbing. Granny came into my room early one morning and sat on the edge of my bed.

"Richard, what is this you're putting in the papers?" she asked.

"A story," I said.

"About what?"

"It's just a story, granny."

"But they tell me it's been in three times."

"It's the same story. It's in three parts."

"But what is it about?" she insisted.

I hedged, fearful of getting into a religious argument.

"It's just a story I made up," I said.

"Then it's a lie," she said. . . .

"Granny, please . . . I'm sorry," I pleaded. "But it's hard to tell you about the story. You see, granny, everybody knows that the story isn't true, but . . ."

"Then why write it?" she asked.

"Because people might want to read it."

"That's the devil's work," she said and left.

My mother also was worried.

"Son, you ought to be more serious," she said. "You're growing up now and you won't be able to get jobs if you let people think that you're weak-minded. Suppose the superintendent of schools would ask you to teach here in Jackson, and he found out that you had been writing stories?"

I could not answer her.

"I'll be all right, mama." I said.

In the end I was so angry that I refused to talk about the story. From no quarter, with the exception of the Negro newspaper editor, had there come a single encouraging word. It was rumored that the principal wanted to know why I had used the word "hell." I felt that I had committed a crime. Had I been conscious of the full extent to which I was pushing against the current of my environment, I would have been frightened altogether out of my attempts at writing. . . .

At school I inquired among the students about jobs and was given the name of a white family who wanted a boy to do chores. That afternoon, as soon as school had let out, I went to the address. A tall, dour white woman talked to me. Yes, she needed a boy, an honest boy. Two dollars a week. Mornings, evenings, and all day Saturdays. Washing dishes. Chopping wood. Scrubbing floors. Cleaning the yard. I would get my breakfast and dinner. As I asked timid questions, my eyes darted about. What kind of food would I get? Was the place as shabby as the kitchen indicated?

"Do you want this job?" the woman asked.

"Yes, ma'am," I said, afraid to trust my own judgment.

"Now, boy. I want to ask you one question and I want you to tell me the truth," she said.

"Yes, ma'am," I said.

"Do you steal?" she asked me seriously.

I burst into a laugh, then checked myself.

"What's so damn funny about that?" she asked.

"Lady, if I was a thief, I'd never tell anybody."

"What do you mean?" she blazed with a red face.

I had made a mistake during my first five minutes in the white world. I hung my head.

"No, ma'am," I mumbled. "I don't steal."

She stared at me, trying to make up her mind.

"Now, look, we don't want a sassy nigger around here," she said.

"No, Ma'am," I assured her. "I'm not sassy."

Promising to report the next morning at six o'clock, I walked home and pondered on what could possibly have been in the woman's mind to have made her ask me point-blank if I stole. Then I recalled hearing that white people looked upon Negroes as a variety of children. . . .

What would happen now that I would be among white people for hours at a stretch? Would they hit me? Curse me? If they did, I would leave at once. In all my wishing for a job I had not thought of how I would be treated, and now it loomed important, decisive, sweeping down beneath every other consideration. I would be polite, humble, saying yes sir and no sir, yes ma'am and no ma'am, but I would draw a line over which they must not step. Oh, maybe I'm just thinking up trouble, I told myself. They might like me. . . .

The next morning I chopped wood for the cook stove, lugged in scuttles of coal for the grates, washed the front porch and swept the back porch, swept the kitchen, helped wait on the table, and washed the dishes. I was sweating. I swept the front walk and ran to the store to shop. When I returned the woman said:

"Your breakfast is in the kitchen."

"Thank you, ma'am."

I saw a plate of thick, black molasses and a hunk of white bread on the table. Would I get no more than this? They had had eggs, bacon, coffee. . . . I picked up the bread and tried to break it; it was stale and hard. Well, I would drink the molasses. I lifted the plate and brought it to my lips and saw floating on the surface of the black liquid green and white bits of mold. . . . I can't eat this, I told myself. The food was not even clean. The woman came into the kitchen as I was putting on my coat.

"You didn't eat," she said.

"No, ma'am," I said, "I'm not hungry."

"You'll eat at home?" she asked hopefully.

"Well, I just wasn't hungry this morning, ma'am," I lied.

"You don't like molasses and bread," she said dramatically.

"Oh, yes, ma'am, I do," I defended myself

quickly, not wanting her to think that I dared criticize what she had given me.

"I don't know what's happening to you niggers nowadays," she sighed, wagging her head. She looked closely at the molasses. "It's a sin to throw out molasses like that. I'll put it up for you this evening."

"Yes, ma'am," I said heartily.

Neatly she covered the plate of molasses with another plate, then felt the bread and dumped it into the garbage. She turned to me, her face lit with an idea.

"What grade are you in school?"

"Eighth, Ma'am."

"Then why are you going to school?" she asked in surprise.

"Well, I want to be a writer." I mumbled, unsure of myself. I had not planned to tell her that, but she made me feel so utterly wrong and of no account that I needed to bolster myself.

"A what?" she demanded.

"A writer," I mumbled.

"For what?"

"To write stories," I mumbled defensively.

"You'll never be a writer," she said. "Who on earth put such ideas into your nigger head?"

"Nobody," I said.

"I didn't think anybody ever would," she declared indignantly.

As I walked around her house to the street, I knew that I would not go back. The woman had assaulted my ego; she had assumed that she knew my place in life, what I felt, what I ought to be, and I resented it with all my heart. Perhaps she was right; perhaps I would never be a writer; but I did not want her to say so.

(*Richard next found employment for several months as porter and delivery boy in a clothing store operated by a white man and his son. The store sold cheap goods on credit. Richard watched several times, frightened but tight-lipped, as his employers beat Negro customers who had not paid their bills.*)

Each day in the store I watched the brutality with growing hate, yet trying to keep my feelings from registering in my face. When the boss looked at me I would avoid his eyes. Finally the boss's son cornered me one morning.

"Say, nigger, look here," he began.

"Yes, sir."

"What's on your mind?"

"Nothing, sir," I said, trying to look amazed, trying to fool him.

"Why don't you laugh and talk like the other niggers?" he asked.

"Well, sir, there's nothing much to say or smile about," I said, smiling.

His face was hard, baffled; I knew that I had not convinced him. He whirled from me and went to the front of the store; he came back a moment later, his face red. He tossed a few green bills at me.

"I don't like your looks, nigger. Now, get!" he snapped.

I picked up the money and did not count it. I grabbed my hat and left.

(*Griggs, a high school friend, told Richard of another job opening — and also advised him to be more "humble" in his behavior at work. Richard got the job with Mr. Crane, a "Yankee" from Illinois who wanted to train a Negro boy in the optician's trade. Richard met Mr. Pease and Mr. Reynolds, the two workers in the shop, who were supposed to help him learn how to grind and polish lenses. The men seemed friendly. Richard's work for the first month, however, was confined to sweeping and running errands. Neither man volunteered to help him learn the trade. When Richard finally asked Mr. Reynolds to tell him something about the job, he was told that it was "white man's work." From then on, the two men grew increasingly hostile toward Richard.*)

The climax came at noon one summer day. Pease called me to his workbench; to get to him I had to go between two narrow benches and stand with my back against a wall.

"Richard. I want to ask you something," Pease began pleasantly, not looking up from his work.

"Yes, sir."

Reynolds came over and stood blocking the narrow passage between the benches; he folded his arms and stared at me solemnly. I looked from one to the other, sensing trouble. Pease looked up and spoke slowly, so there would be no possibility of my not understanding.

"Richard, Reynolds here tells me that you called me Pease," he said.

I stiffened. A void opened up in me. I knew that this was the showdown.

He meant that I had failed to call him Mr. Pease. I looked at Reynolds; he was gripping a steel bar in his hand. I opened my mouth to speak, to protest, to assure Pease that I had never called him simply *Pease*, and that I had never had any intention of doing so, when Reynolds grabbed me by the collar, ramming my head against a wall.

"Now, be careful, nigger," Reynolds snarled, baring his teeth. "I heard you call 'im *Pease*. And if you say you didn't, you're calling me a liar, see?" He waved the steel bar threateningly.

If I had said: No, sir, Mr. Pease, I never called you *Pease*, I would by inference have been calling Reynolds a liar; and if I had said: Yes, sir, Mr. Pease, I called you *Pease*, I would have been pleading guilty to the worst insult that a Negro can offer to a southern white man. I stood trying to think of a neutral course that would resolve this quickly risen nightmare, but my tongue would not move.

"Richard, I asked you a question!" Pease said. Anger was creeping into his voice.

"I don't remember calling you *Pease*, Mr. Pease," I said cautiously. "And if I did, I sure didn't mean. . . ."

"You black sonofabitch! You called me *Pease*, then!" he spat, rising and slapping me till I bent sideways over a bench. . . .

I wilted. I begged them not to hit me. I knew what they wanted. They wanted me to leave the job.

"I'll leave," I promised. "I'll leave right now!"

They gave me a minute to get out of the factory, and warned me not to show up again or tell the boss. . . . I went to the street and waited for the boss to return. I saw Griggs wiping glass shelves in the jewelry store and I beckoned to him. He came out and I told him what had happened.

"Then what are you standing there like a fool for?" he demanded. "Won't you ever learn? Get home! They might come down!"

(*Richard got a new job at a hotel, and tried to save money toward his growing determination to leave the South. But most of his salary went to feed "the eternally hungry stomachs at home." For the first time, he thought of stealing as a way to get his fare for the trip north.*)

All about me, Negroes were stealing. More than once I had been called a "dumb nigger" by black boys who discovered that I had not availed myself of a chance to snatch some petty piece of white property that had been carelessly left within my reach.

"How in hell you gonna git ahead?" I had been asked when I had said that one ought not steal.

I knew that the boys in the hotel filched whatever they could. I knew that Griggs, my friend who worked in the Capital Street jewelry store, was stealing regularly and successfully. I knew that a black neighbor of mine was stealing bags of grain from a wholesale house where he worked, though he was a staunch deacon in his church and prayed and sang on Sundays. I knew that the black girls who worked in white homes stole food daily to supplement their scanty wages. And I knew that the very nature of black and white relations bred this constant thievery.

No Negroes in my environment had ever thought of organizing, no matter in how orderly a fashion, and petitioning their white employers for higher wages. The very thought would have been terrifying to them, and they knew that the whites would have retaliated with swift brutality. So, pretending to conform to the laws of the whites, grinning, bowing, they let their fingers stick to what they could touch. And the whites seemed to like it.

But I, who stole nothing, who wanted to look them straight in the face, who wanted to talk and act like a man, inspired fear in them. The southern whites would rather have had Negroes who stole work for them than Negroes who knew, however dimly, the worth of their own humanity. Hence, whites placed a premium upon black

deceit; they encouraged irresponsibility; and their rewards were bestowed upon us blacks in the degree that we could make them feel safe and superior. . . .

One of the boys at the hotel whispered to me one night that the only local Negro movie house wanted a boy to take tickets at the door.

"You ain't never been in jail, is you?" he asked me.

"Not yet," I answered.

"Then you can get the job," he said. "I'd take it, but I done six months and they know me."

"What's the catch?"

"The girl who sells tickets is using a system," he explained. "If you get the job, you can make some good gravy."

If I stole, I would have a chance to head northward quickly; if I remained barely honest . . . I merely prolonged my stay, increased my chances of being caught, exposed myself to the possibility of saying the wrong word or doing the wrong thing and paying a penalty that I dared not think of. The temptation to venture into crime was too strong, and I decided to work quickly, taking whatever was in sight, amass a wad of money, and flee. I knew that others had tried it before me and had failed, but I was hoping to be lucky.

My chances for getting the job were good; I had no past record of stealing or violating the laws. When I presented myself to the Jewish proprietor of the movie house I was immediately accepted. The next day I reported for duty and began taking tickets. The boss man warned me:

"Now, look, I'll be honest with you if you'll be honest with me. I don't know who's honest around this joint and who isn't. But if *you* are honest, then the rest are bound to be. All tickets will pass through your hands. There can be no stealing unless you steal."

I gave him a pledge of my honesty, feeling absolutely no qualms about what I intended to do. He was white, and I could never do to him what he and his kind had done to me. Therefore, I reasoned, stealing was not a violation of my ethics, but of his. . . .

During the first afternoon the Negro girl in

the ticket office watched me closely and I knew that she was sizing me up, trying to determine when it would be safe to break me into her graft. I waited, leaving it to her to make the first move.

I was supposed to drop each ticket that I took from a customer into a metal receptacle. Occasionally the boss would go to the ticket window and look at the serial number with the number on the last ticket I had dropped into the receptacle. The boss continued his watchfulness for a few days, then began to observe me from across the street; finally he absented himself for long intervals.

A tension as high as that I had known when the white men had driven me from the job at the optician's returned to live in me. But I had learned to master a great deal of tension now. . . .

While I was eating supper in a near-by cafe one night, a strange Negro man walked in and sat beside me.

"Hello, Richard," he said.

"Hello," I said. "I don't think I know you."

"But I know *you*," he said, smiling.

Was he one of the boss's spies?

"How do you know me?" I asked.

"I'm Tel's friend," he said, naming the girl who sold the tickets at the movie.

I looked at him searchingly. Was he telling me the truth? Or was he trying to trap me for the boss? I was already thinking and feeling like a criminal, distrusting everybody.

"We start tonight," he said.

"What?" I asked, still not admitting that I knew what he was talking about.

"Don't be scared. The boss trusts you. He's gone to see some friends. Somebody's watching him and if he starts back to the movie, they'll phone us," he said.

I could not eat my food. . . .

"It'll work this way," he explained in a low, smooth tone. "A guy'll come to you and ask for a match. You give him five tickets that you'll hold out of the box, see? We'll give you the signal when to start holding out. The guy'll give the tickets to Tel; she'll resell them all at once,

when a crowd is buying at the rush hour. You get it?"

I did not answer. I knew that if I were caught I would go to the chain gang. But was not my life already a kind of chain gang? What, really, did I have to lose?

"Are you with us?" he asked.

I still did not answer. He rose and clapped me on the shoulder and left. I trembled as I went back to the theater. Anything might happen, but I was used to that. . . . Had I not felt it when I walked home from the optical company that morning with my job gone? . . . Had I not felt it all a million times before? I took the tickets with sweaty fingers. I waited. I was gambling: freedom or the chain gang. There were times when I felt that I could not breathe. I looked up and down the street; the boss was not in sight. Was this a trap? . . .

The man I had met in the cafe came through the door and put a ticket in my hand.

"There's a crowd at the box office," he whispered. "Save ten, not five. Start with this one."

Well, here goes, I thought. He gave me the ticket and sat looking at the moving shadows upon the screen. I held on to the ticket and my body grew tense, hot as fire; but I was used to that too. Time crawled through the cells of my brain. My muscles ached. I discovered that crime means suffering. The crowd came in and gave me more tickets. I kept ten of them tucked into my moist palm. No sooner had the crowd thinned than a black boy with a cigarette jutting from his mouth came up to me.

"Gotta match?"

With a slow movement I gave him the tickets. He went out and I kept the door cracked and watched. He went to the ticket office and laid down a coin and I saw him slip the tickets to the girl. Yes, the boy was honest. The girl shot me a quick smile and I went back inside. A few moments later the same tickets were handed to me by other customers.

We worked it for a week and after the money was split four ways I had fifty dollars. Freedom was almost within my grasp. Ought I risk any more? I dropped the hint to Tel's friend that maybe I would quit; it was a casual hint to test him out. He grew violently angry and I quickly consented to stay. . . .

I went through another week. Late one night I resolved to make that week the last. . . . I bought clothes, shoes, a cardboard suitcase, all of which I hid at home. Saturday night came and I sent word to the boss that I was sick. Uncle Tom was upstairs. Granny and Aunt Addie were at church. My brother was sleeping. My mother sat in her rocking chair, humming to herself. I packed my suitcase and went to her.

"Mama, I'm going away," I whispered.

"Oh, no," she protested.

"I've got to, mama. I can't live this way."

"You're not running away from something you've done?"

"I'll send for you, mama. I'll be all right."

"Take care of yourself. And send for me quickly. I'm not happy here," she said.

"I'm sorry for all these long years, mama. But I could not have helped it."

I kissed her and she cried.

"Be quiet, mama. I'm all right."

I went out the back way and walked a quarter of a mile to the railroad tracks. . . . An hour later I was sitting in a Jim Crow coach, speeding northward. . . . Well, it's my life, I told myself. I'll see now what I can make of it.

QUESTIONS
FOR
DISCUSSION

1. *Humiliation.* Richard objected that the housewife "assaulted my ego" when she said, "You'll never be a writer. Who on earth put such ideas into your nigger head?" Do you think it is morally wrong for people to insult or humiliate each other through such statements? Why or why not?

It is possible to file suit against those who maliciously slander or libel one's name in public. Should laws be passed that make private, person-to-person insults or humiliation illegal? (Recent urban riots have been allegedly sparked by policemen and firemen who insulted ghetto dwellers.) Consider the problem that truthful, sincere statements can often assault one's ego (e.g., it *was* unlikely that a black child would become a writer in Richard's lifetime; also, a guidance counselor can be completely honest and still inform a student that he has low ability and low probability of success in certain fields).

2. *Expectations and Morality.* Was it right for Richard to steal in his job at the movie theater? Consider the following statement:

"In deciding whether something is right or wrong, we can consider two basic ideas: (a) we should do what people expect us to do; or (b) we should behave according to some natural or moral law that may differ from what people expect. The Ten Commandments are an example of (b), and if we follow them we must conclude that it was wrong for Richard to steal. However, the whites in the South deliberately put the Negro in a situation where he had to steal in order to survive; the whites could then look on the Negro as a poor, immoral lawbreaker. This helped the whites feel superior. Because the whites' own feelings of superiority depended on the Negroes being poor, petty thieves, we can say that the whites really expected and wanted Negroes to steal. Thus it was right for Richard to steal."

3. *Responsibility.* Who was responsible for Richard's plight? (A) The whites who insulted him and refused him a decent job or education; (B) blacks (e.g., his grandmother and playmates) who laughed at his writing and reinforced his feelings of inferiority; (C) blacks who taught him to keep quiet, not make trouble, to survive within the system, rather than strike out against it; (D) Richard himself who could have stood up for his rights and improved himself? Use these alternatives (and possibly others) to arrive at some general explanation of a *network* of responsibility.

HALBERG GOES NAZI

The Barten family feels difficult pressures as their town begins to change.

MARCH 25, 1930

The sky darkened as the sun slid behind the hills surrounding the town of Halberg. Halberg looked best at twilight, and to Greta Barten it seemed a town out of *Grimm's Fairy Tales.* It was an old town, small enough to sit primly within ancient walls built when there was a castle on the same spot. Its houses were made of white stucco, crisscrossed with dark oaken beams that showed how solid they were. As the lamps were turned on, each house gave off its warm yellow glow of pride. Fourteen-year-old Greta was sure that her town must be one of the nicest places in the world.

Greta stopped before the door of her house to pull up her knee socks — Mama would want her to look neat. She opened the heavy door, and the thick, sweet smell of baking pastry mixed with the clear evening air. Greta burst into the kitchen and ran to hug her mother. Frau Barten kissed her daughter and went back to spreading pastry dough with her heavy rolling pin.

"Hello, Walther." Looking up from his geography book, Greta's twelve-year-old brother nodded. He really did not have much time for Greta. It was Karl whom he idolized; his sister, he thought, was silly.

"And Karl, how are you today?" Greta's elder brother was standing by the stove, obviously impatient at being interrupted in what he had been saying. He and Greta usually got along well together, but tonight his greeting was terse:

"You're just in time to listen to the end of an argument, Greta. . . . Mama, I've done my homework. Captain Hersing is speaking. Won't you let me go?"

"You must wait until Papa comes home, Karl. These things are up to him." Frau Barten worked hard at being a good mother, the wife of a respected merchant, and a loyal member of her ladies' club — and those were the limits of her interests. And she disliked arguments.

Karl would not relent: "Mama, why must I always wait for Papa's decision? Nothing happens without the almighty word of Papa."

This case is taken from Donald W. Oliver and Fred M. Newmann, *Nazi Germany: Social Forces and Personal Responsibility,* American Education Publications, Columbus, Ohio, 1968. This fictional case authentically represents events in a German town.

"Karl! That is quite enough!" Frau Barten was angry now and Karl winced at her words. He sulked in the corner, saying nothing more.

The children heard Herr Barten's tired step along the hallway. Papa was home, and he, too, would come to the warm kitchen before doing anything else. He was shorter and heavier than his elder son, and he always walked home from the shop—limping slightly from his old war wound — with his pipe in his mouth. Puffing smoke in rapid spurts from his worn briar, he barely nodded hello to his family before starting his comments on a poor day:

"My God, business is awful! Only two customers today. No one is buying hardware. No one is building anything. Look at the papers! The Socialists publish huge unemployment figures and still tell us everything will be all right!" Herr Barten threw the *Volksblatt*, the Socialist paper, on the table. "The *Times* pretends nothing is wrong and writes about weddings and dances." He threw the paper of the local Civil Servants party on the table. "And the Nazis," with this he waved their paper in the air, "are good at shouting, nothing else! Why do I bother buying papers? I know what I need to know."

Frau Barten, for whom two outbursts in one day were more than enough, calmed her husband, "Now, now, Papa, it's never so bad as you think. Look what we're having for dessert — strudel. Walther, put away that book and get your papa's slippers."

Herr Barten sat down at the table. Immediately he felt better. He had been through the Great War; he had built a prosperous business; he had raised a fine family. Politics were not so important after all, and they certainly weren't going to starve this night. "Well," he said, more to himself than to his family, "we have always voted Socialist — even my grandfather voted Socialist — and we have not done too badly."

Karl, who had been waiting his chance, asked, "Papa, may I go to the rally at the Cattle Auction Hall tonight? Captain Hersing is speaking. They're letting students in at half price."

"Which meeting is that, Karl, the one spon-sored by the Nazis? I thought we had finished discussing politics."

"Papa, it's not really a political meeting. Captain Hersing is a U-boat hero from the war. It'll probably be my only chance to see him."

"You don't have to tell me who Hersing is, Karl. I know the figures of the war all too well. . . . But I guess you can go."

"Can I go, too, Papa?" asked Walther hopefully.

"Of course not. It will be past your bedtime."

"Come, let's sit down to dinner," said Frau Barten before Walther could object. "Greta, is the table set?"

At 8:15, Karl stood in line amid a huge crowd outside the barnlike Auction Hall. The walls were plastered with posters announcing a program of three speeches. Karl was gratified to see that Captain Hersing was first on the program. "Perhaps I can leave after his speech," he thought as he filed through the door.

The scene inside was chaotic. The crowd was much larger than the hall could accommodate, and milling people stirred up clouds of dust from the dirt floor as they waited for more benches to be brought in. A hired band blasted a patriotic song into the crowd.

Karl found himself cramped on a bench between two rather foul-smelling old men. Many of Halberg's derelicts were in the crowd, he noted — admission was free for the unemployed, and the hall was heated; these fellows would otherwise have been roaming the streets, trying to keep warm until they were allowed, at 11, to sleep in the waiting room of the railroad station.

The chairman introduced Captain Hersing in glowing terms. Karl leaned forward to hear the great man's words:

"Comrades, it brings me joy to know that so many are concerned with the fate of the Fatherland. For these are difficult times — times when all Germans must unite to dispel the shadow of disaster, to free their country from the enemies who lurk not only at its borders but within the very heart of the country itself. As the captain of a ship, I would not tolerate one dishonest, surly, or lazy seaman. Yet our nation is like a ship full of just such men. In a time of crisis, these men do not help the country — they must be thrown overboard. . . ."

The crowd listened raptly. Karl felt himself absorbed by the Captain's words. "We are surrounded by enemies! We must unite!" Karl did not know who the enemies were, but that mattered little. This fine man — this war hero — knew. He asked only for strong men to stand for Germany. When the crowd rose to cheer Captain Hersing, Karl's voice was among the loudest.

The next speaker, Herr Blankenmeyer, spoke with even more flair than the Captain. Karl forgot that he had meant to leave after the first speech. Blankenmeyer was not content merely to speak of Germany's enemies — he named them:

"From within and without, Germany is being undermined by Jewish financiers. They have brought all of Europe into a depression, and yet the Jewish merchants of Germany still prosper. They are men who have no country but live off all countries. And what of our friends, the Socialists? Instead of preserving the purity of our country, they speak of an international brotherhood of workers. Instead of preaching loyalty to the Fatherland, they preach the myth of democracy. . . ."

The applause was slightly cautious this time. Some of Halberg's well-established citizens were Jews, and the Socialists had long been the most popular political group. As if to dispel such doubts, the chairman quickly brought forward the final speaker, Pastor Timmerbaum. The Lutheran minister of the neighboring town of Bachheim was a dignified, grey-haired man, about fifty. In measured tones he described the purposes of the NSDAP—the National Socialist German Workers' party. Liberalism and socialism, he declared, were poisoning the youth of Germany. Christianity and German Folkdom, on the other hand, were inseparable and would together bring glory to the German people. At the end of his speech, Reverend Timmerbaum closed his eyes as if praying and almost chanted words of praise for the NSDAP.

The band struck up the Nazis' "Horst Wessel" song. The Cattle Auction Hall rocked as more than a thousand Germans sang chorus after chorus, each time with greater enthusiasm. Then the crowd filed out to the martial rhythms of "Sieg Heil."

Karl had just stepped out the door into the cold air when he saw Gunther Holbern also leaving the rally. Gunther was a year ahead of Karl at school and one of the best athletes. Although he had hardly even nodded to Gunther at school, the spirit of the rally made Karl bold, and he waved and walked over to the older boy. Somewhat to his surprise, Gunther greeted him enthusiastically. He put his hand on Karl's shoulder, looked approvingly at him, and said, "Karl, wasn't that a fine meeting!"

The two boys fell in step, walking toward the part of Halberg where they both lived.

Gunther gestured with a sweep of his arm. "Look at this town. It's getting run-down. The parks are becoming crowded with bums; the markets are selling lousy meat; there's talk of a soup kitchen being opened up! We need men like Herr Blankenmeyer, who can point to the evils and tell us how to get rid of them. We need to organize. Look, we've come to your turnoff. Let me give you this, and I hope I see you next Tuesday."

Gunther pressed a folder into Karl's hand and strode off into the darkness. Karl could make out the bold print at the top, which announced a meeting of the newly formed Nazi youth organization.

As Karl continued his walk home, the words of the rally echoed in his thoughts. This had been a momentous evening. The boy he admired most in the whole school had talked to him like a comrade. And questions that had been building up in his mind about his family, his town, his country, seemed to be at least partly answered. His father's complaints about business, the haggardness that was beginning to haunt the town — the causes were pointed out tonight. And solutions were given: "We must be strong and unite. We must make heroes again — people like Captain Hersing. We must devote ourselves to the Fatherland. I can help in the movement. Yes. I am young. I am strong. I can help."

FEBRUARY 1931

During the months after the rally, the Nazis were heard from more and more in Halberg. Karl became involved with Nazi youth activities, and Gunther Holbern, whom Karl now considered his best friend, became a Nazi youth leader. Karl and Gunther told Herr and Frau Barten they belonged to a "rifle club." Yet Karl, excited by the ideas he heard at Nazi youth meetings, found it increasingly harder to mask his irritation at his parents' attitude toward politics. One evening Herr Barten mentioned an article in the Socialist paper, and Karl shot back:

"Papa, why do you vote Socialist? Just because Grandpa did? Don't you realize that they are really Marxists who want to divide everything up among the poor? You're a merchant. You don't want that." Karl was like a preacher trying to convert someone. He had decided, as he said to himself, to "make Papa and Mama face the issues."

Frau Barten was astonished. "Karl, you don't talk like that to Papa!"

"No, no, Mama, it's all right." Herr Barten sucked slowly on his pipe. "These young people today feel they have to speak. It won't hurt us to listen. Go on, Karl."

"Well, you remember the old days; the army was strong, factories hummed, the country was united. We've lost that and it's the fault of the Socialists."

"Karl, we also lost the war, even with our huge army and busy factories. Now we have democracy . . . we can be proud of that." Herr Barten spoke calmly, but Karl became more excited.

"We lost the war because of foreigners who undermined Germany. Democracy only means that everyone, Jews, foreigners, everyone, tells us how to run the country. It's no good. We need Germany united under Germans!"

Herr Barten was no longer calm. "Karl, you

sound like a Nazi! And you don't know what you're talking about."

The boy nearly shouted now. "It's better to be a Nazi with a plan to save Germany than to be Socialist and help Germany dry up to nothing."

"Karl, you go to bed now. This is quite enough." Frau Barten was nearly in tears.

"Your Mama's right, go to bed." Herr Barten turned toward the fireplace to hide the expression on his face.

Karl made his way heavily up the stairs.

The quarrel was over, for a while.

Herr Barten's hardware store was ideally located on the main street of Halberg. In twenty years he had built up a loyal clientele; faithful customers were important now that times were hard.

On Monday, as Herr Barten was opening up his store, an NSDAP party member, marked by the badge he wore on his lapel, approached him. The Nazi carried a roll of posters under one arm.

"Good morning, Herr Barten, I hope you had a pleasant weekend." The man's smile was broad, and he held out his hand. "I'm Ernst Schwartz."

"Good morning, Herr Schwartz. What can I get for you?" Herr Barten could hardly believe he had business so early in the day.

"I'm not buying today, Herr Barten, but I've come to ask a favor. Would you mind putting a poster in your window?"

"A political poster? I'm sorry. My customers are of all parties, so I don't advertise for any."

The man's attitude changed: "Listen, my friend, I'm from the NSDAP and we want these posters up in all the stores on this street. Do not, Herr Barten, refuse us, please."

Herr Barten still did not take the rolled-up poster, which was now poked into his stomach like a gun barrel.

"I'm sorry, I can't do it. Business is bad. I may lose customers. You must understand."

The other man smiled slightly. "You shouldn't refuse," he said, and turned on his heel.

Herr Barten was trembling slightly as he tried

to put the key into the lock. Once inside the store he sat heavily in his chair behind the counter. He asked himself, "Why am I frightened? This is a democracy. A man does what he wants with his own shop."

That night hoodlums shattered the front window of Herr Barten's hardware store, smashed and scattered merchandise, and scrawled obscene words on the door with soap. Herr Barten reported the incident to the police. A week later they informed him that they could find no witnesses and no clues. NSDAP officials appeared outraged at the idea that they could have been responsible. They even showed the police their membership lists.

Later in the month Herr Barten received another visit from the Nazis. This time there were two men, visiting, as before, just when Herr Barten was about to open his store for the day.

"Herr Barten, we have a small favor to ask." The man who spoke was frail, but his voice was strong. Herr Barten thought he recognized him. Was it this man's picture — "Accused Arsonist" — he had seen in the Socialist paper?

The other man, taller and stronger-looking, spoke: "We ask you not to do business with the Jews Rosenbaum and Hoeltermann. The NSDAP is instituting a boycott of Jew merchants."

Herr Barten gasped in spite of himself. He needed steady customers and one of the best was the jeweler, Saul Rosenbaum, for whom Herr Barten obtained the small tools and lubricants used in watch repairing. Nicholas Hoeltermann — and he was only part Jewish, an immigrant from Holland — bought brass fittings for his prosperous furniture factory.

At that moment a beggar came up to the three men and held out his hat, smiling through toothless gums. The Nazi who had just spoken dug into his pocket and gave the man a coin. "Look, Hans," he said to his companion, "Germans starve while the Jews grow fat." Both men turned back to Herr Barten.

"Well, Herr Barten, will you comply with the boycott?"

Herr Barten did not look into their eyes. Despite his fear, he answered: "But Herr Rosenbaum is one of my best customers, a good jeweler, a respectable citizen. And Herr Hoeltermann is. . . ."

The thin man cut him off. "You must know, Herr Barten, that it doesn't pay to be uncooperative."

Both men turned abruptly and walked off down the street.

For the second time in a month Herr Barten's fingers trembled as he fitted the key to the lock. "Why should this happen to me?" he thought. "I defended Germany in the war. I have a family. I am a good German. I need my business. Jews don't hurt us. Why?"

Two days later, on Thursday, Herr Rosenbaum came in for his monthly supply of jeweler's saw blades. Herr Barten hardly looked up from the counter, but shrugged his shoulders and muttered, "I am sorry, my friend, I . . . cannot do business with you. . . . I must protect my shop . . . my family. . . ."

Herr Rosenbaum merely stood silent. Then he smiled a half smile and said softly, "Yes, Herr Barten, I understand."

Hoeltermann, the furniture maker, must have heard, for he did not come in for the fifty gross of brass screws he ordered each month. Herr Barten had no more Jewish customers.

QUESTIONS FOR DISCUSSION

1. *Self-interest and Social Justice.* Do you think it was right for Herr Barten to refuse to trade with Herr Rosenbaum? In justifying your opinion on this issue, take positions on the following analogies:

a. In an overcrowded lifeboat that is about to sink, the first mate (the highest ranking officer) asks the two heaviest men to jump overboard in order to save the lives of seventeen other people in the boat — twelve of them women and children. Should the two men jump into the sea?

b. Dave observes a group of his classmates breaking into an auto supply store. The group discovers that Dave is the only witness and threatens to beat him if he tells the police. The next day Dave is questioned by the police. Should he tell the truth?

c. Roger, a new student in the school, sees some classmates provoking and beating up younger students of a different nationality. He feels this is wrong, but believes that if he interferes he'll lose the friendship of his classmates. Should he try to stop the fight?

In what ways are these analogies similar to and different from Herr Barten's case? Develop a general position that helps you decide when a person would be expected to make some self-sacrifice to help others or to correct social injustice.

2. *Responsibility*. Do you feel that Herr Barten, by giving in to the Nazis, was partially responsible for the ultimate Nazi seizure of power and the extermination of six million Jews? Why or why not?

3. *Force versus Voluntary Exchange of Favors*. It might be claimed that it is immoral for a political party to "force" a person to give his support, but moral for the party to gain support by allowing the individual voluntarily to exchange favors with the party. Consider the following techniques:

a. A Storm Trooper promises not to destroy Herr Barten's store if Barten cooperates with the Nazis.

b. An employer promises a salary raise to employees who work for the Nazis.

c. An employer promises not to fire employees who work for the Nazis.

d. A Nazi member offers food and shelter to starving and homeless people if they will cooperate with the party.

e. A Storm Trooper threatens to beat a man's wife if the man testifies in court against the Nazis.

f. A bank president says he will give a businessman a loan if the businessman refuses to trade with Jews.

Discuss the morality of each technique of political persuasion. To what extent does the distinction between "force" and "voluntary exchange of favors" help you to distinguish the more and less moral practices?

Chapter 5

Equality

I. Diverse
Illustrations

That all men are created equal and are entitled to equal opportunity and treatment is mentioned not only as the cornerstone of democracy, but even as the basis of justice and morality itself (see Scriven, 1966). Blacks protest against discrimination in housing, employment, and education. A Jew or Catholic might feel that the state, through federal aid to public education, gives special advantage to Protestant children. Students demand voting rights equal to adults. Laborers demand an equal say with management. The poor claim the right to medical care and legal service equal to that available to the wealthy. Women charge that they are not judged on the basis of ability or merit, but on irrelevant criteria such as sex or appearance, that they are denied privileges and responsibilities normally available to men. Politicians want equal time on television. Opponents of college student exemptions from military service claim that all citizens have an equal obligation to serve their country. Members of some minority groups (e.g., artists, homosexuals, the Amish) object that the society will not allow them to live by styles that deviate from the norm.

We use the term "equality" in at least three distinguishable senses. (1) *Availability of Resources and Power.* This interpretation emphasizes equal access to "necessities of life" such as income, food, shelter, medical care, legal protection, and education. There is continuing debate on the responsibilities of those in positions of power to supply such goods and services equally to all. Although goods and services may be equally available in some areas, the powerless increasingly demand equal political decision-making power. This latter interpretation of equality will be treated more thoroughly in Chapter 7. (2) *Dignity and Respect.* Although it may be hard to imagine ways in which public policy might guarantee a psychological sense of dignity

129

and self-respect for each individual, a familiar moral claim states that all are equally entitled to such respect from their fellowmen (because they are all "equal" in the eyes of God or under natural law). Encouraging courtesy, kindness, friendliness, common human decency, and following the "golden rule" can be seen as attempts to inculcate this interpretation of equality. Equal self-respect, however, cannot be attained without equal access to resources. (3) *Individuality or Creative Development.* Stressing the importance of individual freedom to grow, develop, and live according to one's unique interests and abilities, creative development primarily concerns removing arbitrary constraints or limitations. It assumes that all men should be equally free to develop themselves according to personal standards, ambitions, and tastes. Public policy in this regard implies equal rights to be let alone, to have one's privacy protected from intrusion by society, a laissez-faire attitude that encourages freedom of personal choice.

The three interpretations of equality are related. Both resources and opportunities for creative development seem necessary to develop dignity, which may help further creative development. Although the three seem logically inextricable, distinguishing among them allows us to observe different policy approaches aimed at achieving equality. In some areas public policies take positive action to provide specific goods and services (e.g., medical care, education, counsel for the indigent); in others, the government remains almost completely detached, leaving the realization of equality to informal social sanctions (e.g., the absence of laws requiring courtesy or prohibiting insults and humiliation); and in certain contexts the government may act to encourage unique development (e.g., protection and even support of religious minorities; tax exemptions for cultural institutions; scholarships and special programs for talented students).

A. Equal Versus Identical: Human Nature and Treatment

The general mandate that individuals deserve to be treated equally has often been traced back or derived from descriptive statements about inherent qualities or characteristics of all men. But because most agree that men are equal neither in physical and biological endowment, nor skills, talents, and tastes, the claim that all men are created equal is not intended to mean that all men are *identical* in all respects. Yet many have claimed that in certain respects men are universally alike, if not identical: e.g., in the possession of a soul; the capacity to reason; the potential for being virtuous; the tendency to feel pain, to desire affection; to make moral judgments; the wish to be judged by one's moral worth, rather than by superficial considerations of status; or the desire to exert control over one's destiny.

One might continue to explore the nature of man, asking in what respects, if any, all men are identical. Yet this will not necessarily define what is meant by equal treatment or justify why equal treatment is right. We might discover that men have certain identical characteristics, but whether these establish the need for equal treatment is quite another philosophical issue. The question — whether equal treatment is a valid moral principle — involves most issues discussed in Chapter 4.

Assuming that all men are entitled to equal treatment and equal opportunity, we must realize that this is not necessarily a mandate for *identical* treatment.[1] We do not believe that all men should receive the same income, have the same clothes, raise their children the same way, believe in the same religion, work at identical jobs, read the same books, or have the same opportunity to make love to a given woman. On the contrary, to believe in universally identical treatment would contradict that sense of equality that emphasizes opportunity to develop individual differences. Most controversies concern the extent to which equal treatment must entail virtually identical treatment. This interpretation is evident in the following widely accepted positions: two persons convicted of the same crime in similar circumstances should be given identical punishment; each person's vote in an election should receive identical value in the tallying; auto safety standards should be identically enforced with different manufacturers (as should safety and health standards for other products); a doctor or hospital should give identical treatment to people with the same symptoms and illnesses; income tax rates should be identical for different individuals with the same income and dependents; a given quantity of goods in a given store should be priced identically for all customers.

Although equal treatment may entail identical treatment, a more complicated concept of equality specifically advocates differential treatment in order to achieve equality. The wealthy are taxed at a higher rate than the poor; people who commit the same crime are treated differently by motivation and circumstances; low ability students receive instruction different from high ability students. Justifying unequal or nonidentical treatment has several ramifications in public issues.

II. Justifying Unequal Treatment

According to Stone (1965, p. 334), "Our choice is not between equal treatment and the making of distinctions; it is between making (or tolerating) distinctions which we can justify, and making (or tolerating) distinctions which we cannot justify."

One can justify unequal treatment in two ways: (A) We can claim that the action that creates inequality does not infringe on those rights that should

---

[1] Benn and Peters (1965) suggest *impartiality* as the central concept in morality and justice. For them equal treatment is closely related, if not synonymous, when interpreted as a mandate to treat all men alike in those respects in which they are alike and to give different treatment only in response to "relevant" differences among men or their conditions. The challenge, of course, is to ascertain under what conditions a given difference among men should be considered "relevant" enough to warrant different treatment.

be guaranteed to all men (inalienable rights): for example, refusing a stranger admittance to a private social gathering. (B) We can show that differentiated or unequal treatment in one sense leads to greater equality in another more important area: for example, the graduated income tax that places a heavier financial burden on the wealthy.

A. Discrimination Allegedly Irrelevant to Basic Equality

Certain privileges or opportunities are given to some people and denied to others on several bases. Yet for many, it would be difficult to charge that the constitutional or public sense of equal opportunity had been violated. A Broadway director denies the lead role to an auditioner who, he says, can't act. A university faculty denies employment to a prospective professor, because it judges his research to be inferior. A suburbanite complains that he can't afford two cars and a trip to Europe like many of his friends. Some teen-aged girls refuse to invite those from the other side of town to a party. Women are prohibited from membership in a private hunting and fishing club. Immigrants must pass a literacy test and residence qualifications before they are admitted to United States citizenship. A private school admits only those who can afford a $3,500 yearly tuition. A defeated candidate for mayor protests that his party will not have an equal voice in the city's government.

1. General Explanations of Limited Opportunities

These inequalities or denials of opportunity reflect different ways in which access to goods or privileges may be limited (Williams, 1962).

(1) Some positions, goods, or experiences are limited by their *nature*. An inherent characteristic of a lead role in a play is its singularity; the mayor of a city is by definition only one person; a unique experience (e.g., calling plays in football, listening to a concert, raising a child) by its nature occurs only once in a given time or place. Thus, certain opportunities cannot be universally available.

(2) Other experiences are *contingently* limited. Although they are theoretically available to all, certain qualifications or skills are requisite to their enjoyment or performance. Whether a person is entitled to function as a doctor, engineer, architect, scientist, baseball player, film editor, printer, plumber, or comedian depends largely upon whether he can demonstrate necessary competencies. The right to drive a car, operate a restaurant, attend college, or vote is also contingent upon one's meeting certain qualifications and following specified procedures. Those privileges or opportunities limited by contingent qualifications present two major problems: first, opportunities to acquire the needed skills often are limited (e.g., poor people trying to gain necessary education); and second, whether a given requirement is *relevant* to the desired opportunity can become a major issue of public debate (e.g., at what age is a person old enough to vote). One might

construe historical attempts to gain equality as protests against the relevance of specific qualifications considered contingent to specific opportunities. In the following section, "Criteria for Discrimination," we deal with specific contingencies or criteria for limiting opportunity.

(3) *Scarcity* limits opportunities; in some situations there are simply not enough goods, services, or experiences to go around. Because Cadillacs, good colleges, lawyers, or lobsters are scarce, all people cannot equally obtain them, and a system of rationing develops, usually based on money. Whether money is an appropriate or relevant criterion for distributing scarce items is often a controversial question. The Supreme Court says, for example, that though lawyers are scarce, accused criminals are entitled to them even if they can't afford the fees. Evidently some scarce items (e.g., legal defense, medical care, or education) are considered more relevant to equality for all than others (e.g., color television, trips to Europe, or automobiles).

(4) Finally, we recognize limitations on opportunities that arise from *personal choices* considered to be *private matters* and thus out of the realm of public rights: for example, choices regarding one's friends and social companions, business and professional associates, or works of art. The choices, where discrimination and selection seem legitimate, are necessary to realize that aspect of equality which emphasizes everyone's equal right to self-fulfillment. That is, if one was coerced into giving equal consideration to all women in choosing a spouse, all models in choosing a car, all humans in the choosing of friends, or all occupations in choosing a career, he could not exercise the individual preferences that presumably make him unique. The exact boundaries of legitimate personal discrimination can be hotly debated: for example, does the woman who runs a "private" boarding house have the right to exclude travelers by race; should a businessman refuse to hire someone because of religious or ethnic prejudice? There is continuing controversy on whether specific decisions are solely private personal choices or whether they involve public obligations.

2. Criteria for Discrimination

Humans consciously prescribe qualifications, conditions, or criteria that grant goods, services, or opportunities to some people and deny them to others. Many criteria are considered legitimate; some are more controversial than others, depending upon the context in which discrimination occurs. Some more "respectable" or commonly accepted bases on which unequal treatment is justified follow.

Age. School attendance, military service, voting, driving a car, purchasing alcoholic beverages, holding public office, right to work, rights in judicial proceedings, or social security benefits all are determined to some extent by age.

Birth. The right of children to inherit their parents' fortunes leads to considerable inequality yet is widely considered a legitimate basis of privilege. Similarly, the parent by giving birth to a child retains certain rights over the child that are not equally available either to the child himself or to other adults.

Income. As mentioned previously, possessing money is considered a valid way for differentiating between those who are entitled to a large amount of goods and services versus those who should do without them.

Competence. The right to have a particular job (television repairman or surgeon) and the right to engage in certain activities (e.g., driving a car) depends to some extent on demonstrating particular skills, such as literacy, mechanical dexterity, verbal fluency, or physical strength. Those who have demonstrated achievement in business, politics, or the arts are given special privileges and responsibility.

Religious, Political, and Social Belief. In recognizing the right of a minister or priest to deny his services to heretics, the right of the state to deny rights to those who refuse loyalty oaths, the right of organizations to deny membership to those who refuse to subscribe to certain beliefs, we allow ideology in certain cases to be a criterion for privilege.

Obedience to the Law. Those with a criminal record are presumed unworthy of such opportunities as holding public offices, or, in some cases, serving on boards of corporations. Those who commit more serious crimes may be deported, imprisoned for life, or executed.

Physical Attributes. One's physique, sex, or general appearance might exclude him from certain jobs (airline hostess, lumberjack, priest or rabbi, midwife, fashion model, or locker room attendant); schools (those accepting only one sex); and social gatherings (men's and ladies' clubs). Although recent legislation aims toward more equal treatment of the sexes, several areas of discrimination based on sex or appearance are still accepted.

Human Greatness and Progress. Certain achievements of man — the building of pyramids, cathedrals, industrial empires, exploration of space — are usually accomplished at the considerable social cost of denying equal resources and services to large segments of the population. The sacrifice in equal opportunity borne by the masses is conventionally justified by the "greatness" of the achievement, its contribution to "progress' or its monument to "human potential."

Much public controversy in America has involved attempts to abolish race, sex, religion, national origin, or political ideology as grounds for denying people public office or for limiting their access to basic goods and services. As suggested previously, however, such criteria (and others) are considered valid grounds for discrimination in areas that are deemed irrelevant to those rights to which all men are equally entitled. Discrimination or unequal treatment can also be justified because some kinds of discrimination are necessary to *achieve* equality.

B. Discrimination Intended to Achieve Equality

A doctor arriving at an auto accident must decide whether he should first treat a young child or an elderly victim. Although in theory people of all ages should be equally entitled to medical care, the doctor would probably not be criticized for choosing to save the child (i.e., discriminating by age). He could justify this discrimination by citing the value of equality: "The elderly person had already lived a long life. To give the child an equal chance to live, I had to treat him first." Programs in compensatory education for disadvantaged city youth can spend many times the amount per child spent in suburban public schools. This unequal distribution of resources is justified by claiming it is necessary to give the disadvantaged an equal start in life so they will be able to compete with those children from affluent families, who, because of childhood and preschool enriched environments, are educationally far ahead of the ghetto children. Welfare payments to the ill, the unemployed, and women with no other support may also be seen as unequal resources given to those whose condition or plight puts them in an inferior position relative to the larger population.

Veterans' benefits that give preferential educational, financial, and medical benefits are justified by referring to the unusual risks and time that GI's have sacrificed for the country while the general population lived in relative comfort. To even the score, veterans deserve special treatment. The graduated income tax forces the wealthy to pay a higher percentage of its income to the government, yet the objective is equality. If the percentage were equal for all income groups, the poor would have to bear a relatively greater burden. Nonprofit charitable organizations receive the special privilege of tax exemption, on the assumption that such organizations are financially disadvantaged, that the "good" they do for society is valuable (like GI's), and, to give them an equal chance to hire talent and perform services, it is necessary to relieve them of burdens of taxation. Motorists with accident-free records are given lower auto insurance rates than accident-prone drivers because one should pay an amount equivalent to the risk he brings to the company. Differentiated rates result in each motorist bearing a burden equivalent or proportional to the financial burden each is likely to bring to the company.

As the last example suggests, the notion of equivalence or proportionality is crucial to justify otherwise apparently unequal treatment. The unequal treatment when teachers give different lessons to different students is justified on the ground that to treat people equally, it is necessary to provide what is appropriate for, equivalent to, or proportionate to one's needs, abilities, or burdens. Examples from criminal justice are instructive. Different persons commit the same deed — killing a human being — but are punished differently. The child would be treated more leniently than the adult; the premeditated murder would receive harsher punishment than an accidental death or killing in self-defense. Such differentiated treatment signifies that all defendants are not equally responsible for the victim's death. Only if each could be ascribed equal responsibility would each deserve equal treatment. Otherwise one's punishment should be proportionate to the nature of the crime and the responsibility of the defendant.

Price determination is a less obvious area for proportional equality. We rightly would object if someone proposed that the prices of all goods and services be equal per unit: that is, if a pound of bread cost the same as a pound of steak; or if a Volkswagen cost the same as a Jaguar. Why? Because we assume that consumer price should be proportional or equivalent to cost. Paying the same for everything would impose unfair economic burdens on the consumer, wage earner, businessman, etc. To achieve equity, the price must bear some equivalence with the actual cost or worth of the product, and because worth varies, then prices must vary to be truly "equal."

These illustrations suggest that justifying unidentical treatment in the name of equality is the essence of equity. To point this out, however, does not establish which discriminatory or preferential treatments are consistent with equality. Should business firms encourage preferential hiring for blacks? Should colleges and universities give preference in admission and scholarships to blacks? Should interest rates, bail, and fines be based on ability to pay, rather than standard amounts? Should Peace Corps or Vista volunteers be exempt from military service? Controversy continues on whether given forms of unequal treatment are in fact likely to achieve equality and whether given forms of equality are desirable.

III. Problems in Attaining Equality

A. Assessing the Extent to Which Equality is Achieved

Additional issues are involved in working toward or attaining equality. First is deciding what particular sense of the concept is meant. Here we shall assume equality of opportunity and equal treatment, or equal access to resources and services, as prerequisite to the more general interpretations stressing creative individual development or an equal sense of dignity. How can we measure or assess the extent to which this goal is achieved?

There is a problem in defining some standard or baseline against which various opportunities and treatment can be compared. Two general metaphors provide different approaches to defining a standard. Hofstadter (1956) speaks of "running a race" in which the objective is to make sure that all people have a fair chance in competing with others; they should all be equal at the "starting line" of life, and whatever inequalities that develop during the race would result from such natural endowments as imagination, energy, intelligence, or virtue, but not from environmental advantages that favor some people over others. He contrasts the race metaphor with that of a garden. In the garden, people do not compete with one another along a single dimension or racetrack. Instead, each person (flower) has unique aspirations and needs largely unrelated to competition for a single goal, as opposed to the race where there can be only one or a few winners. The garden is obliged to provide the varying resources (lightness, darkness, soil, water, temperature) required by each to blossom to its fullest. The race suggests harsh competition for scarce rewards in which all people seek the same outcome, while the garden emphasizes diversity in goals and needs, and insulation rather than competition between the aspirations of various participants.

Although the metaphors clarify different conceptions of equal opportunity, they do not solve the assessment problem. If we use the race notion, then at least we have a common starting line for all that might consist of specific resources and services: for example, nutritious diet; opportunity for training, shelter, and clothing; medical treatment; and developing competitive attitudes to seek the desired goal. The garden concept, however, suggests a more complicated "standard." That is, each individual seeks different goals and by definition has different needs, so no starting line is common to all. With no common standard, it is more difficult to compare the extent to which each person is treated equally, not only because each would be treated differently, but also because each individual would judge whether his needs are fulfilled.

We might agree that there should be some baseline or minimal level of goods and services to which all are entitled, regardless of one's preference for the race or garden metaphor. Choosing the specific standards presents great difficulties. The Supreme Court ruled that in criminal cases indigents must be provided with counsel, but does this really give equal treatment? The state usually has investigating and legal resources far superior to those of the defense, and in civil proceedings, the wealthy plaintiff or defendant can secure more competent legal help. Similarly, the wealthy family can afford the most prestigious doctors, hospitals, and nursing care, while the poor person often endures inferior, impersonal, and inefficient clinical care. Although everyone is said to have an equal voice in government (one man, one vote), those with money, the time to participate, and personal connections with people in high office have more opportunity to influence policy than, for example, an average blue-collar worker. Can equal educational opportunity be achieved simply by guaranteeing to each child the right to attend public school from age six to eighteen; or should equal achievement be guaranteed in basic skills, exposure to certain ideas, and in opportunities to be taught by dedicated and imaginative teachers? Finally, does an equal right to shelter involve only protection from weather, or should it also involve equal rights to fresh air, space, and privacy within one's home? Much disagreement on public issues concerns setting the specific baseline or equal standard against which opportunity and treatment should be measured.

Once a baseline is established, it is often difficult to measure the extent to which equality is achieved. Even if we agree that adversaries in court should be entitled to equally competent lawyers, we would have difficulty determining whether any two lawyers have "equal" skills. The same problem applies in providing equally competent teachers or doctors. On another matter, many would agree that a person should not be discriminated against by race in looking for a job. Yet how can we determine the extent to which race has influenced a personnel director's judgment; whether coaches, admissions officers, bank officials, or landlords act impartially? Although certain blatant cases of discrimination can be documented with objective reliability, more subtle forms are hard to detect. Another interpretation of equality holds that only those who "try" deserve equal resources. It seems reasonable to assume that a person will not "try" unless he feels some sense of control over the environment (that trying will pay off). If people deserve an equal right to try, they must have a prior right to a psychological sense of efficacy or control over their lives. This entails providing not just tangible goods and services, but psychic resources as well. But how are we to measure a person's sense of control over his destiny, and should policies be devised to equalize psychic resources? Such assessments involve the difficulties inherent in quantifying human behavior or motivation.

B. Scarcity

Apart from assessing the extent to which equality exists, scarce resources and opportunities stand in the way of achieving the general goal. There are relatively few competent doctors, lawyers; few outstanding schools and colleges (and those can educate only a small proportion of those who aspire to them); few acres of unspoiled countryside for healthy living; the cost of good theater, interesting travel, or running for political office in effect bars such opportunities to most people; relatively few people can afford to spend much time off the job away from routine compulsory activities; and for a significant segment of the United States and most of the world, basic food, clothing, and shelter are scarce indeed.

One could claim that scarcity does not necessarily imply denying equality. Although there might be only one quart of water for two hundred people stranded in the desert, conceivably they could divide the quart into two hundred equal parts and achieve equality in spite of scarcity. All would perish, but equality would have been achieved. Scarce goods, services, and opportunities might be equally distributed, yet such action would be opposed for at least two reasons: First, social equality does *not* emphasize the negative sense that all people have equal rights to mediocre, deprived, or inferior conditions resulting from wide distribution of scarce things. Instead, it looks to a more positive, upward mobile, affluent implication which assumes that equal opportunity is relevant primarily to *improving* one's lot — distributing abundance more justly. Second, people often contend that only under exceptional conditions is it legitimate to infringe on the freedom of persons, nations, or corporations by coercing them to give up possessions or render services to spread scarce resources more equally.

C. Conflict Between Equality Versus Freedom and Diversity

Prohibiting a company from racial or ethnic discrimination in hiring; requiring an individual to pay tax money used to help those less affluent; denying special funds and privileges to friends of public officials; forcing a community to accept racially integrated schools and transportation; banning news media from courtroom or jury deliberation; and requiring all children to attend school — all these policies designed to promote equality tend to infringe on the liberty of persons, corporations, and communities. Such constraints restrict the extent to which any given person or group may exercise free choice. They allegedly prohibit actions that deny equal treatment or opportunity to others.

If our concept of equality is influenced by the "race" metaphor, then we would advocate public restrictions or constraints to establish equal opportunity for all competitors at the start. Once the race begins, however, equal opportunity entails a laissez-faire posture that clearly allows some contestants to win and others to lose. Such equal freedom to compete (as in the history of free enterprise in the United States) results in vast inequalities of condition among future competitors. To preserve equal opportunity at the starting line, it is therefore necessary to regulate the tactics of competitors during the race and to limit the power they would gain by winning.

There is the possibility that enforced equality will lead to conformity and homogeneous culture. To the extent that "equal" becomes interpreted as "identical," then opportunities for equal housing, education, culture, recreation, or religious expression could result in sameness, standardization, and lack of diversity. The specter of a *1984* or *Brave New World* suggests a standardized society of interchangeable parts where, although everyone may be equal, opportunities for variation and unique individual development have vanished. This conflict can be viewed not merely as a contest between equality and individuality, but also as a contradiction between two different senses of equality itself: that sense emphasizes objective goods, services, and resources versus the sense that stresses equal chances for creative individual development.

D. Determining Responsibility for Inequality

A fourth general obstacle to attaining equality is locating sources of inequality or discrimination in a complex, interdependent society, and then assigning responsibility to proper sources for correcting the injustice. Focusing on the plight of the Negro, an obvious equality problem, we are constantly reminded by whites that they have never intentionally done anything to discriminate against Negroes. In northern cities it is hard to find laws that can be directly blamed for ghetto conditions. The businessman claims he has nothing against Negroes, yet he cannot hire them because they do not have sufficient education. The teacher claims he cannot give a respectable education to students who come from broken families, with little opportunity to concentrate and study, poor housing, and diet. Loans for the breadwinner are difficult to obtain, not because of race, but simply because the unemployed Negro with few skills doesn't have sufficient credit. The landlord says he has nothing against Negroes; his building is run down because they don't respect his property, and he can't get enough money in rents to cover expenses for remodeling. No single factor seems to cause the problem (although some assert the main cause to be the Negro's laziness and delinquency, while others describe the cause as "white racism"). The unequal position of the Negro results from interdependent forces, all part of a complex social system.

People are reluctant to share the burden for correcting inequality when they honestly feel they had nothing to do with causing or creating the problem. Without observable individual discriminatory acts, or *de jure* inequality, responsibility is hard to ascribe both because of difficulty in viewing the situation as a result of a total system, and the perennial controversy over whether a person's unequal condition is due primarily to his own inferior endowments or environmental inequities over which he had no control. The problem can be clarified by ascertaining whether a given inequality seems to be *de jure, de facto,* consciously intended, a product of differing natural abilities, actually desired by the victims (e.g., missionaries who choose to live in less developed societies), or a result of a complex system of forces.

Plamenatz (1956) suggests that equality in the sense of traditional libertarian seventeenth- and eighteenth-century thought is virtually impossible within a technologically advanced industrial society. In a simple, nonindustrial society, one finds considerably less differentiation among roles and opportunities. Few options are available for differing occupations or life styles, and meeting basic material needs renders most people equally dependent upon each other. There are relatively few status differentials or organizational hierarchies in which privileged people exercise authority and power over others. The industrial society, however, depends upon an organizational hierarchy, specialization, and division of labor. This creates unequal power relationships and differing opportunities so extensive that one person cannot even be equally aware of all options, let alone given an equal chance to engage in them all. The technological society, in offering wider variety, seems to lend more potential to individual creative development, but it seems to decrease the possibility for people sharing power equally or giving equal consideration to life's diverse options. Traditional society, while lacking diversity and numerous opportunities, allowed men at least to perceive common and stable baselines against which equality could be judged; style of life was more equal in the sense of being identical; and, because power rested in smaller family or local units, perhaps it was shared more equally among citizens than is possible in a bureaucratic, industrial system. These generalizations remain open to historical and sociological investigation, but they help to stimulate more careful definition of equality within a modern postindustrial environment.

RACIAL SEGREGATION: THREE CASES

The Case of Homer Adolph Plessy

Can Louisiana force blacks and whites to travel in separate railway cars?

On June 7, 1892, Homer Adolph Plessy walked into the New Orleans station of the East Louisiana Railway and bought a first-class ticket to Covington — a small Louisiana town north of Lake Pontchartrain.

He boarded the train and took a seat. Within minutes a conductor approached him and said: "You'll have to move to the next coach. This one is for white passengers only."

Plessy was, as reported later, seven-eighths white and one-eighth black. In the cosmopolitan atmosphere of New Orleans he had often been regarded by casual observers as "white."

Plessy refused to move from his seat. The conductor called a policeman. Plessy was forcibly removed from the car and taken to the Orleans Parish jail to await trial on charges of violating an 1890 act of the Louisiana General Assembly, which read in part:

". . . all railway companies carrying passengers in their coaches in this state shall provide equal but separate accommodations for the white and colored races."

The law further stated that "officers of such passenger trains shall have power and are hereby required to assign each passenger to the coach or compartment to which such passenger belongs."

Any passenger or railway official who refused to follow this law was subject to a fine of $25 or 20 days in jail.

Plessy might have paid his fine, or served his short jail term, and been forgotten. But his case was to become a stormy landmark in American history — one that would set a pattern for racial

These cases are taken from Donald W. Oliver and Fred M. Newmann, *Race and Education: Integration and Community Control,* American Education Publications, Columbus, Ohio, 1969.

relations in the U.S. for more than half a century, especially in the public schools.

When Plessy appeared before Judge John H. Ferguson of the Orleans Parish criminal district court, his case was handled by two crusading white lawyers determined to challenge the basic principles of the South's new segregation laws. They were Albion Tourgee and James Walker.

In brief, the lawyers argued that the railway segregation law was contrary to the U.S. Constitution; that it established "an insidious distinction and discrimination between citizens of the United States based on race, which is obnoxious to the fundamental principles of national citizenship, perpetuates involuntary servitude . . . and in further respects abridges the privileges and immunities of citizens of the United States and the rights secured by the 13th and 14th amendments to the Federal Constitution."

Judge Ferguson complimented Plessy's lawyers for their "great research" but he denied their arguments, upheld the law, and found Plessy guilty.

Plessy's lawyers then appealed to the Louisiana Supreme Court. The Louisiana court upheld Judge Ferguson's decision. Plessy's lawyers then made their final appeal — to the U.S. Supreme Court.

They were to wait four years for a decision. But the highest court in the land agreed to hear the case — which by now had become known as *Plessy* v. *Ferguson* (for Judge Ferguson).

THE ARGUMENT:

In their appeal to the U.S. Supreme Court, Plessy's attorneys made these main arguments:

1. Plessy's condition of being *almost* white was a "property right" because of the privileged situation occupied by white people.

There was no law defining with scientific accuracy who was or was not "colored." Therefore, the railroad denied Plessy an important property right by stamping him as a colored person.

2. The railroad segregation law violated the 14th Amendment guarantee of "equal protection of the laws." A law forbidding blacks to sit in the same railway coach with whites is "unequal" on its face. It was adopted to keep black people in a lower status and clearly stamped them with a "badge of inferiority."

3. If the court should approve the principles of "separate but equal" facilities for white and black races, then there was nothing to prevent states from separating any groups they chose — on the basis of language, customs, color, national background. Could they not require people with blue eyes to ride on one coach, those with brown eyes on another?

THE COURT'S RULING:

The court ruled against Homer Plessy. By a vote of 7 to 1, the justices said that "separate but equal" facilities for white and black people were constitutional.

The majority opinion was delivered on May 18, 1896, by Chief Justice Henry Brown, a Northerner from Michigan. The lone dissenter was Justice John Marshall Harlan, a Kentuckian whose family had once owned slaves.

In answer to the argument that Plessy had property rights in being *almost* white, Justice Brown said that if Plessy were indeed white he could sue the railroad.

Did the law stamp black people with a "badge of inferiority"? No, said Justice Brown. If it did it was only "because the colored race chooses to put that construction on it."

But an essential point in Justice Brown's opinion — one that was to become a precedent for segregated schools as well as other Jim Crow laws — was the question of whether the law was "reasonable." In reply to the argument that states might segregate people on the basis of such differences as hair color or national origin, Justice Brown said the state's exercise of police power must be "reasonable."

He then proceeded to define "reasonable" laws as those that are in accord with "the established usages, customs, and traditions of the people, and with a view to the promotion of their comfort and the preservation of the public peace and good order.

"Gauged by this standard," he added, the Lousiana railroad law was *"no more obnoxious to the 14th Amendment than the acts of Congress requiring separate schools for colored children in the District of Columbia . . . or the corresponding acts of state legislatures."*

HARLAN DISAGREES:

In his vigorous dissent, Justice Harlan argued that the Louisiana law interfered with the "personal freedom of citizens, both white and black.

"The destinies of the two races in this country are indissolubly linked together," he said, "and the interest of both require that the common government of all shall not permit the seeds of race hate to be planted under the sanction of law.

"What can more certainly arouse race hate, what more certainly create and perpetuate a feeling of distrust between these races, than state enactments which in fact proceed on the ground that colored citizens are so inferior and degraded that they cannot be allowed to sit in public coaches occupied by white citizens?"

Harlan added that the Constitution should be "color-blind," regarding "man as man" and taking no account of color "when his civil rights are involved."

Can Separate Be Equal?

The question moves from equipment to people, and another Supreme Court decision stirs the nation.

In a crowded federal district courtroom in South Carolina in the spring of 1951, an attorney and a psychologist were talking about dolls.

The psychologist, Dr. Kenneth Clark, had just concluded a study of Negro schoolchildren — ages six to nine. An excerpt from the court record follows:

Q. Now, Dr. Clark, you had occasion, did you not, to test the reactions of the infant plaintiffs involved in this case by . . . methods that determine sensitivity to racial discrimination?

A. Yes, I did . . . I used Negro and white dolls, which were identical in every respect save skin color. And I presented them [the Negro children] with a sheet of paper on which there were these drawings of dolls. . . .

I asked them . . . "Show me the doll that you like best or that you'd like to play with. Show me the doll that is the 'nice' doll. Show me the doll that looks 'bad.' "

I found that of the [sixteen] children . . . that ten of those children chose the white doll as their preference — the doll they liked best. Ten of them also considered the white doll a "nice" doll — and I think you have to keep in mind that these dolls are absolutely identical in every aspect except skin color.

Eleven of these sixteen children chose the brown doll as the doll which looked "bad. . . ."

The conclusion which I was forced to reach was that these children in Clarendon County, like other human beings who are subjected to an obviously inferior status in the society in which they live, have been definitely harmed in the development of their personalities; that the signs of instability . . . are clear.[1]

The South Carolina court case was one of five challenges to racial segregation in elementary and

[1] Testimony from case filed as *Briggs* v. *Elliot*, 1951.

secondary public schools that built up between 1949 and 1952 and were destined to reach the Supreme Court of the United States.

The case had not started primarily with psychology. Forty Negro parents in South Carolina's Clarendon County School District 22 were angry about the glaring inequalities in the *physical* facilities between the Negro and white schools.

The all-white schools had modern plumbing and sanitation. Children at the all-Negro schools had to haul water from outside pumps and use outside toilets.

Each white student had his own desk. One Negro school had no desks at all; in another, students had to share desks or tables. The white schools had charts, maps, slides, stereopticons and globes. The Negro schools had no visual aids except blackboards.

Between the testimony of the psychologist and the clear evidence showing unequal physical equipment, two legal questions were raised:

1. Did not the obvious inequalities in plumbing, desks, educational aids, etc. violate the "separate but equal" doctrine that the Supreme Court had laid down in 1896, in the *Plessy* v. *Ferguson* case?

2. More importantly for future legal cases — even if the physical facilities *had* been equal, was not the very fact of separation of the races an inequality and therefore unconstitutional? Could *separate* schools ever be *equal?*

With one of the three judges dissenting (J. Waties Waring of Charleston, S.C.) the district court ruled that the South Carolina law separating races in the schools was constitutional.

However, the court agreed that the physical facilities of the schools were not equal. It gave South Carolina six months in which to correct the inequalities — *i.e.,* to live up to the accepted separate-but-equal principle.

The Negro plaintiffs appealed to the U.S. Supreme Court. The Supreme Court sent the case back to South Carolina for a report on whether the physical facilities in the schools were, in fact, being made equal.

On March 13, 1952, the federal district court in South Carolina reported back that the state was making satisfactory progress in remedying the inequalities.

The Negro plaintiffs conceded that physical improvements were being made. But they renewed their appeal to the Supreme Court solely on the basis that *segregation itself* was unconstitutional.

Between 1950 and 1952 other cases from other states posed similar questions:

In Prince Edward County, Virginia, and in Delaware Negroes charged that their segregated schools had inferior facilities. In both cases, lower courts ordered that the physical inequalities be corrected.

In Kansas the challenge was made on the basis of segregation alone. Negro parents in Topeka (one of nine Kansas cities that had segregated schools under a local choice law), conceded that the schools for the two races were substantially equal in teachers and equipment.

One Negro father explained to the court why he had entered the case:

"It wasn't for the sake of hot dogs. It wasn't to cause any insinuations that our teachers are not capable of teaching our children, because they are supreme, extremely intelligent, and are capable of teaching my kids or white or black kids. But my point was that not only I and my children are craving light; the entire colored race is craving light. And the only way to reach light is to start our children together in their infancy and they come up together."

NAACP attorneys in the Kansas case produced several social scientists who testified that segregation itself imposed serious social and psychological handicaps on the Negro children.

The federal district judges in Kansas agreed that "segregation with the sanction of law . . . has a tendency to retard the educational and mental development of Negro children." Nevertheless, the court ruled, it was still constitutional — at least under previous Supreme Court rulings. The Negroes, like those of the other states, carried an appeal to Washington to see what the present Supreme Court would say.

By the fall of 1952 the U.S. Supreme Court had before it five cases challenging the constitutionality of segregated elementary and secondary public schools: the cases from South Carolina, Virginia, Delaware, and Kansas, along with a fifth case from the District of Columbia.

The Supreme Court heard arguments in the cases. Then, at the end of its term in June 1953, the Court put them over for further argument in a new term beginning the following October.

The four state cases now rested primarily on two lines of argument:

1. The equal protection clause of the 14th Amendment allows states to classify and treat citizens in different ways, for legitimate legislative objectives, *only* if there are *real differences* in the people themselves. For example, young children might be sent to a different school than one for adults; or students with serious mental retardation might be assigned to special schools. However, *race alone does not constitute such a difference.*

2. The 14th Amendment guarantee of equal protection of the laws includes equal educational opportunity. Segregation inflicts mental harm on Negro children, and therefore by its very nature is *inherently unequal.*

When the arguments came before the Supreme Court in the fall of 1953, two of the chief opposing attorneys were Thurgood Marshall, a Negro lawyer who was later to become a Supreme Court Justice, and John W. Davis, a noted New York corporation counsel and onetime Democratic presidential candidate, who had been hired to argue the case for South Carolina.

Davis argued that South Carolina was acting in sincere "good faith and intention to produce equality for all of its children of whatever race or color."

Marshall, on the other hand, argued that the intent of the 14th Amendment was to outlaw "caste" lines in America, and also that segregation had no "rational" foundation.

On May 18, 1954, the front page of *The New York Times* flared with an eight-column, two-line headline:

HIGH COURT BARS SCHOOL SEGREGATION; 9–0 DECISION GRANTS TIME TO COMPLY

On the preceding day, in one of the most momentous decisions in its history, the Supreme Court had issued two unanimous rulings — one covering the four state segregation cases, another for the District of Columbia case. (Because the Kansas case had been first in line when the 1953 arguments resumed, the decision became known as *Brown* v. *Board of Education, Topeka,* et al.)

In effect, the Court accepted the view that segregation itself meant inequality. Schools separated solely on the basis of race were "inherently unequal" and therefore unconstitutional.

The decision affected every public educational facility in the U.S. Millions of Americans were shocked or delighted, reassured or worried, depending on their previous attitudes.

Almost immediately, especially from the Southern states, there were outraged attacks on the decision as "sociological" rather than "legal." If an earlier Supreme Court (1896) had said that separate but equal facilities for the races *were* constitutional, the critics asked, how could this Supreme Court say they were *not?*

Beneath the immediate furor, thoughtful people on both sides of the issue pondered the provision expressed in the second line of *The Times* headline: ". . . DECISION GRANTS TIME TO COMPLY."

How much time? In the following year, 1955, the Supreme Court directed lower federal courts to proceed with "all deliberate speed" in requiring admission of Negroes to previously all-white schools. In many cases lower courts accepted *plans* for gradual desegregation as evidence that states were proceeding with "all deliberate speed." On paper many of the plans looked promising.

Yet a new battle was just beginning.

Facing the Mob in Little Rock

What it was like when nine Negro teen-agers came to a school surrounded by angry crowds—and bayonets.

Six days after the Supreme Court issued its decision outlawing school segregation, the school board of Little Rock, Ark., announced a long-range plan for gradual integration of Negroes into previously all-white classrooms. The plan was to start in three years — in 1957 — beginning with the senior high schools.

As the deadline approached — Sept. 3, 1957 — nine Negro students were assigned under federal court order to enter Little Rock's all-white Central High School. On the preceding day, however, Arkansas Governor Orval Faubus went on radio and television to repeat a warning that his state was not yet ready to integrate its schools. The Governor predicted violence and added:

"It will not be possible to restore or to maintain order . . . if forcible integration is carried out tomorrow in the schools of this community."

To "maintain order" he called up troops of the Arkansas National Guard to surround the high school. Little Rock's mayor and school officials denounced the Governor's action. But on the morning of Sept. 3 when the nine Negro students reported for school, they faced not only National Guard bayonets but also an angry white mob.

One of the nine Negroes was 15-year-old Elizabeth Ann Eckford. Later, in the following words, she told a writer what it was like for her:[1]

You remember the day before we were to go in, we met Superintendent Blossom at the school board office. He told us what the mob might say and do but he never told us we wouldn't have any protection. He told our parents not to come because he wouldn't be able to protect the children if they did.

[1] Elizabeth Ann Eckford's story is reprinted from *The Long Shadow of Little Rock,* by Daisy Bates, New York: David McKay, 1962. Reprinted by permission of David McKay Company, Inc.

That night I was so excited I couldn't sleep. The next morning I was about the first one up. While I was pressing my black-and-white dress — I had made it to wear on the first day of school — my little brother turned on the TV set. They started telling about a large crowd gathered at the school. The man on TV said he wondered if we were going to show up that morning. Mother called from the kitchen, where she was fixing breakfast, "Turn that TV off!" She was so upset and worried. I wanted to comfort her, so I said, "Mother, don't worry."

Dad was walking back and forth, from room to room, with a sad expression. He was chewing on his pipe and he had a cigar in his hand, but he didn't light either one. It would have been funny, only he was so nervous.

Before I left home Mother called us into the living room. She said we should have a word of prayer. Then I caught the bus and got off a block from the school. I saw a large crowd of people standing across the street from the soldiers guarding Central. . . .

Superintendent Blossom had told us to enter by the front door. I looked at all the people and thought, "Maybe I will be safer if I walk down the block to the front entrance behind the guards."

At the corner I tried to pass through the long line of guards around the school so as to enter the ground behind them. One of the guards pointed across the street. So I pointed in the same direction and asked whether he meant for me to cross the street and walk down. He nodded "yes." So, I walked across the street conscious of the crowd that stood there, but they moved away from me.

For a moment all I could hear was the shuffling of their feet. Then, someone shouted, "Here she comes, get ready!" I moved away from the crowd on the sidewalk and into the street. If the mob came at me I could then cross back over so the guards could protect me.

The crowd moved in closer and then began to follow me, calling me names. I still wasn't afraid. Just a little bit nervous. Then my knees started to shake all of a sudden and I wondered whether I could make it to the center entrance a block away. It was the longest block I ever walked in my whole life.

Even so, I still wasn't too scared because all the time I kept thinking that the guards would protect me.

When I got right in front of the school, I went up to a guard again. But this time he just looked straight ahead and didn't move to let me pass him. I didn't know what to do. Then I looked and saw that the path leading to the front entrance was a little further ahead. So I walked until I was right in front of the path to the front door.

I stood looking at the school — it looked so big! Just then the guards let some white students go through.

The crowd was quiet. I guess they were waiting to see what was going to happen. When I was able to steady my knees, I walked up to the guard who had let the white students in. He too didn't move. When I tried to squeeze past him, he raised his bayonet and then the other guards closed in and they raised their bayonets.

They glared at me with a mean look and I was very frightened and didn't know what to do. I turned around and the crowd came toward me.

They moved closer and closer. Somebody started yelling, "Lynch her! Lynch her!"

I tried to see a friendly face somewhere in the mob — someone who maybe would help. I looked into the face of an old woman and it seemed a kind face, but when I looked at her again, she spat on me.

They came closer, shouting, "No nigger bitch is going to get in our school. Get out of here!"

I turned back to the guards but their faces told me I wouldn't get help from them. Then I looked down the block and saw a bench at the bus stop.

I thought, "If I can only get there I will be safe." I don't know why the bench seemed a safe place to me, but I started walking toward it. I tried to close my mind to what they were shouting, and kept saying to myself, "If I can only make it to the bench I will be safe."

When I finally got there, I don't think I could have gone another step. I sat down and the mob crowded up and began shouting all over again. Someone hollered, "Drag her over to this tree! Let's take care of the nigger." Just then a white man sat down beside me, put his arm around me and patted my shoulder. He raised my chin and said, "Don't let them see you cry."

Then, a white lady — she was very nice — she came over to me on the bench. She spoke to me but I don't remember now what she said. She put me on the bus and sat next to me. She asked me my name and tried to talk to me but I don't think I answered. I can't remember much about the bus ride, but the next thing I remember I was standing in front of the School for the Blind, where Mother works.

I thought, "Maybe she isn't here. But she has to be here!" So I ran upstairs, and I think some teachers tried to talk to me, but I kept running until I reached Mother's classroom.

Mother was standing at the window with her head bowed, but she must have sensed I was there because she turned around. She looked as if she had been crying, and I wanted to tell her I was all right. But I couldn't speak. She put her arms around me and I cried.

No black children entered the schools of Little Rock that day — or for several days afterward. The Little Rock school board went back to federal district court to ask that the order admitting Negro pupils be temporarily suspended. The federal judge refused.

The FBI, charged with enforcing federal laws, moved into the situation. The U.S. Department of Justice asked the court for an order to enjoin (prevent) the Governor and the National Guard from blocking the entry of Negroes to Central High. Finally, on Sept. 20, Governor Faubus ordered the remaining National Guard troops withdrawn from the school.

This was on a Friday. By Monday, Sept. 23, the stage was set for a new clash. As the Negro pupils again appeared at Central High, the streets near the school were barricaded against demonstrators. Eighty city policemen and about 50 state troopers were on hand.

What happened that day was described in an eyewitness report by Benjamin Fine in a dispatch to *The New York Times*. Excerpts from his report follow:[2]

A mob of belligerent, shrieking and hysterical demonstrators forced the withdrawal today of nine Negro students from Central High School here.

Despite a heavy turnout of local and state police to see that the Negroes were not molested in Little Rock's newest attempt to integrate the high school, city authorities bowed to the fury of about one thousand white supremacists. They ordered the Negro students to leave the school about noon. The integration attempt had lasted three hours thirteen minutes. . . .

At eight o'clock it was evident that the violence that Governor Faubus had predicted would take place. By this time some five hundred persons had gathered. They appeared in a fighting mood.

"The niggers won't get in," members of the crowd said, time and again.

At eight forty-five the school buzzer could be dimly heard. School was in session.

"Where are the niggers?" one person asked another. "Let them try to get in. . . ."

"We'll lynch them all," several yelled. . . .

Suddenly a yell went up: "There they are, they're coming."

The crowd rushed after four men who turned out to be Negro newspapermen. They were man-handled by the crowd, but managed to escape.

A man yelled: "Look, they're going into our school.

Six girls and three boys crossed over into the school yard. They had arrived in two automobiles and had driven to the side of the school. Mrs. Bates (Daisy Bates, president of the Arkansas branch of the NAACP) accompanied them.

Slowly, almost as though they were entering a normal classroom on a normal school day, the students walked toward the side door of the school. The boys, in open shirts, and the girls, in bobby socks, joked and chatted among themselves. They carried armfuls of textbooks.

The crowd now let out a roar of rage. "They've gone in," a man shouted.

"Oh, God," said a woman, "the niggers are in school."

A group of six girls, dressed in skirts and sweaters, hair in ponytails, started to shriek and wail.

"The niggers are in our school," they howled hysterically.

One of them jumped up and down on the sidewalk, waving her arms toward her classmates in the school who were looking out the windows, and screamed over and over again: "Come on out, come on out."

Tears flowed down her face; her body shook in uncontrollable spasms.

Three of her classmates grew hysterical and threw their arms around each other. They began dancing up and down.

"The niggers are in," they shrieked, "come on out of the school. Don't stay there with the niggers. Come on out. Come on. . . ."

The police were taunted by the mob, well out of hand by now. Instead of tapering off, as it had at previous morning demonstrations, the crowd grew in numbers. By ten o'clock it had grown to about one thousand. . . .

The men and women, augmented by students, surged over the "off limits" line and spread into the street facing the school grounds. For a time it appeared as though the local police would be completely overwhelmed by the angry crowd.

"Come on out of school, come on out, the niggers are in there," the crowd yelled.

[2] From *The New York Times* of September 24, 1957. © 1957 by The New York Times Company. Reprinted by permission.

Four girls slowly walked down the side steps of the high school.

A tremendous cheer echoed through the crowd.

"They're coming out," was shouted time and again.

Soon a group of six left. The students began to leave the school at more frequent intervals.

"I'm going to get my child," one parent said defiantly.

"Sorry, you'll stay right here," the policeman answered.

Quickly this order changed. One by one, mothers and fathers walked up the school steps, and then returned with their children. . . .

At noon the police received this message on their shortwave radios: "This is the Mayor. Tell Principal Jeff Matthews [of Central High] that the Negroes have been withdrawn. Tell Mr. Matthews to announce that to the student body. I've talked with Virgil Blossom [School Superintendent] and the Negroes have been withdrawn."

At twelve-fourteen Lieutenant Carl Jackson of the Little Rock police force stood on the school grounds facing the crowd. Over a loudspeaker set up on the sidewalk in front of the school the officer said, "The Negroes have been withdrawn from school."

"We don't believe you," the crowd yelled back. "That's just a pack of lies."

"If you have any one person in the crowd you believe, he can go in and see, then report to you," Lieutenant Jackson said.

Mrs. Allen Thevenet, of the Mothers League of Central High School, stepped forward across the street.

"Will you accept Mrs. Thevenet's word?" the Lieutenant asked. The crowd gave reluctant approval.

Accompanied by a policeman, Mrs. Thevenet went into the school. On her return she came to the loudspeaker and said: "We went through every room in the school and there was no niggers there."

The Negro students, meantime, had been taken out through a side door and escorted in two police cars to their homes. Despite the rumors that had been flying through the crowd that the students "had been beat up," they were not molested while in school. . . .

Would they want to come back?

"Yes," they agreed, "if we can come here without causing any trouble. The students will accept us once we go with them for a while."

From Washington, President Eisenhower denounced the "disgraceful occurrences" and the "mob of extremists" who were defying federal law. Finally, he ordered Regular Army troops into the area. On September 24, 1,000 men of the 101st Airborne Division moved into Little Rock.

The next morning the nine Negro children entered Central High School under troop escort. By the end of October they were going to the school without escort, and on Nov. 27 the last of the Army troops were withdrawn.

Eight of the nine students remained in school throughout the year. One — a 12th grader at the time of entry — was graduated with his class.

Another, a girl, was expelled from Central High for unruly conduct. White students began to talk in terms of "one down, eight to go." Many others asked themselves if the girl was a real troublemaker or if she only fought back when bothered by the white students.

The experiences of 1957–58 proved to Little Rock that direct opposition to the federal government could not succeed. Yet the town still would not accept integration. It hoped for a solution by interpreting the laws in its favor and by using all legal methods to work around the federal orders.

A vote was taken to determine the degree of public support for segregation. Few were surprised when the town voted overwhelmingly (19,470 to 7,565) to keep blacks and whites separated. While this represented concrete proof that the citizens were behind their local government, it also showed that a large number of people favored integration, or at least preferred it to the crises of the previous year.

Having seen the difficulties of 1957–58, many

favored a delay for integration. Among them were the school committee and Superintendent Virgil Blossom. On June 3, Blossom and other school officials asked Federal Judge Harry L. Lemley for a two-and-a-half-year postponement of integration in order to introduce it gradually. Blossom decided that the public interest demanded this move.

In the court hearing that followed, educators provided evidence to support this view. Mrs. Govie Griffin, who had taught chemistry for 13 terms with "no disciplinary problems," spoke of the tension of the past year, with the presence of Negroes and troops in the school. She commented: "I spent many weekends in bed so I could go back to school on Monday." Her physician said that she had suffered from physical exhaustion. Because of the tension in the classroom, she was able to cover so little chemistry that she could not fairly ask the class to take the usual standard College Board examination; an easier one was substituted.

Although she could not be present, Mrs. Sybil Hefley, another teacher, testified in writing that two of her students had refused to pledge allegiance to the American flag while Negroes remained in the school.

Superintendent Blossom himself stated that the presence of Negroes and armed troops had provoked slugging, pushing, tripping, catcalls, abusive language, and destruction of lockers. Testimony indicated that the school year was characterized by minor accidents (mostly in halls), small fires, destruction of school property, 200 temporary suspensions, two expulsions, and 43 threats of bombs in the buildings. (Each bomb threat meant a search through the buildings, particularly the 2,400 lockers). The faculty, therefore, spent a great deal of time reporting incidents and disciplining students. Persons outside the school threatened teachers by telephone, and spread circulars condemning the Supreme Court and vulgar cards condemning school officials.

In regard to the effect of integration on teachers, Blossom said: "Now you can't take the person who has demonstrated through the years, as these people have, the qualities that they have in education, and pull them out of it . . . and have your total program satisfactory. I am not sure but what that is one of the highest prices we have paid in this."

After hearing the testimony, Judge Lemley approved a delay on integration until February 1961. He commented: "The incidents and other matters just referred to, plus the presence of troops . . . created throughout the school year a situation of tension and unrest . . . which had an adverse effect upon the educational program; and we find that said program was seriously impaired, that the orderly administration of the school was . . . disrupted and that educational standards have suffered.

". . . Now, while you can disperse crowds and can keep the Negro students physically within the school, and while it is possible that, if the troops were deployed in sufficient numbers all over the school, vandalism could be checked, the presence of troops cannot reduce or eliminate racial tensions or create a climate that is conducive to education.

". . . The granting of the board's petition does not, in our estimation, constitute a yielding to unlawful force or violence but is simply an exercise of our equitable discretion and good judgment so as to allow a breathing spell in Little Rock while at the same time preserving educational standards at Central High School."

While many felt relieved to hear the decision, others questioned the morality of disregarding the law of the land, no matter what the practical advantages. Still others maintained that the example of getting around the law provided a poor example of good government for students in Little Rock.

The NAACP appealed the decision to the Court of Appeals for the Eighth District in St. Louis. After the matter was debated, with largely the same arguments used in June, the Court of Appeals reached a decision on August 18, 1958. It reversed Lemley's decision.

The court stated: "We say the time has not yet come in these United States when an order of a federal court must be whittled away, watered down, or shamefully withdrawn in the face of violence and unlawful acts of individual citizens opposed thereto . . . ."

In September the Little Rock school board lost its final appeal. The U.S. Supreme Court unanimously rejected the board's plea for further delays in the racial integration of Central High School.

QUESTIONS
FOR
DISCUSSION

1. *Integration and Equality.* To what extent do you believe that compulsory racial integration is necessary to provide educational opportunities for blacks equal to those enjoyed by whites? In reaching a position, take into account the separate-but-equal doctrine of Plessy versus Ferguson, the 1954 decision that rules segregation inherently unequal, and the experience of racial integration at Central High in Little Rock.

2. *Varieties of Discrimination.* In general the equal protection clause of the Fourteenth Amendment allows states to classify and treat citizens in different ways *only* if there are real differences in the people themselves and if such discriminatory treatment is necessary for the public interest. Consider each following policy and decide whether it seems to serve the public interest and also whether it is discrimination aimed to achieve more equal treatment.

a. Some states have compulsory auto insurance. Rates charged boys under twenty-five years old are much higher than those charged girls and older people.

b. If a man wants to take his wife with him from Boston to Chicago on a commercial airplane, the cost is $37.50, or three-quarters the normal fare. If he wishes to take his girl friend, the cost is full fare or $50.

c. Movie codes discriminate against people between ages fourteen and eighteen. Suppose a fifteen-year-old boy is not allowed to purchase a ticket to a movie with an "X" rating because it contains a nude scene. The boy takes the theater manager to court and argues that the "X" rating brands young people with a "badge of inferiority."

d. Boys and girls between ages sixteen and twenty-one may have the same knowledge of public affairs as older people, but are not allowed to vote in public elections.

3. *Policies for Equal Education.*

a. Today blacks often express the feeling that whites owe them compensation for long years of slavery and exploitation. They do not want simply "equal educational opportunity" but a much better education to make up for years of oppression and deprivation. This may take the form of special teachers and programs, guidance counselors, tutors, special libraries, and social facilities.

Should blacks be given extra funds and support to compensate for the years in which they were segregated and discriminated against? Should blacks be given preferential treatment in admissions to colleges? Should they be given preferential treatment in getting jobs and job promotions? To whom would these opportunities be granted? To all blacks? Only to blacks below a certain income level who were clearly "oppressed"? Only to blacks who could show or "prove" that they had been the victims of discrimination in some specific way?

b. The town of Groton, Mass., had two private high schools as well as one public high school. It is generally agreed that the two private schools enjoy a far higher reputation than the public school. Many of the town's leading citizens send their sons to the private schools for this reason. Suppose the parents of a student in the public high school sue the state for an educational opportunity equal to that of those who attend the private schools. They charge that the private schools are exempt from property taxes, and that gifts are constantly being made to the private schools, which are also exempt from income taxes. In this way the private schools are publicly subsidized or supported, yet parents who send their children to the public schools gain no benefit from this support. Should the state institute financial policies that would wipe out the privileged position of certain private schools?

4. *Black Separatism and Equality.* Suppose that the nine black students who first attended Central High charged that they could not receive an equal education at that school, because of intimidation by white students, and they demanded that a special school (or special classes) be established exclusively for blacks, with outstanding black teachers and resources. Suppose also that white segregationists backed the idea as a way to avoid integration. Do you think the Court decision requiring integration should be forced on the blacks even if they do not desire it? Why or why not?

5. *Defining Equal Education.* How would you determine whether Elizabeth Eckford was getting an education "equal" to white students at Central High? If she took the same courses and had the same teachers, would that be an indication that her education was "equal"? Suppose she earned lower grades than most white children. Would this mean her education was inferior? Suppose some teachers felt that black students were less well prepared for high school than whites. The teachers, therefore, required less difficult work of the blacks and graded them more leniently so as not to fail them. Would this be providing equal educational opportunity? List general criteria by which to determine equal educational opportunity.

Chapter 6	# Welfare-Security

Is killing civilian women and children with napalm or nuclear weapons ever right? Should the police use tear gas and rifles to disperse a crowd? Should a man be forced into military service against his conscience? Should people be forced to pay taxes for medicare and social security, or forced to go to school against their will? Should an employer gather information about an employee's private life? Should the government withhold information from the news media? Should the state remove a child from the home of neglectful parents? Although answers to such questions would be meaningless without reference to more specific contexts, these issues illustrate situations in which personal or group welfare and security are considered important values in justifying a controversial policy. To ensure national security, a society may justify violence against "enemies" and restrictions on the freedom of its own citizens. In the cause of social welfare, it may force people to give up their property or force children to go to school. To protect personal security and welfare, the state may prohibit the police from gathering evidence on crime, prohibit public exposure of personal information, or condone using violence in self-defense. Thus, the value of welfare-security can be used to oppose peaceful, nonviolent techniques and to support infringements on several personal freedoms (privacy, vocational, and educational choice; free enterprise; free speech, etc.).[1] The appeal to welfare-security

[1] We have joined the concepts, because in public issue discussions they tend to be used interchangeably and share common referents. Welfare is perhaps the more general value, connoting such diverse elements as physical safety, medical health, economic prosperity, cultural opportunity, or peace of mind. Security usually implies territorial or bodily defense, and also safety against economic hardship, but security can include protection for everything that one has or wants. All these connotations might be seen as parts of welfare. We hope to clarify several alternative meanings and issues that the hyphenated value suggests.

takes many forms, but the most familiar is national or group (as opposed to individual) welfare-security.

One problem in welfare-security controversies is establishing *whose* welfare is to be preserved or improved. Should an individual risk his personal security for the security of his nation? Is the peace and security of the world as a whole more important than the interests of individuals or nations? Do some individuals or groups deserve more welfare-security than others (compare for example, the president of the United States with a small-town "average citizen," or the government of Red China versus the United States government). The issue becomes a question of allegiance and loyalty: whose welfare-security is one most obligated to defend when the demands of different groups or individuals conflict? Construed in this way the problem involves issues and complexities discussed in Chapter 4 on morality-responsibility: i.e., defining one's moral obligations within social groups.

Those who emphasize national welfare-security as the highest priority have argued that the security of individuals, the security of other nations, and in fact world peace and security cannot be achieved without the security of the United States. All security is, therefore, consistent with United States national security. One should ask whether the realities of military power and politics today necessitate this conclusion, and also whether alternative concepts of security are hypothetically possible. Although the centralized nation state seems to have monopolized the focus on welfare-security in the twentieth century, how much would a decline of nationalism affect the meaning of this value? The growth of nuclear and chemical-biological arsenals, the population explosion, increasing world-wide pollution, and technological breakthroughs in communication and transportation could create the "spaceship earth" in which individuals would be convicted of felonies for endangering world security. Or perhaps in the long run international military conflict will disappear, and the major issues of welfare-security will relate to individual alienation, the breaking up of families, the transiency of occupations, or conflict between the older and younger generations. In any case, the type of welfare-security at stake must be decided.

Even if we accept the emphasis on national power and international relations that dominates thinking about welfare-security today, we may ask another frame-of-reference question: In deliberations on welfare-security that involve international or intergroup conflict, is it appropriate to apply to groups moral standards that would normally be applied in interpersonal relations among individuals? Is the character of relations among large collectives sufficiently different to call for a different "morality"? For example, according to conventional morality, in some situations it would be morally right for an individual to sacrifice his life for the welfare of others. Yet should we ever expect a nation willingly to sacrifice its own survival for the welfare of another? Apparently not. Observers seem to agree that nations should and will place national survival above all other values.

Man has developed a way to apply or enforce traditional morality for individuals. They may be subjected to the judgment of a court or taught so that consciences regulate their behavior. But it is difficult to imagine how this morality can be applied to a nation as a *collective*. Even if a nation is found "guilty" in an international court, and its leaders are ordered to pay reparations, the nation cannot be punished because "nation" is a verbal abstraction, not a tangible being. For this reason it is perhaps inappropriate to apply the rhetoric of interpersonal morality — e.g., keeping promises, helping one's neighbor, teaching someone a lesson — to problems of international relations. Contrasts between problems of individual versus collective welfare-security should become clearer as we continue.

B. Requisites of National Security

When people justify policy by appealing to "national interest," "national security," or "general welfare," more specific goals may be involved. The following list of the more familiar ingredients of the general objective is not intended as an exhaustive or objectively accurate account of what national interest requires, but rather summarizes what people often believe or argue the requisites to be. Although the items are listed separately, they are interrelated and interdependent: for example, part of the idea of territorial integrity is that the home government is sovereign, and part of the idea of sovereignty is that the home government has complete control over stable real estate (territory).

1. Territorial Integrity

It is generally assumed that a nation needs territory — land with definable boundaries that can be rightfully defended against foreign invasion. The home nation has the right to control the use of its land, and the entry and activity of citizens who "belong" to different lands (nations). Although it is assumed that a nation cannot exist without controlling land, "nations" (or nationalities) dispossessed of a stable geographic area have survived (Jews, Arab refugees, American Indians, Algerians, etc.). Although the issue of territorial integrity usually arises in defense policy, offensive national expansion or imperialism has been justified by territorial needs: Hitler's effort to gain *lebensraum*, British colonialism, or the United States in the Mexican War. Territory may be valued as "living space," providing economic resources or strategic military location, or as necessary to a plan for world domination. The history of colonialism raises the crucial issue: What legitimately entitles a group (or person) to ownership of territory? Although some possible answers will be discussed in more detail in Chapter 8 on property, we should mention here such criteria as length of occupation, contribution to "development" of the land, contract, and sheer physical power or need. Territorial ownership can also be equated with political control or sovereignty.

2. Sovereignty   The liberal tradition cherishes the right to self-government: the political independence of a nation from other political authority. From the American Revolution to the Vietnam conflict, self-determination has been continually proclaimed (though not always realized) as vital to a nation's welfare and security. Although many issues pertinent to sovereignty are discussed in Chapter 7 on consent, here we consider problems most relevant to national interest. A prevailing assumption is that a nation's interest or welfare cannot be secure unless that nation has complete and independent power to make policy on the issues it faces. Conversely its security is threatened if it must abide by decisions of an external power or authority. Opposition to United States involvement in the United Nations or specific treaties with other nations has been based on the desire to retain complete autonomy or sovereignty over United States affairs. The fear that another nation or group will infringe upon national independence is a powerful deterrent to international cooperation.

One problem with the sovereignty argument is the virtual impossibility of a nation's isolating itself from outside influences in an increasingly interdependent world. Although a nation may not be formally or constitutionally subordinate to any other, technological, economic, and political events around the world will impinge upon it and influence its policy. The United States proclaims its own right to independence and sovereignty and even suggests that all nations are entitled to that right. Yet it intervenes in the affairs of others on a vast scale to protect American interests. Sometimes it intervenes allegedly to support the self-determination of others (Vietnam), but it often fails to intervene (Hungary, Algeria). If we believe that complete sovereignty is required for American welfare and security, we must also note that the complete sovereignty of other nations (e.g., China or Panama) may threaten American welfare-security, and we must be prepared to decide whose sovereignty is more important.

Although sovereignty in one sense implies isolationism (i.e., the right to be let alone), it may be necessary for a country to attain power over other nations to exert real control over its own affairs. This interpretation leads to greater interventionism, arms buildup, alliances, economic policies to decrease the dependence of the home country on other nations. To gain international power and hegemony, nations must apparently preserve "prestige" by maintaining a good "image." (How would it *look* to other nations if the United States broke its treaty commitments?) Policies aimed toward increasing national power create controversies about whether this is a legitimate national goal, and also over the desirability of specific means toward that end. Does one "stop communism" in undeveloped lands mainly through demonstrating military strength, economic aid, or what? Does one increase national power by working toward economic self-sufficiency or freer exchange and cooperation among all nations? Are certain restrictions on individual freedom (conscription, taxes, travel limitations) a legitimate price to pay for increased national power? Of course, the value of national sovereignty itself has been questioned: Would you rather be "red" or dead?

3. Economic Welfare

National welfare-security requires a decent material standard of living, which involves access to natural resources, labor, technology, and capital, and an economic system that combines such factors to yield needed goods and services as well as some equitable distribution of wealth throughout the society. In a world of scarcity and population explosion, a nation's economic health is said to depend largely upon policies that stimulate economic growth within a pattern of overall stability. Thus policies are instituted and justified by their contribution to the nation's economic welfare: wage and price guidelines, regulated interest rates, taxes, antitrust legislation, tariffs, safety regulations and standards of effectiveness, laws on collective bargaining and working conditions, and educational programs to influence manpower allocation.

Although there seems to be considerable agreement on the utilitarian objective of "the greatest good for the greatest number," difficulties abound in assessing a nation's economic welfare. How much weight should be given to total value of goods and services produced? Are absolute amounts, per capita, or per family figures most meaningful? How significant is rate of unemployment? How important is the *distribution* of wealth, employment, and services? To what extent should our judgments be based on comparative statistics with other nations or the rates of increase and decrease in these variables? Must we assume that *increases* in GNP, employment, etc., are always to be valued more than decreases? Although a society might eventually become wealthy enough to operate a welfare state in which only a small portion of the population had to work, how desirable would this be? The nation might grow lazy, complacent, uninventive, and without perseverance to face hard times — attitudes that could be detrimental to its long-term economic welfare.

Assuming a continuing effort to increase goods and services, we must assign priorities to the kinds of scarcity that are most in the national interest to relieve. With limited resources and labor, is it most in the national interest to produce guns and planes, TV dinners, snowmobiles, artificial hearts, birth control pills, improved teaching techniques, miniskirts, low-cost housing, or plays and symphonies? Even with modern systems analysis and "cost-benefit" calculations, choosing relative priorities remains highly controversial because it ultimately involves value conflicts inherent in differing philosophies of social welfare. The observation that one man's economic benefit may be another's loss illustrates the difficulty of calculating net economic benefit for a group.

4. Internal Order   Maintaining unity, consensus, and law within a nation is assumed to be crucial to national welfare-security. Thus, riots, high crime rates, unresolved labor disputes, and civil disobedience are often considered threats to the national interest. Although most would agree that violent dissension poses serious threats to national welfare, this does not imply that national interest is increased in direct proportion to the amount of unquestioned unity and consensus. To guarantee order, one might, for example, require all teachers in the nation to use the same textbook for a given subject and entertain from students only officially sanctioned opinions. We might reduce crime by giving the police power to conduct surprise searches and allow widespread electronic surveillance. Nonconformists who disagree with national policy or ideology might be subjected to imprisonment, hard labor, or reeducation. Such policies could be proposed as ways of increasing internal order, yet they would be opposed because strong resistance to their implementation might actually increase strife and because even if they did produce greater consensus, violating personal freedoms (privacy, speech, etc.) would be too high a price to pay for "unity."

It can be argued that pluralism, diversity, and controversy are more in the national interest than unity and consensus. This argument assumes that a group (or nation) cannot arrive at the "truth" or best decisions unless it has the opportunity to consider all possible options or alternative approaches to a problem. To keep many options alive, it is necessary to encourage a free marketplace of ideas and opportunities for widely diverse social experiments. Disagreement and diversity are thereby encouraged as crucial to developing national welfare-security. Consensus is criticized for the danger that it may stamp out inventive thought and bring an approach of unexamined complacency or undue reverence for the status quo.

The problem is not necessarily to choose between pluralism and consensus, but to allow both ideals to enlighten one's choices on specific issues of internal order. How should civil disobedience be handled (draft resistance, striking public employees, prohibited demonstrations and boycotts)? What alternative styles of life are permissible (the Amish, hippie communities, Black Muslim communities)? Should there be uniform standards for sex practices, censorship of obscenity, child rearing, and family organization? In what ways may deviant political opinions be expressed and implemented (controls on extremist groups of the right and left, using federal troops to coerce local government, guaranteeing minority representation in government)? Student attacks on conventional middle-class values tend to upset society, as do militant rebellions in the urban ghetto, but one must ask whether, despite their immediate disturbance of internal order, they might contribute to national welfare-security in the long run.

Thus far we have assumed a frame of reference that places primary value on national welfare-security. Whether national welfare-security should be subordinate to other values (or to the welfare-security of other units) is, of course, still an open question. The "requisites" discussed previously also suggest an alternative moral frame of reference. Perhaps the morality code among nations should not be seen in traditional Judeo-Christian or western values of love, brotherhood, mercy, equality, or honesty. Instead we might judge national policy by the extent to which it achieves territorial integrity, sovereignty, economic welfare, or internal order — criteria possibly more indicative of the actual functioning of nation states. Should nations be rewarded and punished according to how well they fulfill these functions? Such questions again raise the problem of applying traditional interpersonal morality to judgments about collectives or nations.

C. National Welfare-Security Issues

1. Competition and Cooperation

A persisting dilemma in the effort to build national welfare-security is the extent to which a nation should become cooperatively involved with and dependent on other nations (or superordinate organizations) thereby giving up some sovereignty or unilateral right to control its own policy. Should the United States engage in open trade and travel with Communist bloc countries? Should the United Nations intervene against South Africa's *apartheid* policy or America's nuclear buildup? Arguments on the desirability and possibility of world government tend to polarize on the extent to which national security necessitates an independent, self-sufficient posture.

Opponents of the apparent (though possibly not real) sovereignty loss inherent in greater international cooperation tend to argue that international affairs, like politics in general, is essentially a struggle among competing self-interests in which a nation must maintain enough power so that other nations may not hinder its pursuit of self-interest. The object is to gain resources in a world of scarcity, to win the allegiance of large populations, protect one's wealth and freedom from other nations seeking the same. Competition and rivalry is a zero-sum game, in which one nation cannot win without another losing. Although some nations may try to maintain their power by refusing to "play," (e.g., through isolationism or neutrality), it is impossible to remain immune from the effects of the battle.

To place national self-interest above international cooperation is most rational according to the premises of such competition. For example, five men in a "state of nature" realize that they might improve their chances of killing a stag if they all hunted together. Midway through the hunt one man sees a rabbit and takes up the chase, leaving the group, to assure himself of at least this food. If he had ignored the rabbit, perhaps another man would have taken it, which would have left the rest of the group foodless yet provided the individual with his needs. Assuming that each person will act in a purely self-interested way, it is rational not to trust the group. Similarly, the United States refuses to disarm without strict international inspection because it assumes it would not be in the self-interest of its rivals to disarm if they could gain an advantage over the United States.

One principle of survival in such a competitive situation is that one should not become involved in a situation where it is necessary to trust or depend on anyone but oneself. Opponents of free trade fear that the United States will become dependent on whims of the world market, over which we have little control; similarly, the reluctance to submit international disputes to compulsory third party arbitration. Denying United Nations membership to Red China is often construed as prudent refusal to risk becoming subject to the enemy's influence. On the other hand, in several situations, alliances and reciprocal agreements among nations apparently *are* assumed to be in the national self-interest: e.g., NATO, nuclear test-ban treaty, participation in the United Nations, or cases submitted to the World Court. Even if one assumes the "competitive struggle" interpretation of international affairs, he may decide that for some issues, cooperation, involvement, and foreign entanglement are more in the national interest (selfishly construed) than policies aimed at total self-sufficiency, isolation, or domination. We then have the paradoxical argument that a nation can increase its power and sovereignty by giving other nations a voice or some influence in some of its affairs.

Although one might justify a policy aimed toward extensive international cooperation, mutual help, and even world government simply by arguing this to be primarily in the greatest self-interest of one's nation (for example, because the human race is doomed to nuclear annihilation unless nationalism is abandoned), international cooperation can be valued over competitive nationalism for other reasons. Ethical positions that emphasize universal responsibility of love and mutual assistance and that derogate competitiveness, pride, and hierarchies of power among men tend to regard national welfare-security of only minor importance. Instead, the most sacred entities are "human beings" or the "world." The desire for international cooperation, peace, and good will take priority over national loyalty or welfare-security. The position may be rooted in both religious ideology (Bahai, Ethical Culturists, Quakers) and "secular" philosophies. It offers an alternative to the power struggle or competitive orientation.

Competition and cooperation are not mutually exclusive. We do not mean to imply that people are consistently committed to one or the other, nor that any given policy can be interpreted as implying only one of the two frameworks. Arguments over national welfare-security are often deadlocked, however, on conflicts over these frameworks. In a sense they reflect different notions of the nature of man, different explanations of human (and group) behavior. Competition can be identified with Hobbes's description of life as nasty, brutish, and short; with Machiavelli's assumptions about political behavior; with the "Protestant ethic"; and with contemporary political scientists' emphasis on power politics. Cooperation derives from a more optimistic view of human nature as characterized by Rousseau and the humanistic tradition that stresses man's innate goodness and perfectability.

Whether we are discussing the merits of social welfare legislation that guarantees income for the poor; allowing Communists to take over an underdeveloped country; using international troops to stop racial discrimination; or unilateral disarmament, certain issues of human nature continue to arise. To what extent is man basically lazy, selfish, prone to violence or industrious, charitable, and peaceful? What aspects of man's nature are unchangeable and what may be shaped by society? Answers to such general questions will probably influence positions on more specific issues. For instance, can people be trusted to use their freedom wisely (self-determination for nations; personal freedoms of speech, property, political association, etc.) or should there be restrictions to guarantee desired behavior (strings attached to foreign aid or welfare payments, forceful intervention to stop racial injustice or subversive activity)? Can one person (or nation) trust another not to infringe on his human rights (disarmament, invasion of privacy, cutthroat business practices, intervention in wars of self-determination)? When discussions begin to focus on questions of this sort, it is helpful to recognize how competitive and cooperative conceptions of human nature affect one's position.

2. Loyalty and Treason

Although issues of loyalty and treason usually concern national internal security, such problems as espionage, political asylum, immigration, and travel extend questions of internal security to international conflict. We will examine some controversies on internal security in the United States and suggest possible international ramifications.

Under the assumption that a nation should not be expected to tolerate acts that threaten its own survival, nations have punished or eliminated persons deemed guilty of treason, a crime allegedly different from other crimes because acts of treason pose a rather clear threat to the state's existence. However, defining the types of behavior most dangerous to the state's security is difficult. Such phrases as "aid and comfort to the enemy," "clear and present danger," "advocacy of violent overthrow of government," have been suggested to distinguish between subversive or treasonous, as opposed to loyal, behavior. Yet applying such criteria remains controversial. Is a person who has opposed United States policy in Vietnam giving aid and comfort to the enemy and, if so, should he be denied the right of free speech? Is a labor leader who prolongs a strike in the transportation or communication industry creating clear and present dangers for the society? If X belongs to a political party whose spokesmen advocate the use of violence by a deprived minority, should he be judged a traitor?

There have been attempts to make such concepts more precise. In seditious speech, for example, it is commonly argued that a person should not be punished for disloyal *beliefs*, but only *actions* or *advocacy*. It is also argued that criticizing specific government policy is permitted as free speech; that people may try to change leadership in the government through constitutional processes, and even may amend the Constitution through the process it provides. But incitement or conspiracy to overthrow constitutional government by violence is not allowed as a free speech provision. Despite these distinctions, marginal cases abound. A soldier with vehement objections to the foreign policy of his commander-in-chief may weaken the morale of his comrades to defend his country, and this might treaten national security although no conspiracy took place.

In recalling historical situations in which people have been punished not only for extreme acts of treason, but for "disloyalty," we find cases in which disagreement with or disobedience of specific regimes and policies have been considered threats to national security and treated harshly. Dictatorships, totalitarian regimes, or revolutionary juntas tend to treat the slightest dissent as treason. It can be asked if individuals should be loyal to individual regimes, to governmental structure and process, or to general ideals (equality, self-determination, etc.). The Nazi underground worker proclaims a loyalty to Weimar democracy and is executed for disloyalty to the Nazi regime. The Nazi army officer proclaims loyalty to his government and is sentenced to death by the Nuremberg court for disloyalty to the ideal of human rights. Even if one decides that universal ideals or moral values are the ultimate source of loyalty or allegiance, one must still face the dilemma that ideals may conflict with each other in certain situations. Allegedly, both the North Vietnamese and Americans have fought for the right of the Vietnamese people to self-determination.

Some will object to almost any dissent or opposition to the status quo and argue that the individual for his own and society's good must conform to the will of the group or regime currently responsible for law and order. This can lead to a philosophy of consensus and homogeneity enforced by policies that try to stifle diversity through restrictions on political dissent, immigration, trade, and travel. Although this general argument is often a persuasive way to justify limitations on eccentric displays of individual freedom, it has at least two difficulties. First, as shown previously, one must decide which "group" or society most deserves one's conformity — a nation, family, world, or what? Second, one must define more concretely what is meant by the "good" of the group or individual, and whether this involves nonviolence, luxury, autonomy, or other possible values.

If heretics may be deported from Puritan Massachusetts, French colonialists from Algeria, capitalists from Red China — all denounced as threats to the national welfare-security or "good" of their respective societies — are other societies obligated to receive them? If an American citizen refuses to vote, or to testify before a Congressional committee, or to fight in the armed services, should he be deported or denied freedom? A more general way to frame the loyalty-treason question is: To what extent should one's claim to basic human rights and freedoms depend upon unswerving conformity to a regime's policies and the norms of the groups to which he belongs? If one agrees that nations are not morally entitled to handle their loyalty problems as exclusively internal or "domestic" questions, then controversies will cross national boundaries and be debated from an international or universal point of view. United States draft dodgers who escape to Canada or seek political asylum in Sweden create dilemmas not only for the United States government, but for the host country as well (e.g., what rights should refugees have as "aliens" in the foreign country?).

Our conception of major issues in internal security stresses the conflict between individual rights and the state's welfare-security, assuming that the personal welfare-security of individuals may not always be served by policies aimed toward protection of national security. In the following section we discuss welfare-security issues from a personal or individual point of view.

II. Personal Welfare-Security

A. Definition and the Problem of a Standard

As in national welfare-security, individual welfare-security has several components. A concern for the individual's physical health and safety is evident in public policies that provide police protection, standards of sanitation, emergency medical services, immunization, etc. An emphasis on one's right to a certain level of economic welfare is reflected in pension benefits, aid to dependent children, unemployment insurance, minimum wage laws, tax exemptions for dependents, etc. Various freedoms and immunities may also be critical to a person's welfare, such as privacy or security from public surveillance, rights to due process of law, and First Amendment freedoms of speech and religion. Finally, emotional or psychic security is asserted — "freedom from fear" or "a sense of worth" are commonly mentioned personal needs. Emotional security may be seen as the most general objective, encompassing more specific aspects as "means" to the end. That is, unless a person is assured physical health and safety, economic necessities, and basic freedoms and immunities, he will not *feel* safe, secure, or dignified.

Recent manifestations of discontent and "alienation" among youth or blacks, for example, suggest that attaining personal welfare-security is not simply meeting obvious material and economic needs. A home in the suburbs with a cottage at the lake evidently is not sufficient to make all people content or satisfied with their lives. In the midst of economic affluence, personal insecurity, anxiety, and despair abound.

Public controversy is created by the very assumption that personal welfare-security is not merely a problem for individuals to solve privately, but that the society at large also has some responsibility to help persons attain welfare-security. To decide more precisely what the state's role is, one must not only distinguish between different aspects of welfare-security, but he must also judge specifically "how much," what degree, or what level of personal security in its various forms the state should guarantee. Should all people be equally entitled to a minimum standard of living? What qualifications entitle a person to this standard — diligence and work competence, obedience to law, family planning, length of residence, etc.?

Arguments over the appropriate level of welfare-security necessitate distinctions between subsistence needs versus luxuries and between material versus emotional welfare. These distinctions vary according to the relative wealth and economic development of a country, state, or locality and prevailing attitudes regarding the essentials of life. The "essentials" of life might be defined more generously in an affluent country than in an "underdeveloped" one where the majority of the population struggles for bare subsistence.

Even within a country, adequate welfare-security will differ from time to time according to variations in national prosperity. We see those who acquire what were formerly considered fundamentals (food, clothing, and shelter) continuing to strive for ever-increasing material goods — color televisions, boats, second cars, or country homes. One asks if man has an insatiable appetite for worldly goods. Will his vision of the essentials of life continue to expand with his increased powers of acquisition? Perhaps "poverty" should be measured not in standard material baselines (e.g., $3,000 per year for a family of four), but as the discrepancy between one's actual attainment of goods and services and his aspirations or expectations of what he deserves. One might also measure poverty by the *disparity* between a nation's poorest and richest members.

Affluence may reach a point where it becomes necessary to define personal security primarily in emotional, rather than material terms. If personal security is equated with a healthy or secure personality, new and complex problems arise. What are the requisites for a sense of personal worth or "identity" in a postindustrial society? To what extent does psychic security depend on complete predictability and certainty in one's life, on a lack of risks to one's well-being? To guarantee highly stable emotional peace might bring tedium. To feel truly secure, man, paradoxically, may need the challenge of risks and problems. Perhaps he gains security only from having confronted and mastered severe tests of commitment, intelligence, or ingenuity. Whether one plans social policy to provide healthy tension and challenges or whether one tries to make life continually easier and challenge-free depends on one's conception of psychological security.

It has been argued that the best sense of personal security is gained when one becomes materially *self-sufficient,* i.e., in a subsistence farming context where each man is totally responsible for his own (or his family's) material needs. The industrial technological society creates a system of specialized interdependence in which it is impossible for individuals to feel they can depend completely upon themselves. To the extent that one's sense of security is inevitably rooted in man's ability to provide his own material needs or more generally to exercise power and control over his destiny, complex technological society (despite affluence and development) poses serious threats to personal welfare-security.

B. Collective and Individual Responsibility for Personal Welfare-Security

Controversies over the state's role in ensuring personal welfare-security may involve situations in which the state prohibits or limits actions of an individual or group because certain acts infringe upon the personal welfare-security of others. Laws against theft, trespass, forgery, kidnapping, and assault protect personal property and life. Constitutional prohibitions against self-incrimination, unreasonable search and seizure, cruel and unusual punishment, infringements on free speech or religion, along with regulations for industrial health and safety, and antitrust and fair business practices legislation may all attempt to protect the individual's welfare-security from encroachment by other people or the state. Disputes about which prohibitions are justified continue to arise. Should cigarette manufacturing and sale be prohibited if smoking's harmful effects on health have been demonstrated? Should police use physical force against uncooperative suspects? Should the government sanction electronic surveillance of suspected criminals? What restrictions should be placed on selling and possessing firearms? Restrictions or prohibitions made to increase personal welfare-security for a certain class (cigarette smokers or innocent law-abiding citizens) often curtail the autonomy or even the welfare-security of the people who are the target of the restrictions (cigarette manufacturers, police, hunters, and gun dealers). Such conflicts might be viewed as contests that decide whose welfare-security is more important.

Some government policies can be construed as coercive infringements on personal freedom, justified only because they allegedly contribute to welfare-security. Is it right to force people to contribute to the social security system; to compel children to attend school; to conscript young men into the armed services; to commit people to mental institutions; to subpoena citizens to testify in court and to serve on jury duty; to compel tax payments to support foreign aid, poverty, and space programs; or to take personal property for urban renewal and highway construction? Some such compulsory policies, although they infringe on personal freedom, allegedly enhance individual welfare-security; for example, schooling, hospitalizing the mentally ill, or social security pensions. Other infringements assume that individual freedom must be sacrificed for the good of the larger group. In the long run, so the argument goes, benefit to the individual depends upon benefit to the society at large. Therefore, taking a person's property for a highway, forcing him into the armed forces, or allowing police to search his home actually increase his welfare-security, although in the short run they seem to be a threat.

Opposition to welfare-state policies that protect and nourish the individual "from the cradle to the grave" need not be based on sentimental commitment to rugged individualism or traditional laissez-faire economics. Sociological or psychological analysis may suggest that public attention to certain personal needs is inherently detrimental to personality development or social structure. Aside from the standard claim that socialistic welfare programs tend to reduce initiative, we can also ask, "Should the state concern itself with improving the quality of love, devotion, and mutual understanding shared between man, wife, and children?" Assuming that certain child-rearing practices are more likely than others to enhance feelings of self-worth and psychic security, to what degree should the state control how parents relate to their children? Assuming that personal worth may also depend upon one's religious or spiritual orientation, his sense of ultimate goodness, and the worthiness of his "soul," in what ways should the state intervene to facilitate this dimension of welfare-security? We may argue that certain decisions should be left in the control of the family or church or voluntary social group, because their contribution to personal welfare-security depends on their immunity from public attention. Merely emphasizing *personal* security conveys by definition a qualitative difference and a concern for reserving certain areas of choice to individual, idiosyncratic, nonpublic, nonstandardized processes.

The following problem may illustrate difficulties in defining the boundaries between individual and collective responsibility for personal welfare-security. It is argued that a person's sense of belonging to a family helps to create a sense of security, both through the love he receives and responsibilities he undertakes for others. A father amasses a fortune so that his children will "have it better" than he did. Inheritance brings grossly unequal opportunities to children of poor parents, disadvantages for which poor children cannot be held responsible. It is argued that part of a personal sense of worth for the wealthy father is the feeling of contributing to the future material security of his offspring. To deprive children of their "birthright" (e.g., by abolishing inheritance) might also deprive the parents of a mission that gives their life meaning. Inheriting the family home or business may give a unique sense of identity to the youth. But what about the welfare-security of youth who inherit nothing? Is state interference justified to secure more economic equality? Problems of this sort will be discussed more extensively in Chapter 8 on property.

III. Violence

Violence prevention and the justification for violence are perhaps the most familiar and passionately argued issues related to welfare-security. Whether we are concerned with national security or individual safety, we shall in some situations openly advocate using violence, even to achieve peace or nonviolence, and in other situations deplore its use as unjustified and inhumane. How do we reach such apparently inconsistent conclusions? Although public rhetoric suggests a duty always to exhaust "peaceful" means of solving a problem before using violence, history has shown that national and individual interests may be pursued in many cases only by deliberate violence. In this section we discuss justifications of collective and individual (or person-to-person) violence together, although it may be useful to distinguish between these types in specific controversies.

A. Justifying Violence

Assuming a prima facie duty to avoid violence, we have a special obligation to justify its use. At least four general approaches can be used:

Self-Defense. That France was justified in using violence against Nazi Germany or the United States in attacking Japan is widely accepted. An innocent civilian attacked by a thief on the street has a right to use violence to subdue his assailant. The general principle holds that victims of unprovoked attacks may use violence to protect or defend themselves against aggressors. Although these cases are easily decided, the self-defense principle does not provide clear guidance when it is difficult to determine whether one's safety is threatened or difficult to decide whether a group (or person) should be classified as a provoker or aggressor. Did Hanoi commit aggression or was the nation of Vietnam fighting a civil war? Would Russian escalation of the arms race be sufficient provocation for the United States to start a preventive war? There is also the question of deciding on the degree or intensity of violence that is justified: Should the United States have used the atomic bomb on Japan? Is it necessary for police to use night sticks against demonstrators? Perhaps the major difficulty with the criterion of self-defense is in deciding what can be legitimately defended with violence. Presumably a nation could argue that Communism, Christianity, or some other ideology presents a severe threat to its own values, and in order to defend a heritage, way of life, economic prosperity, or colonial empire, it is necessary to wage preventive war for self-defense.

Social Ideals. People will fight not only to defend their bodies or property, but apparently also for many other reasons, which leads us to search for values, ideals, or rights that have served as their own justification for violence. Earlier we mentioned the importance of *sovereignty* or *self-determination* as a national interest sought by violent means (American Revolution, Algerian war). *Equality* also serves as a legitimate goal of revolution (French or Bolshevik revolutions, Negro rebellions in the United States). The need for *economic resources* has also been considered sufficient to justify violence in the form of slavery, colonialism, wars of expansion, and revolutions of the dispossessed. Violence waged for *retributive justice* or vengeance is used to justify punishment of individuals (capital punishment, Nuremberg trials), as well as nations (Versailles Treaty). Religious or political ideologies have justified violent conquest of heathens or deviants (crusades, execution of traitors or disbelievers). Violence in pursuit of such intangible ends brings the most heated public disputes.

A classic dilemma for groups seeking such ideals is the extent to which they work peacefully within the status quo: e.g., Negroes using nonviolence to gain the right to vote; obeying white employers and tolerating indignities temporarily while they work their way to the top. A contrasting approach is violent revolution, seizing power and resources and overthrowing the system responsible for one's oppression. The argument is made that conforming to or working within the system is not merely a temporary concession for the sake of victory in the long run, but that by conforming or becoming an "Uncle Tom," one will eventually adopt white middle-class values contrary to one's original intent. To avoid corrupting or perverting one's mission, one must reject the normal legal "channels" that tend to perpetuate white tyranny. Whether we are concerned with the struggle for racial equality and economic equality or the censorship of underground newspapers, we must debate the alternatives: reform within the system (implying peaceful gradual change) versus revolution (implying rejection of the legitimacy of the system, rapid change, and probably violence). Arguments on the pace of change give considerable attention to the tactical question, "Which techniques are most likely to bring the desired ideal?" Many blacks will argue that violent revolution is strategically foolish, because they could never win a race war. Those who protest the Vietnam war and the military-industrial complex may balk at resistance to the draft mainly because in serving a jail term they could not be politically effective.

Involuntary Violence. Violence has been excused or condoned when it is shown that the individual or group seemed to have no real choice or control over violent behavior, such as a child or mental patient unable to control his impulses or ignorant of the difference between "right and wrong"; a person who is "coerced" into violence (the pilot ordered to bomb a city); or people who have no knowledge or intention that their acts lead to violence (hotel keeper provides meeting place for criminals or revolutionaries). Although involuntary violence condones certain acts that would be otherwise unjustified, there is continuing controversy in deciding whether a person had control of his actions, whether he was coerced or could have been reasonably expected not to obey orders, and whether he *should* have known the consequences of his actions.

Violence as Part of Human Nature. It has been suggested that man has unalterable instincts toward aggression and violence; even that certain types of violence are necessary to enhance one's security or sense of worth. War provides a setting in which man can test himself, can develop courage, inventiveness, endurance, self-sacrifice, and loyalty — virtues that give meaning to life. Lorenz's observation (1966) that man is unique as a species that engages in intraspecific aggression to the point of killing one's adversary implies dim prospects for avoiding human violence. We must ask whether the apparent tendency to violence stems from unalterable instinct, or whether perhaps violence and aggression are symptomatic reactions to anxiety and frustration. If the latter is true, perhaps the more basic cause of frustration can be treated. William James spoke of the moral equivalent of war; McDougall spoke of man's tendency to pugnacity being replaced by healthy economic competition. If the more basic need is a test or challenge — whether it be intellectual, economic, artistic, political — then the problem is to arrange for nonviolent ways in which men can compete, demonstrate their skill and superiority, their courage and cleverness. Whether man's nature requires constant struggle or whether he can be satisfied with a life of peace, tranquility, and ease is a fundamental issue relevant to positions on justifying or preventing specific kinds of violence.

B. Definitional
Problems

Which of the following actions are most violent? Police use tear gas to break up a demonstration; police fire rifles at snipers; soldiers force citizens at gunpoint to leave a village; a mother spanks her child; a mother scolds her child who then breaks into tears; a mother threatens to beat her child if the child does not behave. One might define violence as inflicting physical harm or property damage, but this might unnecessarily restrict the definition. Hitler's armed occupation of Czechoslovakia apparently involved very little actual destruction, yet we tend to call this violence because of the substantial threat to use armed force. If the threat to use force, as well as actual physical injury, is part of the definition, then the definition may become too broad. We would not wish to say that we obey the speed limit, because the government will use violence against us if we do not. Another complication is suggested by the mother scolding the child. To what extent can violence be construed as inflicting psychological as well as physical pain? Insults and verbal indignities in certain situations can be considered legitimate provocation for physical retaliation. The self-defense of one's psyche may be as important as physical safety. This is not to suggest that the definition of violence should be broadened to include *any* sense of wrong or injustice, but merely to illustrate problems of conventional definitions.

Other definitions of violence stress forcing someone to perform acts against his will. New technology will make it possible to control human behavior through means more subtle and less painful than, for example, traditional rifles, tanks, and bombs. Using chemicals and drugs on a mass scale may subdue rioters or conquer large populations with minimum physical pain. Perhaps future definitions of violence will emphasize physical pain less and the dangers of "peaceful" methods of control against human will more.

Another futuristic interpretation of violence emerges from escalation of the arms race. Postulating a condition in which annihilating the human race is within the power of hundreds of states (or even individuals who have privately produced H-bombs and missiles), violence might be defined as any act that increases the probability of nuclear holocaust. Acts that increase tension among nations or that tip the balance of power could be considered violent because they could push the world over an "annihilation threshold."

THE PULLMAN STRIKE, 1894

In Chicago, railway workers confronted not only resistant employers but the troops and courts of the U.S. Government.

In 1880 the Pullman Company quietly bought a tract of 4,000 acres in the town of Hyde Park, which adjoined Chicago. It was to be the site of a dream fulfilled — the first model town in industrial America. It was to become a showplace, drawing admiring visitors from all over the world. And finally — in May 1894 — it was to become a dream exploded.

The vision of a model workers' community belonged to George M. Pullman, one of the great

This case is taken from Donald W. Oliver and Fred M. Newmann, *The Rise of Organized Labor: Worker Security and Employer Rights,* American Education Publications, Columbus, Ohio, 1967.

industrialists of the age. Since the 1860's Pullman's name had been famous throughout the nation. Who had not heard of the ingenious, luxurious railway sleeping cars produced by the Pullman Palace Car Company? Railroads everywhere clamored to obtain the prestigious cars for their lines. The Pullman Company established plants from New York to California. Shares in the company doubled in values.

George Pullman worried about the labor troubles that beset many other companies. If he gave workers a decent place to live, he reasoned, he would get a better class of workmen, labor turnover could be reduced, and unrest would turn into contentment. If he owned the entire town, he could insulate employees from corrupting influences.

Pullman thought the town could pay its way as well. He expected every dollar invested in it to yield a 6 percent return (though this was modest in an era when business profits of 100 percent and more were not uncommon).

The first homes of Pullman were erected on 300 secluded acres. The little community was a beautiful place, especially when compared with Chicago, the filthy industrial giant just to its north. One-tenth of the area of Pullman was occupied by its parks. A lake was created for boating and swimming. An island in the lake was dotted with athletic fields.

Every street in town was paved with macadam. The sidewalks were paved too, usually with wood, and were lined with shade trees. The front lawn of every house in town was landscaped by the company. The buildings were nearly all yellow brick, made in Pullman itself of clay dredged from the bottom of Lake Calumet. By 1885 the town had 1,400 dwelling units.

Schooling was free through the eighth grade, the only condition being that all students had to be vaccinated against smallpox. Another pioneering feature was the kindergarten for children between the ages of four and six. An evening school offered such commercial subjects as bookkeeping and stenography. A library was opened

in 1883 with an initial gift of 5,000 volumes from George Pullman.

Pullman's paradise grew year by year. It achieved its peak in 1893, just before the depression struck, when the population of the town was 12,600. At that time employment in the Pullman shops was 5,500, with many workers drawn from surrounding towns. The town grew in value too. The land had cost $800,000 in 1880. Twelve years later George Pullman proudly estimated its worth at $5 million.

But he had his problems with the town. It never earned the 6 percent return he had expected from it. For years it paid only about 4.5 percent. In 1892 and 1893 the return further declined to 3.8 percent.

Pullman also had problems with his tenants. He thought that liquor was bad, so he banned it from the town. He kept his eye on everything. He had informers in every lodge, in every social group; sometimes it seemed that he had them in every parlor on Saturday night. He wanted to know everything that happened, and to model his town on the traditional Puritan virtues of thrift and hard work and sobriety.

But many of his workers came from traditions other than Puritan. As early as 1884 more than half of the residents were foreign-born. Eight years later 72 percent were foreign-born, including 23 percent Scandinavian, 12 percent British, the same proportion of Germans, 10 percent Dutch, 5 percent Irish. Many of them could see no harm in a pint of beer. Many of them wanted to worship in their own faiths.

George Pullman had his firm ideas about that too. There was one church building in town and Pullman owned it. It was available to any religious group, but the rent set on it by Pullman was so high that no congregation in town could afford to pay it. The Presbyterians tried it for a few years and went bankrupt. The church then stayed vacant.

In 1893 the company could boast that its typical workers were "40 percent better in evidence of thrift and refinement and in all the outward indications of a wholesome way of life" than any comparable group in America.

But one worker voiced the bitterness within the people: "We are born in a Pullman house, fed from the Pullman shop, taught in the Pullman school, and when we die we shall be buried in the Pullman cemetery and go to the Pullman hell."

As depression took hold in 1893, orders for Pullman's railroad cars dried up. George Pullman responded vigorously with a program of layoffs, reduced hours, wage cuts. In July 1893 the shops at Pullman employed 5,500 men; the following May only 3,300 remained at work. Wage rates were slashed an average of 25 percent. Yet stockholders' dividends were actually increased, and the company had an undistributed surplus of $2,320,000 for the year 1893–94.

For Pullman workers and their families the winter of 1893–94 was a long, hard one. In some homes the children lacked the shoes and coats needed to go to school in the severe Illinois winter; in other homes children were kept in bed all day because there was no coal in the house.

And then came a voice of hope. The previous spring, June 1893, just as the depression was beginning, 50 railroad workers had met in Chicago to form the American Railway Union. Prior to that time the only trade unions on the railroads had been the various Brotherhoods, a separate one for each of the main occupations — engineers, brakemen, firemen — in railroading.

By 1893 some of the more radical officials in the Brotherhoods were disgusted with quarreling and competition among their organizations. They decided to try to unite railroad employees in a single American Railway Union. Chief among these dissidents, and the first president of the ARU, was Eugene V. Debs, a secretary-treasurer of the Brotherhood of Locomotive Firemen for the preceding 12 years.

Debs, 38 years old in 1893, was a man of awesome vigor. His life was one perpetual organizing trip. Debs was also a visionary who spoke eloquently of a coming era of peace and prosperity.

The new union received floods of applications and by 1894 had 87 local lodges. The workers in the Pullman shops were eligible for membership in the ARU because the Pullman Company operated a few miles of railroad leading to its shops. Man by man, they joined.

After complaining without satisfaction to the vice-president of the company, a local committee of workers voted a strike. On May 11, 1894, more than 90 percent of the workers in the Pullman factory walked out. The company promptly laid off the others. Eugene Debs had advised against the strike. But after visiting the town, he realized that it had been an act of desperation.

The strike dragged along until June 12, when the first national convention of the American Railway Union met in Chicago. In one year the organization had enrolled 150,000 members. But knowing that the union was loosely organized and had little money, Debs was not sure it would win against the mighty Pullman Corporation. At the suggestion of Debs, the convention chose 12 men, including six strikers, to go to the company and propose arbitration of the wage dispute.

The company said that there was "nothing to arbitrate." Its position was that wages and working conditions should be determined by management, with no interference by labor. Several efforts by the ARU to alter this position failed. So the ARU convention voted a boycott which Debs had tried to avoid. Switchmen in the ARU were ordered to refuse to switch any Pullman cars onto trains. If the switchmen were discharged or disciplined for this refusal, all ARU members of the railroad line were pledged to cease work at once.

The boycott began at noon on June 26, 1894. The railroads saw this as their chance to cut the ARU down to size. Unified by the General Managers Association, the 24 railroads running out of Chicago declared that their contracts with Pullman would be honored at all costs, and that they would operate no trains without Pullman cars.

By June 29, 20 railroads were tied up. An estimated 125,000 men had quit work. Agents of the General Managers were busy in eastern cities hiring unemployed railroaders as strikebreakers.

Leaders of the Railroad Brotherhoods were denouncing the ARU. Eugene Debs was sending telegrams all over the Great Plains advising his union members to use no violence and to stop no trains forcibly, but simply to refuse to handle Pullmans.

When the Illinois Central claimed that its property at Cairo, Illinois, was in danger, Governor John P. Altgeld, with the permission of the local authorities, sent three companies of the state militia there. A crowd stopped a train at Hammond, Indiana, and forced the crew to detach two Pullmans. Two other trains were temporarily stopped by mobs in Chicago. But there were no major riots. No mail had accumulated in Chicago. As late as July 5, total strike damages to railroad property were less than $6,000.

Yet the federal district attorney in Chicago wired Washington on June 29 that conditions there were so bad that special deputies were needed. At the urging of the General Managers, Richard B. Olney, Attorney General of the United States, appointed Edwin Walker as special federal attorney to handle the strike situation. Walker was an attorney for a railroad that belonged to the General Managers Association.

Olney also sent Walker some pointed advice: The best way to cope with conditions was "by a force which is overwhelming and prevents any attempt at resistance." Olney believed that a national railroad strike was illegal by definition, and that the local and state officials in Illinois could not be trusted to handle matters. In his judgment, the strikers were impeding interstate commerce and the movement of the United States mails.

On July 2 in Chicago, Edwin Walker and the federal district attorney drafted an application for an injunction against the strike leaders. They based this action on the Sherman Antitrust Act, which Congress had passed in 1890 to control monopolies by big business. The law declared illegal "every contract, combination in the form of trust or otherwise, or conspiracy, in restraint of trade or commerce among the several states, or with foreign nations." Now Olney used the law as a weapon against "combination" and "conspiracy" by the people of organized labor.

Federal judges granted the injunction immediately. The range of the court's order was breathtaking: The strike leaders were enjoined from any deed to encourage the boycott; they could not send telegrams about it, or talk about it, or write about it.

If the ARU leaders obeyed the injunction, the boycott would collapse; central coordination was essential. But if they did not obey it, all strikers would be in active opposition to the federal government, and the leaders might well go to jail for contempt of court. Debs and his colleagues decided to ignore the court order.

Olney hit a snag when he proposed sending federal troops to Chicago. The Secretary of War and the Army Chief of Staff both opposed the move. But on July 3 Olney received a telegram saying that no agency but the U.S. Army could protect the mails. The telegram was signed by Judge Peter Grosscup — one of the judges who had granted the injunction — Edwin Walker, and the federal district attorney in Chicago. President Grover Cleveland ordered the entire command from Fort Sheridan turned out for active duty in Chicago on the morning of Independence Day.

The ARU was incensed. So was Governor Altgeld. He protested to the President that neither he nor the state legislature had asked for help. Local and state authority was adequate to cope with what little violence had occurred, he said. "At present some of our railroads are paralyzed," Altgeld told the President, "not by reason of obstruction, but because they cannot get men to operate their trains. . . ."

The President's reply was brief. He wired back that the postal authorities had asked for the removal of obstructions to the mails, that Judge Grosscup had asked for help in enforcing the injunction, and that there was "competent proof that conspiracies existed against commerce between the states."

Any of these conditions, President Cleveland contended, was ample to give him power to order federal troops into Illinois.

Governor Altgeld reasserted his position forcibly and at length. The President closed the discussion curtly. The federal troops took over — and along with them, 5,000 special federal deputy marshals. Of this latter group, two-thirds were chosen by the railroads and were responsible to them (although the marshal's office gave them commissions and badges).

The result was chaos. On July 5, the day after the Army reached Chicago, violence was more serious than before. The next day it reached its peak when incendiaries ignited railroad cars with torches and waste taken from axle boxes. Fanned by breezes, the flames swept through row upon row of cars tightly packed in the outlying yards, to which fire hoses often could not reach. In the evening a mob of about 6,000 people pillaged the Panhandle yards in South Chicago, destroying 700 cars. Total damage in that one day was $340,000, although on no other day was it more than $4,000.

On July 7 another crowd of several thousand gathered on Loomis Street, where federal troops were guarding a train being moved by non-union men. As the onlookers showered the guards with abuse and stones, ignoring the troop commander's warning to disperse, the troops loaded their rifles. This gesture only incited more showers of stones.

Immediately the commander ordered a bayonet charge; several person fell to the ground bleeding heavily. Then the mob regrouped and tipped over a flatcar. With four soldiers badly wounded and no reinforcements in sight, the commander ordered his men to fire at will. They continued shooting until the mob had fled; 20 people were wounded and four killed.

Eugene Debs, continuing his efforts to prevent violence, again told the strikers: "Our men have the right to quit, but their right ends there. Other men have the right to take their places, whatever the opinion of the propriety of so doing may be. Keep away from railroad yards, or rights-of-way, or other places where large crowds congregate. A safe plan is to remain away entirely from places where there is any likelihood of an outbreak."

Debs repeatedly argued that the rioting was being done by hooligans, not by strikers. During the entire boycott, not a single ARU member in Chicago was killed or wounded by law-enforcement authorities.

In Chicago, newspaper headlines read:

UNPARALLELED SCENES OF RIOT, PILLAGE

Anarchy Is Rampant

THIRSTY FOR BLOOD

Frenzied Mob Still Bent On Death and Destruction

On July 10, with the boycott obviously on its last legs, a federal grand jury in Chicago delivered another serious blow by indicting Debs and three colleagues for conspiracy to obstruct a mail train on the Rock Island Railroad.

The mayors of Chicago and Detroit made a futile call on the vice-president of the Pullman Company to again request arbitration. They found him unyielding. "The issue at question, which was simply that of reopening the shops at Pullman and carrying them on at a ruinous loss, was not a proper subject for arbitration," he was reported to have said.

The boycott dragged along another week, while at Pullman the leader of the original strikers announced that they were being starved into submission. Then, on July 17, Debs and his associates were again arrested, this time for violating the July 2 injunction. They refused to post bail and were imprisoned. A day later a notice was put up on the gates of the Pullman shops: "These gates will be opened as soon as the number of operatives is sufficient to make a working force in all departments." It was the end of the Pullman Strike.

Of the men now hired at Pullman, one of every four had not worked there before the strike. Every applicant was forced to sign a pledge that he would not join any union. A thousand former employees were left destitute. Governor Altgeld appealed to the Pullman Company to help them.

He got no reply. Altgeld then called upon the public for a relief fund.

Tried for alleged contempt of court in violating the injunction, Debs was found guilty on December 14, 1894, and sentenced to six months in jail. The United States Supreme Court, which heard the case on a petition of habeas corpus, upheld the conviction on May 27, 1895. The Supreme Court, ignoring the Sherman Act on which the injunction had been based, reached its unanimous opinion by stressing the power of the federal courts to prevent interference with the mails and interstate commerce.

Debs spent much of his time in jail reading and thinking. He emerged after six months as a convert to socialism. Over a long and active career that followed, Debs was a candidate for President five times on the Socialist party ticket.

QUESTIONS FOR DISCUSSION

1. *Worker Security, Employer Security, Public Interest.* Were the strikes called by Pullman workers, and the boycott and strike called by the American Railway Union justified means for workers to press their demands for greater economic security? In discussing this issue, consider such problems as:

    a.   What alternatives did the workers have?

    b.   What was Pullman's responsibility to guarantee economic security to workers?

    c.   What responsibilities did workers have for not interfering with the security of Pullman?

    d.   What responsibilities did both sides have for not threatening general welfare or public interest?

    e.   What responsibility do workers in one company have for not threatening the jobs of workers in other companies?

What limits, if any, should be placed on workers' rights to strike? The line below represents a *continuum*, ranging from no right to strike (i.e., under *no* circumstances would strikes be permitted) to absolute right to strike (i.e., strikes would be permitted under any circumstances). Indicate for each occupation the extent to which you think its right to strike should be limited, and tell why you place more limits on some occupations than others.

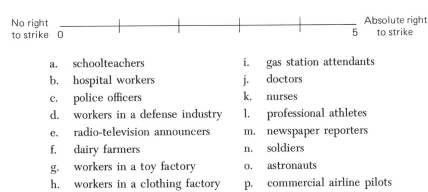

| No right to strike 0 | | | | 5 | Absolute right to strike |

    a.   schoolteachers

    b.   hospital workers

    c.   police officers

    d.   workers in a defense industry

    e.   radio-television announcers

    f.   dairy farmers

    g.   workers in a toy factory

    h.   workers in a clothing factory

    i.   gas station attendants

    j.   doctors

    k.   nurses

    l.   professional athletes

    m.   newspaper reporters

    n.   soldiers

    o.   astronauts

    p.   commercial airline pilots

2. *Defining a Level of Worker Security.* Employers such as Pullman opposed collective bargaining because they feared that unions might force the company to give workers everything they wanted. Below is a list of possible union demands. Which do you think should be granted and which denied? For what reasons?

a.   No worker may be dismissed without approval of an elected union committee.

b.   All workers are to receive an annual wage increase of 3 percent.

c.   The company will provide clean rest rooms, showers, lockers, a lunchroom, and cigarette and coffee machines.

d.   All workers will receive, in addition to their wages, annual dividends from company profits.

e.   The company may not hire a person who refuses to join the union.

f.   Union members will have a regular voting representative on the company's board of directors.

g.   The company will pay for union members' health and life insurance, and a guaranteed pension after retirement.

h.   Workers absent because of illness will receive full pay.

i.   The official work week will be limited to thirty-five hours, with time-and-a-half for overtime.

j.   Workers are not to be hired without approval by a union committee.

k.   A union representative will approve all work assignments and production quotas.

l.   Workers will receive a guaranteed annual wage.

m.   Workers will receive their birthdays off with full pay.

n.   Automatic raises will be geared to the rise in the cost of living.

o.   Any worker whose job is to be eliminated by automatic machinery will be trained for new work.

3. *Federal Intervention.* Intervention of federal troops might be justified when a local authority needs help in handling a *local* law enforcement problem or when a local authority faces an essentially national problem. To what extent was federal intervention justified in the Pullman strike and how significant were each of these grounds for intervention? To what extent do you believe federal troops tended to subdue or incite violence?

OPPENHEIMER: SCIENTIST ACCUSED

A physicist who led the project to develop the first atomic bomb is charged with being a risk to the security of the U.S.

Few modern scientists have ever matched the brilliant career of J. Robert Oppenheimer. He started collecting minerals when he was five years old and became a member of the Mineralogical Club of New York at the age of 11. After attending Harvard for three years, he graduated with the highest honors. He then spent four years in Europe, studying under distinguished scientists and earning his doctorate.

Home in the U.S. again in 1929, he began his teaching career. Although he read widely and in several languages, he paid little attention to politics. He later said: "I had no radio, no telephone; I learned of the stock market crash in the fall of 1929 only long after the event; the first time I ever voted was in the presidential election of 1936. . . . I was interested in man and his experience; I was deeply interested in my science; but I had no understanding of the relations of man to his society."

But, beginning in 1936, Oppenheimer started dabbling in politics because of the Nazi persecution of Jews in Germany (where he had relatives), and because of friends and students with political interests. Many of Oppenheimer's associates, including a woman who was his fiancée for a time, had strong left-wing ties. Soon he was contributing money to a variety of political groups, including some run by Communists. In this he was joined by other prominent American educators and artists who sympathized with Stalin's Russia during the 30's.

Oppenheimer ended his flirtation with Communist-backed causes by the early 1940's. In 1942 he began studying the possibilities of developing an atomic bomb for the war effort of the U.S. Government. The following year he became head of the Los Alamos Project in New Mexico, where he assembled and led a group of some 4,000 scientists, technicians, and experts.

The achievements of Oppenheimer at Los Alamos place him among the most notable scientist-administrators of all time. He persuaded many of the country's top scientists to live in remote isolation in the West. His tact and insight enabled him to keep this group of individualists working together as a team. The successful test of the atomic bomb on July 16, 1945, was considered a tremendous achievement, a fitting climax to the years of self-sacrifice endured by Oppenheimer and his community on that bleak New Mexico desert.

But during this period — in 1943 — he also made a famous false step that would hurt him in the future. While mixing martinis in his home, he was asked by a visiting friend named Haakon Chevalier to pass secret scientific data to an agent of the Soviet Union. In the atmosphere of tight security that prevailed then this was a dangerous suggestion, and Oppenheimer turned it down. However, he failed to report the incident immediately as security regulations required. Only several months later did he report the incident, and then he tried to protect Chevalier by inventing a false story. Security officers finally obtained Chevalier's name from him.

Although Oppenheimer resigned from Los Alamos three months after the atomic explosion, he continued to serve the government in a number of capacities. He was on the science panel of the Secretary of War's Interim Committee on Atomic Energy, on a committee to consider classification policy on atomic matters, on a panel to advise on armaments and their regulation, and

This case is taken from Donald W. Oliver and Fred M. Newmann, *Science and Public Policy: Uses and Control of Knowledge,* American Education Publications, Columbus, Ohio, 1969.

on other official committees. From 1947 to 1952 Oppenheimer was chairman of the General Advisory Committee to the Atomic Energy Commission (AEC).

Meanwhile, the explosion of the first Soviet atomic bomb in 1949 set off a new controversy. Edward Teller, one of the nation's leading physicists, had long been working on calculations for an even bigger bomb, nicknamed the "super." Teller now argued that the U.S. should go ahead with a project to produce this bomb — not only to preserve a military edge over the Soviet Union but also to have equality when the Communists might produce a superbomb of their own.

But Teller was shocked when the AEC General Advisory Committee under Oppenheimer unanimously decided against any expansion of work on thermonuclear weapons. Their reasons were technical, military, and moral. In the light of the knowledge then available, they doubted that a superbomb could be successfully designed. Two committee members felt overwhelming horror at the destructive power that would lie in such a weapon. And, finally, a majority argued that the Soviet Union was only trying to catch up with the U.S., that the Soviet Union would not try to develop new weapons unless the U.S. did. Oppenheimer, as the world's foremost nuclear scientist, led the opposition to expansion.

President Harry S Truman finally decided in favor of developing what would become the hydrogen bomb. The project encountered difficulties, however, and a year and a half passed before Teller made a major breakthrough. At about this time Oppenheimer also contributed an idea that turned out to be so useful that it is still embodied in H-bombs.

The explosion of the American H-bomb in 1952 officially closed the controversy about whether it would be possible to build such a weapon. And the explosion of a Soviet H-bomb less than a year later seemed to refute the main arguments of American scientists who had urged this nation to shun the weapon.

Early in 1954 a former executive director of the Joint Congressional Committee on Atomic Energy sent FBI Director J. Edgar Hoover a letter charging Oppenheimer with opposing development of the H-bomb because he was a Soviet agent. This charge, which was not substantiated, led to a Government hearing on whether Oppenheimer should continue to have security clearance to work on secret Government projects.

A special Personnel Security Board conducted the Oppenheimer hearing. Members of the Board were Gordon Gray, former Secretary of the Army; Thomas A. Morgan, president of the Sperry Rand Corporation; and R. Ward Evans, professor of chemistry of Loyola University. Each of these men served out of sense of public duty. The hearing took place in Chicago from April 12 to May 6, 1954.

A variety of charges were lodged against Oppenheimer and examined during this hearing. These included claims that Oppenheimer:

• Contributed regularly to Communist causes in 1940–42.
• Had been intimately associated with Communists and former Communists, including his former sweetheart, wife, brother, and sister-in-law.
• Gave contradictory evidence to the FBI about attending Communist meetings in the early 40's.
• Recruited Communists and former Communists to work at Los Alamos during World War II.
• Failed to report promptly the attempt by Haakon Chevalier to obtain secret information for the Soviet Union.
• Strongly opposed the development of the H-bomb as chairman of the General Advisory Committee of the AEC, and continued to oppose this development even after President Truman's go-ahead.

Several of these charges had special bite at the time they were made, because Senator Joseph McCarthy of Wisconsin still exerted massive influence in national politics. His charges that hundreds of Communists had infiltrated the State

Department, Central Intelligence Agency, and other offices of the Federal Government were widely believed — though never proved. Some Government officials were ousted on the grounds of behavior that might indicate sympathy with communism. Dozens of other people were denounced before the national and local press, often on slender or questionable evidence. Some state employees and others lost jobs for refusal to sign loyalty oaths.

McCarthy's power was curbed late in 1954 when the Senate censured him, but he still had great influence during the Oppenheimer security hearings. The commentator Richard Rovere has described the political climate of the time: "McCarthyism rampant managed, for a time, to make politics in America seem almost entirely a matter of idotic chatter about 'loyalty risks' and 'security risks.' "

During the three and a half weeks of testimony, the counsel for the Security Board hammered away at Oppenheimer's failure to be candid about security at several points in his career.

The Haakon Chevalier case was the key incident in charges that Oppenheimer had associated with Communists in a way harmful to security. Roger Robb, counsel for the Personnel Security Board, queried Oppenheimer about this in the following exchange:

Robb: . . . Would you begin at the beginning and tell us exactly what happened?

Oppenheimer: Yes. One day, and I believe you have the time fixed better than I do, in the winter of 1942–43, Haakon Chevalier came to our home. It was, I believe, for dinner, but possibly for a drink. When I went out into the pantry, Chevalier followed me or came with me to help me. He said, "I saw George Eltenton recently." Maybe he asked me if I remembered him. That Eltenton had told him that he had a method, he had a means of getting technical information to Soviet scientists. He didn't describe the means. I thought I said, "But this is treason," but I am not sure. I said anyway something, "This is a terrible thing

to do." Chevalier said or expressed complete agreement. That was the end of it. It was a very brief conversation.

Robb: In other words, you thought that the course of conduct suggested to Eltenton was an attempt at espionage, didn't you?

Oppenheimer: Sure. . . .

Robb: Now let us go back to your interview with Colonel Pash [security officer]. Did you tell Pash the truth about this thing?

Oppenheimer: No.

Robb: You lied to him?

Oppenheimer: Yes.

Robb: What did you tell Pash that was not true?

Oppenheimer: That Eltenton had attempted to approach members of the project — three members of the project — through intermediaries.

Robb: What else did you tell him that wasn't true?

Oppenheimer: That is all I really remember.

Robb: That is all? Did you tell Pash that Eltenton had attempted to approach three members of the project?

Oppenheimer: Through intermediaries.

Robb: Intermediaries?

Oppenheimer: Through an intermediary.

Robb: So that we may be clear, did you discuss with or disclose to Pash the identity of Chevalier?

Oppenheimer: No.

Robb: Let us refer, then, for the time being, to Chevalier as X.

Oppenheimer: All right.

Robb: Did you tell Pash that X had approached three persons on the project?

Oppenheimer: I am not clear whether I said there were three X's or that X approached three people.

Robb: Didn't you say that X had approached three people?

Oppenheimer: Probably.

Robb: Why did you do that, Doctor?

Oppenheimer: Because I was an idiot.

Robb: Is that your only explanation, Doctor?

Oppenheimer: I was reluctant to mention Chevalier.

The questioning continued, and Oppenheimer repeatedly had to confess his folly.

Another dramatic point in the proceedings came when the prominent physicist Edward Teller was called to testify about his colleague, friend, and scientific adversary. Teller was born in Hungary, but came to the United States as a refugee in the 30's. The freedom and warmth he found in this country made him permanently grateful and determined to do everything in his power to help his adopted country. He had given years of his life to the cause of U.S. defense. Now he had to evaluate a scientist who had worked on similar problems.

Asked by the Board whether Oppenheimer was disloyal to the U.S., Teller replied:

"I do not want to suggest anything of the kind. I know Oppenheimer as an intellectually most alert and very complicated person, and I think it would be presumptuous and wrong on my part if I would try in any way to analyze his motives. But I have always assumed, and I now assume, that he is loyal to the United States."

Questioning then veered toward Oppenheimer's role in the development of America's nuclear weapons. After giving Oppenheimer lavish praise for leading the work on the atomic bomb, Teller described how the situation changed when it came to developing the hydrogen bomb:

"It is my belief that if at the end of the war some people like Dr. Oppenheimer would have lent moral support, not even their own work — just moral support — to work on the thermonuclear gadget, we could have kept at least as many people in Los Alamos as we then recruited in 1949 under very difficult conditions.

"I therefore believe that if we had gone to work in 1945, we could have achieved the thermonuclear bomb just about four years earlier. . . ."

Critics felt that Oppenheimer placed his own ideas of morality above those of national security.

And there is some evidence that of the three arguments he used against the hydrogen bomb — military, technical, and moral — the last may have been the overriding one.

Gen. Kenneth D. Nichols, general manager of the AEC, had written to Oppenheimer shortly before the hearings about the charges being lodged against him. In his reply, Oppenheimer explained his actions, including the position he took on the "super":

As to the super itself, the General Advisory Committee (of which he was chairman) stated its unanimous opposition to the initiation by the United States of a crash program of the kind we had been asked to advise on. The report of that meeting and the Secretary's notes reflect the reasons which moved us to this conclusion. The annexes in particular, which dealt more with political and policy considerations — the report proper was essentially technical in character — indicated differences in the views of members of the committee. . . .

It would have been surprising if eight men considering a problem of extreme difficulty had each had precisely the same reasons for the conclusion in which we joined. But I think I am correct in asserting that the unanimous opposition we expressed to the crash program was based on the conviction, to which technical considerations as well as others contributed, that because of our overall situation at that time such a program might weaken rather than strengthen the position of the United States.

After the report was submitted to the Commission, it fell to me as chairman of the committee to explain our position on several occasions, once at a meeting of the Joint Congressional Committee on Atomic Energy. All this, however, took place prior to the decision by the President to proceed with the thermonuclear program.

This is the full story of my "opposition to the hydrogen bomb." It can be read in the records of the general transcript of my testimony before the joint congressional committee. It is a story which ended once and for all when in January

1950 the President announced his decision to proceed with the program. I never urged anyone not to work on the hydrogen bomb project. I never made or caused any distribution of the GAC reports except to the Commission itself. As always, it was the Commission's responsibility to determine further distribution.

But the newspaper columnist Joseph Alsop, who defended Oppenheimer after the security hearings, quotes him as saying later about the H-bomb: "I guess I concluded it wouldn't work because I wanted it so much not to work."

Critics suggest that if Oppenheimer's attitude had prevailed, the U.S. might have suddenly found itself in a disastrous military situation. Soviet dictator Joseph Stalin, for example, could have used a monopoly on the H-bomb as international blackmail against the Western democracies.

Even so, Oppenheimer's opposition was not clear-cut. At several stages he gave Teller valuable suggestions on how to proceed with work on the bomb. Furthermore, Oppenheimer was only one of many leading scientists who agreed that the H-bomb was, or should be, unworkable.

The fact that so many scientists had endorsed Oppenheimer's position and strongly sympathized with him as he went through the security hearings later hurt Teller's position in the scientific community. Teller's own uncertain attitude toward Oppenheimer can be seen in his testimony about whether Oppenheimer could safely be given security clearance:

"I believe, and that is merely a question of belief and there is no expertness, no real information behind it, that Dr. Oppenheimer's character is such that he would not knowingly and willingly do anything that is designed to endanger the safety of this country. To the extent, therefore, that your question is directed toward intent, I would say I do not see any reason to deny clearance."

But Teller added:

"If it is a question of wisdom and judgment, as demonstrated by actions since 1945, then I would say one would be wiser not to grant clearance. I must say that I am myself a little bit confused on this issue, particularly as it refers to a person of Oppenheimer's prestige and influence. May I limit myself to these comments?"

His testimony completed, Teller walked over to the leather couch on which Oppenheimer was seated, shook hands, and quietly said: "I'm sorry." Oppenheimer replied incredulously: "After what you've said, I don't understand what you mean."

Several days and many pages of testimony later, the Personnel Security Board voted 2 to 1 that Oppenheimer's security clearance should be revoked. One principal reason was his failure to be more forthright about the Haakon Chevalier episode. Professor Evans of Loyola dissented, arguing that: "He did not hinder the development of the H-bomb and there is absolutely NOTHING in the testimony to show that he did!"

The AEC then voted 4 to 1 to confirm the Board's findings. In conclusion, the AEC stated:

"These episodes separately and together present a serious picture. It is clear that for one who has had access for so long to the most vital defense secrets of the Government and who would retain such access if his clearance were continued, Dr. Oppenheimer has defaulted not once but many times upon the obligations that should and must be willingly borne by citizens in the national service.

"Concern for the defense and security of the United States requires that Dr. Oppenheimer's clearance should not be reinstated.

"Dr. J. Robert Oppenheimer is hereby denied access to restricted data."

Denial of security clearance not only removed Oppenheimer from association with American military matters, but it also effectively ended his influence in the Government. He retired to his position as head of the Institute of Advanced Study in Princeton, badly wounded by the stigma of unreliability. For years afterward he was trailed by Government agents when he traveled, his phone was tapped, and his family exposed to public embarrassment.

But before his death in 1967, a kind of reconciliation took place between Oppenheimer and the nation to which he had given so much of himself. In 1962 President John F. Kennedy invited him to a dinner at the White House for Nobel Prize winners. The following year J. Robert Oppenheimer received the AEC's coveted Enrico Fermi Award for his contributions to the development of atomic energy. Among the leading U.S. scientists who had nominated him was Edward Teller.

QUESTIONS FOR DISCUSSION

1. *Weapons Development and National Security.* Oppenheimer's opposition to the H-Bomb was apparently a major reason for denying him security clearance. A number of public figures have opposed antiballistic missiles and chemical-biological warfare not only on moral grounds but on the claim that such weapons endanger world security and, therefore, threaten rather than strengthen United States security. Suppose the president orders the development of new superweapons in the ABM and CBW arsenal, and four scientists express their opposition as follows:

A is employed by the Defense Department. He makes public speeches against developing new weapons, but reveals no classified information.

B works on classified research and leaks information to United States newspapers so they can expose the horrendous nature of the weapons, particularly their dangers to the American population.

C works on classified research and leaks information to foreign "enemies." This, he maintains, will prevent each nation from launching a military attack based on ignorance of its adversary's weapons, thus helping to preserve a balance of power.

D is called to Washington to give advice on the weapons project. He refuses to cooperate with the government on the grounds that the proposed weapons are "immoral and a threat to world peace."

Add Oppenheimer to the list and rank the five from most to least threat to national security. What criteria would you use to define national security and security risk?

2. *Preserving Security and Preventing Smear.* The Oppenheimer hearings attracted nationwide attention and cast great doubts on Oppenheimer's competence and loyalty. Many argue that his reputation was smeared, especially because of the publicity given to accusations that were not proven and accusations that were considered irrelevant to his role in the H-bomb project. It is argued that once the press reports accusations against someone, even if he is later found completely innocent, the damage to his reputation is impossible to repair. One suggestion for preventing public smears is to ban the public from all security investigations, to hold inquiries in secret sessions,

and to dismiss security risks without public notice. What is your opinion of this policy?

Case: Suppose it was learned that the new wife of Dr. Bradley had deep sympathies for the North Vietnamese and the mainland Chinese people. She contributed money to welfare organizations in those countries, and often opposed what she called United States imperialism in Asia. Bradley, a physicist working on a classified weapons project, was quietly dismissed from his job as a possible security risk. Although all his superiors praised his accomplishments and ability as a physicist, an agency regulation prevented them from recommending him for employment elsewhere. There was no publicity, but his record showed that he was dismissed for reasons of security. He applied for jobs in universities and in business, but was continually denied employment because of his dismissal from the government project.

Should some public policy guarantee that Dr. Bradley will not be denied a job elsewhere because of his dismissal from a classified government project? If so, what policy would you recommend and why?

3. *Security and Privacy.* It is argued that citizens do not have unalienable rights to participate in classified projects and that this is a special privilege open only to those willing to work under certain conditions. Suppose a government agency decided that personnel with access to classified information would be electronically bugged and that all their conversations would be monitored around the clock. Although they would not be told the specific form of eavesdropping, they would be warned before they accepted employment that "you will be subject to electronic surveillance on and off the job." Suppose also that the Supreme Court ruled that evidence gathered by this process could not be accepted in court unless it was relevant to violation of a security regulation. Would you favor or oppose such a practice and why? Do you believe such a policy would have resulted in a more equitable treatment of Oppenheimer?

Chapter 7 # Consent

I. Illustrative
Issues and the
Ideal

A theme recurring through historical accounts of political upheaval and revolution is the struggle of individuals and groups for the "inalienable" right of self-government. This ideal inspired American patriots to battle the British, Algerians to expel the French, and the Confederacy to secede from the United States. Residents of urban ghettoes who demand community control of schools, college students who press for a voice in university policy, and California voters who frequently modify their constitution by referenda all struggle to implement their notion of "consent of the governed." Vietnam war opponents object that the American people or Congress did not formally consent to administration policy. Conscientious objectors refuse to go to war and kill without the "consent" of their individual consciences. Laws prohibiting homosexuality or adultery are opposed by those who argue that the mutual consent of participants should justify such acts. An embittered Negro disavows loyalty to the United States government because he never voluntarily chose to become part of this society.

Despite differing definitions, applications, and phrasings, these problems have a common concern — the felt need or right of individuals and groups to control (or at least have the power to influence) their destiny. This is perhaps the most general meaning of "self-government," the persistent desire for which manifests itself in controversies between colonies and mother countries, labor unions and employers, churches and the state, students and schools, and even child and parent. Disputes on applying the consent ideal usually revolve around two broad issues: (1) To what extent does a given policy result from a process of consent of the governed? This factual problem cannot be resolved without also dealing with the definitional issue — what are the different and more or less appropriate meanings of consent? (2) To justify a given policy, how important is it to demonstrate that a par-

184

ticular consent process was followed? Perhaps other values will be held more important than consent in certain situations.

One major source of confusion and disagreement is the idealized notion of consent taught in the schools and adhered to by laymen and professionals alike. The historical context is a small seventeenth-century agrarian community, Puritan meetinghouse, or even the Mayflower. Citizens voluntarily band together and decide to give up certain individual freedoms in return for the security provided by collective government.[1] Community members have equal voice in town or church meetings in which policies are decided through open discussion by almost all citizens, each of whom maintains active and informed interest in public affairs. When consensus cannot be reached, majority rule is accepted. In such settings individuals actively participate in forming policy that affects them. Those minorities who cannot adjust are free to form their own communities.

We question the extent to which any communities of the past conformed to this classic democratic model. Perhaps small agrarian communities of the past were ruled largely by elites, backed in silence by general apathy. Perhaps those citizens who did participate in policy-making formed their opinions through irrational personal concerns or jealous and selfish opportunism rather than through impartial study and rational discussion. Despite doubts about the historical authenticity of the classical consent model, and despite numerous threats to the model's operation in modern technological society, Americans continue to construe the general ideal of self-government in terms of the traditional historical image.

Although the democracy suggested by the town meeting or Puritan congregation seems unworkable in complex mass society, even the most cynical would wish to retain certain aspects of the model: for example, the right of each citizen to an equal vote; majority rule; efforts to keep the citizenry informed through freedom of the press; restrictions that make the majority, at certain times, subject to the consent of individuals or minorities. In what kinds of controversies does a particular aspect of consent seem to be possible or desirable? Many problems fall into three general categories: issues involving the ability of an individual to influence policy in such powerful institutions as government and business; issues involving the balance between majority rule and minority rights; and issues of personal choice that relate less directly to public policy.

---

[1] Earlier versions of contract, applicable to English restrictions on the monarch's power, stressed the ruler's abdication of absolute power in return for obedience and support of the ruled. Thus the ruled delegate their powers of self-government to the ruler, who, in turn, agrees to rule in their interest. In addition to the importance of mutual obligations between ruled and ruler, contract has come to mean that governmental power should not be exercised arbitrarily. That is, one must justify or give reasons for infringements on others' rights to consent or self-government. For a more thorough historical analysis, see Plamenatz (1968).

II. Individual's Relationship to Institutional Policy	Although consent theory focuses primarily on the relationship of the individual to government, the issues can be generalized to nongovernmental institutions that influence the individual's life — business corporations, labor unions, churches, hospitals, or universities. Problems arise as to "how much" or what kind of consent the individual should have in his dealings with the institution. We can distinguish different possible degrees of consent.
A. Active Participation (or Assent) in Particular Policy	At one extreme are those who claim that all citizens should have a right to formulate or at least vote on almost all specific policies or decisions made by a governing body, whether the decision concerns street cleaning or declaring war on a foreign country. One should not be morally bound to obey any given policy unless he himself has assented to it. Extreme formulations of this position tend to be quickly dismissed as impractical at best, or even leading to anarchy in complex mass society. Nevertheless, parental efforts to gain community control of school policy or student efforts to share in governing universities should be seen as serious attempts to apply this interpretation of the consent ideal. It does work apparently in small voluntary associations (social, religious, and business groups) that make policy decisions only after all members have had the opportunity for extensive discussion: e.g., in certain Quaker meetings.

The "purest" form of direct democracy also requires *consensus*. The group cannot act without the unanimous assent of all individuals (at least dissenting individuals cannot be forced to obey the majority opinion). Opposition to this interpretation of consent stresses two points. First, it would be impossible for the average citizen to undertake detailed study of all specific issues that involve complex and numerous public policy decisions. Therefore, special individuals with the time and commitment to study public issues are designated "representatives." Representatives chosen by election must presumably carry out the citizens' will in order to stay in office. Second, because of large populations and the diverse interests of groups within governmental units, unanimous consensus would be a virtual impossibility. To avoid anarchy, the group must act and dissenters must obey. Majority rule thereby replaces unanimous consent.

B. Representation	To meet the problems posed by direct democracy, we can define a consent process based on representation and majority rule (see the following section on majority rule–minority rights). But who is to be represented? Should children be allowed to choose their own representatives on school boards? Should consumers be guaranteed representation on business corporations? Should aliens and criminals have the right to vote? Should public welfare recipients be represented on welfare boards? Should the military be represented in allocating foreign aid? What representation should students have

in determining school policy and curriculum? Should citizens be represented on police review boards? A major criterion for establishing whether someone deserves to be represented in governing an institution is to ask whether he is affected by the policies of the institution. If so, he is presumably entitled to representation because "people should have a voice in policies that affect them." On this basis students claim a voice in governing schools and universities. Universities also affect other "constituencies": blue-collar service workers, townspeople, parents of students (who must cope with the "knowledge" and attitudes their children bring home), alumni, government officials who are advised by academic experts, book publishers, and professional athletic teams. All these and certainly other segments of the population are significantly influenced by policies and activities within the university. But should all have a direct voice in the university's government? On what basis should we choose those constituencies deserving the most direct representation? To know that one is "affected" by an institution is an insufficient principle. We need more specific guidelines.

By distinguishing between formal authority and informal influence, we can avoid some problems in creating strict constitutional representation for all people affected by an institution. It is suggested, for example, that children are virtually represented on school boards because their parents have children's interests at heart; or that consumers do influence the policies of manufacturing companies, exercising their votes through spending dollars in the market; or that citizens do control the police by being able to elect city officials. Discussing the problem at this level shifts the question from "who has a right to be represented?" to the factual question of whether the form of representation is sufficiently influential or effective to constitute meaningful consent.

Another problem is to arrive at criteria for selecting those few citizens who act as representatives. Implicit in the discussion so far is the criterion of popular election by majority or plurality. Yet we also delegate power to representatives on other criteria. Choosing *not* to elect vast numbers of leaders, we allow them to be appointed by other elected or appointed authorities (e.g., judges, cabinet members, administrative heads, etc.). We delegate to physicians, engineers, lawyers, and scientists the power to make decisions affecting our lives, because their expertise is considered superior to ours. Seniority, whether in the labor union, the military, or Congress, is often another consideration that earns some people more power than others. Wealth, achievement, or even sex may also discriminate between those people who participate in policy-making versus those excluded from participation. (Chapter 5 on equality discusses in greater detail criteria for unequal distribution of power and privilege.) Whether local parents or professional educators are more "qualified" to run an urban school; whether

General Westmoreland or Senator Fulbright is more qualified to make judgments about United States policy in Vietnam; whether the legislature or the Supreme Court should make national policy in race relations — these are controversies over criteria for selecting those "representatives" who will act for individuals unable and/or unwilling to exercise direct consent to particular policies.

A third issue is the proper role of representatives.[2] To what extent should these officials reflect or follow the will of their constituents? To what extent should they act independently of popular will, or even try to shape public opinion to accept their personal views? Some argue that elected officials have little choice — they must follow public opinion to stay in office. Appointed officials (such as judges), relatively free from public pressure, are more obligated to act independently. Yet what about the elected representative who believes majority opinion to be in serious error or possibly morally wrong? Should he endorse what he considers misguided policy to avoid losing his office? Assuming he does so with the argument that if he stays in office, sometime in the future he will be able to correct past mistakes and implement more justifiable policy, how often can this apparent betrayal of conscience occur before he loses integrity? Similarly, the Supreme Court judge may feel that "legally" a given act is unconstitutional. Not subject to popular election, he should be able to act on impartial legal opinion. But the issue under consideration may be so socially explosive that a court ruling contrary to public sentiment could pose threats to the very existence of stable legal process. To what extent should the judge take public opinion into account in his decisions?

To conclude that representatives have some obligation to follow the opinions of their constituents or the public still leaves the problem of identifying the constituents or the public. Whom should the representative heed? The majority, the most vocal groups, or the group with the most power to influence policy (and the representative's future)? Perhaps the representative's obligation is to construct from the differing views of individuals and groups a somewhat new composite or "compromise" view, not necessarily identical to the position of any power or opinion bloc. Such a combination or composite position could be what Rousseau was suggesting when he used the term "general will." In balancing such views one must decide how much weight to give the wishes of different groups and individuals. Should educated professionals be listened to more than poorly educated laymen? Should organized groups be given more attention than individuals? How relevant are legal-geographical boundaries in defining one's constituents (what obligations does a Congressman from Maine have to the people of Chicago)?

---

[2] Here the term is used broadly to mean any official, however chosen, whose job is to shape the policy in the public interest.

That an elected representative must often speak for hundreds of thousands of constituents and thousands of groups can lead to pessimism or disenchantment not only with the classical model of active participation by individuals, but also the representative system itself. Consent of the governed can be redefined to cope with such difficulties. We may assume that by and large individuals do not have direct access to institutional policy-making through representatives. They may exercise their will in forming policy by joining pressure groups who through collective organization of manpower and funds try to influence public officials. Rather than exercising particular consent, individuals give *general* consent through periodic elections in which each person has an equal vote to choose officials or representatives. The periodic vote is the major act of consent. It means that until the next election, the voter has consented to delegate most of his political power to the representative who will act on his own wisdom, but cannot guarantee that he will follow the will of each individual on particular issues. This view of representation emphasizes the individual's consent primarily as delegation of power, rather than the ability to "speak through" one's representative on specific issues.

C. Disposition of Acceptance

The previous redefinition will not satisfy those who wish to have a more direct influence on public policy. Candidates and their supporters who lose elections do not really wish to be ruled by the victors. Except for original settlers and "founding fathers," most citizens have *not* had any meaningful opportunity to accept or reject the constitutional consent system under which we operate. Each generation does not consciously choose to be subject to this government. Negroes have observed that they did not choose to become United States citizens. To interpret consent in modern society as voluntary social contract is inappropriate, for individuals currently do not have a real opportunity to accept or reject either particular policy or the general constitutional system. Admitting our inability to affirm or deny in discrete and binding acts whether we wish to participate in the existing consent process, some would argue that consent still exists, but is given less consciously. By virtue of our continuous and longstanding obedience and participation in the system, the argument goes, we have consented to it. Without clear protest, revolution, or emigration, we should assume that voluntary individual consent has been given, albeit through a general attitude or disposition rather than discrete affirmation.

This argument transforms the concept of consent from active individual participation (with risks of anarchy) to passive acceptance or lack of protest, with risks of massive apathy. Should we say, however, that those slaves who did not revolt consented to slavery; that because the Germans failed to overthrow Hitler, they consented to the Nazi regime; or that because young people attend school, they consent to compulsory education? The failure to try to alter one's lot can be construed as acceptance of, or consent to, the situation only if one has had a reasonable opportunity to leave or to select an alternative to the status quo. In such cases, a decision not to protest represents a clear choice among options. But to the extent that one is coerced into accepting action or prevented from examining alternatives, this absence of choice amounts to a denial of his right to consent.

III. Majority Rule and Minority Rights

Majority rule has been seen as a device for maximizing individual consent or assent to public policy, assuming that unanimity could rarely be reached and that striving for consensus would imperil the government's ability to act efficiently. Accepting majority rule, however, has not obscured or solved other consent issues.

A. Powers and Rights of Divergent Minorities

It is commonly held that even the majority must place some limits on its own power and that in some areas minorities who do not consent to majority policy should retain powers of consent or self-government. Certain freedoms in the Bill of Rights, for example, are presumably protections for minority groups and individuals against excesses by the majority in Congress or separate states. Religious expression, speech, and property ownership are some major areas in which groups and individuals are said to be immune from majority rule and/or state infringement.

1. Activist, Dissenting, Evangelical Minorities

We can distinguish between active minorities who try to change the majority and those minorities who wish mainly to be left alone: for example, isolated religious communities (the Amish), consciencious objectors, or the American Indian. Activist minorities would include socialists and communists in the United States, student radicals, black revolutionaries, peace-marchers, right-wing extremists. Religious missionaries, economic development experts, Peace Corps volunteers, or community organizers could all be considered "outside agitators"; that is, minorities intervening in "foreign" communities.

Arguments over rights of minorities to intervene in or change majority policies can be clarified by distinguishing between the minority's goals and objectives versus its tactics of persuasion and implementation. Goals are often stated as general values — peace, equality, economic development, religious salvation, self-determination, etc. Minorities who phrase their objectives as general Creed values are often not trusted when the majority (or perhaps a ruling power that does not represent the majority) feels threatened. Activists' motives are often questioned: they are really just stirring up trouble, or destroying the government without providing a better alternative; they are agitating for their own self-interest, rather than the community at large; they seek to destroy values and life styles cherished by the majority;

they are attempting to impose a new totalitarianism that would deny minority rights.

Once the goals and motives of a minority are identified, one can judge its legitimacy. If one disagrees with the purposes, one must decide to what degree the minority should be restrained. If one supports the purposes, one must decide how much freedom to give the minority in implementing its program. The general commitment to freedom of speech, religion, and political association tends to justify allowing minorities considerable freedom to employ various persuasive tactics: mass demonstrations, private and public meetings, canvassing, and using media (newspapers, pamphlets, television, films). Limitations on minority rights to dissent and evangelize are usually justified by arguing that actions which tend to advocate and incite violent overthrow of the government (or bring other seditious consequences) can be outlawed, as can actions that tend to interfere with constitutional majority rights (e.g., private property, free exercise of religion, etc.). Should advocates of black power, socialism, atheism, or free love be given access to the mass media and the schools equal to that enjoyed by "the establishment" (which may or may not represent the majority)? Dissenting minorities, although not openly advocating violence, may cast enough doubts on accepted norms to undermine faith in the existing consent process. On the other hand, the consent process may be strengthened by giving minorities the opportunity to challenge the status quo. The latter cannot occur unless protestors are allowed considerable freedom to disturb the majority's thoughts. At what point, however, does challenge and disturbance become social disruption, constituting a "clear and present danger" to the social system or the preservation of majority rights?

2. Minorities Wishing the Right to be Left Alone

Amish parents refuse to send their children to state schools that allegedly inculcate values and ideas contrary to the Amish religion. Jehovah's Witnesses refuse to salute the flag or say the Pledge of Allegiance. Nudists and hippies wish to form communities radically different from the society at large. Debate continues on the extent to which the majority should require conformity from minorities who wish merely to be left alone. Groups who engage in polygamy, hallucinogenic drugs, homosexuality, or gambling; the South seceding from the Union; or blacks refusing to be bussed into schools of the white majority are other examples of minority factions struggling for autonomy.

In contrast to minorities who wish to secede or withdraw, some minorities have been clearly exploited by the majority. Consider the internment of the American Indian on "reservations," the oppression of the Negro, relocation of Japanese-Americans, or discrimination by local religious majorities (the Puritan banishment of Roger Williams or Protestant exclusion of

Jews in country clubs). In limiting the rights of aliens, in establishing literacy, residence, and age requirements for voting, and in barring criminals or communists from public office, the majority (or at least those in power) has exercised the option to exclude certain groups from participation in the official channels of consent.

Restrictions on "deviant" minorities are often justified by claiming that the minority's action (even though it may not attempt to convert the majority) tends to undermine the majority's institutions. For example, it is argued that Jehovah's Witnesses who refuse to salute the flag destroy the patriotism of young schoolchildren, that gambling leads to immoral and economically dangerous behavior in the larger community, and that drug use results in violence against innocent citizens. Restrictions can also be justified by asserting that a minority should not be permitted to do harm to itself: thus, a Christian Scientist should not deny his child medical care; the Amish should not prevent their children from learning about the "outside world"; and drug users should not be allowed to destroy their minds.

Although civics and civil liberties lessons usually emphasize ensuring that majorities do not deprive minorities of fundamental rights, we have given less attention to the rights of minorities to discriminate against members of the majority. Many would agree that Armenians composing a small minority in a largely Catholic town are justified in excluding Catholics from their church. Similarly, a local bar association should be able to refuse membership to nonlawyers, i.e., a majority of the community. The black separatist movement raises a more difficult issue. Suppose blacks gain control of a neighborhood school (either public or private) and deny admission to whites. Many would oppose this with the argument that *any* racial discrimination is wrong. Others could suggest that the black minority should have a right to exclude members of the white majority from black institutions. This discrimination could be justified by appealing to the need for compensation for previous deprivation and oppression by whites, the need for some discrimination to maintain cultural distinctiveness, and also by pointing out that the minority does not have sufficient power to effectively control the majority or take away its unalienable rights. In considering the extent to which a given minority has the right to be left alone, we must also determine when the minority can exclude the majority from participation in its institutions.

B. In What Sense Does Majority Rule?

In addition to injustices of "tyranny by the majority," powerful minorities can violate the consent ideal: the nobility in feudal society, military juntas, or power elites in "democratic" communities. Studies into the realities of societal power and decision-making claim that major United States policies are determined by small but powerful elites not directly responsible to majority popular will (e.g., Mills, 1956; Kolko, 1962; Domhoff, 1967; Lundberg, 1968). Such research points to the extensive influence of a professional military class, a small group of corporate executives controlling vast proportions of the country's economic assets, a class of highly educated technicians and academicians (Galbraith, 1967) whose advice determines policy for major institutions, and the masters of a media industry who shape public taste and opinion. Studies on citizen participation in the consent process (e.g., Berelson, Lazarsfeld, and McPhee, 1954; Campbell, Gurin, and Miller, 1954; Burdick and Brodbeck, 1959; Hero, 1959; Almond, 1960) claim that only a small minority (perhaps 15 per cent) actively engage in politics and that rarely are officials elected by a majority of those eligible to vote.

Did the majority of Americans choose to defend South Vietnam? Did the majority of Americans choose to reject racially segregated schools in 1954? Did the majority of Americans choose to create a polluted atmosphere, squalid urban slums, or even spray deodorants? Such questions force us to examine dynamics of power that go far beyond representative government, majority rule, or minority rights. In spite of studies just cited many questions remain about the actual influence or net effect of powerful, nonelected elites. To what extent are their interests united? To what extent does apparent collusion signify conscious, willful conspiracy to exploit the public? In what sense do conflicting elites create countervailing forces that protect the public from monopolistic power? Whether war is good or bad for business; whether real competition exists in the auto industry; whether management and labor inevitably have conflicting interests; whether the media industry can express independent positions or must bow to the wishes of its advertisers — these problems deserve continuing study.

In studying the history of a local urban renewal project, the marketing of a new product, the operation of a newspaper or television station, the formulation of a foreign policy decision, or the design of a school curriculum, one can inquire about the extent to which majority opinion tends to influence important events versus the role played by individuals and pressure groups immune from majority will. This should help to differentiate between those decisions in which the majority-rule aspect of consent seems operative, those in which other facets of consent are relevant, and those that violate almost any form of consent.

IV. Consent in Personal Choice

Other interpretations of consent emphasize less the conflict between majority and minority groups and more the freedom of the individual to control his personal destiny, immune from intimidation or coercion by government, other institutions, or persons. Choosing an occupation, a spouse, a type of education, a place to live, books to read, how many children to have, and friends to enjoy are matters of personal "consent" that can develop into broader issues of public policy.

A. State Limits on Personal Choice

Because of the familiar assertion that "personal freedom for the society as a whole requires placing some limits on individual freedom," the state imposes restrictions on the individual's power to control his own destiny: compulsory school attendance, military service, taxes; laws prohibiting racial discrimination, homosexuality, adultery, drug use; regulations on child rearing and adoption; restrictions on those receiving public welfare; compulsory collective bargaining in labor disputes; government policy that rewards and creates more incentives for some careers, e.g., scientists and engineers, than others, e.g., poets and conservationists. It is even unlawful in many states to commit suicide. Proponents of such restrictions can argue that they do not on balance constrain or enslave an individual, but in effect enlarge and expand his power to control his destiny. Objections against state-imposed limits on specific choices must take this argument into account, along with other criteria (e.g., law and order or majority rule) commonly used to justify state limitations on personal consent.

B. Consent and Contracts

One form in which personal consent is exercised is making agreements with and promises to other individuals. The state supports the freedom of individuals to consent to a variety of mutual obligations, duties, and privileges: marriage; payment for services rendered; acceptance and release of legal liability; assigning one's rights to others (e.g., author-publisher contracts). The common law upholds mutual consent by providing that a person cannot claim to have been wronged by the results of an arrangement to which he voluntarily agreed. At the same time, the law acknowledges circumstances to which individuals may legitimately be excused from contractual obligations. Statutory law also prohibits individuals from making certain voluntary agreements: conspiracy to commit a crime; agreements in restraint of trade; and restrictive and discriminatory covenants. Other agreements, although not explicitly forbidden, are simply not enforceable through the courts: a girl breaks a date to a dance; a teacher decides to give a test despite an earlier promise to the contrary; a father, after agreeing to pay his ten-year-old son for mowing the lawn, refuses to pay. We need to establish criteria to distinguish between those personal agreements that the government should honor and enforce; those that should be prohibited by statute; and those that should be neither enforced nor outlawed by the state.

C. Availability and Awareness of Alternatives

Personal choice can be limited not only when specific alternatives have been deliberately prohibited (through statutory action or economic and social sanctions), but also when, through oversight or lack of inventiveness, alternatives have not been created, or when individuals are simply unaware of alternatives that do exist. A mother for the first three years of her child's life read only the story, "The Three Bears." On the child's third birthday the mother was convinced that he was now old enough to select stories on his own, and she asked, "What story would you like to read tonight?" " 'The Three Bears,' Mommy," replied the child. An upper middle-class high school student is asked what he wishes to do after he earns his diploma. "Go to college," he answers with assurance. To what extent do such responses represent free choice, or personal consent to one among several possible alternatives?

If one's ability to choose depends largely on his awareness of alternatives, and if the state is to enhance personal consent, then public and educational policy should attempt to create a broad range of alternatives and to heighten individuals' awareness of them. But to ensure that people entertain alternatives could *inhibit* their choice in the short run. For example, people engaged in specialized endeavors could be required to avail themselves of more diverse experiences. A teacher might be expected to try another occupation while on professional leave. Students could be required to survey several fields prior to choosing a major subject. Citizens might be given opportunities to live in several cultures before they declare citizenship to one. Television networks might be forced to provide programming diverse enough to attract small as well as large audiences, and manufacturers could be enjoined to create a wider range of products. To reduce coercion, we might distinguish between *providing incentives* (e.g., scholarships, stipends, tax deductions, sabbaticals, etc.) and *requiring* the creation and examination of alternatives, which implies punishment. "Voluntary" incentives offer more acceptable manipulation.

We are still left with the contradiction that to maximize freedom of choice, we must restrict it. The child who begins to study the violin after two weeks may conclude he cannot enjoy it. If one believes that genuine enjoyment comes only after achieving some mastery, he might plead with the child to continue: "You won't know whether you like it until you know the feeling of mastery; to decide now would not be an informed choice because you have not yet had the experience of mastery." With this argument one might justify policies that, in requiring people to sample alternatives, could be construed initially as restrictions on personal consent.

Personal consent discussions must recognize the extent to which sufficient alternatives actually exist, policy issues on the ways in which institutions and individuals should be regulated to preserve diverse options, and the more philosophical issue of free will–determinism. As pointed out in Chapter 4, conceptions of free choice have been attacked by psychological theories stressing multiple causation or the overwhelming power of institutions to thwart individual choice, and by theological positions claiming man to be the puppet of divine forces. Unless extreme manifestations of these theories are refuted, it makes little sense to debate the legitimacy of specific public policy designed either to expand or restrict personal consent.

V. Competing Values

We have suggested widely differing contexts in which consent ignites public controversy and situations in which one might reject or violate some facet of consent because another general value is considered more important. Some values commonly used to justify denying consent follow.

A. Competence

Individuals are often denied direct participation in policy-making because their skills are considered insufficient. This deprives laymen, and also well-educated persons who specialize in the wrong field, of opportunities to shape policy in business, the professions, the church, and government. Laymen are not allowed to make specific decisions on the United States space program, nor are space physicists allowed to build dams and highways. Because they are said to be unqualified, students are denied a voice in governing schools. Specialization results in giving differentiated power to those skilled in particular fields, thus making it impossible for citizens to have equal consent power in all areas. Arguments persist, however, on what constitutes competency, or what qualifications are appropriate for given decisions and tasks.

B. Efficiency

Even if we could assume that all men were equally competent to make decisions on all questions, we might still limit direct participation because of the waste of time and effort if every individual were involved in every decision that affected his life. Discussion could continue indefinitely and bring such confusion that few effective decisions would ever be made. Efficiency, therefore, limits the privilege to wield active consent power to a relatively small group of representatives and administrators not only in government affairs, but in most other institutions as well.

C. Wealth and Property

Few seem to question the right of corporation owners to have final authority for corporation policy, although owners may delegate their power to managerial executives. Nonstockholders are not presumed to deserve any formal control over businesses. Homeowners are (within limits) allowed to govern their "castles." Those who can afford membership in expensive social clubs have rights of consent in those organizations from which the poor are excluded. Organizations with large amounts of money may spend it to influence government policy, and are thereby entitled to more consent power than impoverished interest groups. Chapter 8 considers property in greater detail.

D. Legality

The suburbanite who complains that he has no formal voice in city government or the defendant who objects that he is not able to choose his judge or the poor man who argues that the United States system of government allows unfair advantages for the wealthy — all hear a standard answer:

"This is the way our constitutional system operates. We have developed certain offices, duties, and methods of selecting leaders. We have legal-political boundaries that establish the jurisdictions in which individuals may exercise consent power. To call for a modification of the legal system is possibly to cut a critical thread in the time-tested social fabric." The argument that one has a duty not to depart from the legally constituted status quo may be used to discourage demands for types of consent power that the existing system has not provided.

E. Conscience

Each preceding value may be used to deny direct consent power to individuals. Individual conscience and choice, though apparently consistent with the consent ideal, can challenge one important aspect of consent: majority rule. Consent of the governed has both collective and individual interpretations, but its collective form obliges individuals to abide by the will of the group. In some situations, however, individual conscience can be invoked to justify disobedience or violating the group's decisions. The conscientious objector, the person who engages in civil disobedience to protest what he considers an immoral law, the school drop-out who opposes the middle-class achievement orientation of his college, or the lone dissenter who leaves his church to avoid obeying its decrees — all may invoke individual conscience to justify failing to accept policies reached through the consent process of groups to which they belong. Such persons evidently place high priority on that aspect of consent connoting individual choice and control of one's personal destiny.

THE FUGITIVE SLAVE LAW
Abolitionists protest and violate a federal law they consider unjust.

A fugitive slave clause had been one price demanded by Southern delegates for approval of the U.S. Constitution in 1787. This clause (in Article IV, Section 2) provided that:

No person held to service or labor in one State, under the laws thereof, escaping into another shall in consequence of any law or regulation therein, be discharged from such service or labor, but shall be delivered up on claim of the party to whom such service or labor may be due.

The constitutional provision was backed up by the Fugitive Slave Law of 1793. This law said

This case is taken from Donald W. Oliver and Fred M. Newmann, *The Civil War: Crisis in Federalism,* American Education Publications, Columbus, Ohio, 1969.

that slaveholders could go into other states to recapture their slaves with the aid of state officials. But the Supreme Court decided in 1842 that state officials were not obligated to help in recapturing slaves. After that, several Northern states passed "personal liberty" laws that *forbade* state officials to help in catching runaway slaves.

Slaveholders were furious over such actions and over the increasing success of the "Underground Railroad," which eventually made possible the escape of as many as 100,000 slaves, worth about $30 million in Southern markets.

The Fugitive Slave Law of 1850 made not only state officials but also *all* citizens responsible for the capture of runaway slaves.

It provided that a Negro accused of being a runaway slave would be returned to his owner without the rights to a trial by jury or to testify in his own behalf. The truth of the accusation against him would be determined by a commissioner chosen by a federal circuit court. If the commissioner decided in favor of the owner (or the owner's agent) he received a fee of $10, paid by the owner; if he decided against the owner, the fee was $5. The law required "all good citizens" to "aid in prompt and efficient execution of the law," and allowed federal officials to "summon bystanders to their aid." Any citizen who aided a slave to escape could be heavily fined.

The passage of the Fugitive Slave Law angered Northern foes of slavery.

When Thomas Sims, an escaped slave, was arrested in Boston, broadside posters of the following kind began to appear around the city:

CITIZENS OF BOSTON AWAKE! A free citizen of Massachusetts, free by Massachusetts laws until his liberty is declared to be forfeited by a Massachusetts jury is Now imprisoned in a Massachusetts Temple of Justice. The compromises . . . are to be crammed down the throat of the North. The kidnappers are here. Men of Boston! Sons of Otis, and Hancock and the brace of Adamses! See to it that the Massachusetts laws are not outraged with your consent! See to it that no free citizen of Massachusetts is dragged into slavery without trial by jury.

But all was in vain. At three o'clock on the morning of April 13, a United States marshal and a guard of 300 police led Sims to a ship in Boston Harbor. The ship took Sims to Savannah, where he was publicly whipped and kept in a prison cell for two months. He was later sold to a Vicksburg brickmason.

But even this excitement was tame compared to Boston's agitation over the case of Anthony Burns. On the evening of May 24, 1854, Burns, a 24-year-old Negro, left the Brattle Street clothing store where he had been working for a month since his escape from slavery in Virginia. As he passed the corner of Hanover and Court streets, a man touched him on the shoulder. "Stop, old boy!" the man said, and then explained that he was under arrest for having robbed a jewelry store. Burns halted in bewilderment. Instantly, six or seven men surrounded the Negro, picked him up by the arms and legs, and carried him down the middle of the street to the court house.

At the entrance, a United States marshal was waiting with a drawn sword. The men then hurried the prisoner up several flights of stairs to a jury room that was to serve as a cell. Suddenly Burns realized what had happened: he had been arrested, not as a jewel thief but as a fugitive slave.

This suspicion was immediately confirmed when Colonel Suttle, his former owner, entered the jury room. "How do you do *Mr.* Burns?" Suttle sarcastically greeted him. "Why did you run away from me?" The Negro replied: "I fell asleep on board the vessel where I worked, and, before I woke up, she set sail and carried me off." That was enough: Burns had recognized Suttle and tried to justify his escape; in effect, he had confessed that he was a fugitive slave.

Soon afterwards, Burns was taken before Commissioner Edward Loring who was to rule on the case. According to the law, Commissioner Loring declared, the case was perfectly plain and the decision totally inevitable: Burns must be given over to his former master. Many Bostonians urged resistance to the Commissioner's decision.

"See to it . . . that Anthony Burns has no master but his God!" said Wendell Phillips, a lawyer famed for his oratory, as he addressed a meeting at Faneuil Hall on May 26.

The Rev. Theodore Parker followed Phillips' speech with one still more passionate:

"Well, gentlemen, I say there is one law — slave law; it is everywhere. There is another law, which also is a finality; and that law, it is in your hands and your arms, and you can put that in execution just when you see fit. Gentlemen, I am a clergyman and a man of peace; I love peace. But there is a means, and there is an end; liberty is the end, and sometimes peace is not the means toward it."

By this time many in the crowd were ready to launch an attack on the court house that very night. Phillips managed to quiet them down, until suddenly a man at the entrance door shouted: "Mr. Chairman, I am just informed that a mob of Negroes is in Court Square attempting to rescue Burns. I move that we adjourn to Court Square." No one waited for a vote. The crowd poured out of Faneuil Hall, surged around the court house and began to assault it with a battering ram.

The door soon was broken enough for two men at the front, the Rev. Thomas Wentworth Higginson and a nameless Negro, to enter. They quickly reappeared, cut by the swords and clubs of the defending officials inside. The mob pressed forward with new anger. Then one of the marshal's men within the court house fell beside the door with a mortal stab wound. The crowd now drew back, dismayed by this flow of blood. They soon dispersed.

Meanwhile, the more peaceful antislavery people had begun negotiating with Colonel Suttle for the purchase of the captive Negro. Suttle's price was $1,200 cash. The money was raised and a bill of sale was about to be drawn up when the United States district attorney intervened. He

objected that the sale should not be made until the commissioner had decided the case. He also pointed out that Massachusetts law forbade selling a man. The bargain fell through.

Now the antislavery forces had only one more chance of saving Burns: to prevent the federal officers from getting the fugitive onto the ship moored in the harbor, one-third of a mile away from the court house. Handbills were circulated through the city, urging the people to "Watch the Slave Pen!!" Notices were mailed to residents outside of town: "Sons of the Puritans," the message declared, "come to watch the removal of Burns with courage and resolution in your hearts; but, this time, with only such arms as God gave you."

At 8:30 on the morning of June 2, the troops (which the fearful federal officials had requested) paraded on Boston Common. In all there were 22 companies, including two cavalry units, totaling over 1,000 soldiers.

By 11 o'clock, Court Square was packed with sullen Bostonians. Above them, at the eastern door of the court house, stood a loaded cannon pointing at the crowd. The tension grew. Finally, at 2 o'clock, the troops formed a column and began to march toward the wharf, followed by Burns in the middle of an armed posse. Thousands of people lined the route. So did the symbols of their feelings: a black coffin hung from a window opposite the Old State House, decorated by a banner reading "The Funeral of Liberty." Nearby, an American flag was draped in mourning.

In the end, however, Burns was put aboard the ship and sent to Richmond. There he stayed in a cell, his wrists and ankles shackled, for four months until he was sold to a North Carolina slaveholder.

Massachusetts did not forget the incident. Wendell Phillips persuaded the state legislature to petition the governor to remove Commissioner Loring from his judgeship. The governor refused. But the legislature persisted. It passed a "personal liberty law" prohibiting the seizure of any fugitive slaves. No other fugitive slave was ever again arrested on Massachusetts soil.

A week after Burns was shipped to Virginia, James Freeman Clarke, a Unitarian minister, voiced the feelings of most of his fellow Bostonians:

"So the Slave Power . . . has come North to Boston, has taken possession of our Court House, of our City Government, of our whole Police Force, our whole Military Force, and suspended and interrupted the business of our citizens until its demands could be satisfied. . . . Now would be the time for this community to put on mourning — to wear black crepe on the arm; because Honor is dead, because Humanity is dead, because Massachusetts has been placed by her own acts beneath the feet of Virginia."

QUESTIONS FOR DISCUSSION

1. *Consent in a Federal System.* Do you think Boston citizens should have obeyed the federally passed fugitive slave law even though they opposed it vigorously? If so, should the people who resisted federal enforcement have been punished? After Massachusetts passed its own law prohibiting the seizure of fugitive slaves, which law were Massachusetts citizens most obligated to obey?

If you believe that Massachusetts citizens were justified in resisting federal law, would you also support the right of southerners to pass "Jim Crow" laws that violate federal statutes? Why or why not?

In 1964 the voters of Akron, Ohio, added an amendment to their city charter, which repealed a fair-housing law that had been passed by the city council and said that before a fair-housing law could take effect in Akron, it had to be approved by a majority of the voters in a citywide referendum.

In 1969 the United States Supreme Court decreed the charter amendment to be unconstitutional. The Court held that by singling out fair-housing laws as the only ones subject to the special referendum requirement, Akron had denied its Negro citizens the equal protection of the laws guaranteed by the Fourteenth Amendment to the Constitution.

A dissenting opinion of the Court said, "there is no constitutional provision anywhere which bars any state from repealing any law at any time it pleases."

Do you think Akron voters should be allowed to pass such modifications of their charter? What additional information would you need to help you decide? How is this controversy related to the conflict on the Fugitive Slave law in Boston?

2. *Uniformity and Diversity Among States.* "If the North had been tolerant enough to allow the existence of slavery in the South," one might argue, "the Civil War could have been avoided. All states should not be forced by the federal government to have the same laws and customs. The federal government must be tolerant and respect diversity in the states' ways of doing things."

Article IV of the Constitution includes the following provisions:

Full Faith and Credit shall be given in each State to the public acts, records and judicial proceedings of every other State. . . . The Citizens of each State shall be entitled to all Privileges and Immunities of Citizens in the several States. . . .

Suppose you were President of the United States, concerned with preserving the Union, but also favoring self-government and freedom for different people. As you look around the nation, you observe that states follow differing policies on certain matters and some groups urge practices quite different from the national majority. For example:

a. States differ in the age at which people become eligible to vote, drive a car, or buy alcoholic beverages.

b. Gambling is prohibited in most states, but allowed in some. Although all states prohibit prostitution, suppose one or a few states voted to legalize it.

c. In some states it is easy to obtain a divorce, although in others, people seeking divorce suffer serious legal problems.

d. Most public schools in the country are racially segregated; only a few are integrated with proportions of black and white students reflecting the national racial percentages.

Try to list rules or principles that tell you for what problems a uniform national policy is desirable and for what problems it would be better to let states do as they wish. In what ways are these questions related to the problem of Anthony Burns in Boston, May 1854?

RELIGIOUS FREEDOM: TWO CASES

The Case of Sharon Garber

Does religious freedom include the right to be let alone — even from laws enacted for the public welfare?

In 1965 when the fuss began, Sharon Garber was a petite and pretty 14-year-old. She lived in the Kansas farming community of Yoder (population 275) about nine miles southeast of Hutchinson. Her father was a successful farmer. He provided well for his wife and four children.

Sharon lived a way of life quite different from that of most American teen-agers, a way that hadn't changed much in 250 years. She was a member of a small, tightly knit religious minority known as Old Order Amish.

At the heart of Amish belief is a biblical command: "Be not conformed to the world." To the Amishman this means that one should not dress and behave like the worldly (in effect, the rest of society) who are considered to be dominated by a Satanic Kingdom. Thus Amish doctrine forbids intimate contact with persons outside the community.

To help them keep "unspotted from the world," the Amish have established a strict code for church members to follow in their personal lives. The "Plain People," as they are called, wear somber, modest, old-fashioned clothing. Women wear ankle-length dresses and full bonnets. They may not wear bright clothing or high heels, or wave their hair. Similarly, the men wear dark clothing, broad-brimmed black hats, and beards.

The Amish shun almost all modern conveniences. They drive horse-drawn buggies. In their homes the Amish get by without large mirrors, pictures, overstuffed furniture, electrical appliances.

The traditional occupation of the Amish is farming, which they consider the purest means of earning a livelihood. Amish children are brought up and educated to become farmers. They are immersed in Amish religion from their earliest days. Because the Amish do not seek outside converts, they must pass down their religion and culture to their children if their way of life is to survive.

The Amish consider public education, with its worldly environment, not only evil but also a threat to their existence. This reasoning impels the Amish to forbid formal education beyond the eighth grade. That is how Sharon became the center of a case called *Kansas v. Garber*.

Sharon's father, LeRoy Garber, refused to send Sharon to Partridge High School, a coeducational public school about ten miles from her hometown. Kansas school officials said that state law required her to enroll there.

Were Sharon's rights to practice her religion being taken away by Kansas school laws? A group of prominent educators and church leaders said they were. They organized the National Committee for Amish Religious Freedom to carry the legal battle to the U.S. Supreme Court if necessary.

The controversy began on October 18, 1965, when the Reno County Court charged Sharon's father with "failure to have his daughter attend continuously a public school or a private denominational or parochial school taught by a competent instructor."

Sharon had finished eighth grade in May 1964. She attended the small public school that serves Yoder. Then Sharon left school to follow traditional Amish education around home and farm.

This case is taken from Donald W. Oliver and Fred M. Newmann, *Religious Freedom: Minority Faiths and Majority Rule*, American Education Publications, Columbus, Ohio, 1967.

Sharon was studying basic subjects — math and languages — every Friday morning at Harmony School, a private Amish school at Yoder. Her teacher was Amos Borntrager, an Amish farmer who had an eighth grade education. There were nine other students.

The rest of Sharon's education went on at home. She spent an hour a day on correspondence courses from a school in Chicago and hours of on-the-job training in home and farm management, taught by her mother.

This education did not meet state requirements. A few years before there would have been no problem. But the Kansas legislature in the summer of 1965 had amended the old law, which required only an eighth grade education, to say that children must remain in school to the age of 16.

Amish leaders at Yoder tried to obey the law by establishing Harmony School and setting down rules for home study. A leading Amish spokesman had summed up the major reasons for such actions:

We want to keep our boys and girls on the farm but we can't do it if we permit them to mingle with things of the world. Their minds become filled with all these new ideas. . . .

E. Dexter Galloway, a Hutchinson lawyer who defended LeRoy Garber against Kansas state charges, said, "This is what the outside world doesn't understand. . . . The rest of us, we separate — I'm a Methodist and a lawyer, for example. But with the Amish there is no separation. They live their religion. . . . When you get into big consolidated schools there are kids from all areas. The Amish youngsters are thrown in with strangers. Their dress is unique. They are picked on, discriminated against."

Glenn Seaton, the superintendent of public instruction in Reno County, took another view. He had visited the Partridge school, where about 25 Amish were enrolled. He said the school was "bending over backwards to make them welcome."

He described the Amish people of Yoder as "pretty resolute. They just won't go along. I have

nothing against these people at all. But I took an oath to uphold the law and they're not meeting it." Mr. Seaton also asked, "Suppose this child grows up with an eighth grade education. Are the parents doing a justice to that child?"

The county court did not think so. The judge fined LeRoy Garber $5 for allowing Sharon to violate the law. The conviction was upheld by the Kansas Supreme Court. On Nov. 5, 1966, the court said:

The natural rights of a parent are subordinate to the police power of the state and may be restricted by municipal law providing minimum educational standards. . . . The individual cannot be permitted upon religious grounds to be the judge of his duty to obey laws enacted in the public interest. . . . Religious liberty includes the absolute right to believe but only a limited right to act.

Donald A. Erickson, a college teacher and a member of the new committee for Amish freedom, disagreed. He defended Amish education in the *Saturday Review:*

In terms of the Amish culture, the Plain People's approach to education may be one of the most effective yet devised. Their success in training the young to be farmers has impressed many agricultural experts. . . . Amish prosperity and self-sufficiency are legendary. These are not the characteristics of a preparation for adulthood that has failed.

The Amish have lived with problems like Sharon Garber's throughout their history.

In the early 1700's the Amish-Mennonites left Switzerland, their founding place, for greater religious freedom in Germany. They left Germany for an even larger measure of freedom in America. (In recent years some Amish may have concluded that America, too, is not a safe haven. A group of them recently left Arkansas for South America.)

The Amish situation in Pennsylvania illustrates a pattern of development. For years, the Amish were left alone to educate their children as they saw fit. But in 1937 Pennsylvania passed a law that raised the age for compulsory education to 16 in rural areas. The state called Amish schools inadequate and ordered many of them closed.

In 1949 an Amish appeal came before the Pennsylvania Superior Court. The court ruled that the children might stay at home.

The victory was short-lived, however. A few months later, in another case, the court reversed itself. The decision left the Amish subject to arrest if they failed to send their children to school up to the age of 16. The early 1950's was a time of arrests, fines, and jail sentences for the Amish.

In 1954 a compromise known as the "Home Study Plan," similar to that under which Sharon Garber studies, was generally accepted. Some Amish communities avoided trouble by simply holding students in the eighth grade until the age of 16. From time to time Pennsylvania applied the school laws to the Amish, but always found them unyielding. Pennsylvania compromised by fitting the school code to the Amish.

Today about 45,000 Amish live in 19 states, 80 percent of them in Pennsylvania, Ohio, and Indiana. Some states have viewed the school laws broadly in regard to the Amish.

But other states, like Kansas, insist that the Amish send their children to school as required by law. In these states the issue is a vital one: Which comes first, public law or private belief? The Amish, for their part, hold and practice one view.

The Case of William Murray

Can public school prayer exercises really be "voluntary"? A ninth grader turned that question into a national issue.

William Murray, III came home one day in September 1960 from Baltimore's Woodbourne Junior High School. He was upset. As young teenagers sometimes do, he nagged his mother.

The incident might have been taken as a matter of course in most American homes, ending in a short spat or a few soothing words. But because the Murray household was different, the 14-year-old's complaint stirred up a constitutional issue that had remained cloudy for more than a century.

Bill protested to his mother that prayers were being recited in his ninth grade class. He said, his mother later recalled, "that he was an atheist and could not participate in school prayers. If I made him do it or allowed him to do it, I was a hypocrite."

Mrs. Madalyn Murray was not a person to let such taunts go by. She was a divorcee, a social worker with college degrees in sociology and law, and a past worker in various civil rights causes. Her general ideas were "against authority," and she extended these ideas to her two sons, Bill and his younger brother Garth.

Atheism was not one of her causes. She had until 1960 described herself as simply "unconcerned" about religion. Her son's needling changed that, and she took the step that would ultimately cause her to be billed on magazine covers as "the most hated woman in America."

This case is taken from Donald W. Oliver and Fred M. Newmann, *Religious Freedom: Minority Faiths and Majority Rule*, American Education Publications, Columbus, Ohio, 1967.

Mrs. Murray petitioned the Baltimore Board of Education to have her son excused from the classroom during the daily five-minute Bible reading and recitation of the Lord's Prayer.

The board's answer came through Dr. George B. Brain, the superintendent of Baltimore schools. He said that the Bible reading and prayer were required by a 1905 rule of the board, which had never been challenged. He said that Bill could remain silent, but could not be excused.

On October 12, 1960, Mrs. Murray informed the board that her son would stay out of school in protest. She accepted legal help in her action from the American Civil Liberties Union.

Bill returned to school on October 28 after the board agreed to refer the case to Maryland Attorney General C. Ferdinand Sybert. On November 2 the Attorney General ruled that objecting pupils could be excused from the classroom during Bible and prayer exercises.

That might have ended it but for the public response to the wide publicity about the case. Bill became the target for kicks and punches by fellow pupils as soon as he got back to school. Stones were thrown through the windows of the Murray home, and paint was smeared on it. The windows of Mrs. Murray's car were broken and the tires slashed. Harassing telephone calls and violent letters began to flow in upon her.

"I decided," said Mrs. Murray, "that the whole country was sick, and one relatively sane person had to make a stand."

Mrs. Murray sued for the end of school prayer exercises in Baltimore.

Help came for Mrs. Murray's cause from Leonard J. Kerpelman, a lawyer who agreed to serve without guarantee of fees. Mr. Kerpelman himself described the case as "nutty." On the other hand, he was an Orthodox Jew and he had felt some personal discomfort over the religious exercises when he was a student in Baltimore schools.

The court dismissed the case on April 28, finding it "abundantly clear" that Mrs. Murray's "real objective is to drive every concept of religion out of the public school system."

Mrs. Murray took her case at once to the highest state tribunal, the Maryland Court of Appeals.

Arguments went on for months before the Court of Appeals. Finally, on April 6, 1962, the Court decided 4–3 against her appeal. The majority opinion said that "neither the First nor the Fourteenth Amendment was intended to stifle all rapport between religion and the Government."

Five weeks later, Mrs. Murray filed her petition with the U.S. Supreme Court. Within 24 hours she was dismissed from her job as a Baltimore social worker. The vandalism of the Murray home, the vicious telephone calls, and the vitriolic letters reached a new pitch. The letters did little to soften the crusty tone of Mrs. Murray's conversation. Her temper rose more to suit her self-imposed nickname: "Mad" Murray.

But Mrs. Murray had at least one thing to even her temper on June 25, a month after she filed her petition. Several New York taxpayers had brought a suit called *Engel v. Vitale* to the Supreme Court. They objected to a prayer recommended by the New York State Board of Regents and required as part of opening exercises in one district's schools. The short prayer went this way:

Almighty God, we acknowledge our dependence upon Thee, and we beg Thy blessings upon us, our parents, our teachers, and our country.

Defenders of the prayer called it "nondenominational." Some of the opponents of the prayer called it a "to-whom-it-may-concern" prayer. The Court voided the prayer requirement as a violation of the First Amendment. The 6–1 majority opinion granted that the prayer was "relatively insignificant," but repeated the old warning of James Madison that "it is proper to take alarm at the first experiment on our liberties."

The decision made Mrs. Murray's chances of success look far better. Still her case led to crackling debate when it came to the Supreme

Court for lawyers' arguments on February 27, 1963.

"If we strike this prayer down," Justice Potter Stewart suggested to Mrs. Murray's lawyer, "we are interfering with the majority's right to free exercise of their religion. . . . Why not just walk out? You are not required to participate."

But William Murray had been excused, Mr. Kerpelman replied, and had been "spat upon, insulted, actually assaulted" by some of his classmates as a result.

Justice Hugo L. Black broke in to question Justice Stewart's point: "The free exercise clause," he said, "does not give a right to pray in a public setting with governmental support and funds."

Francis B. Burch, Baltimore city attorney, made a rather unusual argument. He claimed that, though the Bible reading and prayer had religious origins, they were in fact required because of their "sobering influence" on students. The exercises established an atmosphere of good discipline and morality, he told the Court.

"You could just give them tranquilizer pills if that's the purpose," snapped Justice Potter Stewart.

Attorney General Thomas J. Finan of Maryland argued that the majority of the people in any area should be free to use their prayers in schools. Questioned by the Justices, he agreed that this could include Mormon prayers in Utah or Buddhist prayers in Hawaii.

"Then," commented Justice William O. Douglas, "the big contest would be to see which church could get control of the school board."

On June 17, 1963, the Supreme Court ruled in Mrs. Murray's case, together with the case called *Abington School District v. Schempp*, in which a Pennsylvania couple challenged their state's law requiring Bible reading exercises to start the school day. The Court held, 8 to 1, that both the Pennsylvania and Baltimore laws violated the establishment clause of the First Amendment.

The majority opinion repeated the Court's recognition in an earlier case that "We are a religious people whose institutions presuppose a Supreme Being."

The Court added its support of Bible reading and comparative religions courses "when presented objectively as part of a secular program of education." The Court found, however, that:

. . . the states are requiring the selection and reading at the opening of the school day of verses from the Holy Bible and the recitation of the Lord's Prayer by the students in unison. These exercises are prescribed as part of the curricular activities of students who are required by law to attend school. . . . We agree . . . as to the religious character of the exercises. Given that finding, the exercises and the law requiring them are in violation of the establishment clause. . . . Nor are these required exercises mitigated by the fact that individual students may absent themselves upon parental request. . . .

Thus William Murray's jibes at his mother culminated in a court decision that touched students in every state. Mrs. Murray's court victory brought a strong reaction from editorial commentators and religious and social groups who charged that the nation's public schools were being made "godless." But congressional hearings on the issue turned out an equally strong support for the decision by spokesmen of major Protestant, Roman Catholic, and Jewish church groups.

School prayers continued to win the majority support of Americans polled in public opinion surveys. The Court decision, however, had answered the question of majority support in advance by quoting an earlier opinion:

The very purpose of a Bill of Rights was to withdraw certain subjects from the vicissitudes of political controversy. . . . One's right to . . . freedom of worship . . . and other fundamental rights may not be submitted to vote; they depend on the outcome of no elections.

1. *Consent Power and Religious Freedom.* Do you think the Kansas decision requiring Sharon Garber to attend public school violated her religious freedom or her right to consent? Was the Baltimore Board of Education requirement that William Murray be present during prayer reading an infringement of his religious liberty or consent rights? What are the important similarities and differences between the cases?

2. *Consent Rights of Chidren versus Parents.* Suppose in each following situation that the commands of parents, based on religion, go against the wishes of a child. Do you think the state should step in and overrule the parents in any cases? Why or why not?

a. A Christian Scientist denies medical aid to his child.

b. A parent of one faith prohibits his child from associating with children of other faiths.

c. A father forbids his daughter to date boys of other faiths.

d. A Seventh Day Adventist prohibits his child from going to Christmas parties and exchanging gifts with other children.

e. A parent prevents his child from visiting services with a friend of a different faith.

f. A Jehovah's Witness refuses to allow his child to salute the flag in school.

g. An atheist refuses to allow his child to enroll in a high school comparative religions class.

h. A father forbids his child to dance at school social affairs.

3. *Coercion to Enhance Choice.* Suppose an Amish child argued with his parent: "You have no right to prevent me from exploring other religions and systems of belief. How can I choose one religion as best unless I have some awareness of other alternatives. The state should force you to allow me to sample experiences beyond our Amish tradition." Would you agree or disagree?

Suppose that a high school established a required course in comparative religions to help inform students (of all faiths) about varieties of religious belief. Mrs. A, the teacher of the course, explains that she has tried to present a "broad and positive view" of religion by inviting spokesmen for nine religious denominations and an atheist group to express their views before the class. She has asked each representative to speak "with feeling" about his own religion, but not to debate or criticize other religions. She has also encouraged class members to go together, on a voluntary basis, to the weekend services of the religious groups represented.

Some parents have protested that such a course infringes on religious freedom. Others argue that it increases religious freedom by making people more aware of alternatives. Would you support or oppose such a required course? Why?

4. *Majority Rule–Minority Rights.* It is argued that minorities (such as atheists or Jews) by trying to have school prayers outlawed are in effect depriving the majority of religious freedom. What is your view of this argument as a rebuttal to court decisions that have outlawed religious exercises in public schools?

Chapter 8   # Property

"We are by nature stubbornly pledged to defend our own from attack, whether it be our person, our family, our property or our opinion. . . . The little word *my* is the most important one in all human affairs and properly to reckon with it is the beginning of wisdom" (James Harvey Robinson, 1932).

I. Illustrative Issues

By extending our imagination, we could construe virtually all public issues as economic conflicts over the distribution of wealth and rights of ownership attached to personal and collective "possessions." The word *my* implies that ownership or possession (of intangible as well as tangible "property") creates rights, liberties, and obligations that would otherwise not accrue to a person or group. In this chapter, we discuss problems relevant not only to distribution and ownership of real wealth, but also those problems that arise when we include as "property" a person's children, his skills, his reputation, or his potential economic value.

Consider a sample of the wide range of problems to which concepts of property can be applied. (1) A colonizing power (e.g., England) takes land from primitive tribes (Africans or American Indians) who claim legitimate ownership because of years of prior occupation. Later, when the conquered natives demand independence, the colonists claim rights to some wealth because the investment and labor they provided stimulated economic development. (2) A labor union demands higher wages and better working conditions because their physical labor gives them a just claim to the company's profits. The company refuses to capitulate because it legally "owns" the business. (3) A merger is dissolved by the government and fined for unfair

209

business practices. (4) A program that taxes the wealthy to uplift the poor is opposed by those who claim that giving handouts will destroy the poor's initiative and willingness to work. (5) An urban renewal program is applauded for its efforts to beautify and modernize a city, yet opposed because it takes private property and dislocates a closely knit community. (6) Laws against prostitution or child labor are criticized for restricting the freedom of an individual to sell his services as he wishes. (7) A landlord or restaurant owner, prohibited from discriminating by race, complains that he should be able to choose his clients as he wishes. (8) A parent objects to compulsory schooling, or to the curriculum offered by a school, because it interferes with the parent's right to raise his child his own way. To clarify any issue within this broad constellation, one should first identify the particular conceptions of ownership and property rights that the case implies.

II. Establishing Ownership

What are various ways by which a person or group can legitimately acquire or claim possession of property? Controversial issues arise in part from applying conflicting criteria for ownership.

A. Conquest

Although the rhetoric of modern democracy rejects violent conquest as a way of legitimately acquiring property, we must acknowledge its acceptance in the past: e.g., American preemption of Indian claims, the Spanish-American War. To the extent that one accepts a social Darwinist view of reality — or even a "white man's burden" viewpoint — then conquest seems a justifiable means to acquire territory or scarce resources. Conquest is also considered an acceptable response to provocation or imperialistic aggression by an outsider: e.g., America's right to "reconquer" the Pacific in World War II or its right to prevent Communists from conquering Korea or South Vietnam. The question of when conquest becomes legitimate is interwoven with issues of national welfare–security discussed in Chapter 6.

B. Occupation

Ownership of unoccupied property can be established by those who inhabit it, on a first-come-first-served basis. Land holdings acquired by "squatters' rights" illustrate this principle, as does the familiar claim that America belonged to the Indians, or Africa to the Africans, because "they were there first." Although the principle of prior occupation seems persuasive in a frontier, nonindustrial setting, it can be challenged. (1) How much land or property can a person or group claim as "occupied" by them — must they physically settle on every inch, and if not what are their rights to land used very seldom or not at all (e.g., hunting grounds, undeveloped oil fields, or the moon)? (2) Assuming that several groups claim land almost simultaneously, would it be just to award the property to A and deny it to B simply by arrival time — should a minute or an hour really make the difference?

(3) Other principles are often more important: for example, a tenant who occupies property is not entitled to the property, because his contract allows him only limited rights; occupied land can be taken if it is needed for "community benefit"; through inheritance, a person can acquire land he never occupied.

C. Labor and Productive Use

Colonialists have justified their claim to property previously occupied by natives by arguing that colonial settlers worked to develop the real estate, adding to its productivity and economic value. The person or group who creates or increases the value of property is thereby entitled to proportional ownership. Marx makes a similar argument about the rights of the working class. The worker is entitled to own the means of production and distribution, because his efforts and sacrifices created the economic value of the final goods and services. These principles reflect a general ethical maxim, "as ye sow so shall ye reap," which can be interpreted in at least two ways: the harder one works, or the more *effort* he contributes, the more property he deserves; or regardless of the intensity or pain of one's labor, the more he contributes to the objective value of property, the more he is entitled to ownership.

These principles raise additional prblems. How are we to assess the economic value of various kinds of labor? How should profits in the auto industry, for example, be distributed among factory workers and managers who manufacture the product, patent holders who invented it, capitalists who take investment risks to produce it, advertisers who help create demand, etc.? Why should a secretary be paid less than an executive? Usually in making judgments about the *economic* value of a given job or service, we rely on certain criteria for determining its *social* value as well.

Arguments over whether steelworkers, teachers, doctors, artists, or public officials deserve higher compensation for their services can be clarified by recognizing criteria used to measure economic-social value. Some criteria used to justify various rates of pay follow: (1) The pain-effort criterion assumes that the more unpleasant or undesirable the job, the more one should receive in compensation for having to endure it; thus refuse collectors are said to have a "harder" job than secretaries. (2) Positions involving considerable responsibility for others' actions (e.g., executives and managers) should be more lucrative than jobs in which people merely follow orders, or make decisions that have no significant impact on others. (3) Training and expertise as in medicine, engineering, law, or other professions presumably establish a right to compensation higher than that deserved by unskilled labor. (4) Social service, whether in teaching, social welfare work, public office-holding, or the armed forces is said to deserve higher pay than occupations aimed primarily toward profit. Such criteria need to be explored in greater depth to determine whether they (or some redefinitions thereof) are sufficient for assessing the economic-social value of one's labor.

D. Contract

One can establish ownership through purchase: i.e., a house, land, automobile, livestock, or television set. One can also purchase less tangible property rights: a tenant rents a house or farm; an employer pays laborers for their work; a publisher buys the right to print an author's work; a man purchases the right to marry a woman. Purchase is essentially executing a contract in which buyer and seller exchange property and/or obligations. Persons may lose ownership or rights to property if they violate the terms of their contract. We must distinguish between those contracts or exchanges that seem fair or justified and those that should not be considered legitimate or should not be enforced. Should prostitutes be allowed to sell their services? Should child labor be prohibited? Should each seller guarantee the buyer a safe and effective product (cars and drugs)? Should a doctor agree to perform an abortion? In Section III below we explore limitations imposed on rights of contract (see also Chapter 7 on personal consent).

E. Birth and Inheritance

Parents have such extensive powers over their children that children appear to be treated virtually as property — possessions with few rights of their own. Although children are legally emancipated at age eighteen or twenty-one, the rights of parents (and the state) to control children before emancipation should be examined. How far should parental rights extend? Should parents make and enforce any rules they wish on dating, driving, drinking, smoking? Should they have the power to determine schooling for their children? Should parents have the right to commit abortion or mercy killing of their own children? The extent to which the larger community should have the power to make decisions on such issues or the extent to which children should be given more autonomy are questions of increasing worldwide importance.

Children or other relatives and legatees establish ownership through inheritance that perpetuates and compounds vast disparities in the distribution of wealth. Although one might not dispute the right of a parent to reap as he sows, and thus earn a large fortune, it can be seriously questioned why the child of a poor parent should begin life at an extreme disadvantage to the child of a wealthy one, when neither child has had a chance to "sow." Although Americans have tried to prohibit inequality arising from the inheritance of political power (as in a system of government by nobility), gross inequality in economic power because of family fortune is readily accepted. If we accept equality and equity regarding the distribution of wealth, can we justify the present inheritance system as a legitimate basis for property rights?

We might expect considerable future controversy over ownership or property rights in space, under the sea, or perhaps at the earth's poles. Should any group (private business or nation) be allowed exclusive rights over a given area and if so, on what basis? To what extent would criteria just discussed prove useful in settling disputes over property in these frontier areas?

III. Limitations on Acquiring and Using Property

Various explicit reasons, values, or arguments justify restrictions and limitations on acquiring and using property. Those who ardently endorse "free enterprise" and "property rights" may need to qualify their commitment because of some following considerations.

A. Conflicting Criteria for Ownership

In a sense the quest for property can be seen as a zero-sum game in which ownership or freedom of property for person A automatically excludes or denies property rights to person B. As A and B scramble for unreserved seats at the ball park, they know that prior occupation bestows rights on one person and denies them to another. Prior occupation will not guarantee rights, however, if A and B scramble for a *reserved* seat. C's ticket is a contract that entitles him to the reserved seat, legally superseding all other criteria for ownership. Limits on property rights result largely from choosing some criteria for ownership (outlined previously) as more valid than others in specific situations.

A strong labor union limits the freedom of businessmen to distribute earnings. The freedom of nonunion workers and employers to make individual contracts is sometimes restricted by laws that make collective bargaining compulsory. Although arguments persist over how much control labor should exercise over owners and management, a general commitment to just desert for one's labor, reinforced by political power, limits the property rights of those who own or manage enterprises in which productive work is done by hired labor.

The belief in just desert for one's labor can itself conflict with other bases for acquiring wealth. Servants who work diligently to maintain and increase a millionaire's estate are not thereby entitled to a portion of his inheritance. The wealth may be given to family members who contribute virtually no labor or value to the estate. In this instance property rights based on inheritance prevail over rights based on just desert for labor.

Acquiring property through conquest has historically infringed upon property rights gained through occupation, contract, and inheritance: for example, white settlers who displaced American Indians, or the English who colonized Kenya. Native African property rights were usurped by conquests that brought slaves to the United States. Later the North's "conquest" of the South expropriated from southerners their slave property. Although contemporary domestic property disputes seem to be based on values other than occupation or conquest, these criteria remain important in discussing international issues.

B. Liberty

Disputes over property rights arise not only in conflicts among the criteria for ownership, but also through concern for other general social values such as liberty or general welfare. Personal liberty and equal opportunity have been used to justify acquiring large personal fortunes and economic power. However, unregulated and unrestrained economic liberty produced concentrations of economic power that in effect destroyed opportunities for entrepreneurs to compete. In the late nineteenth century it became apparent that laissez-faire policy originally intended to preserve property rights led to monopolistic control in which a few giant corporations held the power to appropriate property rights of less successful businessmen or of those who had not yet entered the economic struggle. Antitrust laws, attacked by some as encroachments on property rights, were supported by others as necessary to preserve the liberty of businessmen to engage in free enterprise. In the name of economic liberty, restrictions were imposed on businessmen. Antitrust laws aim to limit the market that any single firm can control; they prohibit monopolies and contracts that tend to "restrain trade"; and they prohibit certain business practices (e.g., rate discrimination to eliminate competitors) as "unfair competition."

One persisting problem is to determine what kinds of regulations on business are justified to preserve equal liberty for businessmen, and what kinds are unjustified infringements on their property rights. (Regulations on property designed to protect the consumer will be discussed later.) Mr. Tuttle, a barber in a small town, claimed he was maliciously run out of business by a local banker who, for personal animosity alone, set up a competing barbershop and used his influence to divert customers from Tuttle's shop. Should the banker's privilege to set up a barbershop be limited if his motives are considered malicious? Should supermarkets be prohibited from charging low prices to run small independent grocers out of business (or should the supermarkets be taxed to support subsidies to the small grocers)? Should General Motors be denied the opportunity to control 95 per cent of the auto market if it suddenly made a technological breakthrough that allowed drastic reduction in auto prices and improved quality?

Limitations on property rights, based on a concern for equal liberty, also manifest themselves in prohibitions against ethnic, religious, racial, and even sexual discrimination. It is argued that the innkeeper should not deny a traveler accommodations because of race; the landlord or real estate broker should not discriminate in housing sale or rental; the employer should not discriminate in hiring. If these are justifiable infringements on property rights, would it then be right to require property owners to give people of all races and religions equal access to private homes and social clubs? Should the government establish a racial quota system for neighborhoods and compel vast redistribution of whites and Negroes to bring about integration in housing? Should churches be allowed to ban from their facilities members of other religions considered "heathen"? Should an Irishman be given equal opportunity to work in a Chinese restaurant? Should employers exclude women from jobs that have been traditionally held only by men (e.g., taxi drivers or jockeys)?

To provide equal opportunity for economic mobility, it may be necessary not only to prohibit discrimination, but also to take property from the wealthy and distribute it more equitably throughout the population. Debates on taxation, deductions, and incentives for "charitable" uses of wealth may be seen as controversies over the priorities given to property rights of different social classes or income groups. Is equal economic opportunity for low-income families important enough to justify spending *more* public funds per child to educate the economically disadvantaged? By taxing upper-income groups at a higher rate and spending less per child on them, we are essentially depriving them of property rights to enhance such rights for low-income classes. Approaches to the poverty problem will be discussed in greater detail in Section V.

C. General Welfare

By referring to general welfare or community needs one might justify several other infringements on property rights. Advocates for consumer protection stress business regulation to guarantee the safety and effectiveness of food, drugs, cars, airplanes, and household appliances. Building and zoning codes place restrictions on construction and maintenance for the benefit of the community and the safety of inhabitants. Large amounts of property are taken from owners through eminent domain for public projects (highways, parks, airports, etc.). When the "security" of the nation is at stake, price and wage controls, along with rationing, restrict economic liberty. Truth-in-lending and other controls on financial transactions impose further limitations on both the buyer and seller in business dealings.

One could propose even more severe control of business and property for consumer protection or general welfare. Health and safety standards in industry could be far more stringent (e.g., prohibiting the sale of cigarettes). Heavy penalties could be imposed for polluting air and water. One might even require all companies to cooperate with a centralized consumer information bureau that would select for every shopper the best product available at the lowest price, thus eliminating hardships for deceived consumers or those unable to shop thoroughly. Finally, one might propose to eliminate profit and other devices that allegedly lead to exploitation. Proposals like these evoke enough opposition to illustrate that despite our accepting many restrictions on property for general welfare, there are points at which rights of ownership are considered more sacred than marginal increments to general welfare. The challenge is to define these points in specific public policies and to justify them through qualified general principles.

IV. Basic Issues in the Distribution of Wealth

Thus far we have not detailed general arguments or social theories behind some more specific criteria used either to defend property rights or to advocate their limitations. Major points in the case for free enterprise or private property and the case for socialism raise issues that tend to recur in discussions over the extent to which ownership and property rights should be limited. Recognizing the dangers of oversimplification, we will try nevertheless to identify and summarize the most commonly stated arguments and schools of thought.

A. The Case for Private Property and Profit

1. Appeal to Tradition and Law

The fact that private property has been one of the oldest and enduring human institutions, that it is considered in the natural law tradition to be an inalienable right, and that it has been legally protected both in common law and in the United States Constitution serves for many as sufficient justification for the sanctity of free enterprise. The right is legitimated simply by its traditional acceptance in law and custom. There are, however, more complicated arguments.

2. Human Nature and Needs

Studies of the animal kingdom (Ardrey, 1966; Lorenz, 1966) have produced evidence that a phenomenon known as the "territorial imperative" is essential for survival of the species. The animal is said to require physical space or territory all its own, from which uninvited intruders must be excluded. The human version — "a man's home is his castle" — has been inferred from findings in animal studies that show actual biological and psychological harm to animals whose territory is invaded or reduced. A more positive psychological argument has also been made: man gains personal worth and dignity by combining his labor with his property. Whether we consider a farmer tilling the soil, a banker lending money, or an industrialist building an airplane, satisfaction and personal achievement seem to hinge upon the individual's right to own and work with property as he chooses. It is argued that if these rights are taken away, men will lose the incentive to work in productive and creative enterprises. A final argument suggests that although we may not be able to prove that ownership and property rights are essential to human worth or that their denial would be biologically harmful, nevertheless, men do desire property rights and profit. To contradict or attempt to modify human nature would bring violence and social disintegration.

3. Social Benefit

In addition to fulfilling individual psyches or survival, private property has been defended for its contribution to social progress or advancement. The American free enterprise system is hailed as the most effective way to bring about economic development and to ensure such benefits as longer life spans, increased leisure, and improved health and education. "Progress" is attributed to a system of free competition that provides lucrative profits, which stimulate investment, hard work, and creative thinking to meet consumers' needs. It is also claimed that through the free market system, consumers receive highest quality for the lowest price, and the widest range of choice. To limit ownership or profit-taking in ways that decrease competition among rival producers would infringe not only on the freedom of the business community, but would also slow social progress, limiting benefits and services for the consumer. Those committed to the general values of free enterprise, private property, and profit use these arguments to oppose limitations on rights of ownership.

B. The Case for Socialism

The general case for socialism (there are of course many varieties) includes arguments favoring restrictions on property rights, which may be minor (rules for fair business practices) or extensive (abolition of all private property), depending upon the extent to which private property is viewed as a social evil.

1. Inequality and Exploitation of the Worker

Beginning with their historical protest against laissez-faire capitalism, socialists have continually objected to the vast economic inequality between owners of property and the workers they hired. Those who control the means of production and distribution of goods and services have the power to exploit working classes, and the profit motive rewards and encourages such exploitation. The capitalist will reap increased profits (and power over the workers) if he lowers costs (through low wages and minimum investment in safety and comfort for the workers) and raises the prices that the workers, as consumers, must pay for goods. This keeps workers in perpetual poverty and debt to the wealthy who control credit, as well as jobs and natural resources. Inheritance and property ownership vested in the family unit further exacerbates the exploitation by forcing children of the poor into an inferior economic position before they have a chance to compete.

It is argued that a man deserves income and property in proportion to his needs, his working ability, and his effort, not according to his success in exploiting others. To prevent exploitation and to guarantee distribution of goods and services according to some combination of needs, effort, and ability, profit and the social control attendant to property rights must be either abolished or severely limited. The commitment to economic equality that this protest reflects has been justified by reference to natural law (unalienable rights of all men to an equal chance), Biblical doctrine ("blessed are the meek. . . ."), and other moral sources.

2. Economic Efficiency

Apart from an ethical concern for equality, it is argued that a free enterprise system, encouraging competition among several private firms, each producing similar products, is economically wasteful. Duplicating production facilities and the large amounts of money and talent spent on advertising or taking business away from competitors exhausts valuable resources. Centralized planning and control would eliminate the costs of competition, substantially reducing expenditures for the consumer.

3. Public Interest

Because entrepreneurs are not chosen by the public at large, and they must act primarily to increase profits, they cannot be expected to serve the public interest. If the means of producing and distributing goods and services were owned jointly by all people and controlled by their elected representatives, then the system would be more responsive to public needs.

4. Avoiding Conflict

In a world of scarce resources, the capitalistic system aggravates conflict between "haves" and "have nots." It fosters greed, cutthroat competition, aggressiveness, and lack of trust, rather than peace and cooperation. Not only are workers exploited, but small businessmen and farmers are ruined, large classes are unemployed, professionals and artists become pawns of the relatively few industrialists who control much of the nation's assets. Vast disparities in the distribution of wealth can generate violent conflict that could be avoided if profit were abolished, if property were held in common by all, and if each person were remunerated on the principle "from each according to his ability, to each according to his needs." Such a system would provide material security without economic exploitation.

C. Summary of Issues

Arguments on both sides raise several issues yet to be resolved. (1) What evidence do we have for conflicting claims about the relationship between economic policy and human behavior? Are rights to private property and profit critical incentives required for productive and creative work or do they engender greed and selfishness — undesirable motives that would diminish if private property were abolished? (2) What should be the relative importance of a person's needs, the energy he expends, his native ability, the responsibility he shoulders, his actual contributions to society, or his competitive economic performance in determining how much income or property he "deserves"? (3) To what extent does a free market system built on private property and competition versus a planned or regulated system bring the most social progress at the lowest possible cost? (4) In serving the public interest, what is our frame of reference: a family, a particular social class (workers or owners), an industry (automobile production or telephone service), a town or a country or the world? Why, for example, should a person's native state have more claims to the wealth of a deceased person than poverty-stricken human beings in other states? (5) Although we might reduce disparities in economic power, will it ever be possible to eliminate inequalities of power arising for other reasons (e.g., technical skill, or supervisory role in a bureaucracy)?

Controversies about ownership and property may become less salient in the future. Some have argued that increasing affluence would diminish economic conflicts found to be so pressing in a world of scarcity. Although one might agree with the psychological benefits of man's mixing his labor with his property, perhaps this conception of self-worth must be abandoned in a modern economy where vast, diffuse corporate organization and occupational specialization take people far away from the concrete involvement with property known in rural self-sufficient economies. Those who manage large businesses today do not own them. Even the boards of directors and stockholders rarely have personal holdings large enough to claim exclusive ownership. Workers in government, the professions (medicine, education, engineering, law), and business are increasingly involved in providing human services rather than making or selling goods. Are such salaried workers unable to gain mission or purpose simply because the object of their labor is not something they own? Restrictions on business and professional practices, although they may be construed as limitations on personal freedom or autonomy, perhaps should not be seen as violations of property rights.

V. Approaches to Poverty — An Illustrative Problem

Suppose we are asked to to discuss the general problem: What public policies should be undertaken to cope with the problem of poverty in the United States? In outlining three general approaches (all short of socialist revolution), we can illustrate the relevance of concepts mentioned previously.

A. The Bootstrap Approach

This suggests that each individual should be held responsible for his own economic condition, that the government has no particular obligation to give to the poor, that poverty is primarily caused by lack of motivation, poor morals, etc., and that very little can be done to correct these human failures. However tragic it may be, the poor will be always with us; those with initiative and courage will be able to rise above misfortune. The position could be bolstered by most arguments used to defend an extreme version of the free enterprise philosophy.

B. Incentives for Voluntary Charity

Some would argue that it is certainly not wrong, and on the contrary would be admirable, if some segments of the population voluntarily aided the poor. Accepting that part of the bootstrap argument that opposes requiring the rich to give to the poor, one could still support policies that provided incentives for voluntary contributions from the wealthy. Tax exemptions, low interest loans, monopolistic franchises, matching grants, and rent supplements are various devices that might entice private enterprise to provide housing, jobs, and education for the poor — either as a matter of social conscience or as "enlightened self-interest" to reap financial benefits.

Policy along these lines might stress the notion that wealthy classes should have the right to do social good, so long as they are not compelled or assumed to have a *duty* to do so. Contrary to the bootstrap approach, the incentive approach assumes that improvements can be made; that the poor, with help, can be encouraged to stand on their own feet. Even outright handouts and long-term support to those unwilling or unable to work could be justifiable "charity," if the help is given voluntarily. The distinction between public policy designed to stimulate voluntary giving versus that designed to compel economic assistance can be hard to draw, especially when the funds to support "incentives" are taken as compulsory taxes from the public at large.

C. Massive
   Public
   Assistance

The extreme, most "socialistic" alternative might be heavy progressive taxation on personal and corporate income and property. Wealth would be distributed equitably according to some formula based on needs and work. This approach places economic equality above private property. The moral argument states that owning property, instead of increasing the person's autonomy and freedom, places more social responsiblity upon him. He is morally obligated to share his wealth with the less fortunate. It is denied that this approach will slow economic growth or encourage sloth and indolence. Most proponents argue that such assistance should get the poor on their feet as independent, economically productive people eventually able to care for themselves. Some, however, would advocate permanent handouts for people who choose to work in occupations that fail to provide adequate income (e.g., the arts, or such obsolescent crafts as blacksmithing or cabinet building) or even for those who prefer not to work for a living. Using public funds for people able but unwilling to work is vigorously opposed. But some day it may be necessary to pay masses of people for what is recognized as nonproductive activity. Prospects of increased leisure have led to predictions that eventually it will be impossible to find economically productive jobs for a large part of the population. People already spend much of their lives "learning" instead of "earning," and substantial public funds are dispensed to support students.

Although some have proposed outright grants to the poor or a guaranteed income without strings attached, most public assistance schemes do place limitations on the recipient. Should public welfare recipients be penalized for having additional children or illegitimate children? Should they be required to work in *any* job that becomes available? Should they be prohibited from holding jobs to supplement public assistance funds? Should they be free to spend welfare funds in any way they choose (whether for rent or liquor)? In sickness should the poor patient be entitled to the best medical talent or only second-rate clinical service? In what ways should welfare recipients be prohibited from acquiring certain property: e.g., real estate and "luxury" consumer goods? What "eligibility" requirements are justified: residence, age, employment status, income, dependents, criminal record, an oath to support the government? Should the recipient be expected to give something in return: for example, extra years in the military, Peace Corps, or other public service? Conditions or strings attached to assistance may be seen as restrictions on the property rights of the recipients, whether we have in mind the urban poor of the United States, countries receiving foreign aid, or college students benefiting from government scholarships. The donor may claim as part of his rights of ownership the right to dictate the terms on which he contributes his wealth for the benefit of others. Finally, to what extent should granting or denying welfare benefits be subject to normal due process requirements enforced ultimately by the courts rather than administrative agencies?

The approaches outlined are not mutually exclusive and specific public policies can be consistent with more than one general view. Proponents of different emphases will disagree on such issues as: whether poverty should be attributed to willful laziness and irresponsibility or to complex social forces for which victims should not be held responsible; whether a given form of economic aid is likely to increase or decrease the dependency of recipients; the extent to which using aid should be controlled by the donor or the recipient; definitional problems in establishing a minimal standard of living; distinctions between "necessities" and "luxuries," a job versus a "decent" job, or employment versus "underemployment."

BUSINESSMEN: THE NRA

In the early days of the New Deal the National Recovery Administration helped marshal the cooperation of business.

RECOVERY BY COOPERATION

In an effort to improve the economic condition of the country, Congress in June 1933 passed the National Industrial Recovery Act. Immediately after signing the bill into law, President Roosevelt created a National Recovery Administration (NRA) to carry out its purposes. One primary goal of the new agency was to raise prices to a profitable level by limiting production, since prices tend to go up as goods become more scarce. Another goal was to guarantee to labor a fair work week and a living wage.

Its primary tactic was to obtain the adoption of hours and wages codes by all branches of industry and business, the terms of these codes to be worked out by committees with representatives from management, labor, and the public.

In July 1933, during one of his famous "fireside chats" over the radio, the President explained to the nation how the NRA was functioning:

The proposition is simply this:

If all employers will act together to shorten hours and raise wages we can put people back to work. No employer will suffer, because the relative level of competitive cost will advance by the same amount for all. But if any considerable group should lag or shirk, this great opportunity will pass us by and we will go into another desperate winter. This must not happen.

We have sent out to all employers an agreement which is the result of weeks of consultation. This blanket agreement carries the unanimous approval of the three boards which I have appointed to advise in this, boards representing the great leaders in labor, in industry, and in social service. The

agreement has already brought a flood of approval from every state, and from so wide a cross-section of the common calling of industry that I know it is fair for all. It is a plan — deliberate, reasonable and just — intended to put into effect at once the most important of the broad principles which are being established, industry by industry, through codes. Naturally, it takes a good deal of organizing. . . .

The essence of the plan is a universal limitation of hours of work per week for any individual by common consent, and a universal payment of wages above a minimum, also by common consent.

BOTTLE CAPS AND BLUE EAGLE

A blue-gray canopy of smoke tangled among the light fixtures over the conference room.[1] John Stearns pressed the stub of his cigarette against the edge of an ashtray, then added it to the white mound of other stubs. "Okay, I think everybody understands the general framework within which we're to operate. So let's roll up our sleeves and settle on the terms of a code. Perhaps we'd do best to start with the proposal Simmons mimeographed for us."

Stearns looked around the large oval table at the half dozen men. Most of them were nodding in agreement. The electric light shone palely on their faces, accenting the lines around their mouths and eyes. They were tired. So many statistics, so many arguments had crisscrossed the table during the last two hours. It was hard work to draw up a code for the entire bottling industry of the East Coast.

But most of these men had come well-prepared.

[1] This case is fictional, but it accurately reflects the conditions of the time.

This case is taken from Donald W. Oliver and Fred M. Newmann, *The New Deal: Free Enterprise and Public Planning,* American Education Publications, Columbus, Ohio, 1968.

Henry Simmons understood the New England side of things better than any one single man; that wasn't surprising, since for 35 years his company had done more business than all the other New England bottlers put together. Then there were Fairfield and Carlos from the South, Sand and Abrams from the Middle Atlantic area, and of course Stearns himself from New York. These men knew the industry "inside-out"; every day they handled the details of costs, volume, sales, profits. Their knowledge and energy had earned them the honor of leading the Bottling Trade Association, Eastern Divsion.

And now in this smoky conference room in New York City, with a warm July rain beating on the windows, the six men were preparing to draw up a code for the NRA. "It sure isn't any picnic, making up a code." Fairfield's drawl had a soft, musical quality. "It's like being in charge of every factory from Maine to Florida all at once."

Simmons' smile did not change the hard expression of his eyes. "If it's a choice of this or the cut-throat competition of the last three years, I'll take this." He leaned back in his chair, rolling his tie around a pencil. "Roosevelt's been in office almost five months now, and I still have no doubt whatever that he's a reckless radical. But I'll give him credit for this NRA. It's giving businessmen a chance to get back on their feet. Maybe our prayers have been heard at last, and the trust-busting fantasy has finally been busted. We can get together again without worrying about the Justice Department's antitrust people getting on our necks for it."

Stearns cleared his throat. "Excuse me, gentlemen, but I'd like to get this over with before midnight if possible."

It was a summer day in 1934. Even the shade of the New York skyscrapers did little to relieve the soggy-shirted population. The smell of sweat, the waves of heat rippling upwards from the asphalt, the lethargic flow of bodies moving along the sidewalk — all were marks of a city slowly burning up. On the 16th floor of the Gilbert Building, separated only by a wall from the simmering outdoors, the office of the Bottling Industry Code Authority shared the sluggish summer rhythm. Two fans whirred at each other with a lazy monotony from opposite corners of the room.

"Mr. Claiburn is off the phone, Mr. Hanley. You can go in now."

Marc Hanley slid out of the chair. "Thanks, Mary." He gave the secretary a quick smile as he passed her desk and knocked on the walnut door with its golden Gothic letters, "Deputy Administrator."

"Come in. Oh, hello, Marc. What's the problem?" said Claiburn, looking up from a pile of papers.

"Well, we just got a telephone call from the Potts Company. They claim that S. L. Gross and Company isn't living up to the minimum-wage sections of the code, and that this is permitting them to undersell their competitors."

"Sounds bad," Claiburn replied, squinting his eyes and chewing his lower lip. "Have you checked Gross's monthly reports?"

"I did that as soon as I received the complaint, but—at least according to the material they sent us — everything they're doing is on the up-and-up. I hope they aren't lying."

"I think we had better assign some investigators right away, and go check this out."

"Right, I'll go out myself this afternoon. If this law isn't going to be enforced properly, it might just as well not be on the books at all."

"That's the spirit, Marc." Claiburn murmured, already studying his documents again.

"God, it's hot," thought Hanley as he walked down 15th Street, dabbing a large blue handkerchief across his forehead. "Here we are, number 33, and there's his sign: S. L. Gross & Co." As he climbed to the third floor, he heard the churning of the factory's machines and pictured the long steel thumbs pressing the little cork discs into their scalloped tin containers.

He stated his business to a yawning secretary.

"I'm sorry, sir." she finally responded. "Mr. Gross is unavailable today. Perhaps Mr. Pfeiffer, the general manager, can deal with your questions."

"Well, all right. Where is Mr. Pfeiffer's office?"

She pointed with pink fingernails. "Right through that door and on your left."

"Thanks."

Pfeiffer's door was open, and almost before Hanley was aware of it, he found himself in the chair to which the general manager gestured him. The collar of Pfeiffer's shirt was wilting against his flushed, thick neck. Perspiration dampened his round face.

"I'm from the Bottling Code Authority, Mr. Pfeiffer. We've received a report that you've violated the code for bottle caps, and I just thought I'd stop around to check it out."

"That's completely absurd," Pfeiffer replied. "I'd no more think of violating the code than I would of cheating on my taxes."

"Do you mind if I interview some of your employees?"

"Of course I mind. Who do you think you are, coming into this office and questioning my honesty like this?"

"I don't remember saying anything about your 'honesty.' I merely want to find out whether you are living up to the code."

"Code, code, code . . . that's all I ever hear! Let me tell you about your code. In the old days, before the code, a man had a competitive chance. We didn't have a labor union and that meant that we could really give the opposition a run for their money. If they were silly enough to let all those working stiffs push them around, they had a tougher time of it — and they deserved to have a tougher time of it. What's the old saying? They made their bed, now let them lie in it!" His blunt-ended fingers drummed on the desk blotter.

"I'm really very sorry you feel that way, Mr. Pfeiffer, but you know there is an industrywide agreement, and after all, the majority rules . . . that's the American way. I'm afraid we'll simply have to stop selling you Blue Eagles for your products."

"Well isn't that just too bad!" Pfeiffer sneered. "Blue Eagles! Who cares? Most of the public will buy my product if they can get it cheaper. And besides," he chewed the end of a pencil, "with all the counterfeit emblems, do you think anyone really pays much attention to what should be a *'red'* eagle? That's what your NRA is anyhow, a Communist notion of how to end free enterprise. My workers don't care. They know we're not in the code. But times are tough. They're proud men; they don't need the Government to molly-coddle them. They're not afraid of a little hard work."

"Well, if that's the way you feel. . . ." Hanley rose slowly to his feet. Pfeiffer also stood up, leaning his short body over the desk.

"And besides, if the going gets too rough, I can always get back on the bandwagon. All I have to do is [he snapped his fingers] change a few hourly rates, and you guys will come running back, just throwing those eagles at me."

"Don't you bet on that," Hanley blurted out with irritation. "We're working on schemes to enforce this even better. Before we are done, every loophole is going to be plugged."

"Sure, sure. Maybe the Government wants to take over the business altogether."

"Good-day, Mr. Pfeiffer," Hanley said over his shoulder as he opened the door. "I'll be reporting your code violation to the Administrator."

"Yeah, good-day indeed."

The cardboard sign had been tacked clumsily to the door, so the letters seemed in danger of spilling over the doorknob: "NRA Compliance Division. Hearing in Progress." A secretary clattered breathlessly down the hall, clutching a pad of paper in one hand, and pushed open the door just as the chairman's gavel began thumping on the table. The murmur of the crowd inside the room suddenly evaporated, a few chairs squeaked.

"The meeting will come to order," intoned the chairman, performing a final emphatic rap with his gavel. His thin blond moustache twitched as he surveyed those seated in front of him. "Before the hearing proceeds, Mr. Gross," he said after a moment, "do you wish to make any statement for the record?"

"No, just fire away," Gross replied quickly with a casual wave of his cigarette. One corner of his mouth lifted in a smile, but his dark eyes stared impassively at the chairman. His thick black hair and hooked nose gave him an aggressive, capable appearance.

"Is it true, Mr. Gross, that your company has violated the Bottling Industry Code for bottle caps?" the chairman questioned.

"No, it is not."

"Do you know that on August 15, Mr. Marc Hanley of the Bottling Code Authority visited your plant?"

"Yes."

"And do you know that on that date he spoke with your plant manager, Mr. Pfeiffer?"

"Yes."

"And are you further aware that Mr. Pfeiffer not only admitted that you were violating the code, but that he said—in so many words—that you would continue to do so?"

"Yes, I know all these things. But I should like to make certain other things clear at this point. First, while Mr. Pfeiffer is a trusted and able manager, he does not speak for the company's policy. Second, Mr. Pfeiffer has always felt a great deal of resentment against the Code Authority and does not hesitate to say so. You can't condemn him for that. Third, while I was at first rather unhappy with the idea of a Code Authority, I am a law-abiding citizen and would not purposely break with the industry once the code was enacted." Gross presented these points rapidly and with obvious confidence. Then he paused, lowering his voice into a more conciliatory tone. "Now it is true that we are paying some of our workers less than the minimum wages approved by the code. But — and I want to make this absolutely clear [he rapped the table] — our wage scale is not intended as a challenge to the Code Authority. Rather, we are paying less money to those workers who are making tops rather than caps and who therefore are outside the authority of the code."

"You mean to say that tops are different from caps?"

"Exactly. You see, caps have little cork insets and are pressed onto bottles. Tops, on the other hand, are all metal and are screwed onto jars. Bottle caps and jar tops, you see?"

"Well, I . . . I'm not. . . . ."

"It has seemed to me right along that — since there are a number of manufacturers who make tops and not any caps, and since these manufacturers are not organized under a code — then for that part of my production which involves tops I'm under no obligation to the Bottling Code Authority. Neither legal nor moral obligation."

The chairman opened his mouth as if to speak, then rapped his gavel. "The hearing will recess for deliberation." The audience began murmuring with excitement as it filed out of the room.

Two hours later the group reassembled to hear the decision of the Compliance Investigating Division.

The chairman called the meeting back to order. "Having considered the issues of the case, we have arrived at certain decisions. First, we feel that Mr. Gross has acted in good faith in this matter. Second, we are nevertheless convinced, in view of the fact that Mr. Gross's plant manufactures both caps and tops, that he must apply the wage scales in the Bottling Code to all his workers. It would be mere splitting of hairs, it seems to us, to distinguish between a cap and a top. More important, to make such a distinction would, in our view, be inconsistent with the spirit of the NRA, which is to effectively organize industry to preserve certain price and wage levels. The NRA was not set up in an effort to play word games about who shall or shall not belong simply because in one case an item is pressed rather than turned."

A voice from the back of room yelled, "Fascist!"

"Therefore," the chairman continued in a louder voice, "we hereby forbid the placing of the Blue Eagle seal on any cartons containing the caps or tops of S. L. Gross & Co. until that company complies with the rules of the Code

Authority and shows itself ready to abide by the code's spirit."

"But what about all the other top manufacturers?" Mr. Gross blurted out.

"We'll take care of them in due time. Meeting adjourned."

BLUE EAGLE TO SICK CHICKEN

A National emergency productive of widespread unemployment and disorganization of industry, which burdens interstate and foreign commerce, affects the public welfare, and undermines the standard of living of the American people, is hereby declared to exist.

This was the first sentence of the National Industrial Recovery Act. What followed justified the establishment of codes such as that adopted by the bottling industry. Automobiles, textiles, lumber, coal, shipbuilding, laundry and dry-cleaning, dog food, pecan shelling, barber shops, flexible metal hose and tubing — these were only a few of the hundreds of industries and enterprises that sent draft codes to the NRA. Between the summer of 1933 and early 1935 the NRA approved 557 basic codes and more than 200 supplementary codes.

The chief administrator of the NRA in Washington was one of Roosevelt's brain trusters, General Hugh Johnson. Johnson had grown up with the Army; he was tough and sentimental at the same time — and smart enough for the Army to have sent him to law school. After World War I he retired from active service and became an official of a plow company. Then he moved into bigger business circles, finally becoming the administrator of hundreds of codes, coordinating production, price, and employment activities in virtually every industry in the country — industries that employed more than 20 million workers. Since the NRA had a legal life of only two years — from June 1933 to June 1935 — General Johnson and his assistants had to work fast.

The NRA's program seemed successful. Merchants throughout the country pasted the Blue Eagle on their windows and products. Newspapers and magazines reprinted the emblems on the corners of their front pages. Speakers, motorcades, mass meetings, and brass bands proclaimed to every American his patriotic duty to adopt and honor the symbol of economic recovery.

As the code provisions went into effect, letters began to pour into the NRA offices — many of them laboriously pencilled notes. A woman factory worker in a large industrial city, for example, wrote:

Before the New Deal came into effect we was compelled to work 15 hours of each day during the rush and no overtime and fired if you get a [union] card. Now we got our union and we got our decent work-week and we got more girls working here and we got better wages.

According to the United States Bureau of Labor Statistics, wages increased by 33.5 percent between June 1933 and December 1934. At the same time, production increased by 20 percent and employment rose by 16 percent. As for the earnings of business, the NRA's Research and Planning Division reported that a selected group of 639 corporations had increased their net earning by 519 percent between 1932 and 1934.

But despite these indications that it was succeeding, the NRA became the object of increasing criticism. Small businessmen and manufacturers complained about codes that, they said, were written and administered by big business in order to benefit only big business. Many consumers grew increasingly angry at what they considered to be unfairly high prices; they blamed the NRA codes for encouraging businessmen to keep prices and profits up and to keep production down. And within the NRA itself there was bitter disagreement: Some staff members argued that the program had failed because businessmen had virtually taken over the program and were using it to build up monopolies and enormous profits. Others, agreeing with representatives of labor unions, looked only at the other side: Wages had gone up and they intended to keep them that way.

Unemployment, which reached a peak in 1933, slowly began to decline.

Economists, looking at the progress being made in recovering from the depression, were divided on whether the NRA was a real help to the economy. By keeping production limited and prices high, there were not as many jobs for the unemployed as there might otherwise be, and people couldn't afford to buy many of the goods. Maybe it would be better, they thought, to return to a completely competitive system.

In March 1935 *The New York Times* observed: "The friends of NRA are halfhearted. They are like people who have a tired bear by the tail and are not sure whether it is safe to let go or not." But President Roosevelt spoke in unmistakably firm words when he asked Congress for a two-year extension of the Recovery Act. "The fundamental purposes and principles of the Act are sound," he asserted. "To abandon them is unthinkable. It would spell the return of industrial and labor chaos."

It is hard to say whether industrial and labor chaos were really prevented by the NRA. In any event, there was no need to discuss the problem in practical terms again, for in May 1935 the Supreme Court handed down a landmark decision.

The case before the Supreme Court involved the four Schechter brothers — Joseph, Alex, Martin, and Aaron — who operated A.L.A. Schechter Company and the Schechter Live Poultry Market, Inc., in Brooklyn. The brothers competed against other poultry wholesalers in the booming New York marketplace — the poultry center of the country.

Along with their competitors the Schechters displayed the NRA Blue Eagle, for which they had promised to obey a code that regulated working hours and wages, outlawed the selling of diseased fowl, and required that birds be sold by the coopful rather than singly.

But the Schechters soon were accused of flouting NRA regulations. Their worst offense was to sell large quantities of sick chickens to the people of Brooklyn. In addition, they had reportedly been commiting enough other offenses so that they were indicted on 60 separate counts.

Government lawyers described how one of their agents followed one of the Schechter delivery trucks to a retail shop and there bought a diseased chicken that had just arrived. It was argued that a housewife buying such a chicken would tend to switch to other foods and persuade her friends to do the same. The cumulative effect, the Government argued, tended to hurt the flow of interstate commerce in poultry.

Despite a spirited defense, the brothers were found guilty on 17 counts and sentenced to jail — Joseph for three months, Alex for two, and Martin and Aaron for a month apiece.

Lawyers for the convicted men appealed the sentences to the Supreme Court on the following two grounds:

The NRA violated the traditional American doctrine of separation of powers. Congress had, in effect, turned over its lawmaking authority to the Executive branch by allowing it to draw up the details of codes that had the effect of law.

The poultry business was a local business, and it did not affect interstate commerce. The Schechters bought most of their poultry, and sold all of it, right in New York State. Congress had the power to regulate only interstate — not *intra*state commerce; even the opening sentence of the Act admitted this.

The Court agreed with these arguments. *Schechter v. United States,* popularly known as the "Sick Chicken Case," was decided unanimously against the Government. The era of the Blue Eagle ended. Within a short time after the decision, May 27, 1935 — about a month before the NRA would have expired — the innumerable code authorities across the nation ceased their operations. They packed and sealed their records; they dismissed their staffs. The most innovative and massive governmental experiment affecting the competitive economy in America had come to an end.

1. *Free Enterprise and the NRA*. It has often been charged that the NRA violated the free enterprise system by imposing codes that infringed on the property rights of businessmen like S. L. Gross and the Schechter brothers. To what extent do you agree or disagree with this charge? Be sure to make explicit the criteria you use to define free enterprise.

2. *Free Enterprise Applied to Schools*. One major purpose of the NRA was to establish standard prices and quality for certain products, and standard wages and working conditions. This was done through planning by businessmen within an industry. Except that it is a *public* service within a single community, the school system is organized along lines similar to those set up by the NRA. All teachers are commonly on the same salary schedule (all teachers with the same education and experience make approximately the same amount of money). Teaching schedules are established through planning and negotiation between teachers and administrators. This approach to work organization was rejected when the NRA was discontinued.

Imagine a school in which the principles of free enterprise would be followed. Parents would be allowed to bid for the teachers they wanted their children to have. Very popular teachers would make a great deal of money; unpopular or dull teachers would make much less money. Parents who could afford to bid the highest could get the teachers they wanted for their children; poor parents would have much less voice in selecting their children's teachers. Very popular teachers might bargain to teach only two or three classes, while less popular teachers might have to teach more.

a. What do you consider the strengths and weaknesses of the "free enterprise" approach to school as opposed to the "planning" or NRA approach?

b. Would you say that medical doctors are organized on the "free enterprise" system or the NRA system? Why?

3. *Property Rights and the AAA*. The Agricultural Adjustment Act, passed in 1933, gave relief to farmers by attempting to ensure high prices for farm products. To keep prices high, the government established quotas that prevented farmers from cultivating land or raising hogs. That is, to reduce the farm surplus (the major cause of low farm prices), farmers were paid *not* to produce. Money to pay the farmers high prices for their goods and bonuses for limiting production came from a tax levied on processors of agricultural products. In 1936, the Supreme Court declared the AAA unconstitutional because it imposed a tax on one group (processors) to benefit another group (farmers). What do you think of this decision? Using similar reasoning, would it be unconstitutional to tax cigarette manufacturers to support research on lung cancer? Would it be unconstitutional to tax liquor distributors to help

rehabilitate alcoholics? In what ways would such taxes be similar to and different from the AAA tax?

An Analogy: In 1976 a successful and practical electric car was developed by Westinghouse. Although the center of automobile manufacturing remained in Detroit, where the giant automobile companies converted to manufacturing new electric cars, there was a revolution in the fuel industry. The demand for oil declined.

Most cars were fueled by metered electric outlets conveniently placed in private homes and parking garages. Commercial trucks over one ton still used internal combusion engines. As a result there seemed to be a surplus of gas stations and gasoline.

The petroleum refineries said that it would be dangerous to disassemble the refineries and put the gas stations out of business, because the new cars were not fully proven, and gas stations were still needed for trucks. Moreover, they argued that the small businessman who ran the corner filling station was an American institution. If these stations were allowed to go out of business, thousands of men would have to be relocated and reeducated. The federal government responded by paying oil companies *not* to pump oil, because there was a large surplus. The government also built storage facilities and purchased surplus gasoline that the companies could not sell to private customers. The government, further, paid the small service station operator a subsidy to ensure his staying in business.

a. If you were in Congress in 1976, would you vote for subsidies for oil companies and gas station operators? Why?

b. If you were in Congress in 1933, would you have voted for subsidies for farmers? Why?

A TALE OF THE TUSCARORA

To generate electric power, a state agency plans to flood an Indian reservation.

On April 17, 1958, William Rickard sat in jail in Niagara Falls, N.Y., and cursed at the bars around him. What good were treaties, promises, agreements, or civil rights laws? It seemed to Rickard that he was caught in a grim but familiar play, fighting a battle he had no chance of winning. How could a tiny band of American Indians hope to defeat the New York State Power Authority, and its energetic and powerful director, Robert Moses?

Early in 1958 Mr. Moses had announced a vast project to harness Niagara Falls for the produc-

This case is taken from Donald W. Oliver and Fred M. Newmann, *Colonial Kenya: Cultures in Conflict*, American Education Publications, Columbus, Ohio, 1968.

tion of electricity. The generators and other facilities were to cost $750 million, but would ultimately provide power at great savings to the entire state and the whole Northeast. Moses proclaimed an ambitious and rigid construction schedule, to begin immediately. He urged citizens to support the project.

As the full plans were revealed, it became clear that some people would see no benefits at all in the plan. About 1,300 acres of the Tuscarora Indian Reservation (one-fifth of its area) were to be flooded to form a reservoir against dry seasons in the main river. The reservation site involved about 175 Indians living in 37 houses. The only alternate site for the reservoir was in the town of Lewiston. It included a million-dollar school, two cemeteries, and about 350 homes.

During preliminary work on the project plans, engineers had visited William Rickard's father, Chief Clinton Rickard, to ask permission to test soils on Indian land. They assured him that there was nothing behind their request except a need for complete maps of the area. The Chief called a council, which refused permission and made clear that the Indians were not prepared to "sell, lease, or negotiate for any land transactions of any kind." The Indians heard nothing more until they read in the papers that 20 percent of their reservation was to be flooded. Several months later they learned at the last minute that hearings on the subject were to be held the next day before the Federal Power Commission in Washington. Chief Rickard dispatched his son William to Washington.

Rickard explained to the commissioners that the reservation was not for sale, that its "inalienable" use had been guaranteed by 18th-century treaties, and that according to tribal religion, the land ,"did not belong to us, we were only the custodians of it, and we were to preserve it for the coming generations. *As such the land cannot be sold and is priceless;* there can be no value placed upon it."

Soon afterward, Mr. Moses tried to persuade the Tuscaroras with an open letter:

. . . Obstructions in the way of the project have already caused unconscionable economic loss to the whole state. Absence of cheap power is aggravating the general business recession. Ten thousand constructions jobs which will be provided when the project is fully under way are badly needed to offset rising unemployment. You yourselves have as much at stake as your neighbors, since the local industries where most of you are employed cannot invite much longer the economic difficulties resulting from increased power costs and uncertainties as to the completion of the project. . . . It will be necessary in the very near future for our engineers to enter your property. . . . We are carrying out an urgent project of vital public importance, under State and Federal law. We have no more time for stalling and debate. . . .

In case his persuasion failed, Mr. Moses also had a bill passed in the New York State Legislature giving the Power Authority the right to confiscate, without any prior legal procedure, any land needed for the project. The Authority had merely to file a map of the territory with the State and deposit with the State Comptroller a sum equal to the land's market value.

But the Tuscaroras began to fight through the courts. With trials still pending in April 1958, it came as a shock to the tribe to hear on the radio that Power Authority surveyors were to enter their land under police protection the next morning. True enough, ten carloads of State troopers, deputy sheriffs, and plainclothesmen arrived the next morning, armed with tear gas and submachine guns, to protect the handful of surveyors. The Indian women were greatly upset, and wept at the prospect of losing their homes. Many lay down in front of the trucks, while others gave way to their feelings by punching and scratching the officers. Two Indian men were jailed on charges of "unlawful assembly," and the leader of the demonstration, William Rickard, was charged with disorderly conduct and dragged to the paddy wagon.

As the agents of Mr. Moses finished their first day's surveying, William Rickard sat in a dark cell wondering where his tribesmen could turn now.

1. *Establishing Rights to Property.* What rights should the Tuscarora and the New York State Power Authority have to the disputed territory on the Indian Reservation?

An Analogy: Fogg Island is a small island off the Carolina coast. It is densely wooded except for about five acres of lush fields and a mile of sandy coastline. Most people on the mainland thought it deserted, but "hermits" were rumored to live there who went on "rampages" shooting wild game. In reality, the island was populated by two peace-loving brothers in their early sixties, Alvin and Calvin Hermit, who had lived there alone for forty years. They spent most of their time cultivating a vegetable garden.

During two weeks in the fall the brothers' quiet was disturbed by hunters who came annually to hunt the deer, pheasant, and rabbits that are so abundant on the island. The Hermit brothers resented these intrusions but they did little about it, because the hunters actually had fired at the brothers when they tried to stop the shooting.

That was the condition of Fogg Island until Leroy Smith decided to make it into a resort. Upon careful investigation, Leroy found that the federal government thought it was under state jurisdiction and the state thought it was under federal jurisdiction. Neither government cared to become involved in determining how it was to be used. Smith then hired an attorney who composed a legal-sounding letter to the Hermit brothers, informing them that they would have to vacate because they had no legal claim. Letters were also sent to the hunters (who were actually wealthy oilmen from Texas).

The Hermit brothers were shocked when they heard that they were supposed to leave the island. Alvin immediately wrote to his cousin Thomas in New York, who was a prominent clergyman in the Ecumenical Church. Thomas quickly viewed the island as having a great deal more potential for the good of humanity than it would have as a vacation resort, or, for that matter, as a haven for his two unsocial cousins. He wrote back saying that he would be glad to find lawyers for them, but they would have to join his church and work to make the island into a religious retreat for clergymen and laymen who wanted to get away from the hurlyburly of city life.

Alvin and Calvin refused to go along with Thomas. But Thomas had become engrossed with his idea. Because no one had clear rights to the land, including his cousins, he thought, why not work to obtain it for the church?

Jonathan Pembroke heard of the dispute over the island and had a vague hunch that he had heard of this island before. One day he dug through some old papers and found a very old parchment, which stated that the chief of a small Indian band who had once lived on the island sold it to James Pembroke, who had later deeded it to George Pembroke. Jonathan was a direct descendant of these Pembrokes.

"Ha," thought Jonathan, "the island clearly belongs to me. There is no legal basis for anyone else's ownership. Of course, the deed is not made out to me, but it was clearly my relatives who bought it from the Indians. If it hadn't been for them, it would still belong to the Indians."

So the dispute over who owned Fogg Island grew. No one dared take the matter to court, because no claimant was sure enough that he could win, and none knew what court had jurisdiction. At first all wrote nasty threatening letters to one another. Finally, all agreed to meet and talk. The basic arguments follow:

The Hermit brothers: "We have lived on the island for forty years. During that time no one bothered us and we bothered no one else. We care for the land and leave it pretty much in its natural state. At the very least, we have a right to live out the rest of our days there without being disturbed."

J. P. Oildrip, a hunter: "We consider the island our private game preserve because we have used it, without incident, for many years. We let the old Hermit brothers stay there as long as they don't bother us. Anyone who tries to claim it is going to contend with some first-rate sharpshooters."

Leroy Smith, resort king: "I have already invested considerable money having the island surveyed and interested some investors in its possibilities as a vacation and resort area. This is the best purpose to which it can be put, because it is uneconomical to farm, and it would allow the maximum number of people to enjoy its fine beach and quiet woods."

Thomas Hermit, clergyman: "The best purpose to which the island can be put is something that is obviously in the public good: a religious retreat. My close relationship to Alvin and Calvin has some bearing on my claim to the island."

Jonathan Pembroke, descendant of original "owner": "The parchment, establishing me as heir to the original owner, clearly gives me the right to the land."

What general criteria for owning land are implied by the various people involved in the dispute? Which seems to make the most persuasive case for legitimizing his ownership? How would you apply these criteria in settling the Tuscarora dispute?

The Reconstruction
of Controversy

Chapters 4 through 8 convey a rather disjointed, kaleidoscopic — almost impressionistic—view of values, arguments, concepts, and theories by which to construe various public issues. We offer no all-inclusive model to explain social controversy; no coordinated, step-by-step formula to control it. The seemingly fragmented style through which dozens of ideas have been presented reflects our belief that public controversy is so complex that it cannot be explained by any single model, no matter how comprehensive it claims to be. Perhaps the day will come when some global systems analysis yields a comprehensive scheme that explains and interrelates the legal, ethical, political, economic, and sociological aspects of any and all public issues. Until then, however, we must function with a piecemeal approach, searching for ways to construe and reconstrue specific conflicts, collecting and selecting ideas from several sources that may or may not fit into a larger internally consistent scheme.

The seminal ideas that ignite controversy and form the basis of citizens' opinions change with time, which is particularly evident in the history of judicial opinion. The Constitution prohibits states from denying persons life, liberty, or property without due process of law (Fourteenth Amendment). For decades, however, this clause was never interpreted to ensure equal rights to Negroes or the poor. Instead it was used primarily to invalidate pro-labor legislation by Congress and the states. That is, maximum hours and minimum wage laws were seen as infringing upon liberty of contract between employer and employee (or as unjustified Congressional

233

regulation of intrastate commerce). From 1898 to 1954 public schools racially segregated by law were judged to fulfill the states' obligation to provide "equal protection under the law," but in 1954 racially separate schools were declared to be inherently unequal, and, if legally established, violating the equal protection clause (Fourteenth Amendment). Similarly in government regulation of free enterprise, the right to counsel, free speech and assembly, government aid to religious schools, and compulsory loyalty oaths, court opinions and legislation have made major changes in interpreting basic rights. The slaveholder's right to human property vanished as did the employer's right to refuse to bargain collectively.

In Chapters 4 through 8 we have suggested a few ways in which ideas, concepts, and values critical today might become obsolete, radically reinterpreted, or totally replaced by new human concerns. Here we wish to further emphasize the possibility that many of our comments on the substantive problem areas may become irrelevant to future controversies.[1] Several examples illustrate.

1. In an affluent age dominated by what we now consider leisure activities, work and self-sacrifice as criteria for acquiring material wealth might be abandoned. People would deserve a comfortable life as an inalienable right, not because they "earned" it, but because they are human and the economy can provide it. With guaranteed abundance for all, competition for material property might disappear as a source of human conflict.

2. Breakthroughs in communication and transportation can accelerate the "shrinking" of the earth and a heightened sense of economic, social, and political interdependence among all people. The population explosion and environmental pollution could create a feeling of urgency characteristic of the "spaceship earth." Conflicts between states and nations would have to be controlled for human survival. Political movements espousing national sovereignty or territorial integrity could threaten the safety of all. World government would replace current geopolitical boundaries. Collective security would come to mean protecting man from himself rather than from "foreign enemies."

3. Deliberate medical intervention in the functioning of mind and body will create new challenges to conventional ethical-legal reasoning. Who will be responsible for a child artificially conceived and gestated in a laboratory? If parents become able, through genetic manipulation, to control the intel-

---

[1] The ways in which we have construed social conflicts may be irrelevant not only because "times change," but also because they are insensitive to the real concerns of certain groups. It makes no sense to speak of the importance of respect for law and order to individuals who perceive the law as consistently perpetrating repression and violation of human dignity. To speak of one's ethical obligations to others is ludicrous if one's audience feels that the only way to survive is through cutthroat competition.

ligence, sex, personality, and tastes of their offspring, what limits should be placed on right to privacy associated with procreation? Suppose that safe, mind-altering drugs make it possible for individuals to change their personalities at will. What impact would this have on one's legal identity and on enforcing contracts (e.g., marriage and employment)?

4. Because of increased capabilities for widespread electronic surveillance, controlling aggression through chemicals and drugs, and computerized information processing that makes crime impossible to hide, violence in the sense of physical destruction of life or property may diminish substantially. Doing harm or violence to another might take on such new meanings as invading privacy, excessive psychological manipulation, or inflicting psychic damage. What would cries for "law and order" mean in response to this sort of violence?

5. Youths rebelling in the universities and elsewhere reject not merely "establishment" policies, but authority itself. Even the revolutionary rhetoric of the Declaration of Independence recognized *some* authority as legitimate. What would happen to dialogue on controversial issues in which participants rejected all authority, and instead recognized brute power ("might makes right") or immediate subjective feelings as the only legitimate grounds for obedience?

6. Finally, we can even question whether the value of human dignity might be superseded by other ideals. Though we have assumed a framework that places ultimate value on man as a species, does man really deserve such reverence? Should he be looked upon as the center of the universe? When we examine the violence he has done to himself and, more important, the destruction he has wrought upon other species by raping the physical environment, we seriously can suggest that man's own extinction might be a healthy evolutionary step for the universe. The value of human life can fade in significance when one contemplates the aesthetic grandeur of nature, or of forces (reproduction, movement, light, evolution) that transcend human experience.

Although these observations may seem all too distant from the headlines, they offer some perspective on our constructions of immediate issues. The conceptual reconstruction of reality is a task not only for curriculum makers and social scientists. We believe it to be a critical component in personal growth for each individual, akin to what George Kelly (1955) called "constructive alternativism." Kelly investigated how people used the categories by which they described reality. He felt that the essence of human communication and psychological health lay in a person's ability continually to refine the categories or cognitive lenses through which he views the world. One must strive to modify one's categories (constructs) to make them sensitive to many diverse events and to both discard and supplement them to create alternative visions. In many ways our work in curriculum development is a process of continually changing constructs. We hope that the constructs presented in the previous four chapters have stimulated the reader to reconsider some of his own.

PART III   # Implementation

I. Introduction   How can teachers translate Chapters 1 through 8 into a coherent curriculum plan and specific classroom pedagogy? To what extent can the AEP *Public Issues Series* (developed from the Harvard Project) be used effectively within existing curriculum? Is it possible to consider public issues meaningfully in a typical school classroom isolated from realities of the larger community? In this section we discuss concrete problems in implementing a jurisprudential approach to public issues. First it would be useful to summarize main elements in the approach.

II. Juris-prudential Approach   The main objective is to teach students to clarify and develop rational justifications for positions on public policy through oral dialogue. This assumes heavy emphasis on discussion with correspondingly less emphasis on writing, library research, and other skill objectives commonly claimed for social studies instruction. The teacher should be a listener, questioner, and clarifier of what students say, rather than a "truthgiver" or guide to student "discovery" of preselected truths. Typically this involves more attention to the clarification processes taking place in a dialogue than the topic of the dialogue. Progress tends to be measured in an increasing awareness of the complex implications in an issue rather than "solving the problem" or "giving the right answer."

A "rational" justification demonstrates awareness of value, definitional, and factual disagreements relevant to policy issues, and employs specific intellectual strategies for dealing with each type: for example, providing specific evidence to support general factual claims; anticipating and rebutting arguments of opposing positions; and — the operation most critical to jurisprudential thought — developing general principles of judgment that are

237

sufficiently qualified to take account of exceptions that otherwise would render one's application of principles inconsistent (see Chapter 2).

To develop a rational position through discussion, one must demonstrate specific attitudes toward and skills in discussion: for example, listening and responding to statements of others, stating the issues, summarizing positions, guiding the discussion toward relevant issues, conceding points when appropriate (see Chapter 3).

Public issue interpretations and positions can be illuminated by concepts, generalizations, and theories from history, social science, philosophy, and law. Chapters 4 through 8 discuss substantive distinctions and viewpoints relevant to diverse issues.

Just as legal principles emerge from judicial responses to specific cases, so general views on public controversy arise from debate on concrete case studies. Case studies investigate single institutions, decisions, situations, or individuals to gather detailed information about a relatively small class of phenomena, such as the growth of a corporation, the decision to drop the atomic bomb, the living conditions of a Negro family in an urban slum, or the behavior of a politician seeking election. Case studies focus intensively on limited situations rather than on sweeping sets of events because it is assumed that examining a limited incident will yield conclusions applicable to a more general class of incidents.

Case materials can vary considerably, and the AEP *Public Issues Series* include a wide range:

Stories and vignettes, written like novels, portray concrete events, human action, dialogue, and feelings; they tell of episodes about individuals and may represent authentic events, as in historical novels, or they may be totally fictitious. The vignette is a short excerpt, or slice of a story, without a complete plot. For illustrations, see "Oliver Wiswell" (*American Revolution*); "Black Boy" (*Negro Views of America*).

Journalistic historical narratives are told as news stories or narratives of concrete events. Relatively little individual characterization is used. Hour-by-hour descriptions or eyewitness accounts might describe the actions of institutions as well as individual people. For illustrations, see "Incident at Pettus Bridge" (*American Revolution*); "Battle at the Overpass" (*Rise of Organized Labor*).

Research data report experimental and survey studies, with statistics that can be used as empirical evidence to test factual claims. For illustrations, see "Statistics on Racial Differences" (*Negro Views of America*) and "Meeting of Railroad Presidents" (*Railroad Era*).

Documents include court opinions, speeches, letters, diaries, transcripts of trials and hearings, laws, charters, contracts, and commission reports. Public documents are formal and legally valid records. For illustrations, see

"Vanderbilt's Defense" (*Railroad Era*); "Mr. Livermore's Testimony" (*Rise of Organized Labor*).

Texts are general statements of institutional trends and history, excluding details about individuals except to illustrate generalizations. A text would be considered a "case" only if it described relatively limited events and if it were critically analyzed. The text usually explains as well as describes events by giving definitions, causal theories, and explicit "reasons" for events. It presumably offers objective knowledge, and will usually be accepted by the student at face value because he assumes it to be unbiased truth. The introductions and overviews in the AEP unit books illustrate text material.

Interpretive essays, clearly intended as explanation and evaluation, reach interpretive conclusions on such issues as: "Who caused the American Revolution?" "Are there genetic differences between races?" Essays, unlike texts, attempt to develop and support a position, not just to report and explain it. For illustrations, see "Three Theories of Political Process" (*Municipal Politics*); "Theories of Racial Differences" (*Negro Views of America*).

These different materials ascend from personal, dramatic, concrete human stories (story, vignette, journalistic historical narrative), to more "objective" abstract facts and generalizations about individuals and institutions (documents, research data, text), to highly abstract interpretations (interpretive essay). As we progress through this order, the material increasingly provides its own construction of a problem, rather than laying out the raw experience and challenging the student and teacher to construe the problem.

For the most part the teacher should use an inductive approach by stimulating and guiding the student in reaching his own conclusions, rather than transmitting to the student conclusions that the teacher has previously determined to be correct. We wish to distinguish between two interpretations of "inductive" teaching.

The open-ended approach occurs when the teacher has not previously decided what knowledge or conclusions the students are supposed to gain from studying a case. The teacher himself is willing to entertain whatever issues and approaches the students suggest, so long as these issues and approaches seem serious and relevant. For the teacher to be truly committed to this idea, we think he himself should be somewhat tentative or undecided about issues raised by the case material.

In contrast, the closed inductive approach occurs when the teacher already has in his mind the knowledge, structures, or conclusions that students are expected to discover. The teacher will, with varying degrees of sublety, lead or prompt the student to reach the "right" conclusions. Suppose, for example, in studying the growth of railroads, the teacher wants to emphasize reducing costs as a way to increase profits. If the student suggests that one may "raise the price of the goods," and thereby increase profits, the teacher will not really be satisfied. "Think of another way," he will prod.

Most stories, vignettes, and persisting questions in the AEP unit books assume the use of an open-ended inductive approach. There are many possible ways to construe most issues, and we are unable to tell teachers which are the best or "right" ways for their particular situation. It is also possible, however, to use cases as material for closed inductive teaching: i.e., when the teacher can specify the particular lessons, generalizations, or morals that he believes the cases illustrate or confirm.

Novelty and flexibility in teaching technique and organizing content is crucial. As discussed in the introduction to Part II, public controversy could be conceptualized according to many themes, topics, disciplines, periods, areas, etc. Because we believe that no single structure is most useful for studying public controversy, our curriculum lacks a conventional plan for scope and sequence. For this reason the pamphlet series has been criticized as lacking in organization. The flexible format in which cases are made available to the public is not meant to imply that teachers should simply choose issues at random. Certainly it is reasonable for teachers to try to organize content into a scheme that creates some order and structure. We believe, however, that teachers are competent to create their own structural plans, and that organizing apparently chaotic material offers an important opportunity for teachers to use their own intellectual resources. Some alternative approaches to selecting content are discussed in Chapter 9.

Because we emphasize teaching discussion skills, some observers express concern that "kids will get tired of constantly discussing in class." There may be an implication that most class periods would involve tough-minded debates, with the teacher always behaving as a Socratic gadfly. We deny this implication and emphasize the significance of novelty in the classroom and teacher sensitivity to varying motivational student needs. There are times when a teacher's lecture would be more appropriate than student-led discussion, when a film would be more useful than a debate, when silent reading and study in class would be more productive than any talking whatsoever, when traditional recitation of facts of a case would be more helpful than arguments over ethical dilemmas, when role-playing would make more sense than writing systematic briefs for a position, or when a field trip would teach more than a classroom lesson. For public issue study to be meaningful, teaching techniques as diverse as these should be deliberately planned. Unfortunately, we are unable to advise teachers on how much class time to spend on each technique or in what circumstances they could be most successfully employed. Experience convinces us, however, that success is unlikely without considerable novelty and variety in classroom technique.

Chapter 9   # Problems in Classroom Application

We cannot demonstrate empirically that some schemes for organizing content are more effective than others, nor can we show that certain teaching techniques or styles accomplish given objectives more efficiently than others. Hence, we do not offer precise recipes on how to teach public issues. Although we have arrived at no final answers, through several years of experimental teaching (in public school classrooms) we have learned a good deal about the complexity of the "jurisprudential" approach. We shall draw together observations here on several instructional problems: selecting and organizing content; factual information in studying public issues; using analogy; evaluating student discourse on public issues; and the teacher's posture in dealing with value issues.

I. Selecting Content and Curriculum Organization

What controversies should one study and in what order? How much time should be spent on certain value issues or substantive concepts? The study of public controversy has not yet evolved into a "discipline" with concepts, generalizations, theories, and models that build cumulatively upon each other to form a conceptual system (as has been claimed for such subjects as math, physics, and even economics). Thus, we cannot recommend for public issues a sequence in which mastery of certain "fundamentals" should precede the study of more "advanced" problems. It is important, however (for both intellectual and pedagogical reasons) to strive for some order and structure, rather than to approach public issues in a completely random fashion. In groping for general syllabus outlines and organized plans for specific lessons, we have dealt with several approaches in selecting content.

241

A. Crisis-Event Orientation

We seemed to oscillate continually between a *crisis-event* orientation and a *thematic* orientation. The two can be interrelated and hard to distinguish in curriculum planning and argument, but for purposes of analysis we can characterize them starkly. According to the crisis-event orientation, one begins with important happenings — those controversies that are significant in history and/or relevant to present-future problems. One identifies those major crises or events (e.g., American Revolution, Civil War, depression, Watts riot, Little Rock controversy, Brown versus Board of Education decision) that involved much controversy; then one "teaches" the events. Themes, issues, and value conflicts will emerge in teaching and discussing the events, but to identify these in advance or to use them to guide selection of what will be studied is not critical. The fact that an event (or series of events) is associated with public controversy is considered sufficient reason for including the crisis or event in the curriculum. The crisis-event orientation has the major advantage of reducing the tendency to preconstrue and preanalyze through the teacher's categories, hopefully providing more opportunity for open-ended analysis by the students. If a teacher decides in advance to use the 1937 Ford strike as "an example to show the importance of employer recognition of unions," the controversy might well be construed from only this point of view, leaving students with a narrow conception of the strike. Other issues that could be explored include the value conflict between private property and the public interest; legitimate methods of protest for social change; effective techniques for controlling violence; criteria for determining a fair wage; right to work versus closed shops.

The crisis-event orientation alone, however, does not provide sufficient criteria for selecting content. Because it would be impossible to teach all controversial crises-events in history, how does one choose which to include and exclude in the curriculum? Are controversies that involve violence more important than those argued peacefully? Are national controversies more important than local ones? Should current or recent controversies take precedence over those in the remote past? Should the controversies we study represent a wide range of value conflicts? Should controversies in different cultures be studied? If one has to justify including some crises-events and excluding others, additional criteria are needed. The need for criteria suggested in these questions is expressed in what we call a thematic orientation.

B. Thematic Orientation

One can select events because of their relevance to themes, topics, questions, problems worthy of study (e.g., labor relations, racial conflict, violence, political power). Because themes can be seen as abstract cognitive responses to concrete crises-events, we do not wish to imply that one first dreams up thematic ideas in total isolation from specific events, and then searches for events to illustrate the themes. Nevertheless actual curriculum planning often begins with teachers attempting to identify themes or concepts they wish to teach. The data or events used to teach the concepts are often considered of secondary importance to the thematic principles. In thinking about content selection for a particular course, we may consciously begin with a thematic orientation or be forced into it at a later stage when it becomes obvious that a crisis-event orientation cannot resolve all the decisions in content selection. Several thematic routes might be followed in organizing a public issues curriculum.

1. Historical Topics

Topics usually included in history courses can help in selecting material: revolution, labor, immigration, race, business, the frontier, foreign policy, colonialism, or farming. The Harvard Social Studies Project developed several units on such topics, but did not confine itself to this approach. AEP unit books include such titles as *American Revolution, Civil War, Railroad Era, Rise of Organized Labor, Immigrant's Experience, Nazi Germany, The New Deal, 20th Century Russia,* and *Colonial Kenya.* Although cases are grouped under historical labels, they are presented in such a way as to lead to various public issue disputes, not primarily to teach historical facts or arrive at historical explanations and generalizations. The book on railroads, for example, involves such issues as government control versus private enterprise; defining the "public interest"; the ethics of business competition; and the effect of technology on changing social customs and roles. Diverse issues are related by their connection to a common topic — the railroad industry.

2. Topics in Social Sciences and Other Disciplines

Those who prefer social science disciplines can select cases by their relevance to such topics as: authority, power, sovereignty (political science); scarcity, competition, self-interest (economics); conformity, deviance, values-norms (sociology); or identity, prejudice, attitude change (psychology). Urbanization, industrialization, specialization, bureaucratization, the individual in mass society, pluralism, and cultural identity reflect concerns deserving interdisciplinary attention. Although such topics have recently been included in history courses, they represent a departure from teaching historical narratives, and we recognize in them a concern for social science themes. The five problem areas discussed in Chapters 4 through 8 could be used to help select and group public controversies. Morality-responsibility, equality, consent, welfare-security, and property reflect perspectives not only of social science, but combinations of ethics, law, and philosophy as well. They represent ideas and problems that do not clearly belong to any single scholarly heritage. AEP unit books on *Municipal Politics, Negro*

Views of America, Community Change, and *Race and Education* use concepts from social science and law to illuminate controversial issues, with less emphasis on traditional historical topics.

3. Value Conflicts and Persisting Issues

We could organize content by value conflicts represented in persisting social choices: for example, majority rule versus minority rights; liberty versus order; equal opportunity versus national security. Issues need not be phrased in dichotomous value priorities. One's topics might be stated as problems in (1) the use and control of violence; (2) providing for dissent and constructive change; (3) achieving economic welfare; (4) creating an equitable system of privilege; and (5) protecting privacy. The AEP book, *Religious Freedom*, for example, includes cases from several historical periods raising different issues relevant to freedom of religious expression — Christian martyrs in Rome, Puritans in seventeenth-century Massachusetts, Amish and Jehovah's Witnesses in twentieth-century America.

The categories one uses to define the most important conflicts and issues will vary depending upon the social-ethical framework of the teacher. Our construction of the issues is strongly influenced by a conception of the American Creed and an interdisciplinary perspective. By labeling this a separate, issue-oriented route to thematic organization, we do not mean to imply that other frameworks ignore issues. This orientation is unique only in its attempt to define issues at the heart of public controversy, denying any obligation to cover problems that happen to be included in courses (especially history and the disciplines) in which analyzing public controversy is not the primary objective.

4. Current Problems

Here the guide to selecting content is primarily the daily news report. Topics could include student disruption on campus, race riots, pollution, drugs, birth control, Vietnam war, Biafra, crisis in the Middle East, police brutality, organized crime, war on poverty, and medicare. As with each other approach, content decisions still remain — we cannot teach all current problems. Another difficulty is the possibility that selecting problems from the mass media may leave unexplored many important but currently unrecognized issues. If by controlling what comes to public attention, the media not only reports but also *creates* public issues, those who rely on current problems as their guide will have to scrutinize the media with care to decide what the important issues are.

The thematic approaches we outline are by no means mutually exclusive. History-minded teachers may emphasize social science findings. Social science teachers may use history and both may focus on value conflicts and current problems in selecting content. Almost any idea or event could be studied from each or all approaches we mention here. We must, however, distinguish between using public controversy cases to illustrate historical problems, social science concepts, or value conflicts — where teaching concepts would be the major purpose — versus using thematic content to help categorize and order various public issues that in themselves are the major focus of teaching. Our intention here is to suggest the utility of different thematic routes for the latter purpose. It must be noted, however, that teachers concerned primarily with teaching economics or "the colonial period" could use cases in the AEP books for the former purpose as well. For example, *The Railroad Era* contains plentiful data to illustrate competition, profit, price determination, or market. *Negro Views of America* contains clinical information to illustrate the psychological notion of self-concept. As narratives of human experience, cases in the unit books can be construed through various concepts and used as vehicles to "teach" those concepts.

C. Relationships Between Crisis-Event and Thematic Orientations

A most demanding intellectual challenge in planning curriculum is deciding how to construe crises-events in themes, topics, or issues. Imagine a conversation among teachers: "We ought to begin with the American Revolution." "Why?" "Because it involves a persisting theme: the conditions under which violent overthrow of established government might be justified." "I think we also ought to teach the New Deal, because of the theme of government intervention to help the poor." "Let's put all this on the board."

CRISIS-EVENT	THEME
American Revolution	Overthrow of established government
Depression and New Deal	Emergence of federal planning for social welfare

The initial outline gives little instructional guidance. Teachers ought to discuss whether they wish to "cover" the revolution simply to make the general point that colonists declared their independence and fought to overthrow the British, or whether they wish to focus on more specific events — Stamp Act, Boston Tea Party, drafting the Declaration of Independence, raising an army. They should also consider whether to introduce explicitly other issues into classroom discussion: definitions of equality, consent of the governed, political representation; alternative techniques of political protest; the roles of elites and the common man in revolutionary struggle. Although teachers may generally agree on the importance of the initially stated event and theme, their execution will differ according to varying emphasis given to more specific events and themes. After some discussion, their outline might become more complex:

CRISIS-EVENT	THEME
American Revolution	When is violent revolution justified?

English economic policy
   Stamp Act
   Boston Tea Party
	Rights to property versus right to political representation

Battle at Lexington-Concord	Responsibility for starting the violence
Oliver Wiswell	Irrational mob behavior
Signing the Declaration of Independence	Where is the source of legitimate authority to speak for a group? Definition of unalienable rights

Teachers interested but inexperienced in teaching public controversy often fail to see "where to go" or "what to do with" controversial cases, except to ask for each student's opinion on the most obvious issue. By trying to anticipate various issues before discussion begins, the teacher can create many avenues to follow. To help formulate issues, we recommend using the grid presented in the Introduction to Part II, or the three-dimensional version of it on page 247.

Suppose we are studying the controversy at Central High in Little Rock, Arkansas, in 1956. We can begin with categories on the grid as a stimulus to articulating issues. That is, we can ask what legal, political, sociological (or other discipline) issues seem to emerge; what substantive problems of equality, consent, or morality are involved; and which problems would be policy, value, definitional, or factual issues? For example, we might list:

Legal issue: Did Eisenhower have a constitutional right to send in the troops? (fact: welfare-security; political science)

Consent issue: Should a local majority be able to go against the will of the Supreme Court? (policy; political science; law)

Definitional issue: What is equal educational opportunity? (equality; sociology)

We should note the relevance of these issues to other categories and dimensions, as indicated in parentheses.

Once an issue is listed, we can search for those categories that might provide assistance, or raise additional subtleties not evident in our initial phrasing. Suppose we wish to explore the issue, "Was violence likely to occur, as Faubus originally claimed, if he integrated the school?" According to the analytic categories this is a factual issue (thus requiring attention to problems of empirical verification). On the discipline dimension, this appears to be a historical question, directing us to historical accounts for evidence and interpretation. The substantive welfare-security area might provide insights on alternative interpretations of violence and law and

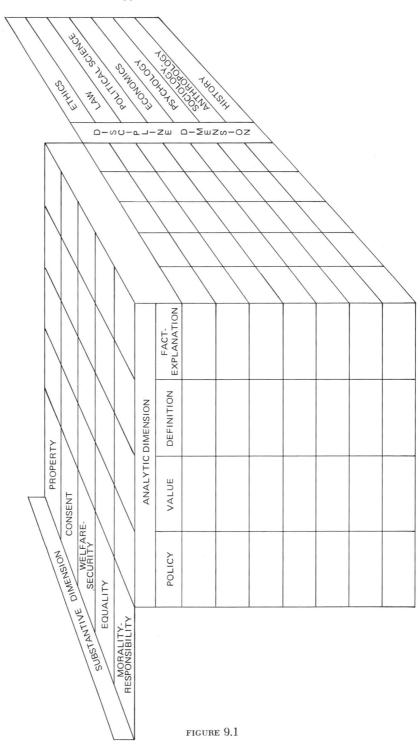

FIGURE 9.1

order. In this way, we can "locate" an issue on three dimensions and enter it in appropriate cells in the grid. Other examples:

1. Which is more important, peace and order or enforcing federal court rulings? (value; ethics, law; welfare-security)
2. Who was responsible for the violence in Little Rock? (fact-explanation; history, law, ethics; morality-responsibility)
3. Should Faubus have closed the school? (policy; law, political science, sociology; consent, welfare-security)
4. Is racial discrimination a form of violence? (definition; sociology, psychology; equality, consent, property)

The grid is intended as an issue-raiser, a heuristic to help expand the ways in which a given event might be studied. The dimensions (and categories within them) are neither completely independent nor all-inclusive. Because cases will raise different issues, they will differ in the types and numbers of cells that can be filled in.

Teachers primarily trained in a single discipline may have difficulty in broadening their perspectives along lines suggested in these different thematic routes. We feel, however, that a generalist, interdisciplinary approach with continual reconstruction of issues is critical not only to enrich teaching in this area, but to resolve actual controversies themselves.

D. Order and Sequence

We have not suggested methods of ordering or sequencing. Because of the lack of logical or cumulative structure requisite to comprehending public issues, we find it difficult to recommend any such guidelines. We see no reason why problems geographically close to home should necessarily be studied before issues in distant lands. Nor has it been shown that studying the past must precede studying the present or future. The meaning and relevance of controversial problems depends, we suspect, on other variables: for example, whether the situation presented contains a classical or persisting human ethical dilemma, whether it is dramatically told, or whether it invites the student to translate personal experience into more general societal issues. We are accustomed to thinking in chronological terms, and thus chronologically ordering events often contributes to the structure we seek. To the extent that one wishes to explore questions of cause and effect, a chronological approach may seem especially appropriate (although a "flashback" technique, reverse chronology, can also be used). If it is possible to distinguish the simple from the complex aspects of an issue, it would seem reasonable to allow the student to approach simpler problems first, gaining mastery over these before dealing with more complicated matters. The situation in the Mutiny Act, for example, involves fewer conflicts, groups, roles, and decisions than does "The Fight for Parsons Point"

(*Municipal Politics*), in which the interaction of numerous forces in a community is traced as the city makes a decision on land use. Before trying to comprehend ethical issues related to several groups and various events, it seems reasonable first to try to understand conflicts that can be expressed in a few clearly defined issues that do not span several levels of abstraction or disciplinary framework. The dimension of *simplicity-to-complexity* might thereby aid in arriving at a sequential outline of content. Finally, we mention the obvious criteria of *student ability and readiness:* for example, reading comprehension and the ability to reason hypothetically. To the extent that students mature through different stages of cognitive functioning (see Piaget, 1962, or Kohlberg, 1968), we must try to arrange our curriculum accordingly.[1]

E. The Problem of Bias in Organization of Content

Choosing to organize content in one way rather than another closes off alternative approaches to issues, and thus no curriculum can be considered completely open-ended. Oliver and Shaver (1966, pp. 140–41) discuss this problem:

> However one goes about selecting and organizing specific materials for the teaching of contemporary political controversy, he should realize that once a problem is classified and described, even in a tentative way, the student is already predisposed to deal with it as the writer or teacher has seen and presented it. This is unavoidable. Even when we decide to deal with content as "controversial," and therefore seek to present and justify various sides of an issue, we are not necessarily immune from bias or distortion. The problem of the instability of central Europe, for example, which has plagued the Western world for the past 1500 years would be framed and taught quite differently by a Russian, a German, or a Pole, although all would probably agree that it was controversial and that there was a problem. Social and political problems begin with the emotional reactions in the minds of people, not within an analytical framework. Only after these visceral reactions make their presence known are intellectual structures built by which to understand and resolve them. The description of a problem should flow initially from this fundamental source of controversy.
>
> We are thus faced with something of a paradox in building a curriculum. A framework is necessary to "make sense" out of problematic data and deal with them systematically. But the framework tends to predispose us to include some aspects of the problem and to exclude others. Obviously, although we hope to teach the student our particular frame of reference, it is necessary to be alert

---

[1] For the most part, unit books in the AEP series cannot be arranged in order from simple to complex, nor along a dimension of student cognitive growth. That is, no unit books are composed solely of "simple" or "complex" cases. They are appropriate for a wide range of ability in grades 8 through 12. The teacher, however, can control for level of complexity by the questions he asks in guiding student analysis of the cases.

to the fact that each student will modify it to meet the indiosyncracies of his own personal history. This, of course, is the basic corrective in any social or political theory designed for instruction in the area of public controversy: It can be communicated or taught only imperfectly, thus allowing for growth and change in the theory itself as each new mind struggles to comprehend it and apply it to the facts of the day.

In our approach we see conflicts between social values — both within the individual and between individuals and groups — as the basis of important problems. And although we have tried to guard against distorting reality in order that societal problems can be understood and more easily handled within this framework, our identification and analysis of problems will inevitably reflect our way of looking at political controversy.

To the extent that one is willing to recognize and reexamine those assumptions in his framework that others would dispute, he is less likely to cling permanently to a single conception of public controversy. The plurality of conceivable schemes for organizing teaching public issues provides, in this sense, healthy confusion.

F. Teaching Public Issues in the Existing Curriculum Structure

Where can (and should) public issues be taught in the K–12 program? Because all our work has been done at the secondary level, we shall discuss possibilities there before commenting on the total curriculum span. Public issue analysis can be considered the core of curriculum (or of a single course) or a concern supplemental to other objectives (e.g., historical knowledge, inquiry, skills, understanding a discipline). Most teachers probably prefer the latter. Initially they are less interested in creating entirely new curriculum on public controversy than in bringing public issues into existing courses as enrichment. The titles of almost all social studies courses at the secondary level can be interpreted as consistent with such modification. The "histories" — United States, world, European, black; the "area studies" — Africa, Asia, Latin America; the "disciplines" — economics, political science, psychology, geography, sociology, anthropology; such courses as Civics, American Government, Problems of Democracy, International Relations, and humanities–social studies combinations — could be made more "relevant" if they included attention to persisting public issues. The AEP *Public Issues Series* contains materials that can be used for many of these courses, as Table 9.1 illustrates.

Several teachers have used public issues units occasionally in an ad hoc manner to enliven or give depth to topics in existing courses (e.g., using the *American Revolution* or *Civil War* booklets as supplements to a textbook-oriented course in United States History). Others have attempted more

TABLE 9.1. AEP *PUBLIC ISSUES SERIES* UNIT BOOKS APPROPRIATE AS SUPPLEMENTARY MATERIALS IN SOCIAL STUDIES COURSES

Courses	*Titles*
History	1. *The American Revolution*
United States 1, 2, 4, 5, 6, 7, 9, 17, 18	2. *The Railroad Era*
European 15, 16, 21, 22, 23, 24	3. *Taking a Stand: Discussion Guide*
World 13, 14, 15, 16, 21, 22, 23, 24	4. *Religious Freedom*
Black 7, 17, 18	5. *The Rise of Organized Labor*
	6. *The Immigrant's Experience*
American Problems	7. *Negro Views of America*
	8. *Municipal Politics*
Civics, Problems of Democracy 4, 7, 8, 10, 11	9. *The New Deal*
American Government 12, 18, 19, 20	10. *Rights of the Accused*
	11. *The Lawsuit*
Area Studies	12. *Community Change*
	13. *Colonial Kenya*
Asia 14	14. *Communist China*
Africa 13	15. *Nazi Germany*
	16. *20th Century Russia*
Disciplines	17. *American Civil War*
	18. *Race and Education*
Economics 2, 5, 9, 12, 14, 20	19. *Science and Public Policy*
Political Science 1, 4, 5, 8, 9, 10, 12, 17, 18, 19	20. *Status*
Sociology-Anthropology 7, 8, 12, 13, 14, 15, 16, 18, 20	21. *The Limits of War*
	22. *Revolution and World Politics*
Psychology 6, 7, 12, 13, 14, 15, 18, 19	23. *Organizations Among Nations*
Law 4, 10, 11, 18, 21, 23, 24	24. *Diplomacy and International Law*
International Relations	
21, 22, 23, 24	

thorough curriculum reorganization to make public issues a substantial focus. Statements from teachers in three different school systems indicate some variety in the way AEP units might be used.

An eleventh-grade United States history teacher reports:[2]

> The three experimental sections did not use the standard textbook, nor was their main objective to impart knowledge of the facts of American history to students. The main purpose of the course was, instead, to better serve the needs of students who were not necessarily going to become historians, but who were being asked to make sense out of an increasingly complex society. . . .
>
> The materials and methods used were organized around four general concepts.
>
> 1. Students need to develop clearly defined procedures that will aid them in

[2] Information received from Mr. William R. Shirer, Downers Grove South High School, Downers Grove, Illinois.

the areas of critical thinking, logical analysis, and working together in groups to solve problems.

2. Students should be able to understand the nature of a pluralistic democratic society. Further, they should be able to relate some of the important events and ideas that formed the outlooks prevalent in that society to their own experience.

3. Students should clarify their own views on various issues, and learn to support those views by rational means.

4. Students ought to be more involved in the process of their own education. They should, therefore, be put in classroom situations where it is difficult, if not impossible, to ignore the ideas being discussed, or the people discussing them.

In order to implement these concepts, we emphasized the three strategies of *ordering values, logical analysis, and group work.* . . .

The first semester dealt with movements, concepts, or events that are generally regarded as important in shaping basic American assumptions and values. During the second semester, issues important in the twentieth century were studied. Outline of materials used:

Semester I

1. *The American Revolution* (AEP)
2. Logic, Analysis, and Discussion
   Taking a Stand (AEP)
3. Fundamental American Values
   The Constitution
   Religious Freedom (AEP) or *Liberty Under Law*[3] (AEP)
4. Independent Study: The Westward Movement, Slavery,
   The Civil War
   The Pioneer vs. the Wilderness (Scholastic Great Issues Series)
5. Immigration
   The Immigrant's Experience (AEP)

Semester II

6. Organized Labor
   The Rise of Organized Labor (AEP)
7. The Relationship between Business and Government
   The Railroad Era (AEP)
   The New Deal (AEP)
8. American Foreign Policy in the Twentieth Century
   MacArthur vs. Truman (Scholastic Great Issues Series)
9. The Problem of Race in America
   Negro Views of America (AEP)
10. Who Makes the Decisions: The Individual and Society
    Municipal Politics (AEP)

[3] Because *Liberty Under Law* is not part of the *Public Issues Series*/Harvard Social Studies Project, it is not listed in Table 9.1.

Supplementary Materials

Avenues to America's Past, Bowes, ed., Silver Burdett
The American Political Tradition, Hofstadter, Vintage

A teacher describes a ninth-grade Civics course developed by a teaching team in the St. Louis-St. Louis County Social Studies Project:[4]

The basic objectives of our ninth-grade Civics course were to develop the discussion skills and to aid the student in developing positions on some of the major moral-value issues present in our country. In addition to providing stimulating material for aiding the student to develop the discussion skills, we felt that our program enabled the student to gain an understanding of such value dilemmas as: free enterprise in conflict with the general welfare, rights of minorities versus the majority rule, conformity versus cultural pluralism, individual rights and the security of the public. These dilemmas were studied through the AEP pamphlets which formed the core of the Civics course.

There was considerable variety in the manner in which each teacher organized and taught the course. The teachers began with a study and practice of the skills contained in the *Taking a Stand* unit. One teacher used this unit for the entire semester by applying the skills to a wide variety of current issues which the teacher obtained from newspapers and magazines. Using current issues seems to lead to greater student involvement, but this approach does require the teacher to develop a large number of new cases each year. Another teacher did not issue the *Taking a Stand* unit to the students; instead he spent approximately two weeks at the beginning of the year discussing cases of immediate interest to the students. Then he used the pamphlets in the AEP Public Issues Series, teaching the discussion skills when appropriate. Most teachers spent one or two weeks on introductory cases after which they taught *Taking a Stand* for three to five weeks.

The variety of programs increased with the other units of the course. One teacher selected some cases from each unit and omitted the rest. Other teachers taught the unit booklets in their entirety, adding supplemental material either for the purpose of providing more content background, or for providing the students with relevant cases which were omitted or occurred after the unit was published. For example, in the *Railroad Era* and *Negro Views of America* units teachers prepared additional historical overview lessons to make the students aware of significant events which the books omitted. Movies also were used to provide additional historical information.

Examples of additional cases for the *Religious Freedom* unit include the issue of taxation of church property and the question of government aid being provided for parochial and private schools. The question of racial intermarriage was developed into an additional case for the *Negro Views of America* unit. Cases dealing with the French in Quebec and the Ibos in Nigeria dealt with

---

[4] Information received from Dr. Alan Tom, Washington University, St. Louis, Mo.

the issue of conformity which was contained in the *Immigrant's Experience* booklet.

The AEP units most frequently used were *Religious Freedom, Immigrant's Experience, Railroad Era, Negro Views of America. Rights of the Accused, Municipal Politics, Rise of Organized Labor,* and *Community Change* were used in some of the schools. The multiple case units usually were taught from three to five weeks depending upon the amount of extra material for each unit; the single case units lasted from one to two weeks.

A curriculum coordinator explains plans for a course in ninth-grade citizenship:[5]

Theme: Responsibility — personal, political, and legal.

During the course students will look at ethical choices, some of which are highly individual and some of which are more clearly matters of public policy. In addition they will examine legislative process, pressure group formation, public confrontation, judicial process.

Objectives:

. . . to improve student ability to identify issues and use analogies and stipulation to further discussion.

. . . to help students explore the various dimensions in the construct, "responsible." That is, responsible for what? To whom? Keeping one's word? Being liable for one's actions?

. . . to aid students in seeing how processes and systems work. They should be able to read newspaper articles on these processes and make sense out of them, be able to make predictions about what may happen next in the process, be able to suggest ways in which participants could have operated differently to be more effective or to be more just, or more responsible.

AEP books to be used:

Municipal Politics, Community Change, The Lawsuit, Rights of the Accused, Liberty and the Law. In addition we use other cases such as the Genovese case, eminent domain cases, and cases dealing with national legislative politics. *Taking a Stand* is used on an *ad hoc* basis, whenever it seems necessary to work on a given aspect of discussion training.

The Harvard Social Studies Project taught a three-year course based on the following outline as students progressed from tenth through twelfth grade:

CONTENT OUTLINE OF HARVARD SOCIAL STUDIES PROJECT

Level One: Introduction to Social Problems: The Individual within a Community

The general purpose of Level One was to present a few cases, illustrative of the general problems to be considered throughout the curriculum, along with

[5] Information received from Mr. Gordon Neisser, Arlington Public Schools, Arlington, Mass.

legal-ethical, analytic, and social science themes and concepts used to deal with the general problems:

    I. A series of cases to demonstrate general problems: Use and Control of Violence, e.g., "The Mutiny Act"; Standard of Living, e.g., "The Coal Mining Hills of Kentucky"; Priority of Privileges, e.g., "Elmtown's Youth"; Public Conformity and Dissent, e.g., "John Brown"; Privacy, e.g., "The Amish."

    II. A few cases in more complex settings to illustrate the role of humans as instrumental to change within a social system, e.g., "Deerfield," "Christian Martyrs."

Level Two: Revolution, Politics, and Law: Anglo-American Constitutional Development

Having raised a series of problems in Level One, Level Two seeks to show, again through a series of cases, the kinds of legal and political institutions that have been developed to deal with the sorts of issues raised in Level One.

    I. The English Experience: William the Conqueror through the English Civil War.

    II. The American Experience: The American Revolution, Constitution, and American Civil War.

    III. The American Political and Judicial Process.

While Part I established formal, institutional arrangements, Parts II and III introduced informal realities in the functioning of the institutions.

Level Three: Transition and Conflict in American Society, 1865–1930

Having outlined the institutional structure in which social conflict is handled, we next presented examples of more complicated problems and examined the process by which the American constitutional system dealt with these issues. The historical context is generally between the Civil War and the Great Depression.

    I. The Negro

    II. Business and Industry

    III. Immigration

    IV. Labor

Level Four: Crises in World Societies: Five Societies in the 20th Century

The purpose here was to examine periods of crisis using as points of view the perceptions and values of those living in the society under study. The student's own, more Anglo-American, point of view was discussed in the light of different cultural norms and institutions.

    I. The New Deal

    II. Kenya — Colonialism and Independence

    III. Germany — The Rise of Nazism

    IV. U.S.S.R. — The Bolshevik Revolution through the mid-thirties

    V. China — Pre-20th Century Stability to Communist Revolution

Level Five: Introduction to the Problem of International Order

The purpose here is to move from domestic issues to the general problem of world peace and order. Historical background is to be given to demonstrate problems of peace-keeping, national sovereignty, and international law.

    I. Colonialism and the Balance of Power
    II. World War I and Versailles
    III. Diplomatic History through World War II
    IV. Nuremberg Trials
    V. Cases on the Problems of International Order: Israel, Hungary, Berlin, Cuba, Vietnam, Panama, South Africa

Level Six: Contemporary Problems: Attaining the "Good Life"

This was to be the most open-ended part, giving students the opportunity to reconsider, redefine, rethink issues raised earlier, and to examine anew the basic dilemmas of modern man. The problems and dilemmas might be categorized as:

    Economics (production, employment, population, technology)
    Race and Ethnic Assimilation — Isolation-Autonomy
    Politics (sovereignty and the consent process)
    Philosophical, Psychological, and Personal Fulfillment

The Harvard staff did not have enough time to develop materials for and teach Levels V and VI. Materials arising out of Levels I through IV have been adapted into the AEP unit books. Continuing development and experimental teaching will bring unit book titles appropriate for Levels V and VI, along with additional titles and topics appropriate for earlier levels.

A three-year course focusing exclusively on public controversy startles those committed to other educational goals. Some assume this necessitates *neglecting* history, concepts from social science disciplines, or inquiry skills, thereby providing a far too limited curriculum. Those who equate public controversy with sorrow, hatred, bloodshed, injustice, and intense advocacy may find the curriculum excessively dismal, harsh, or lacking in joy and the opportunity for creative aesthetic learning. It is appropriate, therefore, to question how much controversy students (at various ages) can handle productively and what should be its place in the total educational context. Various experiences are important to a "well-balanced" education, and it would be wrong to monopolize a student's education through a single curriculum, whether it be public issues, the disciplines, art, or athletics. As we explain in Chapter 11, we see a critical need to provide opportunities for students to become involved in nonacademic, "action" activities as well as formal reflective activities. We have no desire to impose studying public issues as the primary focus of K–12 or even secondary curriculum. The challenge of the moment is only to make studying public issues an available and exciting *option* for teachers and students.

Effective use of the jurisprudential approach requires students who are cognitively mature enough to think in abstract, hypothetical terms, and who can engage in relatively sophisticated moral reasoning.[6] We believe that these abilities emerge usually during the teens. Thus it may be premature to attempt the jurisprudential approach (teaching students to arrive at general qualified principles to support positions on specific cases) prior to high school. Given this maturation problem, analyzing public issues seems most appropriate for secondary school social studies, and we see no reason why three- or four-year programs on public issues should not be made available.

To answer above criticisms of such lengthy programs, we must remind the critic that our approach includes major concern for history, concepts, and theories in social science and "inquiry" skills. To suggest that we have neglected these is inaccurate. Rather than construe these points of emphasis as ends in themselves, we use them as sources of data, insights, procedures, etc. that can help clarify public issues. We are also aware that disturbing, discouraging, even dismal and pessimistic attitudes can develop through extensive and intensive public problems analysis. The initial intellectual excitement of public dilemmas, if pursued too singlemindedly, can become a wearisome burden. Earlier we mentioned the importance of novelty and the need to depart from a tone of harsh advocacy on "insoluble" problems. Here we reaffirm that and emphasize that "happier" sorts of learning elsewhere in the curriculum are necessary antidotes to the often untasty medicine of public issues.

II. Factual Information in Studying Public Issues

Critics warn that until students acquire a significant body of information, they are not equipped to analyze public issues intelligently. The plea to concentrate heavily on acquiring information is implied in recommendations to study several years of "content" (e.g. history) before approaching public policy questions. Critics also hold that a thorough study of sociological and psychological literature on race relations is necessary before one advocates public policy on that subject; or that one ought to visit Vietnam and read Congressional debate before one takes a stand on United States policy there.

---

[6] According to Levi's analysis (1948), legal reasoning requires the ability to detect logical inconsistencies in arguments, to construe specific cases as illustrations of general principles, and to make fine distinctions among apparently different situations. Kohlberg (1968) suggests that children mature through different stages of moral reasoning, beginning with a "pre-moral" level based only on avoiding punishment and gaining hedonistic rewards, progressing through a stage emphasizing obeying rules and authority primarily to avoid disapproval and censure, and finally arriving at self-accepted morality grounded in a concept of community welfare, social contact, and eventually independent individual conscience. The ability to engage in jurisprudential reasoning would seem unlikely unless a person is operating at least in Kohlberg's third stage. It remains to be seen whether intensive training might accelerate the development of such cognitive functions and stages in moral reasoning.

In this section we examine the significance of factual information, how to acquire such information, and strategies for coping with a lack of information.

We recognize the importance of factual disagreements in public controversy, discussed at some length in Chapter 2. Did the Christians pose a serious threat to stability in the Roman Empire? Did Britain impose sufficient economic burdens upon the American colonies to justify revolution? Will establishing separate black institutions intensify racial polarization? Will an ABM system increase or decrease the chances for world peace? How harmful is marijuana or DDT to the health of humans? To adequately justify most public policies we must be able to verify factual claims, whether they be oriented toward the past, present or future, whether they involve complicated causal relationships ("appeasement causes aggression," "DDT causes death"); descriptive accounts of events and conditions ("who fired the first shot?" "what kinds of economic burdens existed?"); or singular predictions ("How will the Soviet government respond to ABM deployment?"). Considerable information is required to resolve such issues.

Information on historical situations is required if students are to weigh the appropriateness of analogies (as in the discussion between a teacher and Don — pp. 266–268 — in which similarities and differences between the American Revolution and Civil War were examined) and if they are to suggest authentic analogies on their own. Substantial historical background is a necessary but certainly not sufficient condition for productively discussing public issues. Persons may "know" history in the sense of being able to recall details of political-military narrative. This is no guarantee, however, that such persons will also be able to perceive how the known facts might be used to challenge or support more general claims. Nor does historical knowledge necessarily enable one to perceive principles or commonalities among events that could be applied to public issues not yet studied. Information storage is helpful only if complemented by a retrieval system that applies relevant information to new questions (i.e., questions different from those that requested and stored the information in the first place). We must be careful, therefore, not to place too much emphasis on merely acquiring and storing factual information.

A. When to Acquire Information

Unfortunately, the educational debate usually focuses not on "What kind of information is most useful?" but on "Should information be acquired *before* the student deals with problems or *while* he is studying problems?" Should the fundamental knowledge necessary for dealing with issues be taught separately and prior to considering the issues or concurrently as the issues themselves arise? If this choice must be made, we believe that acquiring information should occur as a *response* to the stimulus of a problem, and we have three major objections to the alternative strategy of teaching substantial information as *preparation* for dealing with problems.

Difficulty of Predicting What Information is Useful. It is difficult (if not impossible) to anticipate at time A what knowledge and information will be useful in resolving public issues at a later time B. Discussants of the Vietnam war may clash on such problems as the legality of United States action; the Vietnamese attitudes toward their government; the motivations of United States policy-makers; the possibilities for liberal democracy in Vietnam; the probability of increased communist aggression in Southeast Asia in the face of an American defeat; or the consequences of war on United States domestic conflict. Because the information needed depends largely on what issues appear salient to the discussants, it is difficult to plan precisely what information the discussants will "need."

Information Overload. We could try to provide extensive information on all these issues, thus preparing discussants for any specific question they choose to discuss. This strategy, however, would require spending vast amounts of time acquiring information. Were they to learn "all" information relevant to all these issues, they might never have the opportunity to think about an appropriate United States policy. In a world of exploding knowledge, poor communication results both from lack of access to information (because knowledge is too specialized) and storing excessive information (which we are unable to sort and process). Unless people become more discriminating and selective of information they choose to learn, they will be paralyzed by information overload, unable to apply knowledge gained in the past to solving issues not previously studied. One way to avoid this is to acquire only information for which an apparent or imminent need exists. Because technological advances (printing, radio, television, computers, libraries, indexing) in storing, retrieving, and disseminating information have vastly enlarged our capacity to gather information in response to relatively immediate questions, it is no longer necessary to store information in our minds far in advance of possible use.

Pedagogical Effectiveness. Research seems to indicate that students are more highly motivated to acquire information and tend to retain it longer if it is acquired as a response to solve a problem that interests the student. Much youth revolt today focuses on requirements to learn information for which students see no immediate use. Students who have been permitted to gather information for dealing with issues pertinent to their lives (e.g., drug problem studies by teenagers) have shown great enthusiasm for amassing "the facts."

For these reasons, we advocate acquiring information primarily as a response to or by-product of investigating specific public issues, rather than as a separate, preparatory study for future problems that, at the time of such study, remain unapparent to the student. Yet, we do not wish to overemphasize the distinction between the "before" and "during" approaches. A student in discussing Vietnam may suddenly learn that he knows nothing about procedures for appealing draft board decisions. He then may spend many hours researching this problem to "prepare" himself for the day when he receives his classification. This is appropriate — he should not wait until the day he is classified to investigate appeals. If we wish students to consider public policy on race relations, we do not simply ask, "What do you think about race relations?" We provide a case that dramatizes some specific issues, ask students to read the case, and *then* we discuss the issues. In this sense, we provide "preparation" that helps to create the problems that students will later pursue. Acquiring information "before" or "during" studying an issue represents different points on a continuum, not a categorical distinction between teaching strategies.

B. Recognizing the Need for Information

Assuming that the educator is unable to predict the specific knowledge or information students will need at a future point, the major challenge for curriculum-makers is to teach students to identify and recognize issues on which their knowledge is incomplete and to develop skills for seeking information that is needed. Continuous practice in requesting evidence to support factual claims should help illustrate to students the many questions for which we have no final answers. Continuous practice in explicitly stating the issue of disagreement in discussion should help to isolate those issues that might be solved by accumulating more evidence from those issues that must be resolved through other strategies. That is, the first step in acquiring information must be recognizing the need for specific facts.

The teacher can illustrate through real or contrived discussions how certain information, if introduced into the discussion, might resolve or ignite disagreement (e.g., when new information challenges assumptions that all discussants had assumed to be true beyond reasonable doubt). He can structure exercises in such formats as the following:

1. What information in the case tends to (A) support, (B) refute, or (C) neither clearly support nor refute each of the following claims? 1. "Patriots tried peaceful methods of protest to Britain" etc.

2. What kinds of statistics would you request to determine whether British mercantile policy caused economic hardship to American colonists?

3. List factual issues raised by the case on which there is conflicting evidence.

4. At what point in the following discussion should someone have said, "Wait. We're just speculating on different motivations of the slaveholders. We need some specific testimony from slaveholders to learn what they really thought."

Such activities should help to teach the habit of asking whether the information one has is sufficient and what additional information would be required to support or challenge the claims in dispute.

C. Gathering Information

Once discussants have identified the information needed, they must then seek it. In some cases, it might be wise to terminate discussion and allow for a research period in which participants search for important evidence in libraries, government agencies, or other sources, returning later with additional information that will allow them to resume discussion. In many controversies, however, the information can be readily obtained without significantly interrupting the discussion. The teacher may have information needed by students and be able to settle some controversial claims with a few short remarks (e.g., informing students of recent Supreme Court decisions). Often students have overlooked information available in the cases or textbooks on their desks, and the teacher can suggest taking time out to examine these sources (dictionaries, encyclopedias, almanacs, maps, periodicals, and other documents) that students could quickly consult. Students themselves provide useful sources of information for each other from their specialized experiences, interests, and skills. One day students began to argue about whether the local police ever advised suspects of their right to remain silent. Only one student in the group had ever been arrested, but through his personal report the group obtained specific information.

The teacher cannot anticipate all information that might be needed on certain issues. Even if he could anticipate such needs, he would probably find it impossible to make the information easily accessible to students in the classroom. Therefore, students must learn research skills that will enable them to gather information on their own. Instruction on using a library, gathering information at City Hall, and standard references sources (e.g., almanacs, fact books, historical encyclopedias, government publications) will help equip students with skills needed to "get the facts."

D. Coping with a Lack of Conclusive Evidence

Discussion might be stalled on a factual issue in at least three ways: (1) Discussants do not have access to information that they assume exists and would resolve their disagreement if it were available (e.g., Has the Supreme Court upheld the right of students to demonstrate peacefully in high school?). (2) Discussants realize they need more information to solve an issue, but are unsure if additional research would help (e.g., How much economic hardship did the average American suffer because of British mercantile policy in the eighteenth century?). (3) Factual claims remain controversial because discussants lack conclusive evidence on important problems, but they prefer to continue conversation rather than search for additional information. This decision might be based primarily on convenience, as in (1), or on the necessity to act even though important issues remain unresolved, as in (3). More often than not, we suspect, citizens and officials are compelled to take a stand on public policy before they have all relevant facts. There is insufficient time or resources to complete all conceivable research that would be helpful in settling controversial factual issues, especially predictions. (Decisions to drop the atomic bomb in 1945, to intervene at the Bay of Pigs, to test nerve gas in Utah in 1969 are just a few examples.) Critical to policy justification is accurately predicting *consequences,* but until we can gather enough facts to make airtight predictions on alternative actions, our judgments will always be based on incomplete evidence.

Once the decision not to engage in further research has been made, two major strategies help cope with controversial factual issues. One can *stipulate* alternative conclusions to the controversy, and examine the implications of each alternative stipulation. One could stipulate, for example, various possible costs for the United States to bring democracy to Vietnam, and then inquire what prices the United States would be willing and able to pay. One can also *bypass* or ignore temporarily the issue under contention, requesting that disputants make their cases on grounds other than the unresolved factual problem. In ignoring the cost question on the Vietnam problem, discussants might focus on such issues as American treaty obligations, defining civil war versus foreign aggression, or the probable Russian and Chinese responses to different United States policies. Stipulating and bypassing the controversial claim shifts the agenda to new issues, which can be especially useful if the discussion is "hung up" on irrelevant issues or unanswerable factual questions. In debating the justification of American intervention in Vietnam, suppose a group is preoccupied with whether one discussant's brother has been assigned to a helicopter or an infantry unit. To stipulate a conclusion on this might point out its questionable relevance to the central issue: i.e., justification of United States intervention.

Stipulation and bypass can prevent a discussion from bogging down on unresolvable problems, but they can also be used recklessly to avoid and evade issues that should be faced. It would seem premature for John to cut off discussion on Vietnam war costs by saying, "Let's not get involved in that question, because we don't have all the facts," if the group had been considering the problem for only two minutes. Similarly, Sam could unreasonably stipulate away an argument by suggesting, "Because we don't have all the facts, I will stipulate that the United States could bring peace to Vietnam at a cost of $50,000 per year for ten years." Stipulation and bypass should be used not to avoid troublesome issues, but to move the discussion along after controversial claims have been wrestled with, and when there seems no other way to break a deadlock that is interfering with the progress of discussion.

E. How Much Information Do We Need?

How much does a student need to know about the American Revolution to make an intelligent judgment on its justification? This represents the dilemma faced by most teachers in selecting a finite quantity from a virtually infinite reservoir of information. Although we can offer no prescriptions to ensure appropriate content selection, the dilemma can be approached more manageably if we ask not "how much information," but "what kinds of information seem necessary for dealing with specific questions?" A teacher who wishes students to test generalizations about colonial American society would select facts and data different from the teacher who wishes to focus primarily on a case study of one community. In studying school desegregation, teacher A, concerned with issues in legal reasoning, might emphasize analyzing Supreme Court decisions; teacher B, concerned with sociological effects of desegregation, might focus on data from social science studies; teacher C, concerned with personal, biographical experiences, might select short stories or journalistic accounts of children in segregated and integrated schools. How much and what information the student "needs" cannot be determined by any universal standard, but only by the specific issues on which he is called upon to reflect.

Critics of the "case study approach" often ignore this point. They may assert that students don't obtain much information on the American Revolution from reading a section of Kenneth Roberts's *Oliver Wiswell*, or that a case on the Pullman strike of 1893 does not sufficiently cover the history of organized labor during that period. Most likely the teacher does not intend such documents to convey the general historical knowledge to which the critics refer. The teacher may have completely different issues or questions in mind; "How might it feel to be driven from your home by an angry, irrational mob?" or "What techniques for subduing strikes were available to private enterprise?" If one wishes to generalize conclusions reached on a single case study, then information beyond the case study is obviously necessary. However, merely using a case study (or fictional historical account), cannot be condemned for its lack of comprehensive coverage when such is not the teacher's intent. The major power of case studies included in the AEP *Public Issues Series* lies not in the evidence they provide for substantiating historical generalizations, but in the issues and principles they raise in legal-ethical-political reasoning. Each case following Chapters 4 through 8 provides sufficient information to raise several issues and principles, but certainly inadequate information to support or challenge all claims about the past, present, or future. The teacher must, of course, help students to perceive how specific facts of case studies support, refute, or are irrelevant to broader generalizations.

Another dimension of the information problem is that teachers are reluctant to deal with issues for which they have not been formally educated.

Teachers often feel inadequate in dealing with public issues because the information they have acquired in studying formal academic subjects seems inapplicable to dilemmas, especially ethical problems, raised in controversial public issues. We suspect that feelings of inadequacy are often based on an unrealistic and unnecessary assumption — that teachers must have the answers to all questions a student may ask on the teacher's "subject," that teachers who are unable to tell students solutions to problems are incompetent. Throughout this book, we have tried to indicate the many senses in which conflicts over public issues are not likely to be resolved by final answers or truth. The teacher's role in this sort of curriculum cannot be that of truth giver, but one of provoker, clarifier, summarizer, and facilitator. Because no human being could master all the knowledge relevant to considering public issues, teachers need not be embarrassed when they cannot recall important facts, nor when students provide information that the teacher may not know. The honest recognition of what we do not know (and need to learn) can be equally as instructive as telling each other what we do know.

III. The Use of Analogy

A. The Function of Analogy in Argument

One effective technique for helping students qualify their general value judgments is to introduce an analogy for which the student is likely to take a position different from (or directly contradicting) his position on the original issue.[7] The disturbing feeling of possible inconsistency can lead to more careful consideration of the principles one uses to justify his stand. In a dialogue following "Mrs. Webster's Rooming House," Sam and his teacher argue whether the state should pass a law that prohibits racial discrimination in renting rooms in the landlord's home.

Mrs. Webster's Rooming House

Ever since her husband died, Mrs. Webster had struggled to eke out a living from the small rooming house she operated. She was quite disturbed when the state passed a law that, among other things, prohibited discrimination on the basis of race, religion, or nationality. She didn't really like members of minority groups, especially Negroes. But, more important, Mrs. Webster felt that if she rented rooms to such people her regular boarders might get angry and move out. "It's my property," she told her neighbors, "and no one has the right to tell me whom I must allow to sleep in my house."

One night Mrs. Webster was disturbed at dinner by the ring of her doorbell. "A traveller to occupy my vacant room," she thought happily. When she opened the door she saw a Negro. "My name is Mr. Jones. I've looked all over town.

[7] For our purposes, an analogy is an authentic or hypothetical situation introduced to test the consistency and extent of one's value or policy judgment on an original situation. Analogies can be expressed in shorthand references ("if you favored using the atomic bomb on Japan, why not on North Vietnam?"), or in a detailed narrative describing a situation unfamiliar to the discussant.

Do you have a vacant room for me tonight?" he asked. Mrs. Webster hesitated, "No, sorry, we're all full."

Dialogue	*Dialogue Analysis*
Sam: The government should not tell Mrs. Webster how to run her business.	Implies general value claim: laissez faire, free enterprise
Teacher: Suppose Mrs. Webster ran a restaurant. To save money she served leftovers the next day. Occasionally the food spoiled and customers got food poisoning, but because most customers were transient, moving through town, they never really complained. Do you think the government should force Mrs. Webster to abide by certain health standards?	Introduces analogy to challenge value claim by raising conflicting value: public health
Sam: Yes, of course.	Supports conflicting value
Teacher: Well, that's government control. I thought you were opposed to government interference with a person's business.	Points out inconsistency
Sam: Well, a restaurant is different from a rooming house. It affects a person's health.	Challenges relevance of analogy by showing how it's different
Teacher: Getting a good night's rest also affects your health. If Mr. Jones has to sleep out in the cold, Mrs. Webster is hurting him — maybe even more than a person who just has a stomachache from old food.	Defends analogy by arguing that health is critical to both cases
Sam: But this is in her own home. This would be forcing people to mix with other people socially and that's different from laws that require that food be safe.	Makes a distinction between regulation for social integration versus public health
Teacher: Well, what now is your position on whether the government should be able to tell people how to run their businesses?	Requests reconsideration of original value claim
Sam: Government regulation for the clear purpose of defending public health is okay, but regulation intended to force different people to mix socially is not.	Presents qualification of original position, based on distinction introduced through the analogy

The persuasive power of the analogy depends largely on the human desire to maintain a consistent position. When confronted with a challenging analogy a person will: (1) Reverse his original position. ("Okay, I guess you're right—if they can interfere with restaurants, they should also be able to control rooming houses.") (2) Maintain his original position by showing how the analogy differs from the original situation. ("Interference is justified in the restaurant, but not in the rooming house, because the two situations are different in very important ways. . . .") (3) Qualify his original position. (Mrs. Webster is justified in turning away Mr. Jones only if we construe the rooming house as essentially her private "home" and only incidentally a place of business.)

Students often see a challenging analogy only as a technique for "showing up" or "beating" one's adversary, rather than helping discussants reach more complicated justifications of their views. It is also commonly seen as a rhetorical or sophistic trick used by the teacher (or other students) to put a person on the defensive.[8] The student viewing the analogy as a trick is likely to say "that's different," and assume that he has met the challenge. To this, the teacher has only to ask, "How is it different?" Inquiry into similarities and differences between the two situations helps to provide criteria (e.g., regulation for health versus social integration) for making distinctions and adding qualifications or limitations to one's general positions. That is, apparent inconsistencies can be resolved by showing how value statements previously expressed in a very general form can be modified to exclude implications that the student does not intend. Because of the restaurant analogy, Sam will no longer imply that he opposes all government control over private business; he does favor regulations that protect public health — a qualification not stated in his initial position. In this sense, imperfect but provocative analogies are often as useful as closely parallel situations. The analogy is a valuable tool for clarification precisely because it tends to lead toward distinctions and qualifications. It also tends to lead to confusion, unless the group can go beyond the analogy and arrive at a distinction.

History students often object to using analogy. In the following dialogue, a teacher explores Don's opinion about whether the American patriots were justified in revolting against England.

> Don: I think the patriots had a right to revolt because the British were just not
>   giving them a chance to exercise their basic rights, you know, like the right to

---

[8] To avoid overly defensive reactions by students, the teacher might explain how and why he will be using analogies in discussion. Analogies should be used not only with aggressive, argumentative students, but also with the more subdued, reflective ones. The teacher should avoid posing analogies in rapid-fire succession, because it is difficult to keep many situations in mind at once, and because this encourages gamesmanship ("you handled that analogy, but can you deal with this one?").

be represented. They had the right to levy their own taxes on themselves but not have somebody else come and tell them to pay taxes.

Teacher: Yeah, but don't you see what this means? I mean, this means that they were going to form a new country and break away from England.

Don: So?

Teacher: Well, I'm just wondering whether they really had the right to do that. Now take a look at the South. What about the South before the Civil War in this country? Do you think they had a right to break away from the United States?

Don: Gee, you keep doing this. I mean, you keep bringing up these extraneous, these outside topics. Now why bring up the Civil War? That just gets us off the subject again.

Teacher: No, no it doesn't. It's very relevant. You're saying that when people think their rights are being taken away by the government they have a right to break away or set up a new government. Isn't that what you're saying?

Don: So, what has that got to do with the Civil War?

Teacher: Okay, now. Take a look at the South. They felt that the federal government was taking away the South's rights. They felt the federal government was trying to abolish slavery, and they were placing high tariffs on all these manufactured goods that the South had to buy, and the South really felt that the federal government was taking away their self-government, the self-government for southerners. Now if you say the patriots had a right to revolt but the southerners did not have a right to revolt then you're being inconsistent, because the two situations involve the same principle, the right to revolt if self-government is denied.

Don: Oh, yeah, I see that. I can see the two situations are alike in the sense that they both involve revolt when you want more self-government, but I still think that the Civil War, is, you know, is different, it's just different, that's all.

Teacher: What are the important differences?

Don: Well, let's see, the main difference was the South decided at some point, that is the individual states themselves, like Virginia, North Carolina, and South Carolina, they all decided at a certain point to join the Union, to become a part of the Constitution. When they joined the Union, and became part of the Constitution, they agreed to abide by the decisions of the federal government. They said, okay, we're going to follow the Constitution; that's the supreme law of the land, and then the decisions started going against them and then they said no, we're going to break away. Well, they made an agreement, they made a contract, and then they wanted to pull out after they'd made the agreement. But the patriots were different. I mean, nobody ever asked them to join the British Union, nobody ever asked are they part of some British constitution. That was different. It was imposed on them.

Teacher: Okay, that's very good. This is an important difference and helps to show why your position may really be consistent after all.

Don: Well, I still don't see what the Civil War has to do with my position on the issue of the American Revolution.

Teacher: Well, you said the patriots had a right to revolt because Britain wouldn't grant them basic rights, mainly of representation. But you wouldn't say that people in general have a right to revolt even though they feel their rights are being taken away. Now by considering the South you have clarified that if people voluntarily agree to limit their rights of self-government by joining a union then they have no right to back out of the agreement and they can't revolt.

Don: Oh, I see. The patriots have a right to fight for freedom, because they never voluntarily joined anything, whereas the South voluntarily joined something and so they don't have a right to, I see, so the two situations really are related in that sense.

Is it fair for the teacher to compare the American Revolution with the Civil War? Some historians claim that each historical event is unique, arising from its own conditions and causes that have not been and never will be replicated. To suggest that there are important similarities between the American Revolution and Civil War is, therefore, historically misleading. Such oversimplification can result in disastrous mistakes when used as a basis for social policy: for example, the attempt to justify American military involvement in Vietnam by the analogy of appeasement at Munich. The extreme position holds that *no* similarities exist between any two events. Even if we demonstrate that American patriots and southern Confederates used similar language in defining their rights, this view of history would hold that the "rights" were not comparable because they communicated different *meanings* to those who used them in the two historical periods. A more moderate position holds that while the gestalt, milieu, or ethos of any two historical situations differs markedly, discrete events do contain similar components or elements (e.g., both the American Revolution and Civil War involved violence and in both cases men sought to justify violence by invoking the value of self-government). According to the moderate position, identifying similarities among historical situations is legitimate, but one must take special care to note significant differences that might otherwise be obscured by uncritically accepting apparent similarities.

We reject the assumption of total uniqueness for every historical event. Writers have persuasively illustrated how elements or components of two or more historical situations do resemble each other (e.g., Elkins, 1959; Mink, 1965; Klein, 1967). Comparing and showing commonalities among some aspects of separate events does not imply that the events must be similar in all significant aspects — on the contrary, important differences are likely, should be recognized, and can be as instructive as the similarities. Our ability to demonstrate useful ways of comparing historical situations should be reason enough to reject the "absolute uniqueness" position. In addition, we believe that if many people were to act in accordance with that position, organized society would disintegrate. If every event is unique in all respects, we would not be justified in applying any rule made in the past to any event in the future. The definitions of murder, violence, racial discrimination, speeding, school attendance, divorce, or property would change every instant and vary for each individual. Our ideas, which result from totally unique experience, could not be communicated to others. It would be foolhardy to make predictions or to expect any regularities in human behavior.

We must accept the more moderate view that although the general character of historical situations seems unique, there are often sufficiently similar components so that comparing situations is intellectually legitimate. Comparison involves sorting out relevant similarities and differences. In fact, identifying specific differences is often the most instructive strategy for arriving at qualifications in one's value position. In the discussion of Mrs. Webster's rooming house, the differences between a restaurant and a private rooming house helped Sam to articulate his position on government regulation of business. In the discussion between the teacher and Don, the difference between the relationship of the South to the central government versus the patriots to England helped Don to resolve what appeared to be an inconsistent position. (The teacher could have continued to explore whether voluntary contract was an accurate distinction between the situation of the patriots versus the Confederates.)

The major function of analogy in jurisprudential teaching is to lead the student to articulate distinctions and qualifications that could be used to refine what had been previously vague, gut reactions to public policy. In this sense the major focus for clarification is not history, but why we feel certain ways about history or events. By comparing controversy in Selma, Alabama, in the 1960's or the Confederate secession from the Union in the 1860's to the American Revolution, it should be clear that we do not intend primarily to achieve a more thorough study of the American Revolution. Rather, the analogies are introduced to clarify students' values and positions about the legitimacy of violent revolt against established authority. The "subject" studied is not really a historical period, but the principles one uses to support his beliefs.[9]

The following dialogue is from a class disscussion on the justification for violent protest against the Stamp Act in American colonies:

Betty: I don't think morally speaking that violence can ever be justified.
Roger: It can be justified in self-defense.

[9] Given this purpose for the use of analogy, hypothetical and fictional analogies are as helpful as historically authentic ones. To thoroughly explore one's value commitments it is important to view historical situations as hypothetical possibilities and credible fictional situations as real alternatives. This can be done, we believe, without "distorting" history, though many teachers may squirm at the thought.

Teacher: Any other situation you can think of where violence can be morally justified? Think of a specific situation where it's not in self-defense, but still justified.

Long period of silence. No student response.

Teacher: Let's look at the Civil War in this country. To oversimplify the situation, the North felt that the South was practicing an inhuman institution — slavery. A major justification by the North for fighting the Civil War was that the southerners did not have the moral right to enslave a race of people. They went to war over that issue, but this wasn't necessarily for the self-defense of the North was it?

Leslie: The issue was more whether the South had a right to secede from the Union — preservation of the union.

Teacher: Okay. Certainly both issues were cited as justifications for violence. Do you think these principles are as valid as self-defense?

Chris: I think that if you in your own mind feel that you have a really strong principle and you feel that this violence is going to help you to succeed with your principle and you feel very strongly about it I think that you yourself will feel that you're morally right.

Pat: Let's take the case of Hitler who went against the democracy which was established in Germany. He thought his principle was right so he raised an insurrection and that could be analogous to this situation.

Teacher: Take a person within Nazi Germany who decides that he wants to obliterate Hitler — the people who plotted the assassination of Hitler. It wasn't in their self-defense to destroy Hitler. They were endangering their lives by plotting against Hitler. And they felt there were some more important principles that would justify their assassinating the leader of their government.

Barb: It's sort of picking the lesser of two evils.

Charles: It would be morally wrong to kill him. It doesn't matter who he is — just the fact that you killed someone. You wouldn't necessarily say he was a human being but a facsimile thereof. But you still killed him and that's morally wrong.

Teacher: What about the executioner in those states where capital punishment is practiced? A man is given an order to execute a prisoner convicted under due process of law of the state. Is it morally wrong for the executioner to pull the switch? He commits violence, but not in self-defense.

The teacher helps students to consider different situations in which some basis other than self-defense might justify using violence. The class should eventually try to make explicit additional considerations suggested by the analogies: for example, slavery as an immoral institution, the need to preserve the Union, overthrowing a totalitarian regime, or exercising one's lawful duty. These considerations could elaborate and refine the initial claim that violence can be morally justified only in self-defense.

B. Suggested
   Classroom
   Techniques

Analogies can be exceptionally clarifying, but teacher education programs and conventional social studies curriculum have given virtually no attention to this aspect of inquiry. The following suggestions for using analogies in the classroom are not intended to make the teacher a clever dispenser of analogies. The more basic objective is to help students discover, invent, and evaluate analogies on their own.[10]

1. Outlining
   Substantive
   Issues

Effective use of analogy depends largely on our ability to anticipate how others are likely to feel about specific issues. The teacher introduced the restaurant analogy to Sam, assuming that Sam would probably favor government regulation for public health. Before engaging in classroom discussion, the teacher should try to anticipate in detail the value, definitional, and factual disagreements likely to arise in considering a particular issue. In addition to taking inventory of issues and arguments presented in the media, it is most useful to have discussions with one's colleagues — discusstions that focus not on "How should I teach about open-housing laws?" but on "What kinds of open-housing laws should I support and why?" To anticipate problems likely to arise in the classroom, discussions with colleagues should focus precisely on the substantive public policy issues, not pedagogical problems. Once controversial substantive claims are exposed, *then* considering how these should be handled in class can be profitable. The following plan (Oliver and Shaver, 1966, pp. 155–7) delineates the controversy that arose as colleagues discussed the federal government's role in desegregating public schools.

> I. The Central Issue: Does the white segregationist have the right to control which races his children will associate with in the public schools, or should the right of the Negro to attend racially mixed schools be assured so that he can obtain equal educational opportunities?
>   A. The Value Conflict: freedom of association vs. equal education opportunity.
>   The Legal Conflict: states' rights vs. equal protection under the law
>   B. Important Factual Questions Behind the Conflict
>   1. Do most southern whites actually feel that going to school with Negroes seriously infringes upon their freedom of association? Would most whites feel a personal injury if they were forced to attend school with Negroes?
>   2. Will Negroes get an inferior education unless the southern schools are desegregated?

[10] This section would also fit appropriately in Chapter 10. Because analogical reasoning is significant in jurisprudential thought, we choose to recognize analogy as a special problem and continue theoretical and pedagogical observations here.

C. Definitional Problems

    1. What does "equal treatment" mean? Does it mean that each person should be treated exactly the same? Why isn't separate-but-equal actually equal treatment?

    2. What does the word "associate" mean in freedom of association? Does one have to associate with the Negro when one goes to school with him? Do you associate with a person living in the same community with him, or by walking down the same street he does?

D. Analogies to Make the Value Conflict More Salient

    1. Analogies emphasizing association rights.

        a. If a group of Indians moved into your town and it was known that there was a very high rate of TB among Indians, would you want them to have a special school?

        b. Is the principle justified in segregating boys and girls on the playground?

        c. What if you and your friends enjoy playing football in one corner of the playground every afternoon? Several boys, who can't play very well and who are always starting fights, want to play with you. Do you have the right to exclude these boys from your game simply because you and your friends don't like them? What if this exclusion makes them feel inferior?

    2. Analogies emphasizing equal rights.

        a. Suppose a doctor just doesn't like to associate with people who have dark kinky hair. Does he have the right to refuse to treat such a man who is brought to him for emergency treatment? Does he have a right to refuse him treatment for any kind of medical problem?

        b. Suppose the majority of people in a community decide they do not want to associate in social or school activities with anyone named Smith. Smiths are not allowed to attend the large, well-established local high school; they are, however, given an "equal" education by being sent to a small rural school some 20 miles out of town. Is this equal treatment?

II. The Implementation Issue: Should a whole section of the country be forced to go through a period of increased tension, violence, and civil strife in order to give the Negro equal educational rights, or should the South be allowed to work out the problem itself, perhaps very gradually, so that there will be less threat of violence and less disruption to the normal activities of the community?

  A. The Value Conflict: peace and order vs. equal educational opportunity

  B. Important Factual Questions Behind the Value Conflict

    1. Will there actually be violence and civil strife if we try to desegregate the schools?

    2. Is the violence caused by desegregation itself, or by radical and

unstable people within the community who simply use desegregation as an opportunity to vent their pent-up hostilities?

3. Can the more subtle forms of violence (economic reprisal, intimidation by anonymous phone calls, etc.) be controlled by law enforcement agencies?

4. Will both Negro and white suffer more through attempts at desegregation than if everyone accepted separate-but-equal?

C. Definitional Problems

What do we really mean by violence? Are tensions and threats violence? Are boycotts, economic sanctions, or threats of being fired violence? Is mass picketing and jeering violence?

D. Analogies to Make the Value Conflict More Salient

1. Analogies emphasizing the importance of basic rights and justifying violence.

a. The American Revolution

b. World War II

c. A man is giving a lecture. Several people start shouting him down and heckling him. Do the police have a right to remove these men from the hall?

d. You and your friends enter a public playground. Several boys threaten to prevent you from using the baseball field. Should you go ahead and use the field, even though there may be a fight?

2. Analogies emphasizing peace and order

a. The Hungarian Revolution of 1956. Should we have risked atomic war to free the Hungarian people?

b. The seizure of Tibet by Communist China

c. A store manager is enraged at a clerk for knocking over a box of cans. You know the clerk did not do it. Should you get into the argument too, especially when you know that the manager is likely to become very angry at you?

III. The Issue of Government, Law, and Higher Morality: Do people have the right to break a law or ruling when they think it goes against a higher moral principle? Can the people of the South justifiably ignore or evade the Supreme Court decision on desegregation, by open or subtle means, because they sincerely believe that it is morally wrong?

The outline spells out issues related to the school desegregation controversy, and for each issue discusses factual, definitional, and value disagreements that could arise. In addition it provides analogies that can be used to support or challenge value claims related to main issues. Such outlines are helpful in lesson and unit planning.

2. Alternate Between Specific and General Issues

Problems just outlined arise in response to specific policy choices—should Governor Faubus bar Negroes from Central High School in Little Rock? Should President Eisenhower send federal troops to enforce the federal court order to integrate Central? The Little Rock case provokes and illustrates the more general substantive issues. Because the jurisprudential approach assumes that decisions on specific cases must be justified by referring to broader principles and issues, it is necessary to teach students to construe the specific cases and analogies in broader terms. In comparing cases and eliciting reasons for personal stands on specific policy, the teacher can draw out the more general categories and principles that students (and citizens in general) need to refine. Consider a teacher-student discussion on the case of the Woodville Barber.

The Case of the Woodville Barber

For years Brian Tuttle had been Woodville's only barber, giving good haircuts at reasonable rates. His small income enabled him to live modestly in an apartment over his shop.

Alex Smith, son of the wealthy bank president, decided one day that he wanted to be a barber. As a present, his father built him a modern barbershop across the street from Tuttle's shop. The banker promised to give his son enough money to operate at a loss for a while. By charging half as much as Tuttle, Alex would soon draw customers away from him and eventually have all the business for himself.

Most of Tuttle's customers could not resist Alex's low rates, even though the haircuts were slightly inferior. Tuttle found he could barely support his family on his decreased volume of business. In Woodville, there was room for only one barber.

Tuttle felt Alex's competition was cheating him out of his livelihood. He took his case to court, claiming, "Since law prohibits 'unfair competition and unreasonable business practices,' Alex Smith and his father are acting illegally." How should the court decide?

Molly: I felt that Tuttle did give the best haircuts, and it said so in here that Alex was giving inferior haircuts, and also Tuttle was there longer, and his rates were reasonable. Alex was giving, you know, unfair competition.

Teacher: Unfair competition. What makes it unfair, Molly?

Molly: Because it's hurting another person, and. . . .

Teacher: Competition that hurts somebody else is unfair. Right?

Molly: Right. You just have to take each case as you see it.

Teacher: Let's take another example, the one that was given during the discussion a few minutes ago, where you have a small grocery store. The fellow has been running the store for years and years. It's his only source of income. Then a big new A & P supermarket moves in across the street, right? And the people start patronizing the supermarket. So then, the fellow who owns the little store — let's call him Joe Grocery — goes to the courts, and he says: "Gee, there's this big supermarket, and they're ruining me!" And the court says: "You're a nice little fellow, you've been working all your life hard in the store, that's right." And they put the A & P out of business. They say you can't do that, right, Molly?

Molly: No, no I don't say that.

Teacher: You don't say that?

Molly: I think, some competition is fair, but if it, if it is, if it is really unfair. . . .

Teacher: This isn't fair now, this is more. . . .

Molly: No, not necessarily. Unfair . . . sometimes there's a healthy competition.

Pat: And this isn't a healthy competition, I don't know, this is unhealthy competition, this grocery store thing.

Joe: Yeah, it's gonna destroy him.

Teacher: Well, we've a new principle called healthy competition and unhealthy competition. Now we've got to draw the distinction. Okay, Molly, what makes it healthy?

In examining the barber case alone, Molly concluded (tentatively) that competition that hurts someone is unfair. After considering the chainstore analogy, she is less willing to call all competition that hurts someone unfair. Instead she suggests the principle of healthy competition, implying that harm resulting from "healthy" competition might not be unfair. The next problem was to distinguish between healthy and unhealthy competition.[11]

Such exercises as the following can further develop the ability to relate specific to general issues (taken from the teacher's guide for the AEP booklet, *Negro Views of America*):

Assume that you wish to discuss the issues listed below, but you can pick only one case to illustrate each issue. Which case would you choose to best illustrate each issue? A. *The Younger Family*, B. *Black Boy*, C. *Malcolm X*, D. *Adam Henry*

ISSUES

_____ 1. What is it like to live in a northern urban slum?

_____ 2. Should whites have the right to exclude Negroes from suburban housing?

_____ 3. Is it ever right for southern Negroes to steal?

_____ 4. Would it be right for Negroes to start a violent revolution?

---

[11] Later in the discussion, the teacher introduced the analogy of a shoemaker put out of business by an automated shoe factory. Students were not willing to prevent the factory from producing shoes, even though it would put the shoemaker out of business. Automation (of the shoe industry) was considered "progress" by the students, one criterion in the definition of healthy competition. Forcing a person out of business because of a personal whim (as in the barber case) was considered "unhealthy."

Match each specific issue to the general issue it raises.

SPECIFIC ISSUES	GENERAL ISSUES
—— 1. Should the Youngers move to Clybourne Park?	A. When should a person risk his own security in order to help another?
—— 2. Was it right for Richard to steal money from the movie theater?	B. Does extreme concern for political power of a race necessarily indicate racial hatred?
—— 3. Should Cato have killed the slave?	C. Is it always morally wrong to break the official law?
—— 4. Is Stokely Carmichael a racist?	D. Is racial discrimination in housing ever justified?

3. Exercises

We have illustrated teachers using analogy in dialogue, but we have not suggested how teachers might teach the use of analogy more explicitly. Through structured exercises, and intervention in classroom dialogue, teachers may help students to understand the function of analogy in argument.

Students can be presented with short *prestructured dialogues,* such as that on "Mrs. Webster's Rooming House," and asked to match statements with the intellectual functions performed (e.g., "introduces analogy to challenge value claim," "challenges analogy as irrelevant," "qualifies original position"). The teacher must create a pure or ideal dialogue in which the operations are more apparent than in natural, "sloppier" conversation. Ideal prestructured models are useful for discussing how analogies might be used to make discussion more productive.

Students can be presented with general value claims and invited to suggest analogies *as exceptions or challenges* to the claims (recall the teacher who asked students discussing Stamp Act protest to think of situations in which violence might be justified for reasons other than self-defense). A sample exercise:

For each following value claim think up a situation, a historical event, or a short story that would contradict or pose an exception to the claim.

Value Claim	*Challenging Analogy*
Example: It is wrong to kill	An innocent man is attacked by a thief with a knife. The man shoots the thief in self-defense.

1. You should never tell a lie.
2. The majority should rule.
3. Each person is entitled to an equal share of the necessities of life.
4. We all deserve freedom of speech.
5. We should always obey the law.

In another exercise teacher presents both values and analogies, asking students to match analogies with the values they seem to challenge:[12]

> After reading the statements by Boris and Doris, decide for each analogy whether it challenges Boris' position (mark B); challenges Doris' position (mark D); or does not clearly challenge either position (mark N).
>
> Boris: Opposing sides of public issues should be given equal time so that citizens can decide their views carefully.
>
> Doris: But we should never restrict freedom of the press.
>
> — Analogy 1: Suppose Grand Trunk, a small town, is served by only one newspaper and one television station, owned by the same man. He allows advertisements, news, and speeches favorable only to Republican candidates. He ignores publicity given to Democratic candidates and their views. Shouldn't something be done about that?
> — Analogy 2: All three newspapers in Watertown were accused by the police of publishing information from the secret police files. The police chief filed suit for breach of contract, charging the reporters had broken their promises. Do you think the reporters should be punished?
> — Analogy 3: Representatives from the government of North Vietnam request free time on television and free space to publish editorials in the newspapers to match all the United States opinion against their country. Do you think that should be allowed?

Such exercises question whether a given analogy really does constitute a valid challenge to a given claim. Debating the relevance of an analogy can often be more clarifying than complete consensus on a "right" answer.

4. Analysis-Intervention in Actual Classroom Dialogue

Teachers can point out the functions of analogy and encourage their use during or after discussion (that has preferably been tape-recorded). In the following excerpt, the teacher reviews a previous discussion on public regulation of railroads in late nineteenth-century America.

> Teacher: Okay, then we talked about many of the problems involved in building and operation of railroads. Does anyone remember generally what type of techniques were used in the discussion, especially on my part? For instance when I asked a person if he thought it was right for the government to set standards and you said either yes or no, what did I do then? Do you remember, Elizabeth?
>
> Elizabeth: You either asked for our opinions or value judgments.
>
> Teacher: Right, and once you stated them what did I do?
>
> Elizabeth: Asked us why, asked us to back them up.
>
> Teacher: Okay, then what did I do?
>
> Elizabeth: Somebody else to challenge them or . . . .

---

[12] Though analogies can also be used to clarify definitional and factual issues, here we limit discussion to their influence on value or policy claims.

Teacher: Do you remember my talking about things like airplane factories, and post offices, what function did they serve, what did they have to do with railroads? Go ahead, Dick.

Dick: What if this was so, or what if that was so?

Teacher: Right, does anyone know the name that might be given to something like that? Jane.

Jane: Analogy.

Teacher: Analogy, very good. An analogy is another situation in which the same general issue also occurs. Now what is the purpose of analogy? Why did I all of a sudden introduce questions on post offices and airplane companies into a discussion of railroads? Go ahead, Sonia.

Sonia: It brings it down to our level, it makes it closer to what we are familiar with because railroads are still prevalent today but not under the same conditions. And we can compare them more readily to our lives and the way things are now.

Teacher: Okay, Marie.

Marie: Also, if you give an analogy you have to clarify exactly what you mean, because if you think a post office should be run by the government. . . .

Teacher: Right, and what also might an analogy force a person to do? Elizabeth.

Elizabeth: I think an analogy forces a person to do at least two things. First it pinpoints exactly the thing about the railroad or the thing you are talking about. Since the issue of the analogy is exactly what the railroads and the post office have in common you know what you are talking about. And also analogy makes you, I guess, change the issue a little bit, make it general enough so that you can compare it with other things.

Teacher: Okay, and often an analogy is used to make a person change his opinion. For instance, someone said he thought the railroad should be allowed to do whatever they want because they own the tracks and such. Then I said what if Boeing Aircraft Company made airplanes that crashed after every third flight. As I remember, someone said (it might have been Mark) they should not be allowed to do that. In effect the analogy is making a person change his mind on the issue of government regulation. As I said yesterday, that type of technique is going to be quite common in our classes next week. And analogies, the use of other types of situations which portray the same issue, is a technique which I hope you people will begin to use in talking with each other.

By explicitly noting the function of analogy as a discussion strategy, the teacher tries to alert the class for its subsequent use. Other examples of teacher's explicit recognition of analogy appear in Chapter 10.

IV. Evaluating Student Competence

How can a teacher assess the extent to which he has improved students' ability to clarify and justify their views? Because views on public issues are primarily *opinions* that cannot be substantiated as clearly true or false, can we tell whether students have "mastered the subject?" Although we might be able to assess the quality of a personal statement in an essay, brief, or speech, how can we evaluate the rationality of a dialogue?

A. Theoretical Problems

We see three facets to the general problem of evaluation. The first involves ethical relativism (see Chapter 4). Some claim that we should not make judgments as to whether some views are better, more rational, or more valid than others. Relativists maintain that groups and individuals harbor different standards of goodness, justice, and morality, and that there are no universal absolutes by which one man or group could legitimately judge another. This position is reflected in familiar preaching for tolerating different cultures: "Live and let live," "The natives are not inferior to us, only different — they have their values, we have ours." "You should judge a group by *its* values, not yours, the outside observer." Findings in psychology that demonstrate ways in which individual perceptions and attitudes are influenced by cultural surroundings; findings in anthropology demonstrating various value systems throughout the world; and the democratic value of toleration all have been used to support a relativistic view that, in an extreme form, suggests that no person or group should judge the positions or behaviors of another. "Though we Americans believe in free enterprise, the Russians do not. Their system might be right for them, but wrong for us." "According to Jimmy's values, it's all right to dodge the draft, but according to mine, it's wrong. He has his life — I have mine. Nobody can say whose is "better."

The relativist position tends to be adopted for different reasons. Students, when confronted with difficult choices among conflicting values, can escape the agonizing intellectual dilemma simply by saying — "you have your values and I have mine." Teachers who wish to be completely "objective," wary of indoctrinating students with only one view, will suggest that there are good reasons for all points of view — no single one is really the most valid. Existentialists can retreat from making social judgments for others by affirming that the only meaningful reality is one's subjective experience. However, each represents an escape from problems that we believe must be confronted, which is why we cannot accept a relativist position.

In Chapter 1, we indicated our commitment to basic values that can and should be applied in some universal sense. That people must live in communities requires us to judge persons and groups beyond ourselves. We do not have the liberty to be unconcerned about the actions of others. Because decisions must be made about how public funds are allocated, what constitutes due process of law, whether racial discrimination should be outlawed, what are the obligations of military service, the extent to which business can exploit labor or labor can endanger the public interest — we can see that the subjective-relativist approach provides no assistance in making such social choices. The assumption that all positions are based on unique subjective experience leads to the conclusion that all are equally valid. According to this assumption there would be no point in having dialogue, except possibly to inform each other of different views. To persuade or provide justifications for policy, however, we must be able to refer to some general values to which the community at large will subscribe. These must be values that the community says are "right" in a general sense for everybody, regardless of idiosyncracies in personal or group culture. To avoid the implication that we advocate a narrow totalitarian value system, let us remind the reader of our commitment to a Creed that proclaims the importance of considerable diversity and individual liberty. We must be willing to say, however, that this value is important, not just for us (authors) personally; it is good, in a prima facie sense, for everybody, and we should be willing in some cases to "impose" it on others who may not agree.

It may be impossible to persuade an extreme relativist of the necessity for belief in general values that the individual is willing to apply beyond himself. We have found, however, that most students who begin with a relativistic position do not, upon further thought, stubbornly cling to it. By using analogy we are usually able to show students that they in fact will make universal judgments about the behaviors of other individuals and cultures — that although they may preach toleration and respect for cultural differences, at a certain point or in certain situations they believe they *should* judge the validity of actions beyond their own. The following dialogue illustrates this happening in one class.

> Alice: I sort of have a problem. I don't see how you can judge what was a good thing for people to do at a different time, in a different place, in a different environment than ours. I mean the British did what they themselves thought was right. Americans did what they themselves thought was right. And, you know, how can we sit here and say that the British were wrong? They thought that they were behaving justifiably.
>
> Becky: Well, the South Africans have a policy of apartheid. Now do you think we should make moral judgments about their apartheid policy?
>
> Alice: Well, I think it's wrong.
>
> Dick: And to use another historical analogy, the southerners, at the time of slavery with their moral view of the world and the nature of man, thought slavery was perfectly justifiable, and the best state for the slaves to be in.
>
> Alice: But that's such a clearcut case, I mean this one isn't so clear.
>
> Dick: But it wasn't clear, it wasn't clear back in the nineteenth century. We had to fight a Civil War about it.
>
> Teacher: But if you really believe in your position, you'd say we shouldn't make judgments about South Africa because of their culture. It's a different culture,

it's their values. Well, then why should we make judgments about Southern
culture in the pre-Civil War period?

Alice: Well it's a problem, because I really think slavery is wrong.

Teacher: Well, that's the point. In some situations, you think some values are
"better" than others. In some situations you can judge certain human actions
as being "bad," regardless of what the participants themselves valued.

Alice: I guess that's quite a difference from what I originally said about our not
trying to pass judgments on the values of others. I just realized about a minute
ago when I was arguing with Becky and Dick that I really didn't believe that
was true.

The second facet of the evaluation problem is whether we are able to
distinguish between more and less rational justifications for positions. Because
public policy questions are controversial and because each opposing side to
an issue can be supported by reasons, it is argued that "one opinion is as
good as another." It is often inferred, therefore, that we are unable to discriminate between more and less reasonable justifications for public policy.
Thus, we should be reluctant to evaluate students' arguments and justifications. Suppose that Sue and Jane agree that the state legislature should pass
a law forbidding racial discrimination in all housing sales and rentals. Each
is asked to support her view.

SUE'S POSITION

I favor Bill 976, because it is badly needed and it is now time to act, to make
good on this country's promises. We shouldn't be afraid of the real estate interests or of the racist reactionaries who oppose it. We should have the courage to
stand up and be counted. This country faces a serious racial crisis, an explosive
situation, in which tensions could erupt at any moment into civil war. The
divisions of black against white must be healed, and this bill can heal them.
Its passage will result in the immediate movement of millions of blacks into
white neighborhoods where men will learn to live as brothers rather than enemies. The bill would be a fitting tribute to the efforts of Martin Luther King
and Robert Kennedy who fought for full equality for all. To defeat this bill
would be as blatant an act of racial prejudice as lynching innocent blacks in
the public square. I don't see how we can say we believe in human rights and
still allow some people to refuse to sell or rent their homes to Negroes. Whenever I pass a black man on the street, it makes me feel sick to know that he
would have a difficult time finding a home in my community.

JANE'S POSITION

I support Bill 976 for several reasons. 1. We have a moral obligation to live
up to the ideal of equal treatment under the law as affirmed in the Declaration
of Independence and by the Supreme Court, especially in Brown versus Board
of Education in 1954. The bill, by prohibiting discrimination based on race in

the sale and rental of housing, helps to attack one of the barriers to equal opportunity in this state. By equality under the law, however, I do not mean that all people should have an equal right to live in any house they choose. Certainly the person who makes the highest financial offer for the house should have priority over someone who is broke and can pay nothing at all. If a landlord desired peace and quiet, and refused to rent a room on his premises to a drummer who wanted to practice three hours each evening, this would also be a justified form of discrimination. However, since skin color causes no physical disturbance, and is something a person is born with — had no control over — it would be a violation of equal treatment to deny a person housing because of his race.

2. A major argument against this bill on the part of landlords and owners is that Negroes moving into white neighborhoods would have the effect of decreasing property values, causing economic hardship for owners and sellers. Several studies show (e.g., by the Anti-Defamation League) that property values do *not* necessarily decline when blacks move into white neighborhoods. Declining values have been foisted upon some communities by white real estate speculators who through blockbusting deliberately frighten whites into moving from the neighborhood. There are effective techniques for combating such instability in the housing market.

3. I am aware of the argument that open housing is no panacea or speedy path to racial justice and integration in this state. There will be a problem of enforcement. It is true that most blacks cannot afford housing in the wealthy white suburbs, and true also that many blacks oppose integrating with whites even if they did have the opportunity. Yet experience of nearby states shows that reasonable enforcement is not impossible, if we adopt proper testing procedures. The bill has no intention of instantly integrating our society — its justification rests only on the claim that those blacks who can afford to and who wish to move into white neighborhoods have the legal right to not be barred because of their skin color.

Is one argument clearly more rational and systematic than the other? We believe that Jane's is, and all in a sample of twenty-five students, faculty members, and secretaries agreed. To demonstrate that we can discriminate between more and less rational arguments should convince us that one opinion is not necessarily as good as another — some are clearly better than others in the sense of being more rational or systematic. However, these gross judgments cannot always be as reliably applied as in comparing Sue and Jane. The rationality of most arguments that occur, in or out of the classroom, is much more difficult to rate reliably. Moreover, such gross judgments would not seem to contribute much to instruction. It would not be very helpful to say to Sue, "Make your argument more like Jane's." Sue would need more specific instructions as to what kinds of statements would improve her position. For both evaluative and instructional reasons, we must try to articulate in a rather specific "behavioral" sense those intellectual operations that we believe to be critical to developing a rational position. This is the third and most difficult aspect of evaluation.

We shall not review the extensive literature on critical thinking, problem-solving, rhetoric, and logic here. Complex issues in defining logical, rational thought are treated in detail by Hullfish and Smith (1961), Berlak (1965), Hunt and Metcalf (1968), Ennis (1969), B. O. Smith (n.d), and others. Rather than to justify our scheme in the context of the literature, we shall here simply present it, leaving the task of comparison and analysis to the reader. We must acknowledge the extensive thought and research that have resulted in continuing revisions and refinements of the system. To see how the system evolved, consult Berlak (1963), Ellis (1963), Archibald (1965), Oliver and Shaver (1966), and Levin (1968). We do not consider this scheme final, for research indicates that continuing efforts in revision and refinement are needed.

When we ask "What makes an argument rational?" we can imagine two formats or contexts in which the argument can be expressed. The first is a statement such as a speech, essay, or legal brief in which one party presents a complete argument. The second is a dialogue, debate, or discussion in which two or more persons interact, and in responding to each other create individual and group arguments or justifications. Because our teaching has focused primarily on the discussion context, we have phrased the intellectual operations that follow in terms appropriate for listening to a discussion.[13]

RATIONAL OPERATIONS

1. Issue Stating. Phrasing specific policy issues in terms of more general issues; stating the particular issues relevant to the policy in question (distinguishing these from irrelevant issues); distinguishing among factual, definitional, and value issues.

   Example: "The issue isn't whether we should be in Vietnam, but whether a person should be allowed to protest this by burning his draft card.

2. Summary-Inventory-Agenda. Discussing which issues should be discussed in which order, identifying points of agreement and disagreement on issues that have already been discussed, summarizing (paraphrasing) arguments of participants and the progress of the discussion.

---

[13] Most items seem equally crucial to the rationality of argument in the form of brief or discussion. Though items 2, 3, 4, and 6 seem more critical in discussion contexts, they would also be evident in briefs which address themselves in great detail to counter-arguments of their adversaries.

Example: "We've agreed that the march was illegal. Now I think we ought to discuss whether it was morally justified. Later we can talk about how politically effective we think it was."

3. Clarification-Elaboration. Requesting or providing clarification or elaboration of a statement.

Example: "You got me wrong. I was only saying that students who do intentionally break the law should be willing to take the consequences and not expect amnesty."

4. Relevance. Questioning or substantiating the relevance of statements.

Example: "What does your point abut the Chicago convention have to do with our tactics in Vietnam?"

5. Referring to Qualified General Ethical and Legal Principles. Arguing a policy to be consistent with general values in the society's moral tradition, but stating exceptions, qualifications, limitations on the general values or policies one supports. Using analogy as an effective method of arriving at a qualified position.

Example: "Although we have to preserve law and order, we also have to respect rights of privacy, so I am opposed to wiretapping except by special warrant from the court."

6. Consistency. Pointing out logical and empirical inconsistencies in arguments, and inconsistencies between ideals and actions, means and ends, etc.

Example: "We say America is a land of equality, but the income of blacks is about half that of whites and the unemployment rate twice that of whites."

7. Conditional Reasoning. Raising logical and empirical implications (positive and negative) of policies and claims; stating premises and stipulations assumed in the argument. This operation is most easily recognized in "if . . . then" statements.

Example: "If you want to prohibit marijuana because of possible harm to health, then you should also ban the sale of cigarettes and alcohol."

8. Weighing Opposing and Alternative Positions. Stating and responding to counterarguments, including modifying one's position and conceding points in light of persuasive opposition.

Example: "On one hand, I'm opposed to the widespread sale and possession of guns, but I can also see your point that it would be impossible to stop determined criminals from obtaining them."

9. Defining Terms. Explaining or asking for the meaning of key concepts by using examples, analogies, or general defining criteria.

   Example: "Equality is pretty vague. Are you suggesting economic, political, social equality, or what? Give me an example of what you mean."

10. Comparison and Distinction. Stating the specific bases for similarities and differences among concepts, events, policies, etc.

    Example: "Killing in self-defense is different from killing to conquer new territory. When you're an aggressor you take the initiative and are fully responsible, but when you act in self-defense, someone else has forced you to act."

11. Evidence and Examples. Providing data, specific claims, examples, etc. to support or challenge factual claims.

    Example: "The Supreme Court is making it difficult for police to interrogate suspects. In one recent decision the states were required to provide lawyers for the indigent; in another, the court overturned a conviction because the police failed to advise the suspect that he had a right to a lawyer and didn't need to talk."

12. Using Source and Authority. Citing sources and authorities for claims and evaluating the reliability thereof.

    Example: "I got my facts straight from the Kerner report on civil disorders."

13. Need for Information. Acknowledging those issues for which it would be desirable to have more information.

    Example: "We don't really know much about the effects of DDT. We ought to get some specific facts before deciding what to do."

The operations can be defined more specifically so that they may be reliably identified in content analysis scoring. This was done in evaluating the Harvard Social Studies Project when the staff listened to students' tape-recorded discussions and tallied the occurrence of statements like those just listed.[14] A far more simplified version of these categories appears below (Fig. 9.4), and is more readily usable as a check list for teachers and students who, while listening to discussions, can note the presence and absence of operations considered valuable.

Although the scheme detects the kinds of intellectual operations crucial to rational justification, it is by no means complete. Its categories cannot

---

[14] See Levin (1968) or Levin, Newmann, and Oliver (1969) for the complete scorer's manual.

detect the level of accuracy or relevance in persons' statements. Joe can make the claim, "Whites have never done anything mean to blacks in this country." Then he can support this claim with evidence: "No one in my family ever had any slaves, whipped any Negroes, or even denied them housing, jobs, or education." According to our list, Joe has supported his claim with "evidence," but the evidence he gave really does not adequately verify the claim (although he believes it does). Joe might even give inaccurate evidence: "Once the slaves were freed, they were all given forty acres and a mule" — and still receive credit for using an intellectual operation we admire. Although our scheme gives a framework for reliably observing the intellectual process of argument, it does not provide a reliable system for evaluating statements according to their relevance, their wisdom, or the logical validity of the inferences they represent. Such judgments must be left to teachers and students who evaluate the merits of arguments on specific issues. In this sense our scheme should be seen perhaps as a necessary, but certainly not a sufficient device for distinguishing the more from the less rational positions. An observation scheme that reliably distinguishes the accuracy, relevance, and logical validity of statements on specific issues has yet to be developed.

There are other problems in using the scheme as an evaluation device. Suppose we listen to a discussion between Frank and Eric, scoring the frequency with which each uses the previous operations. The tallies turn out to be equal for each, 20 to 20. In examining distributions, we find that Frank's tallies are concentrated primarily in issue-stating, relevance, and summary-inventory-agenda. Eric's tallies are about equally distributed in all categories. Because Frank and Eric have equal totals (20 to 20), should we conclude that their positions are equally well justified? Are we willing to say that the rationality of a person's justification in discussion is directly proportional to the tallies he receives on these operations? Let us assume that we can solve the content problem — that Frank and Eric are equal in accuracy, relevance, and logical inference. We must then decide whether some operations should be considered inherently more valuable than others. If we conclude, for example, that issue-stating, relevance, and summary-inventory-agenda are more important than evidence, weighing, or source, then the *distribution* of a person's tallies, not just his total, must be considered in arriving at a summary judgment of his competence.

It appeared absurd to assume that rationality depended only on the total tallies in all categories. To inquire empirically how some categories might be weighted more heavily than others, we asked scorers to assess the overall quality of each discussion. This judgment was recorded on a rating scale with five units from "poor" to "excellent." We found that operations 1, 2,

3, 4, 5, 8, 9, and 10 tended to be positively correlated with overall quality judgments, but the statistical relationships were not sufficiently strong for us to recommend weighting such categories in any given amount.[15] Much additional validation research must be done before we could say that some operations (all other things being equal in a discussion) contribute x times the amount of others to the rationality of discourse.

Of what use, then, are these operations to the teacher? Despite these problems, we are confident that such categories aid teachers in labeling and identifying specific kinds of statements that they intuitively consider "good" or valuable when they listen to discussion. The categories may be used to organize *instruction* on developing rational discourse. That is, by noticing their occurrence and practicing their use, students may come to see the clarifying, verifying, and persuasive power that such operations can provide. They should not be seen as ends in themselves, nor as behaviors to master in playing the game of school, but as tools to build rational justifications.

B. Specific Evaluation Techniques

The teacher might evaluate at least three types of student competence.

1. Writing a Logical Essay or Brief to Support Position

Our discussion of what constitutes a rational position provides various criteria that the teacher might combine in his own way for judging and responding to student writing.

2. Construing Issues Analytically

Teachers' guides to each AEP *Public Issues* booklet contain "Level B" tests to assess students' analytical thinking on issues and cases related to the unit. These test student ability to translate abstract into specific issues, to notice relevant similarities and differences among cases, to judge the extent to which various claims are supported or refuted by facts in the cases, to apply analogies in challenging general positions, etc. Figure 9.2 illustrates a Level B unit test. In this and other multiple choice exercises, students should be encouraged to debate alternative answers, which allows the test to serve as an instructional as well as evaluative tool.

3. Dialogue Analysis and Performance

We can test student ability to analyze both oral and printed dialogue. The Al and Marvin exercise illustrates the latter.

    (1) Al: Why shouldn't everyone be allowed to use the drugs he wants to?
    (2) Marvin: What? And walk around knifing people or stealing things to pay the high prices the pushers get?
    (3) Al: But it's the stupid laws that force people to steal. If drugs were legalized

[15] See Levin (1968) for the detailed report of this research; also available in Levin, Newmann, and Oliver (1969).

Unit Test: Level B
The American Revolution

NAME: _____

CLASS: _____GRADE: _____

■ *Assume that you wish to discuss the issues listed below, but you can pick only one case to illustrate each issue. Which of the cases would you choose to best illustrate each of the issues?* **A. Adam Cooper, B. Incident at Pettus Bridge, C. Stamp Act, D. Oliver Wiswell.**

. . . .1. What methods of protest used by the colonists against England were justified?

. . . .2. How did militiamen at Lexington feel about resistance to the British?

. . . .3. Did the patriots abuse the rights of other colonists in their effort to win the war?

. . . .4. In what ways should the right to public demonstrations be limited?

■ *Suppose you are discussing the question: "When is it right to dissent against existing authority?" Place checks before the two terms that are likely to raise the most difficult and relevant problems of definition.*

. . . .1. Patriotism   . . . .3. Parliamentary system

. . . .2. Taxation   . . . .4. Consent of the governed

■ *Decide whether the facts of each case tend to support the claim* (mark **S**); *refute the claim* (mark **R**); *neither clearly support nor refute the claim* (mark **N**).

Claim: Laws passed by the British caused expense and inconvenience to American colonists.

. . . .1. Stamp Act   . . . .3. Oliver Wiswell

. . . .2. Adam Cooper   . . . .4. Account of Lt. Col. Smith

■ *Place checks before the* **two** *most important* **similarities** *between the "Stamp Act" case and the "Incident at Pettus Bridge."*

. . . .1. Protestors have effective leaders who inspire them.

. . . .2. Public demonstrations intended to dramatize issues.

. . . .3. Overthrow of government by force advocated.

. . . .4. Protestors feel they are denied voice in government.

■ *Place checks before the* **two** *most important* **differences** *between Negroes in Selma and American patriots in Lexington.*

. . . .1. Negroes not involved in American Revolution.

. . . .2. Only patriots were asking basic human rights.

. . . .3. Patriots violent, Negroes generally nonviolent.

. . . .4. Negroes within stable system of constitutional government; patriots' rights not clear in British constitution.

■ *After reading the statements made by Boris and Doris, decide for each analogy whether it challenges Boris' position* (mark **B**); *challenges Doris' position* (mark **D**); *or does not clearly challenge either position* (mark **N**).

Boris: If you have a long-standing and serious complaint against your government, and the government does not satisfy the complaint, you have the right to start a violent revolution.

Doris: Obedience to law and order must be preserved. Violence against established government should be avoided at all costs.

. . . .**Analogy 1:** American colonists complained that they had no right to vote. Britain refused to allow them representation in Parliament after peaceful pleas by the Americans. Britain passed laws that did financial harm to the colonists. The colonists were right to revolt, weren't they?

. . . .**Analogy 2:** Suppose a group of people object to the decision of a state government to build a new highway through their property. They bring suit, but the court decides that they have been paid fairly for their property and that the planned highway route is the only possible one. They appeal the decision, but the appeal is denied. They refuse to leave their homes but the police come and evict them. It wouldn't be right for them to form a revolutionary group to overthrow the government, would it?

. . . .**Analogy 3:** Jews in Nazi Germany complain to government authorities that they are being taken from their homes and businesses and sent to labor camps; many are being executed. Nazis explain that, in accordance with government policy and for the good of the country, people must be forced to work hard and long and undesirables must be eliminated. Wouldn't it be right for Jews to join a resistance movement against the government?

. . . .**Analogy 4:** The United States was attacked by Japan at Pearl Harbor. The U.S. armed forces began a determined effort to destroy the power of the Japanese government. Didn't the U.S. do the right thing?

■ *Decide whether each of the following arguments tends to support the position* (mark **S**); *refute the position* (mark **R**); *neither clearly support nor refute the position* (mark **N**).

Position: The mob was justified in harassing Oliver Wiswell's family.

. . . .1. In times of war, people friendly to your enemy cannot be trusted.

. . . .2. Religious freedom should be guaranteed to all.

. . . .3. Innocent people should not be harmed.

. . . .4. British sympathizers should have foreseen the conflict and left the area voluntarily.

■ *Match each of the following incidents with the ideas they illustrate.*

Incidents	Ideas
. . . .1. More than 260 demonstrators are arrested in Selma for parading without a permit.	A. Accidental or "small" event triggers great violence when hostilities are deep.
. . . .2. Federal court order provides 4,000 troops to protect marchers from Selma to Montgomery.	B. Mounting protests and intimidation affect government official.
. . . .3. Shot rings out at Lexington Green.	C. Willingness to take the consequences for civil disobedience and deliberate violation of law
. . . .4. Andrew Oliver resigns as stamp distributor.	D. Guaranteeing freedom of speech and assembly

■ *Place a check before the most important* **difference** *between George Watkins and Adam Cooper.*

. . . .1. One an adult, the other a youth

. . . .2. One a patriot, the other a loyalist

. . . .3. One mainly thinking about his position, the other forced to *act* on one side

. . . .4. One considerably confused and upset, the other taking issues rather lightly

4

Reprinted by permission of American Education Publications.

FIGURE 9.2

the prices would drop and so would the crimes that some addicts commit to pay for them.

(4) Marvin: I don't know where you get your ideas. I think addicts are disgusting people who should be dealt with severely.

(5) Al: Your feelings are irrelevant. The fact is that the illegal dope trade is one of the biggest rackets in the country, and the only reason it exists is because of the strict narcotics laws. Many drugs are legal in England, and their crime rate isn't any higher than America's.

(6) Marvin: Okay, I'll admit that preventing crime isn't the best reason for opposing legalized narcotics. But I think people who avoid the responsibility of working in their society shouldn't be supported by the rest. Why should I pay taxes to support dope addicts who don't have jobs?

(7) Al: Who said anything about supporting people? All I'm saying is that people should be free to choose what they put into their bodies. How would you like it if someone said you couldn't smoke cigarettes?

(8) Marvin: Cigarettes are different. They don't put you into a narcotic daze. We're talking about drugs that take your mind off working and facing your responsibilities.

1. Which of the following best describes what statement 3 does in the discussion?

   a. Clarifies the meaning of a disputed term in the discussion.
   b. Makes a prediction to support a policy recommendation.
   c. Suggests the other person needs further evidence for his viewpoint.
   d. Points out a competing value that has been overlooked.
   e. Shifts the topic to another question.

2. Which of the following best describes what statement 6 does in the discussion?

   a. Gives a factual claim and evidence to support it.
   b. Gives an analogy to challenge the opponent's position.
   c. Concedes a point and makes a general policy recommendation.
   d. Suggests that evidence is unreliable or untrustworthy.
   e. Makes an irrelevant statement.

3. What is Marvin doing in statement 8?

   a. Attacking the motives of his opponent.
   b. Making a distinction to challenge a previous argument.
   c. Conceding a point to move the discussion along.
   d. Making a general value statement to support a policy recommendation.
   e. Defining a term that has been in dispute.

4. The discussion shifts or changes from one issue to another. In which following statement does this shift occur?

   a. 1
   b. 3
   c. 5
   d. 6
   e. None of the above

DISCUSSION EVALUATION SHEET

_____   _____
(Name of Evaluator)   (Date)

_____
(Topic of Discussion)

_____
(Participants in Discussion)

Statement Summary	Rating 1-Excellent 2-Very Good 3-Good 4-Fair 5-Poor	Reason for Rating
(Example) Joe mentioned recent mutinies on other ships	2	Gave evidence for his earlier claim about danger of mutiny on ship
1.		
2.		
3.		
4.		
5.		
6.		
7.		

FIGURE 9.3

DISCUSSION PERFORMANCE LIST

GOOD RATINGS	POOR RATINGS
G-1: Definition Given or Asked	P-1: Claim Excessively Repeated
G-2: Evidence or Example Given or Asked	P-2: Irrelevant Statement
	P-3: Insensitive Statement
G-3: Analogy Given	P-4: Issue Changed Abruptly
G-4: Inconsistency Challenged	P-5: Unclear Statement
G-5: Relevance Questioned	P-6: No Evidence Given
G-6: Issue Stated	P-7: Inaccurate Facts
Factual	P-8: Personal Attack
Definitional	P-9: Loaded Words
Policy or Value	P-10: Other
G-7: Summary Given or Asked	
G-8: Stipulation Made	
G-9: Concession Made	
G-10: Other	

FIGURE 9.4

By using evaluation forms in Figures 9.3–9.6, the teacher can test students' ability to analyze their own oral dialogues. Students are asked to fill out the forms as they listen to oral dialogue. Then the teacher evaluates the students' perceptions as recorded on the sheets.

The teacher may, of course, wish to complete his own independent evaluation of student performance in dialogue. By using tape recordings or on-the-spot observation, he can make judgments based on tallies of the occurrence of the rational operations described on pages 283–285, or in Figure 9.4, or on such rating scales as shown in Figure 9.6.

We cannot suggest how the teacher should translate observations arising from these diverse evaluation techniques into numerical or letter "grades." Our purpose here has been only to illustrate methods for gathering, and categories for describing, student behavior relevant to analyzing public issues. It has often been difficult to isolate evaluation from teaching because many techniques have been useful as *instructional* exercises. The skills we wish to develop cannot as yet be validly assessed through nationally standardized tests. Therefore, much of the burden of devising systematic evaluation remains with the teacher.

At what point does a discussion achieve its purpose and when should it be terminated by the teacher? Several possible "benchmarks" for terminating discussion have been suggested:

When people reach consensus.

TAKING STOCK OF YOUR DISCUSSION

_____   _____
(group)   (date)

1. What issues were discussed?

2. What were major points of disagreement?

3. What positions were taken, and by whom?

4. Was agreement reached on any issues? Which ones?

5. What happened to help move the discussion along?

6. What happened to bog the discussion down or make it unproductive?

7. What did the discussion accomplish?

8. What should be discussed next? Why?

FIGURE 9.5

> When people decide they can never agree — a deadlock.
> When people are just tired or can't think of anything else to say.
> When a person has changed his mind from his original position.
> When some arbitrary time period has elapsed.

In defining the nature of rational justification we have argued that none of these indices are adequate for determining that a discussion has been productive. Agreement or disagreement and reversing one's position or retaining it are less important than developing more complex positions (in the sense of including distinctions, qualifications, evidence, etc.) as a result of the discussion process.

DISCUSSION RATING SCALES

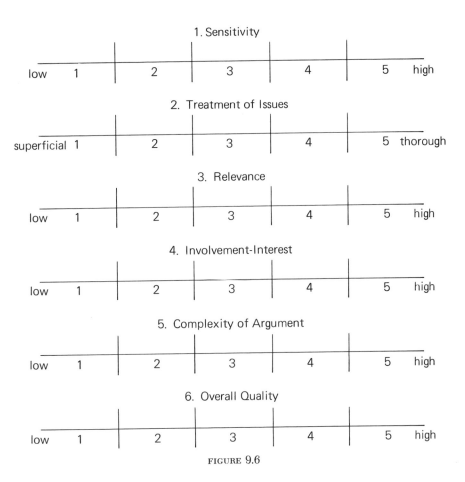

1. Sensitivity

low   1 | 2 | 3 | 4 | 5   high

2. Treatment of Issues

superficial 1 | 2 | 3 | 4 | 5   thorough

3. Relevance

low   1 | 2 | 3 | 4 | 5   high

4. Involvement-Interest

low   1 | 2 | 3 | 4 | 5   high

5. Complexity of Argument

low   1 | 2 | 3 | 4 | 5   high

6. Overall Quality

low   1 | 2 | 3 | 4 | 5   high

FIGURE 9.6

V. The Teacher's Posture in Dealing with Value Issues

School authorities, citizens, and published curriculum materials have traditionally discouraged discussing controversial public issues for different reasons: (1) Value questions are said to be essentially private, personal concerns appropriate for discussion perhaps in the family or church but not in a public, state-controlled institution. This argument implies that, as in protecting religions from state control and establishment, we must also protect other personal values from state encroachment. (2) If the classroom is to be a center for truly open inquiry, where students are free to explore all paths to truth, teachers must be completely neutral, lest they close off alternative intellectual avenues. (3) As mentioned in Chapter 1, it is claimed that teachers are not more competent than others to deal with controversial value problems. Because they lack expertise in this area, they should avoid it. In Chapter 1 we have replied to each point, yet we have not explored the merits of specific strategies or postures that a teacher takes once he has chosen to deal with values in the classroom.

Teachers may choose at least three possible postures. The more effective teacher probably shifts, using each posture when it seems appropriate. (1) The neutral, objective, disinterested bystander is someone who seldom take a personal position on issues. Instead, he states arguments for various sides of the issue, summarizes the progress of discussion, and requests clarification on student views. He is a dispassionate moderator, trying to draw the best from opposing advocates, trying to create a civilized group discussion. (2) The Socratic devil's advocate also refuses to take a firm personal stand, but he is less cooperative and agreeable than the neutral summarizer. The devil's advocate acts as a gadfly trying constantly to expose the weaknesses and confusions in everyone's position. He shifts positions, depending upon what stance is necessary to raise troublesome questions. He is less concerned with producing consensus and closure, and more concerned with demonstrating how none of the advocates have completely defensible views. He tries to point out to everyone complexities and inconsistencies in their positions that they had apparently never considered. (3) The committed advocate is concerned primarily with persuading students that his position on a given issue is the most reasonable one. Although the neutral summarizer and the devil's advocate may inform students of their personal views on an issue, they deliberately attempt to prevent these from influencing the outcome of classroom inquiry. The committed advocate, however, not only informs students about his views, he tries to convince students that his views are right. He might use tactics of the devil's advocate and the neutral observer in doing this, but his major intent is neither producing an interesting discussion nor raising self-searching challenges, but to persuade students to adopt a particular stance on a given issue.

Each posture has virtues and drawbacks. The class of the neutral summarizer benefits from a cool atmosphere in which all opinions are equally respected. The devil's advocate destroys intellectual complacency. The committed advocate demonstrates that moral conviction can be intellectually supported. The neutral summarizer risks a certain lack of passion and intellectual superficiality in discussion (especially if participants are unable to raise difficult and relevant challenges for each other). The devil's advocate might find students interpreting his shifty behavior simply as a game to upset students; they may come to feel that discussion cannot accomplish anything except to expose sloppy thinking. The committed advocate risks suppressing free inquiry as students may feel they must agree with a party line or have to submit to teacher's more forceful arguments.

What principles should we use to help us decide when to adopt each posture? We can suggest only two. (A) Given the objective of open dialogue aimed toward developing complex individual positions, we should adopt whatever posture seems likely to achieve this objective. In general this would imply a combination of neutral summarizer and devil's advocate. (B) In special cases, on certain issues, to meet one's moral responsibilities as a citizen, it is necessary to take a firm stand and even to try to persuade students that a view is most reasonable (implying the committed advocate posture). Because this latter principle is usually vigorously opposed by those who fear it will destroy neutrality and open inquiry in the classroom, we wish to elaborate.

We suspect that teachers who never take vigorous stands on public issues in the classroom inadvertently teach two lessons in a "hidden curriculum": (1) Because all opinions are treated equally, students may see that "one opinion is always as good as another," a myth we have challenged above. People should not fear to make judgments indicating that some positions are clearly more reasonable than others. (2) Assuming that the teacher serves in some sense as a model of human virtue, the objective, neutral analyst presents a somewhat distorted prototype. He can easily give the impression that it is "good" not to take a personal stand and that it is preferable to stay aloof from controversy, always observing as a cool analyst, pointing out complexities that detain us from acting rather than encouraging us to be decisive. This conception of human virtue is repugnant to us on intellectual and moral grounds. It is anti-intellectual when the concern for objectivity prevents students from asking and trying to answer questions of prescriptive personal commitment. Questions on the validity and justification of personal action commitments are of equal intellectual substance as those dealing with more impersonal data. The posture can be immoral when a teacher is silent or neutral about public policy that he knows clearly violates human dignity. Not to take a stand on some issues is thereby a failure to meet one's ethical responsibilities.

Suppose that in studying Nazi Germany, we present students with Allied and Axis documents that evaluate the achievements of the Third Reich. We make a deliberate effort to present data and arguments both supporting and condemning the Nazi movement. After considerable discussion (in which we have played a neutral role) the students conclude almost unanimously that Hitler's slaughter of six million Jews was morally justified because he worked for the good of the country, saving it from depression and disunity. At this point we would be morally obligated not only to inform them that we disagreed, but to oppose their rationale with the most persuasive evidence and arguments we could muster.[16]

On the other hand, if we had been discussing whether a recent slowdown by air traffic controllers was a justified method to redress their grievances, we would be less concerned with the position that the class might reach. As long as alternative public policies do not pose what we consider extreme threats to human dignity, we would try to be open, eager to learn, and willing to tolerate student positions with which we personally disagree. To avoid stifling genuine inquiry in the classroom, the teacher must choose carefully those issues on which he takes a vigorous personal stand. These choices will vary from teacher to teacher, depending upon the individual's moral convictions and interpretations of issues. Although teachers have both an intellectual and moral obligation to take a stand *at times,* if this is done too often, it can stifle the independent and open student dialogue that the teacher has equal professional and moral responsibility to cultivate.

There is a danger in taking these teacher roles too seriously. A teacher who attempts to play roles can easily give students the impression that he is not a natural person, but someone masquerading deliberately to manipulate students. Students will find no intrinsic value in learning when they see teachers behaving like unreal people. Before we trust a person enough to take him seriously, we must have some confidence that he shares our own human qualities, having unique loves, hates, fears, and dilemmas. In line with our comments on the limits of rationality (Chapter 3) and Chapter 11's more extensive critique of artificiality and gamesmanship in school, we must applaud those who are authentic persons first, teachers second — individuals who honestly express their views (however biased, emotional, or extreme) and who treat students not as inferior trainees, but as fellow humans. At times a concern for systematic curriculum analysis obscures the importance of this fundamental need.

---

[16] Although on certain issues we would try to persuade students that our position is more reasonable than theirs, we should not punish them (e.g., by giving low grades) for failing to be convinced. We should evaluate students on the quality and complexity of the rationale for their positions, not on the substance of the position itself. A student with a fascist position might supply better reasons for his stand than a person of liberal persuasion.

Chapter 10

Selected Techniques for Teaching Discussion Skills

Implied in Chapters 1 through 8 are at least three general teaching objectives: (1) to teach analytic distinctions between policy, factual, value, and definitional issues along with appropriate intellectual strategies for dealing with them; (2) to select and teach complexities of substantive concepts central to public controversy (e.g., equality, property, consent, etc.); (3) to teach a style of oral discussion in which the analytical concepts, substantive concepts, and intellectual strategies clarify personal stands on public issues. Our pedagogical experimentation has focused primarily upon developing analytic-inquiry and discussion skills (objectives one and three). Teaching substantive concepts was approached less systematically. That is, how to teach about property, equality, etc., has not been a major concern of the study.[1]

In this chapter we illustrate how a teacher might intervene in discussion to help students construe issues analytically and improve discussion skills. The excerpts should be prefaced by several qualifications. (A) They must be seen only as illustrations, not proven techniques. The difficulties in conceiving, developing, teaching, and evaluating a new curriculum made it impossible to manage a rigorously controlled experiment. We could not define specific teaching techniques that could be reliably replicated and contrasted to different techniques in a control group. Nor could we assess the influence on student discussion competence of the multitude of variables

---

[1] At the beginning of the Harvard project, the collection of substantive concepts that eventually became Chapters 4 through 8 did not exist in an organized form. Only through discussing public issues among colleagues and students did we learn which substantive concepts seemed critical and the nature of their complexities.

beyond the control of our curriculum. (B) Because of insufficient transcripts and limited space here, we cannot demonstrate how a student or group, beginning as untrained, came to master a skill or concept over a period of time. (C) Although we have tried to identify the most salient teaching function in each of the excerpts, most probably illustrate a number of functions and strategies. (D) Though the dialogue is taken out of context from the larger class period or unit, we hope the excerpts are sufficiently comprehensible to reveal specific teaching strategies.

I. Examples of Classroom Dialogue

A. Teaching Analytic Skills

1. What Is a Value Issue?

The class hears a taped discussion made by students in the previous lesson.

Tape: We feel that the workers are not justified in breaking any laws.

Teacher: Okay, we feel that the workers are not justified in breaking any laws. What does that communicate?

Susan: His feelings on it.

Teacher: His feelings, right, and so would that be a factual statement, or a value statement, or a clarification statement, or what?

Susan: Clarification.

Teacher: Clarifying what?

Susan: How he feels about it.

Teacher: How he feels about it. His feelings, right? So first we have a statement of his feelings. Is that really persuasive, does that persuade us that we really should feel the way he does?

Alan: No, but at least we know how he feels.

Teacher: Right. It tells us how he feels but it doesn't really give us any persuasion that we should feel like he does, good.

Tape: When our life is at stake we should be able to break laws.

Tape: Can you prove that your life is going to be at stake?

Teacher: Okay, what does that interchange do? I mean, "if your life is at stake you should be able to break laws." What kind of a statement is that? Is that a factual statement, a value statement?

Carol: Value statement.

Teacher: Value statement, very good. So first we have a statement of personal feeling. Then it says when your life is at stake you should be able to break laws, a value statement. What's the difference between the statement of simple feeling and the value statement?

(*Silence.*)

How about this? What's the difference between "I like chocolate ice cream," and "people should eat chocolate ice cream"? Linda.

Linda: Well, one, you can have two sides to the issue and I'm sure people who eat chocolate ice cream — some people will say they can and some people will say they shouldn't. But if I say I like chocolate ice cream nobody can debate about it. If you like it, you like it.

Teacher: So, "I like it," is a personal preference to me. When you say "should," it suggests what?

Linda: A disagreement, there's an issue.

Teacher: There's an issue in which lots of people have a stake, right, does anybody understand that? What do you think she said, Don?

Don: She said that there is no disagreement in personal opinions, feelings.

Teacher: A personal feeling doesn't necessarily create a disagreement, right?

Don: And the other one could create a disagreement because it's . . . has to do with more people. He tells what someone thinks should be for others.

Teacher: *For others.* Great, so that the value statement is really a recommendation of how others should feel and what others should do. A personal feeling statement is just a statement of how you feel, right? So Linda is quite right. A value statement tends to make people disagree, to polarize people, put them on two sides of the fence.

Although in this excerpt a value statement was defined primarily as igniting disagreement, we must recognize that factual and definitional claims can be equally controversial. The distinguishing feature of a value claim is its recommendation that certain actions or conditions are good, right, just (or their negatives).

2. What Is a Factual Claim?

Students have been suggesting that certain disputable questions (e.g., whether a history teacher is kind or cruel) are issues of opinion, not fact.

Teacher: All right, suppose I say there's a pink elephant behind the blackboard. You can't look, but you say that there isn't one there. Now that's a disagreement. You have different kinds of evidence, right?

Sue: But you can prove it.

Teacher: You can prove it.

Sue: Yes.

Teacher: I see.

Sue: I could prove there wasn't or you could prove there was.

Teacher: I see. A factual question is one in which you could finally develop sure proof that it is one way or the other.

Sue: Yes, the other side has to give in to you.

Teacher: I see. Let me suggest that the earth is a large flat plain and if you sail far enough you will sail off the edge, right? Is that a factual issue?

Sue: No.

Teacher: Can you prove it one way or the other?

Sue: Yes.

Teacher: So it *is* a factual question. Okay, suppose we go back to 1400 — is it a factual question then?

Sue: Sure.

Teacher: Has it been proven one way or the other?

Jerry: Yes.

Teacher: What was the answer in 1400?

Sue: They thought it was flat.

Teacher: It was flat.

Sue: Yes, but they had never really proved it until . . . .

Teacher: But it is a factual question.

Sue: Yes.

Teacher: Even though it was never proven. So you can have factual questions which aren't finally proven.

This conversation failed to provide a complete definition of factual claims, but it did establish that factual claims can be controversial yet susceptible to empirical verification. The point that factual claims answer questions regarding what is, was, or will be (rather than ought or should be) was not dealt with.

3. What Kinds of "Proof" Can Be Given to Support Factual Claims?

Tape: Can you prove that your life is going to be at stake?

Teacher: Ah, here we are. Can you prove that your life is going to be at stake. Now is that a value statement? What kind of a statement is he asking for? Go ahead, Don.

Don: He's questioning a previous statement.

Teacher: He's questioning it in a certain way, right? Now, is he saying that's a poor position to hold?

Don: No, he is asking for proof.

Teacher: All right. You ask for proof regarding what kind of statement: value statements, definitional statements, factual statements, or clarification statements, or what?

Jack: Factual statement.

Teacher: Factual statement. So he's saying that the previous statement is a factual assumption, that somebody's life was really in danger. He is asking for proof of this factual assumption. Okay now, what do we expect that Team A is going to do at this point, the first team. What are they supposed to do now?

Betty: Give some proof.

Teacher: Give some proof, right. Let's see if they give some proof.

Tape: The safety conditions are very poor which have injured the lives of many workers, which has been proven by the deaths of many brakemen.

Teacher: Okay. She says that many brakemen have died and that proves this factual statement that people's lives are at stake, right? Do you think that's true, Kathy?

Kathy: Yes.

Teacher: Okay. Suppose I say that I have a pink elephant behind this blackboard. Then Pete says, "That's pretty ridiculous — go ahead and prove it." And I say, "yeah, he's still there." Now is that proof?

Kathy: No.

Teacher: Gee, I just looked.

Kathy: You could be a liar.

Teacher: You think I might tell lies. But if I look and I report as a witness, that is a kind of proof, isn't it?

Don: I still don't believe it.

Teacher: You still don't believe it?

Don: No.

Teacher: What would I have to do to make you believe it? What other kind of proof could I offer you?

Jim: You would have to show me that it was behind there.

Teacher: Right. You personally would have to look at it. Then you might believe it. That would be the most persuasive kind of evidence. Now Linda has just said that many brakemen have actually died. She has just told you something to prove a prior statement that people's lives were in danger. Okay, now, can she take you back to 1874 and show you all the bodies strewn in the tracks? Sue?

Sue: It was in print, though, in our trusty book.

Teacher: It was in your trusty book. So one kind of factual proof is an eyewitness, and another kind of witness is your trusty book, right? Now has Linda suggested that her proof is based on eyewitness account, or on her trusty book, or what?

Bill: Trusty book.

Teacher: Did she say that in her statement?

Bill: No.

Teacher: She just uttered it like she believed it was true, right? So what's a good way to challenge her statement at this point, Jim?

Jim: Have an eyewitness.

Teacher: Yeah, but it is pretty hard for events in 1874. If we had a time machine that would be okay. What other way can we challenge her?

Jane: Just get her to show where it says it in her trusty book.

Teacher: Very good. Say it louder.

Jane: Get her to show us where it refers to this in her book.

Teacher: Right. Get her to show in her trusty book where she got this idea that brakemen were being killed. Okay, this sounds to me like a very intelligent strategy so let's see if the other Team B does this.

Tape: Taking the job as a brakeman is at your own risk, we are not forcing you to work as a brakeman.

Teacher: Ah, so they didn't challenge her factual claim, instead they took another strategy. They didn't say, "How do you actually know these people are getting killed?" I think later in the discussion people did this, but at this point they questioned not the facts, but what? Go ahead, Jerry.

Jerry: Whether they were forced to work or not.

Teacher: Whether or not it was wrong to worry about people who voluntarily did the job, right?

Ellen: They must have believed the statement, though, if they would actually say a statement like that.

Teacher: Right. They accepted Linda's factual assumption on the basis of her own unsubstantiated claim. So she got away with it, right?

In pointing out two sources of evidence for factual claims (direct, eyewitness observation and books), the teacher tried to show how, in the previous discussion, the discussants had neglected to seek proof for the factual claims that were made. Analyzing tapes made by students has been useful both for teaching analytic concepts and for demonstrating how certain strategies (in this case, asking for proof) might have improved positions in the discussion.

4. Identifying and Resolving a Definitional Problem

Teacher: All right, so you are questioning what?

Elaine: Whether they (the railroad workers) are really being murdered or whether they are just dying in accidents.

Teacher: Right, accidental death versus murder. What kind of dispute is that?

Elaine: Factual, whether it's accidental or murder.

Teacher: But the same facts occurred in either case, so it can't be factual.

Elaine: So then it's values.

Teacher: Nope. It's a new category.

Elaine: It's either accidental death or it is murder.

Teacher: But you get into a big argument about whether this is accidental death or this is murder. What is really at stake? What's that, Sylvia?

Sylvia: A definition.

Teacher: A definitional argument. Okay, so it's over a definition of a term, right? Where can we go from this point? Don, you say it's not really murder, then what are you going to say.

Pete: It's not actually murder, it's manslaughter.

Teacher: Okay, go ahead, Ron, I mean go ahead with the argument. He said it's either murder or manslaughter.

Ron: It could be as much suicide as murder. I mean, it's just accidental death.

Pete: But you can prevent it. (Pete is playing the role of railroad worker.)

Ron: True.

Pete: True. Then why don't you?

Ron: I can prevent some of it, not all of it. (Ron is playing the role of railroad owner.)

Pete: Well, that "some" — that's what I'm talking about.

Ellen: Then what about the rest of the people?

Ron: The rest of it is still accidental.

Pete: You're getting off onto the others.

Teacher: Don, why don't you say what you were getting at earlier?

Don: I was just saying that that's not murder because just because the railroad can prevent it doesn't mean that they had to. Like, say he has this pond — this swimming hole, where all these little kids go in and swim. Well, I could go out in the middle of the pond in a boat or something and wait for someone, wait for him to drown, and I can start saving him, but if he drowns I am not murdering him. I mean I'm not murdering the kid, just because I *could* have saved his life.

Teacher: Right, so you're saying, "just because . . . ."

Don: Just because they could do this, they have the means . . . .

Teacher: Because it was preventable doesn't make it murder. Yes, that's very

persuasive. You're giving kind of an analogy in support of a particular definition. Howie?

Howie: I don't think murder is the right word, but I do think the railroad is
responsible for the deaths, because, like, if someone walks on your property
and there is a loose brick and they trip, you're responsible for that and they
can sue you.

Jim: That's questionable, though.

Howie: It is? They can sue you for something like that.

Jim: That's questionable, though.

Howie: Because you're responsible for your own property.

Teacher: Let's bring the example back to Don's water hole. You have a water
hole with a fence around it and a lot of little kids in the area and you know
if there is a faulty fence a little kid is likely to wander in and possibly drown.
What if he doesn't take care of the fence, and the little kid drowns? Is that
murder?

Dave: No.

Teacher: What would we call that?

Elaine: Negligence.

Teacher: Negligence. So now we have to think of the difference between
negligence and murder. Very good.

Here the class made progress on the definitional issue by using analogies
to illustrate the principle that murder involves more than failing to prevent
death when able to do so. The discussion could continue to search for additional criteria in the definition of murder and how it should be distinguished
from negligence.

B. Discussion
   Process
   Skills

1. Listening to
   and Para-
   phrasing Indi-
   vidual State-
   ments

A serious obstacle to productive discussion is the failure of discussants to
listen to each other. One method for developing greater auditory attention
is periodically to intervene in discussion and request students to tell what
the previous speaker said.

Tape: Dyke knew that the railroad was a monopoly so if he had made plans to
protect himself ahead of time then he wouldn't have been hurt in the raise
of rates.

Teacher: Hmmm. David, what did he just say?

David: If Dyke didn't build a monopoly, he wouldn't raise the rates.

Teacher: Once more, David. Were you listening?

David: Yes, I was listening.

Teacher: Okay, tell me what he said.

David: If Dyke didn't raise a monopoly, make a monopoly, he wouldn't raise
the railroad rates.

Teacher: Listen to it again.

Tape: Dyke knew that the railroad was a monopoly so if he had made plans
ahead of time he wouldn't have been hurt by the raise in the rates.

Teacher: Okay, David, what did he say?

David: Dyke knew a monopoly, I don't know, I forget. It is hard to remember things like that.

Teacher: Kathy.

Kathy: He said that since Dyke knew that the railroad had a monopoly he should have made plans, sort of thinking ahead that the railroad might raise their rates. Then he wouldn't be bankrupt.

2. Stating and Pursuing Issues Separately

Another common roadblock is the tendency to wander from one issue to another without explicitly acknowledging the major points of disagreement. Often each participant has his own points to make regardless of whether they are responsive to the remarks of the previous speaker. To gain any sense of accomplishment in discussion, it is important to identify and pursue issues separately.

Millie: That's not a treaty, a treaty is something you get from a foreign nation. That's a deed.

Jim: Well, a treaty and a deed are almost alike.

Millie: No, they aren't.

Jim: Now if the tollroad decides — we live beside the tollroad — if they decide they've got to widen it to a 16-lane highway and they want to take our land, they can do it even though my father's got that deed. Well, the Indians have the deed to that land, made by the government . . . .

Millie: They've got inalienable . . . .

Jim: Well, the deed is inalienable too.

Millie: It says that?

Jim: It guarantees them the right of the land. Now a deed does the same thing, but the deed can be revoked. But can't this treaty, especially this treaty that was made in the 1700's . . . ?

Millie: It has nothing to do with when it was made.

Jim: Well what about — to change the subject for a second — what about, the Constitution guarantees us the right to bear arms and now they're trying to take that right away from us. The Constitution, you remember, was written . . . .

Millie: Come now.

Jim: Well, they're changing the Constitution.

Millie: That's a whole different . . . that's not even a valid argument.

Jim: Well, yeah, but it's a law, and they're changing it.

Millie: Okay, so what's that got to do with the Indians?

Jim: This law is a treaty, you know.

Millie: Oh no, it's not a law, it's an agreement by a foreign nation. You don't break that.

Jim: Wait a minute, what's this foreign nation bit?

Millie: You don't make a treaty unless it's with a foreign nation.

Teacher: Okay, now just stop for a minute and try to figure out what's happening. That'll help you find your next step. Now just listen for a minute. What is the main thing you're disagreeing on here?

Millie: Well, mostly the definition of a treaty.

Teacher: All right, one is the definition of a treaty.

Jim: Well, wait a minute, I don't think that means so much, because the point I'm trying to bring out is that the deed is not the exact same thing, but very similar to the treaty.

Teacher: You're trying to show that they're similar, and she's trying to show that they're different. You're trying to argue that she would admit it's all right to break a deed, and if they're similar then it should be all right to break a treaty. She's trying to establish that they're different. Now what was one major difference that she has used to show why they're different?

While discussing rights of railroad workers to strike in protest against dangerous working conditions, one team suggested (on the tape) that the railroad owners should have voluntarily improved working conditions.

Tape: We are not discussing whether we should improve conditions. We are discussing whether workmen should break laws, and that has nothing to do with it.

Teacher: Okay, how does that function in the argument? What did he just say? What was the thrust of his argument? Virginia?

Virginia: He is saying it is irrelevant to the issue.

Teacher: Okay, I asked two questions: what did he say and how is he using what he said? And which of those two questions did you just answer?

Virginia: The second one.

Teacher: Right, "how is he using what he said?" He said it's irrelevant. He is questioning relevance. And what he did was restate the issue. He said there are two issues A and B. And we are supposed to be discussing A. What are the two issues that we are mixed up on? What does he want to go ahead on? Jerry?

Jerry: He wants to go ahead on the issue of whether or not it is right for the workers to break laws.

Teacher: Right, he wants to go ahead on the law-breaking issue. And he says now we are talking about what?

Jerry: Whether it is voluntary or . . . .

Teacher: No. Go ahead, Jerry.

Jerry: Whether the employers should provide safety.

Teacher: Safety. Very good, whether they should provide safety measures. Okay, now we are saying you guys are on an irrelevant issue, you are talking about safety and you should be talking about law-breaking.

In each excerpt, the teacher interrupts the discussion, trying to lead students to explicitly state the issue of disagreement. Once the issue is stated, the teacher suggests what directions the discussion might then take to pursue the issue.

3. Analyzing Specific Discussion Moves

A dialogue can be viewed as a developing or evolving process in which specific actions (statements) tend to determine a more general pattern. As we might ask how the outcome of a symphony, painting, or athletic contest would vary, depending upon specific inputs at certain points in its development, we can do the same with dialogue. The teacher can focus student attention on how specific statements affect the progressive clarification of positions.

Teacher: What is the issue of disagreement now?

Joan: What were their legal rights?

Teacher: Yes, who legally owned this land? Now did you ever reach an agreement? Quiet, Bobby, we're trying to figure out where the discussion is going. Now, did you ever reach agreement on that issue? Well, what was your major point, what were you trying to get Rick to admit?

Joan: I was trying to get him to see that the government didn't have any right to the Indians' land.

Teacher: All right, did you get him to admit that?

Joan: No, I gave him every possible reason but he . . . .

Teacher: Well, how could you have convinced him?

Joan: I don't know, but I wasn't doing too well.

Teacher: Well, I think you could have if you had stuck to this point in the case. The case says Indians had inalienable rights guaranteed by eighteenth-century treaty. Now you could have said to him something like this: "Are you trying to tell me that there wasn't any treaty for these Indians?" And he'd say, "No, I have to admit there was a treaty." He couldn't deny that there were treaties. So then after Rick admits that, now what can you do to get him to see your point?

Joan: Just go on the theory of the treaty. Then how can you — don't you consider the treaty valid?

Teacher: That's right, you can say, "Obviously, Rick, you're telling me that we should break the treaty, or the treaty is invalid. Now for what reason can we break a promise like that? And a treaty?" I think you could have followed up on that point.

The class is trying to decide how they might have improved their previous discussion.

Marie: Then Don said that he should have gotten some protection from this monopoly. Then Jan turns around, from the same group and says, no, he shouldn't have signed that early. That makes discrepancy among the group.

Don: I said he should have taken steps to protect himself.

Marie: Well, wouldn't you call that step getting the contract. I'd consider it a giant step.

Don: Jan was talking about the contract between selling his crops to the dealer who makes the beer or whatever he does with them.

Marie: I think Jan is talking about the contract.

Jan: No I wasn't.

Teacher: I think Don is right in that case.

Marie: Oh, okay.

Teacher: Okay, and I think that was part of the problem we had yesterday. One team was talking about one problem and the other team was talking about the other. So you can see that was the difficulty. Jan said two things: one, that Dyke was a stupid businessman and, two, that the agreement wasn't really valid. Now what could Team B respond to this? How might they have confronted Jan's last statement? Sheila?

Sheila: Well, they could have disputed the fact of the contract and kept going on about was there a contract or wasn't there a contract.

Teacher: Yes. Now what issue would you think would have been the best issue for Team B to pick up at this point. Jan has allowed them to pick up either of two issues, the stupid businessman issue, or the validity of the contract issue. Thinking back, what do you think would have been the best thing for Team B to do at this point? Liz?

4. Summarizing To gain a sense of where a discussion is going and what it has accomplished, it is useful continually to summarize.

After extensively arguing whether the Sons of Liberty were justified in using violence to protest the Stamp Act, the teacher calls on Alison, who had earlier been appointed secretary to keep track of issues and positions raised in the discussion.

Teacher: Now, let's try to list the pro and con arguments on the rights of the Sons of Liberty to destroy property and life in protesting the Stamp Act. I'll put up on the board the points you've made. Alison, would you tell us what you've written down for each side of the case?

Alison: Well, the first one we talked about was that the Sons were fighting for their rights and their liberties.

Teacher: Their cause, in other words, seemed to be a just cause — the liberties and rights they were fighting for — just or reasonable or something like that.

Alison: We kind of talked about whether or not they were represented and if they weren't represented, this was something they should fight for.

Teacher: Representation would be an example of one of these basic rights, maybe.

Alison: And also that violence was the only way to get it across to Parliament.

Teacher: Violence was necessary to achieve these rights.

Alison: We talked about how other peaceful methods could be used, but the only one we came up with was the boycott continuing. And also that the colonists — that the tax was only levied on them and not on the other English and that was kind of unfair.

Teacher: Unequal taxation meaning only on the colonists. The people in England didn't have to pay such a tax. That looks like a very persuasive case. What were some of the persuasive points that came up against this sort of activity?

Alison: Well, we came up with that it was legally wrong to be violent.

Teacher: Okay, so their actions were illegal.

Alison: Morally, we felt it couldn't be decided upon and some people thought it was morally right and some people thought it was wrong depending upon the situation and how good the principle was.

Teacher: So you're saying it is clearly illegal and the morality is at least questionable. We didn't reach a conclusion on that. The morality is questionable. Are there any more points that would favor this position that came up in our discussion?

Chris: We stipulated that the boycott had to be supplemented by violence. I think the point that the boycott could have been sufficient as a tactic can be a point on the column against the Sons.

Teacher: That's very good. Even though we made a stipulation, that didn't settle the issue. We stipulated because we couldn't figure out how to solve it.

In another situation, students have been discussing the Woodville Barber (pp. 274–275), without teacher help, in a small group.

Mary: There is no law that says two stores . . . .

Robert: Yes, there is.

Mary: No, there isn't.

Robert: There is. It's called, oh I forget the word, oh, conspiracy — price fixing.

Mary: Okay, we'll assume that what you say is true. That means, if there's this little corner store, in this poor ghetto area that's charging like 75¢ for a loaf of bread—and then there's this other supermarket selling it at 25¢, you mean to tell me that this is all right as long as they don't both go to 75¢.

Robert: One law says that it's illegal to have the same price, the other says it's illegal to have too high a price. The third lays says it's illegal to have too low a price.

Pat: Listen, I know a case where a big large supermarket moved right across the street from this little grocer. And it took less than half a year for this little grocer to decide that he was going out of business, and it closed down. That's the end. And this . . . .

Peter: Wait a minute . . . .

Gail: The exact same thing . . . .

Peter: Wait, wait a minute — I think, Robert, that the point is that they can't have the same price when they've made an agreement to fix the prices, and . . . .

Robert: Yes, but they say it's a tactical agreement. If they have the same price, it is not proof of a conspiracy.

Mary: Is this going to help Tuttle?

Gail: I think that the court could decide a price which both of them would agree is a fair price for a barber to have.

Pat: Yes, but that's not . . . that's not free enterprise.

Gail: Yes, it is.

Robert: It is. Price fixing . . . .

Gail: Well, they could fix it between two things.

Pat: No, you can't.

Mary: Wait a minute. What are we disagreeing about? Let us summarize what we are disagreeing about, first of all. Maybe we can attack each one at a time. Robert, you seem to be saying that the law can do nothing. So the poor barber, he goes someplace else or just stays there and suffers the consequences. Now, Pat, what is your point? You're saying that maybe the court can do nothing but they should at least try, to propose an adjustment for both people to work it out. Right? Now, Gail, your point is that when they do propose this, Alex will not agree. So we're right back to the original problem.

Pat: Right!

Gail: Okay.

Peter: Now we'll have to decide this morally. That's what our decision should be. Stick to what is morally right.

C. What Does Discussion Accomplish?

These excerpts show how the role of the teacher can vary. He may deliberately attempt to teach specific analytic concepts, he may focus on drilling or practicing specific discussion skills (issue-stating, listening, summarizing), he may serve as a resource person to comment on substantive problems (e.g., the legal definition of contract), or he may actively coach individual students in strategies that would make their position more defensible. And, of course, the teacher may assume different postures toward value problems as discussed in Chapter 9.

For reasons mentioned in Chapter 1, people often see discussion at worst as a complete waste of time or, at best, simply as sharing opinions. Overcoming such attitudes is a challenge probably more difficult than training people to perform particular discussion skills. Teachers must make special efforts to demonstrate that student discussion can be productive. To help students gain a sense of intellectual accomplishment or achievement the teacher, through review and summarization, should try to show how class discussion: (1) made explicit complex issues not apparent to students at the beginning of a discussion; (2) helped students increase reasons used to support their position, or supplied reasons that led to revising or rejecting a former position; (3) provided qualifications and distinctions for students' positions; (4) increased student awareness of arguments opposing their position; (5) moved along smoothly (avoided getting bogged down or "hung up" needlessly), because certain discussion strategies were used.

Because students are not accustomed to viewing school achievement or excellence in school in terms of oral behavior (written tests or papers are the major vehicle for achieving grades), the teacher must make special efforts to praise and reward students for demonstrating competence in discussion skill. Teachers can respond with compliments (and grades) when students exhibit the desired skills (giving evidence, using analogy, stating issues, etc.). We do not mean to imply, however, that students can gain a vital sense of intellectual achievement simply from extrinsic teacher reward and praise. Quite the contrary, unless the cognitive operations and discussion skills produce intrinsic intellectual clarification for students, extrinsic reinforcement from the teacher will result in superficial gamesmanship and compliant efforts to please teacher.

At least, the teacher should ask, "what has a discussion accomplished?" By thoroughly and continually examining this question, students may conclude that all discussion is not in vain. The following excerpt occurred after forty minutes of class discussion on the justification of violence used by the Sons of Liberty to protest the Stamp Act. The teacher listed on the chalkboard eight different disagreements (issues) that arose in the discussion.

> Teacher: Today, we began with this question on the justification for violence by the Sons of Liberty. We started off pretty slowly, without much excitement and nothing on the board. Now, however, it looks like we have a very complicated problem. We have both discovered and created complexities in a problem that did not exist in our minds when we began. In a sense that's an accomplishment. I don't know if you personally feel it's an accomplishment. I do, because I think too many people assume problems like this are simple to solve.

Following this statement, teacher and class went on to review positions that emerged in discussing the various issues (see pp. 307–308 for part of this summarizing).

II. Activities for Practicing Discussion Skills

In line with our plea for novelty in classroom technique, we can suggest different formats for conducting classroom discussion.

A. Grouping

Discussion by twenty-five to thirty students can be arranged and managed in several ways:

Teacher as Moderator. Conventional pattern in which teacher moderates discussion of the whole class, attempting to orchestrate diverse views of many students.

Teacher as Interviewer. With most of the class listening, teacher focuses intensively on one or a few students to pursue individual views in depth.

Debates. Teams of two to four students each present their views to the rest of the class.

Evaluation Panel. In five-man groups, two students discuss the issues (an interesting variation is to have one student "coach" for each of the two discussants) and three act as observers or judges. Periodically judges stop the discussion to consider what "progress" is being made and to suggest ways of improving it. This encourages students to listen more carefully.

Two-man Dialogues. Two-man pairs carry on private dialogues in different parts of the classroom. This allows students to explore each others' views in some depth without continuous public surveillance by teacher or class-mates.

When students are split into groups, taking responsibility for their own discussions, teacher can roam about, occasionally intervening as devil's advocate, moderator, or resource person.

B. Deliberate Discussion

One technique for ensuring careful attention to statements is to have a group of students discuss and decide what to say next to a previous statement created by another team or group. After Team A comes up with its "best" statement, it is tape-recorded and played to Team B. Team B is given time to construct a response. It then records the response, which is played to Team A. This technique forces students to think carefully about one statement at a time. Deliberate discussion proceeds much more slowly than a normal discussion, where participants generally talk continuously in a rapid-fire sequence that leaves little time for reflection between statements.

Deliberate discussions can have several objectives:

1. Producing a total "good" discussion.
2. Producing a deliberately poor discussion.
3. Using particular operations within a discussion (e.g., analogy and analogy challenge, stipulation, concession, and evidence).
4. Illustrating different ways to decide on a discussion agenda.

After tape-recording a deliberate discussion, the entire class can analyze it and rethink whether statements recorded were most appropriate.

C. Public Hearing

A group of students becomes a judgmental panel to question students who play the roles of interested parties to a dispute. If the issue is whether to set up a coffee and coke lounge in the high school basement, relevant interest groups such as the vending machine company, parents, teachers, students, and custodians might testify. This technique encourages students on the panel to take initiative in asking questions appropriate to resolution of the major issues.

D. Creating "Model" Dialogues

Teachers and students can develop orally (preferably on tape), or in writing, contrived dialogues to illustrate particular operations or problems. Students might gain more sensitivity to the problem of relevance, for example, if they intentionally constructed a recorded dialogue that contained a high proportion of irrelevant statements. They might learn better how to separate issues if they tried to make a model discussion in which transitions between issues were clearly articulated. They could practice the skill of summarizing dialogue results if they create their own model in which fictional participants try to summarize often. Student teams can present models for their classmates to analyze. Competition among teams to create the best models can increase motivation.

E. Evaluation Forms

Forms similar to those in Figures 9.3–9.6 in Chapter 9 can heighten student attention toward discussion processes. Class discussion of responses recorded on the forms can be as instructive as the discussion itself.

F. Paper-Pencil Tests and Exercises

Structured exercises such as the Level B tests (see Figure 9.2, p. 288) or multiple-choice dialogue analysis (see Chapter 9, pp. 287–289) can be used to teach analytic and discussion concepts as well as to evaluate student mastery.

Many of these activities involve students in *analyzing* as well as producing discussion on public issues. Although we believe that intensive practice in analyzing discussion will help to improve actual discussion performance, we must express the serious reservation that these skills may not necessarily correlate. We have known many experts in the analysis of teaching who fail as teachers. Although analytic exercises may increase students' facility to describe or annotate discussion, we must not neglect the importance of having and participating in discussion of substantive policy issues (as opposed to commenting about such conversations). One's skill in analyzing discourse should not be confused with his skill in engaging in discourse.

Chapter 11

Education and Community

This chapter presents a critique of the American educational system and recommendations for change. Having given so much attention to curriculum designed ostensibly for implementation in public schools, it may seem paradoxical that we conclude with a broad indictment of those schools. However, while teaching the original three-year curriculum to adolescents in a conventional school setting, we became increasingly aware of the obstacles the school environment poses to discussion of public controversy.

In a metropolitan community which makes a substantial financial commitment to education and whose schools are nationally known for innovation, the Harvard staff taught sixty students (two classes of thirty each) for three consecutive years from grades ten through twelve. The staff consisted of at least two and up to four experienced teachers engaged in doctoral study or on the Harvard Graduate School of Education faculty. We enjoyed an ideal teaching arrangement, relatively *immune from censorship by parents or administrators* and free of obligations to teach given content to prepare students for standardized tests. The students we taught had average academic ability (mean IQ about 107), and came from middle- to lower middle-income families. None would attend high prestige, four-year colleges or universities, though many planned to pursue some form of education beyond high school.

We sensed that students enjoyed our classes, and the final evaluation indicated they had achieved some competence in the objectives we sought. It would be obvious to any sensitive observer, however, that after an initial period of creative enthusiasm, the students were "turned off" by school. Though we dealt with "live," "relevant" topics — war, sex, race, politics — the class was approached as an island, detached from mainland reality. Students often showed animated concern and involvement in class discus-

313

sion, but it seemed that clarifying positions on public issues in our course was unrelated to the community beyond the classroom or school.

We asked ourselves why? Why did students seem to switch on separate attitudes and behavior patterns as they moved between the school and the "real world"? The standard, often perfunctory response that courses are irrelevant and teachers uninspiring seemed inadequate to explain the pervasiveness of student disengagement. We found ourselves involved in a more fundamental assessment of the forces shaping American education, examining the usually unstated assumptions and forgotten historical choices that have molded the process of learning into a bureaucratized function that is segregated from noninstructional aspects of community life.

I. Reexamining Premises of Contemporary American Education[1]

A. Education as Formal Schooling

To most Americans education is synonymous with schooling, which is defined as formal instruction carried on in an institution that has no other purpose. In conventional rhetoric one "gets" an education by going to school. One therefore improves education by improving schools. Whether we read progressives (Dewey, 1900, 1902), traditionalists (Rickover, 1960), public educational statesmen (Conant, 1959), prominent professors venturing into curriculum reform (Bruner, 1960), or other analysts of education in America (Kimball and McClellan, 1962), we find almost universal agreement that better education requires better schooling.

Federal and foundation moneys are channeled into hundreds of projects designed to improve instruction in the schools. New approaches to instruction such as team teaching, programmed instruction, nongraded schools, computer use, simulation, or educational television are all designed as methods for improving schooling. Millions are spent — in preschool training programs to prepare the "disadvantaged" for success in school, to prevent adolescents from dropping out of school, to train teachers to teach in schools. In addition to the traditional elementary-secondary-college sequence, we aim to improve education by creating more schools: summer school, night school, and graduate or professional schools.

The proliferation of schools leads one to ask whether it might be possible to become educated without going through conscious formalized instruction in institutions designed only for that function. Bailyn (1960) notes the emergence of formal schools in the Anglo-American colonies as an historical development responding to radical social changes. He boldly suggests that even before formal schools emerged, people acquired an effective education through less formal processes:

> The forms of education assumed by the first generation of settlers in America were a direct inheritance from the medieval past. Serving the needs of a homo-

[1] Sections I and II of this chapter are quoted and adapted from Newmann and Oliver (1967).

geneous, slowly changing rural society, they were largely instinctive and traditional, little articulated and little formalized. The most important agency in the
transfer of culture was not formal institutions of instruction or public instruments
of communication, but the family. . . .

The family's educational role was not restricted to elementary socialization.
Within these kinship groupings, skills that provided at least the first step in
vocational training were taught and practiced. In a great many cases, as among
the agricultural laboring population and small tradesmen who together com-
prised the overwhelming majority of the population, all the vocational instruction necessary for mature life was provided by the family. . . .

What the family left undone by way of informal education the local community most often completed. It did so in entirely natural ways, for so elaborate
was the architecture of family organization and so deeply founded was it in the
soil of stable, slowly changing village and town communities in which intermarriage among the same groups had taken place generation after generation that
it was at times difficult for the child to know where the family left off and the
greater society began. . . .

More explicit in its educational function than either family or community was
the church. . . . It furthered the introduction of the child to society by instructing
him in the system of thought and imagery which underlay the culture's values
and aims. . . .

Family, community, and church together accounted for the greater part of
the mechanism by which English culture transferred itself across the generations.
The instruments of deliberate pedagogy, of explicit, literate education, accounted
for a smaller, though indispensable, portion of the process. . . . The cultural burdens it bore were relatively slight. . . (pp. 15–19).

The modern American, however, no longer construes family, church, or
other community agencies as vital educational institutions. He is in fact still
distilling from other institutions their normal educative functions and transferring them to the school: e.g., vocational training, auto safety and driver
training, rehabilitating the disadvantaged, early childhood training, home-
making. The consequences of assuming that education necessarily takes place
in school, or *should* take place in school, have been profound and far-
reaching, and require serious reexamination.

Allocating the educational functions of society to a single separate
institution — the school — suggests that such an institution must have a
unique responsibility and that the separation must somehow be intrinsically
related to this responsibility. This assumption becomes highly suspect,
however, when we look at three important aspects of the separation: (a) we
conceive of education as necessary "preparation," and we, therefore, carefully separate "learning" from "acting," "doing," or productive work; (b) we
separate the school environment from the "noninstructional" life of the
community at large; and (c) we construe teaching as a specialized occupa-

tion, isolated from the world of action and decision-making — a world that is considered to have no pedagogical function.

B. Education as Preparation

Formal schooling is commonly justified on the ground that we need a specialized institution to prepare children and youth for life as productive adults. The value of education is seen as instrumental, leading to ends extrinsic from the processes of formal instruction itself. We get an education *now* so that at some *later* time we can earn money, vote intelligently, raise children, serve our country, and the like. The preparatory emphasis implies closure — education is begun and finished. Graduation or commencement signifies the termination of learning and the beginning of real life. Education in America most often consists of formal training through discrete courses and programs. How many institutions have we designed to foster education not as preparatory activity but as a legitimate end in itself, insinuated as a continuing integral element throughout one's career?

Preparatory aims of formal schooling are often embedded in a concept of growth. As Bruner (1966, p. 1) remarks, "Instruction is, after all, an effort to assist or to shape growth." To implement such a mandate, schools have isolated children and adolescents from adults and have focused most formal training on young people. This, however, betrays a confusion between biological and mental development. Let us assume that the schools should be primarily concerned with mental-emotional development (they can have relatively minor affects on biological growth). First, we wonder whether it is possible to make a useful distinction between people who are "growing" versus those who have "matured" with regard to mental-emotional development. One could argue that adulthood, far from being a period of stable maturity, is no more than a continuing process of mental-emotional growth (and biological change) presenting conflicts and adjustment problems as stormy and challenging as growth during childhood and adolescence. Marriage, child-rearing, occupational decision, pursuit of leisure, adaptation to geographic and occupational change, and adjustment to retirement and death continually demand growth by adults. With the entirety of a human life cycle before us, we would ask, when is mental-emotional maturity reached? If growth, change, and decay continue until death, then why confine education to the early years of biological development?

Second, by assuming young people to be dynamic and growing and adults to be static and ripe, one is led to postulate that adults have needs essentially different from the needs of young people — that conflicts and differences *between* generations are greater than conflicts and differences within a given generation. We would suggest, however, that members of differing generations do have common problems and educational needs, and the needs of members of the same generation may be radically diverse. Compare, for example, an unemployed man of forty with an unemployed teenage dropout who both lack literacy and vocational skills. Could they not benefit from a common educational experience? Or suppose an oppressed ethnic group is attempting to combat discrimination. Members of that group from all generations face a common problem. Conversely, groups *within* a generation may have quite different educational needs: a thirty-year-old mother on public assistance versus a thirty-year-old attorney attempting to establish a law practice; or a teenage girl from a broken lower-class home versus a teenage boy from a stable upper-class family.

The current exclusive emphasis on preparation raises another basic question: Is it possible that, despite certain commonalities across generations, childhood and adolescence constitute in themselves integral parts of the human career, with certain roles, needs, and behavior that may be largely unrelated to the demands of a future adulthood? Schools are designed mainly to implant in students knowledge, attitudes, and skills revered by adult scholars and educators, yet we can legitimately question why it is necessary to stress almost exclusively adult values before children and youth have attained that biological and social status.

We also note a certain pragmatic folly in education as preparation for future adulthood in the modern world. A leading educational innovator remarks on "the colossal problem of educating youngsters for jobs which do not exist and for professions which cannot be described" (Brown, 1963, p. 14). Is it even possible to prepare children to behave fruitfully in a future world, the dimensions and complexities of which educated adults are presently unable to grasp?

The tendency of formal schooling to isolate children during a period of "preparation" for adulthood has produced a rigid system of age-grading, which has as one effect a fractionation of the human career. This tends to hinder development of meaningful relationships among generations and cultivates a fragmented, rather than continuous, concept of self. The prevailing conception that children can learn only *from*, rather than with, adults and the forced submission of youth to adult rule amplifies the conflict between generations and encourages a posture of dependency, a sense of powerlessness that may carry over from youth to adulthood.

1. School and the Community at Large

A large portion of school training is separated from, and has no significant effect on, students' behavior outside of school mainly because the school establishment is isolated from problems, dilemmas, choices, and phenomena encountered beyond school walls. Teachers readily attest to students' capacity to "tune out" or memorize but not apply lessons taught in school. There is a sense of unreality inherent in living in two discontinuous worlds, if one is to take both seriously.

The progressives tried to handle this separation by bringing more "real life" activities into the school. They tried to match work in school with work in real life, introducing various manual skills and decision-making activities similar to those occurring outside of school. Modern efforts in curriculum reform have pursued the same idea through developing simulation activities — attempts to make school relevant to more instructional life. But simulation still occurs within *instructional* contexts and is, therefore, detached from actual and significant concerns. It may cultivate an attitude that learning or life or both are synonymous with playing games. The attempt to make school "fun" by exploiting the motivational power of competition or curiosity in children simply avoids the challenge of applying learning to life outside the school. In spite of 'the progressives' efforts toward antiformalism (for example, allowing students more individual freedom, emphasizing play and a variety of arts and crafts), they did much to solidify a conception of education as equivalent to formal schooling. In fact, the most dramatic way for the progressive to demonstrate his ideas was to found a new *school*, which soon became isolated from genuine conflicts and decisions of students' lives beyond school walls.

2. Teaching as a Specialized Occupation

Formal schooling provided the basis for a new specialized "profession of education." As Cremin (1964) points out, the profession was quick to isolate itself from other professions and fields of knowledge. It also built an education establishment dedicated to studying, servicing, and expanding formal schooling as a separate and discrete institution, often accumulating powerful vested interests irrelevant to the real improvement of education (Conant, 1963, 1964). As an alternative to the unquestioned policy of requiring professionally trained teachers in schools, one might argue that in fact students could gain valuable education from each other and from various "untrained," though interesting individuals, be they blue-collar laborers, politicians, bureaucrats, criminals, priests, athletes, artists, or whatever. To the extent that schools are staffed by professional educators, learning tends to become isolated from the significant community concerns, and the narrower functions and tasks of the *school* come to dominate the broader purposes of education.

The consequences of equating education with formal schooling have special relevance to teaching public issues. Because adults can vote, hold office, own property, pay taxes, and are legally responsible, presumably they are more vitally concerned with public controversy than young children. Yet, because of the preparatory emphasis of schooling, most educational resources are invested in children. Adults are in effect discriminated against and deprived of opportunities to study social controversy. Although adolescents can be deeply concerned with social issues, their inquiry occurs in the relative quiet of classroom or library, insulated from realities of battle in the legislative committee room, factional disputes in a local labor union or civil rights group, the tumult of a mass demonstration or riot, the ways of justice in night court, the joys of victory or sorrows of defeat at election headquarters. Students learn of public issues from a teacher who has studied education and history or social science at college, not from the practicing politician, judge, lobbyist, dissenter, policeman, or taxpayer. Thus, by isolating students from adults most directly interested in controversy and by providing unequal opportunities for adults to become students, schools as we know them perpetuate an unrealistic view of public issues and inhibit opportunities for the citizen to act responsibly on the positions he formulates.

C. Education as Public Monopoly

The expansion of schooling as a stable and universal service through governmental compulsion rather than private voluntary association raises questions about the system's underlying political philosophy. American political thought has traditionally distinguished between society (a collection of various private groupings) and government (the combination of political and legal organs that make up the state). Lindsay (1943, p. 120) notes the special value that Americans place on voluntary associations:

> The English or the American democrat takes it for granted that there should be in society voluntary associations of all kinds, religious, philanthropic, commercial: that these should be independent of the state at least in the sense that the state does not create them. The state may have to control and regulate them. Questions concerning their relations with the state are indeed continually turning up, but it is always taken for granted that men form these societies and associations for their own purposes; that their loyalty to such associations is direct; that it therefore does not follow that the state will prevail in any conflict between such associations and the state.

This laissez-faire philosophy implies that the state exists to facilitate a plurality of diverse interests inherent in men's *voluntary* associations and enterprises. The commitment of a community representing such pluralistic interests was applied to many domains of experience: to religion where sectarianism flourished; to economic affairs by developing overlapping and competing business enterprises. Traditional notions of ordered artisan industries controlled by disciplined guilds, agriculture controlled by the feudal lords, mercantile trading policies encouraged and regulated by a central government, and monopolistic industry sanctioned by restrictive state charters all fell before the laissez-faire economics practiced in America. It was assumed that the life of the community at large would be infused by the vigor and drive of private enterprise and association, that natural laws of competition and cooperation would prevent any serious conflict between private interests and the public.

But pluralism in the schools was short-lived. The common school, which established firm roots in early nineteenth-century Massachusetts, was later seen as a place where the children of all nationalities, religions, creeds, and economic levels could mix together. As the common school spread to other states and as pressures mounted to establish secondary schools and to open private academies to all, the educational impact of voluntary associations declined. Rapidly increasing immigration from Europe in the latter half of the nineteenth century and the first decade of the twentieth created in the common school a major test for the pluralistic philosophy. Some Americans viewed the floodtide of newcomers as an opportunity to renew and invigorate the national and ethnic dimension of American pluralism. In 1915 Horace Kallen (1953, pp. 29–30) sentimentally envisioned

> . . . a democracy of nationalities, cooperating voluntarily and autonomously through common institutions in the enterprise of self-realization through the perfection of men according to their kind. The common language of the commonwealth . . . would be English, but each nationality would have for its own emotional and involuntary life its own peculiar dialect or speech, its own individual and inevitable esthetic and intellectual forms. The political and economic life of the commonwealth is a single unit and serves as the foundation and background for the realization of the distinctive individuality of each *nation* that composes it and of the pooling of these in harmony above them all.

But not all Americans had faith in the "distinctive individuality" of national groups. In addition to tension created by religious sectarianism, free enterprise, and ethnic diversity, the nineteenth century labored under the severe strain of rapid industrialization. Evidently fearing that continued cultivation of national differences would be disruptive to society, the common schools stressed the need for pooling or assimilating immigrants into a common melting pot.

Eventually public schools attained a virtual monopoly on the life of youth between ages six and sixteen. This development represents a clear shift in political philosophy. It signifies a blurring, if not total rejection, of the distinction between society and government, formerly so crucial to the American democrat; a loss of faith in the ability of a pluralistic system of private associations to provide an education that would benefit both the individual and his nation.

Perhaps at this point in history it was necessary and useful for the common school to serve a cohesive and integrating function by emphasizing a common heritage, common aspirations, common learnings, common dress, and a common routine within the school. One could suggest, in fact, that the school simply reflected the needs and requirements of the society by stressing *integrating* elements in the society, rather than the diversity, so blatant and obvious. Granted that the society might have been on the brink of disintegration and in need of cohesive institutions at that time, uniformity and conformity have been continuously characteristic of public education ever since the development of common and secondary schools. One might argue theoretically that even though education is public and compulsory, it can conceivably encourage and reinforce cultural diversity by providing widely ranging alternative types of education. This, however, has not been true of public education in America. On the contrary, the schools have attempted to file down or erase distinctive cultural traits, denying that important cultural diversity ever existed; the instruction and procedures of the school reflect a mandate to persuade youth that all groups share a common language, common political and economic institutions, and common standards of right and wrong behavior. And although it is somewhat more stylish to recognize the importance of "individual differences," these are construed in psychological rather than cultural terms. Insofar as the recent effort to educate slum children has forced us to recognize cultural differences, these differences are still construed largely as cultural deficiencies (the "black studies" movement is a healthy antidote).

We are concerned with two general effects of the decision to make education an exclusive, compulsory, public function.[2] First, the public monopoly has fundamentally altered the nature of childhood and adolescence in America. Young people spend more than half their waking hours from age six to their early twenties trying to meet demands of formal schooling. This has destroyed to a large extent opportunities for random, exploratory work and play outside a formal educational setting. One could argue that, psychologically, it is most important for youth (and for that matter all humans) to spend a significant portion of their lives in spontaneous, voluntary kinds of activity, as in Erikson's (1962) suggestion of a psycho-social moratorium, rather than in regimented, required, planned learning tasks. By denying to students basic responsibility and freedom, public schooling prevents development of a sense of competency in making personal decisions. Though schooling requires large quantities of work ("industry"), its evaluation system generally assumes the work of youth to be inferior to work of adults (teachers). The public institutional milieu of the school discourages intimacy among students or between students and teachers. Schooling prevents exploratory, experimental activity; it prohibits total involvement in any single interest; it refuses to delegate to students responsibility for seeking their own "education." If public schooling were only one among many

[2] The fact that state laws allow youth to fulfill educational obligations by attending private as well as public schools does not diminish the influence of the public monopoly. A relatively small proportion of children do attend private schools (approximately 16 percent at the elementary level and 11 per cent at the secondary level). Moreover, even private schools must conform to publicly established standards.

major experiences for young people, these would be less important criticisms. What makes the criticisms most significant is the fact that schooling has a virtual monopoly on youth's time and energy, and the power to suppress the quest for individuation through extraschool activity.

In addition to psychological dangers, the monopoly's second major threat is its potential for creating cultural uniformity, destroying diversity in viewpoints, in life styles, in standards of taste, and in underlying value commitments. The standard rebuttal for this criticism is to point out that although we do have required public education, it is controlled by local communities and is not a national system. Therefore, one can have radically diverse types of education, depending upon the unique needs of each community. In theory this seems persuasive, but in fact numerous forces in modern America — mass media, the publishing industry, national curriculum development programs, and professional educators — combine (however unintentionally) to produce overall institutional similarity. If one examines programs in schools throughout the country, one finds an incredible similarity among curricula of different communities. (The apparent differences between schooling in slums and suburbs cannot be accounted for by assuming that slum dwellers have chosen to have one type of education, suburbanites another.) Although public schooling should not bear all responsibility for cultural uniformity, the fact that it has captive control of youth allows it to accelerate cultural standardization. We object to such a trend because we believe that the essence of freedom lies in the opportunity for significant choice, and that choice becomes increasingly limited as individual and cultural differences are blurred or erased.

Given the failure of the school to support a vital pluralistic tradition, one might ask why must education be carried on as a publicly controlled, compulsory activity? Law and medicine, certainly as vital as education for society, have remained largely controlled by the private sector. Powerful, but essentially private media industries (books, newspapers, cinema, television) communicate and transmit knowledge to the community at large, equally important as education. To meet basic subsistence needs, we use a system of production and distribution run largely by private enterprise. Spiritual-religious activities are exclusively reserved for private associations. Curiously, public schools are required to provide ideological indoctrination (the American Creed) comparable to religious indoctrination, yet we have refused public support for "religious" education. In citizenship education, the public schools provide instruction for citizen participation in the political process, but in fact that instruction is obstructed by myths and misinformation. The most effective training for political life occurs within various private interest groups or political parties.

Because education is seen as the responsibility of a public body that must be "impartial" to the influence of private interests, school teachers and administrators seek to avoid controversy and to prevent partisan concerns from influencing instruction. But an institution that tries to be totally nonpartisan and aloof provides an inappropriate arena in which to study public issues, the essence of which is advocacy and the clash among vested interests.[3] As citizens we do not always have the luxury of playing the role of detached, neutral analyzer. We must take a stand. Developing sensitivity to significant issues in a controversy and learning how to pursue one's position demands active involvement by the student in controversies relevant to him as a *citizen* in the community. To this end, we suggest that schools provide released time for students to engage in social action projects. If public officials (i.e., school board members or school superintendents) feel uncomfortable in sponsoring student involvement in private political causes (which can attack school policies and personnel), but also see participation in community affairs as crucial to citizenship education, then they need only delegate this function to on-going voluntary associations in a community. This delegation would reduce the overwhelming control that schools exert on the student's life.

D. Education Modeled after Corporate Bureaucracy

Education, having evolved into publicly sponsored formal compulsory instruction, could conceivably have taken many forms. Public schools might have become coordinating agencies that channeled the students into various educational experiences provided by existing political, economic, cultural, and religious institutions. Schools might have become supplementary agencies, like libraries, appended to small neighborhood communities. In the long run, however, education adopted the prevailing institutional structure in the society at large: the factory served by an industrial development laboratory and managed according to production-line and bureaucratic principles. Architecturally, the schools came to resemble factories (instruction carried on first in rooms but more recently in large loft-like spaces, with different spaces reserved for different instruction) and office buildings (with corridors designed to handle traffic between compartments of uniform size). Conceivably, schools could have been built like private homes, cathedrals, artists' studios, or country villas.

[3] We do not wish to imply that schools are in fact impartial. Curriculum in social studies usually gives implicit partisan support to groups and interests that dominate American culture. Neither do we wish to minimize the importance of dispassionate reflection or periodic retreats from the pressures of social conflict to better understand public issues. There must be a balance between what one learns from the world of action versus "pure" reflection. Schooling as a public monopoly, however, tends to neglect the former.

The schools came to be administered like smooth-running production lines. Clear hierarchies of authority were established: student, parent, teacher, principal, superintendent, and school committeeman, each of whom was presumed to know his function and the limits of his authority. Consistent with the principle of the division of labor, activities were organized into special departments: teaching (with its many subdivisions), administration, guidance, custodial services, etc. The administrator saw instruction as assembling and coordinating standardized production units: classes of equal size, instructional periods of equal length; uniform "adopted" books and materials that all students would absorb; and standard lessons provided by teachers with standardized training. Departures or interruptions in the routine were (and still are) discouraged because they threaten the "efficiency" of the overall process (e.g., taking a field trip, or showing a film that requires two time periods, or making special arrangements to meet with students individually). Conceivably, the schools could have been organized on a much less regimented basis, allowing more exploratory, random, unscheduled activity. However, as Callahan (1962) persuasively argues, the corporate bureaucratic model, guided by the cult of efficiency, exerted a major influence on the organization and program of public education.

In our view, corporate organization in education leads to three major developments that have important contemporary implications: (1) the research and development mentality, which limits its attention to building technology and instrumentation to achieve given specifiable goals, rather than questioning or formulating the goals themselves; (2) the increasingly fragmented school environment, which is sliced according to administrative and subject categories prescribed by educational specialists, rather than according to salient concerns of children, youth, or the larger community; and (3) the trend toward centralized, coordinated decision-making for schools by a combination of agencies in government, business, universities, foundations, and "nonprofit" research and development institutes.

1. The Research and Development Mentality The society seeks to build a highly educated final product (a graduate) at the lowest possible cost per unit. Armed with such a mandate, policy makers and educators scurry to devise and implement techniques that will achieve visible "pay-offs" in the "terminal behavior" of students. Many new devices and programs emerge: nongraded schools, advanced placement courses, independent study, programmed instruction, self-administered television and cinema, computer-based instruction. They are lauded and increasingly in demand for their apparent effectiveness in speeding up the educational process by "individualizing" instruction for students. The federal government invests millions of dollars through universities, research and development centers, and private industry to produce more efficient methods. Administrators use the techniques both as yardsticks to evaluate and as symbols to advertise their schools and build their personal reputations. Policy-makers and curriculum advisers beg for definite answers concerning which methods are best. But who seeks reasons for the emphasis on acceleration and efficiency? Why read at age three? Why learn quadratic equations at age ten? Why study American history a year or two earlier? Why try to think like an MIT physicist or an anthropologist at all? The research and development mentality thrives on gadgets, engineering metaphors, and the fever of efficiency, but rarely questions the purposes to which its technology is applied. The excessive concern with technique, rather than a searching examination of ends, results in a tendency to accept as legitimate those objectives that can be translated into operations and those products that can be schematically and quantitatively measured.

Despite its "practical" outlook, the research and development mentality constantly runs up against the "relevance problem": youth see the content of school as bookish and artificial, unrelated to the decisions and actions that lead to important consequences either in school or in the outside world. Both students and teachers attempt to right the disproportionate emphasis on abstract words and thought by stressing instead concrete procedures — prompt attendance, assignments completed, tests taken — and success. The progressive approach to the relevance problem was to abandon rigid work and grade standards without recognizing that these constraints provided structure, task definition, and consequences of decisions that are palpable and immediate. The new research and development proponent is somewhat more sophisticated; instead of stressing the concrete procedures associated with abstract verbal tasks, he seeks to simulate the real tasks of the outside world. Students play war, peace-making, monopoly, empire building, showing all the involvement of adult poker and bingo players. Although the research and development specialist sees the conceptual relationship between elements of the simulated activity or game and real life decisions, does the student? Perhaps the student simply learns that adults get their intellectual kicks by playing games, rather than dealing with real problems in the noninstructional world. At any rate the danger is that what students learn from playing games is how to play games, not how to construe either academic or world problems more effectively.

The underlying difficulty results from divorcing schooling from problems and choices that have genuine significance for youth and community. Because the kind of learning we prescribe is not intrinsically important to students, we invent trivial tasks and procedures to capture their attention, and we contract with engineers and research and development centers to do this as efficiently as possible. Significant problems and decisions emanate not primarily from research and development laboratories, but from strains and dilemmas in the world beyond school walls.

2. The Fragmented School Environment

In the spirit of Durkheim's analysis of the effects of division of labor, Thelen (1960, p. 215) comments that one of man's most important inventions was the development of concepts about how to organize human activity. But organization requires division and fragmentation that can, at times, have undesirable results:

> We have made hard and fast divisions between thinking and doing, creating and applying, planning and acting, preparing and fulfilling. The age of reason, the development of science, the domination of organization, and the simple increase in density of human population have interacted among each other to create these divisions. But these divisions have made modern life purposeless. For as long as we maintain the division we shall never have to find an organizing principle to integrate the parts. The organizing principle we have thus succeeded in avoiding is *purpose*.

The school, faithful to principles of bureaucratic organization and division of labor, has fostered the development of specialized compartments, many of which have no apparent relationship to, or communication with, each other: English, social studies, science, math, physical education, home economics, industrial arts, and guidance. Boundaries between the departments often arise from legitimate distinctions among subject matter or fields of knowledge, but lack of communication among fields can be attributed to the parochial interests of human beings who place the highest priority on their own area.

Fragmentation also may arise from underlying disagreements over the fundamental purposes of education. In broad terms we might classify differing objectives as: work skills (competencies required for successful careers and breadwinning), socialization (values and skills necessary to perform in the role of citizenship), psychological guidance (developing mental health), intellectual excellence (acquiring knowledge and cultivating various mental abilities). To this list we would add a less commonly stated objective, *social reconstruction* — the effort to justify schooling as a vehicle for establishing a particular social order. Many progressives saw the school as a microcosm of a particular ideal society. Other groups, from Puritans and Amish to Nazis and Communists, have similarly valued schooling as an instrument of social reconstruction.

The corporate educational enterprise tends to minimize conflict among differing objectives and fields of interest; it accommodates many philosophies and priorities by establishing isolated compartments, allowing each to pursue its own goals in peaceful coexistence. The school articulates its "philosophy" by simply *listing* all the differing objectives and course offerings. We have no quarrel with the diversity of objectives and subjects. On the contrary, our commitment to pluralism strongly supports them. We do, however, object to the organizational principle that attempts to minimize conflict by isolating and separating various interests from each other. This attempt aggravates fragmentation in community. It discourages tendencies to relate various purposes of man in community within comprehensive social theory. It stifles healthy ferment that might arise from tough public discussion of the merits of different specialties and objectives.

3. New Corporate Coalitions

Current efforts to construe education as a system of fully articulated components intended to shape terminal behaviors are increasingly evident in mergers among communications, electronics, and publishing industries: Time, Inc., owns television stations, a textbook company, and has become associated with General Electric; Xerox owns University Microfilms, Basic Systems, Inc., and American Education Publications; other mergers include RCA with Random House, IBM with Science Research Associates, and Raytheon with D. C. Heath and Company. These companies or their subsidiaries, often with the assistance of university research and development centers, are planning federally financed programs to solve America's educational problems. Similar government, industrial, and university coalitions have long cooperated in developing America's war hardware and space exploration. The federal government raises research and development funds, university and industry supply engineering talent and laboratories, and industry manufactures and distributes the final product. An educational prototype of this pattern is the urban Job Corps training center, financed by the federal government which contracted with private corporations to recruit staff, refurbish physical facilities, and manage the centers. Industry then turned to universities to help train personnel, and to advise and evaluate the operation. Presumably this type of coalition could expand its horizons beyond special groups (such as dropouts, unemployed, preschool disadvantaged, or Peace Corps and Vista volunteers) and try to reform all public education in the country at large.

We view with suspicion the emergence of national super-corporations' ventures into education production. It signifies a decreasing probability that education might be rooted in the concerns and pursuits of primary communities. It offers unprecedented possibilities for cultural uniformity, as the large coalitions sketch long-range plans for producing standardized educational kits or packages to be marketed throughout the nation. The packages will be designed within professionalized and bureaucratized organizations, singlemindedly devoted to educational "projects" as isolated goals. The society evidently assumes that because a government-industry-university coalition seems to have solved problems of economic affluence and defense, it should therefore be able to solve educational problems.

The resemblance of schools to corporate bureaucracies has a number of unfortunate consequences. (1) Because decisions are made at the top, the consumer or client (i.e., the student) has no assurance that the service offered by the corporate hierarchy (i.e., the school) will be responsive to his particular needs. In a social studies class, one student's brother has just been killed in Vietnam, another student has been harassed by classmates for dating a girl of a different race, the father of a third risks his job and family income by marching in a picket line, and the teacher, following instructions of his superior (the curriculum coordinator), dictates a lesson on the causes of the War of 1812. (2) The bureaucratic ethic discourages questioning and challenging fundamental assumptions. To get a job done, one needs a smooth-running machine that thrives on harmony and consensus, not dissonance and conflict. Students in hot disagreement with each other and even with the teacher could invite the wrath of parents upon school authorities. Such controversy would be seen as dysfunctional to the system. (3) Specialization and division of labor, another feature of corporate bureaucracy, leads to different subjects of study that fragment the student's intellectual experience. Conceivably, math, English, social studies, biology, and foreign language could collectively address controversial community issues — race relations, chemical biological warfare, natural resource pollution, or population control. Unfortunately, training teachers to fill specialized slots in the bureaucracy inhibits a holistic approach. (4) Text and test publishers, attempting to accommodate all interests in a national market, produce in effect a standard national curriculum, insensitive to public issues in specific localities.

Before proposing an alternative model, we will reiterate three major criticisms of the present education enterprise: (1) it fails to support as legitimate the rich educational potential available in noninstructional contexts; conversely, it conceives education narrowly as mainly formal instruction occurring in schools; (2) by becoming a compulsory public monopoly, it neglects the educational value of diverse public and private associations; and (3) it is organized by the model and motivated by the values of corporate industry and bureaucratic civil service.

E. Schooling and the Missing Community

Perhaps the most disturbing feature of contemporary education, aside from the obstacles it poses to studying public issues in schools, is its exacerbation of a more fundamental social malady: the missing community. To clarify our conception of missing community, we will contrast it with a popularized interpretation of America as "the Great Society."[4] A missing com-

---

[4] Gross (1966) presents a variety of interesting critiques.

munity interpretation notices effects of industrialization, urbanization, specialization, and technology that tend to destroy man's sense of relatedness, to disintegrate common bonds, to increase apathy, to depersonalize activities, and to reduce identity and meaning in the human career. In contrast, the vision of a great society exudes a sturdy optimism in man's progress, a desire to accelerate urbanization, technology, and economic development, on the assumption that such inevitable historical forces can be harnessed to make man more free and more secure to allow him to be more "human" than ever before. Education for the great society involves raising teacher salaries, building more schools, and using computers and audiovisual devices to supply training and meet the manpower needs of the "national interest." Seen from a missing community perspective, however, major objectives of education involve creating and nourishing diverse life styles that allow for significant choice in reconstructing community relationships — formal training and "national interest" are of minor importance.

But what do we mean by "community"? Conventional sociological definitions emphasize (1) households concentrated within a limited geographical area; (2) substantial social interaction between residents; and (3) a sense of common membership, of belonging together, not based exclusively on kinship ties. The essential criterion seems to be psychological — "a sense of common bond," sharing an identity, or holding things in common esteem (Inkeles, 1964, pp. 68–69). Communities frequently are identified by references to legal-political boundaries, ethnic groups, occupational classifications, or simply areas of residence. Standard definitions fail to distinguish among more specific criteria that *lead to* developing interaction or a sense of belonging. These criteria, for example, make it difficult to distinguish between a group and a community.

We offer more differentiated criteria, each of which is viewed as a continuum. Greater and lesser degrees of community are possible, depending upon the extent to which each criterion below is fulfilled. These criteria include attributes *valued by the authors* and encompass characteristics beyond those needed for a minimally adequate definition. We are concerned with pluralism in community and have provided for this in the definition (attribute 3, competing factions). Tightly knit groups do not necessarily allow competing factions; for example, the Puritans in Massachusetts Bay or the Amish in Pennsylvania. By our definition, such groups constitute less of a community than groups that tolerate more diverse conceptions of "the good life." A community is a group: (1) in which membership is valued as an end in itself, not merely as a means to other ends; (2) that concerns itself with many and significant aspects of the lives of members; (3) that allows competing factions; (4) whose members share commitment to common purposes and to procedures for handling conflict within the group; (5) whose members share responsibility for the actions of the group; and (6) whose members have enduring and extensive personal contact with each other. This working definition does not require that communities be distinguished from each other by such criteria as residence, political-legal unit, or occupational category.

As we speak of "missing community," we are constantly reminded of the folly of wishing to establish in the modern world communities similar to the traditional rural model. We are told either that such communities never did exist; or they may have existed, but they were certainly not very pleasant — on the contrary, that human life in the bygone community contained anxieties and problems more tragic than the ones we face today; or they may have existed and been delightful, but inevitable forces have pushed them aside and it is impossible to turn back the clock. Our definition, however, makes no such historical claims, nor does it implore a return to days of old. The only claim is that in the modern world, community (as defined above) is missing.

We do not suggest that associations and human groups have decreased. On the contrary, we find more organizations than ever before: professional associations, credit unions, churches, corporations, labor unions, civil rights groups, clubs, as well as families. Yet few, if any, of such groups fulfill our definition of community, mainly because each serves a relatively special and narrow function. The emergence of many institutions, each with specialized functions, has created discontinuities, such as the major one described by Nisbet (1962, p. 54):

> Our present crisis lies in the fact that whereas the small traditional associations, founded upon kinship, faith, or locality, are still expected to communicate to individuals the principal moral ends and psychological gratifications of society, they have manifestly become detached from positions of functional relevance to the larger economic and political decisions of our society. Family, local community, church, and the whole network of informal interpersonal relationships have ceased to play a determining role in our institutional systems of mutual aid, welfare, education, recreation, and economic production and distribution. Yet despite the loss of these manifest institutional functions, we continue to expect them to perform adequately the implicit psychological or symbolic functions in the life of the individual.

What institutions *do* perform psychological or symbolic functions necessary for viable community? In mass society few can be found, and Nisbet traces historical developments that account for their disappearance. He sees at the root of the problem the growth of a centralized economic and political system that, by concentrating on serving *individual* needs, has neglected and eroded community. Objectives of the "great society" provide selected products and services: housing, jobs, food, education, medical aid, transportation, and recreation for individuals; and centralized bureaucracies now meet many of these particular needs. But centralization and specialization have caused the breakdown of communication among differing groups, the rise of transient rather than enduring relationships among people, the disintegration of common bonds, and the reluctance to share collective responsibility. Whether it is possible to create new forms of community appropriate for urban and industrial society should be of great concern in planning for education.

But educators have not addressed themselves to this problem. In their zeal to provide quality education to the masses, they have ignored the effects of their institutions on the nature of community in society at large. Education is seen as a means, not an end, a product for each individual to "get" as he passes from class to class, grade to grade, school to school. This transient process (like the ladder of social mobility) denies students and teachers the opportunity to view each other as total human beings and interdependent community members. In school (and society) individuals relate to each other only for specialized purposes. Learning is compartmentalized into discrete, usually unrelated subjects served up in assembly-line style. Sharp differentiation between the provinces of school, private life, and community affairs militates against sharing responsibility. Students, unrepresented in governing education, and teachers forced to conform within a bureaucracy feel equally powerless. Centralized business and government coalitions create de facto national curricula and national achievement standards that make it difficult for local communities to develop unique approaches. The need for harmony and efficiency minimizes opportunities for competing factions to assert diverse educational models. In each of these ways prevailing assumptions and institutional structures in education reflect and contribute to the more general condition of missing community. The following proposal is a beginning attempt to view educational reform not as the introduction of new curriculum into schools, but as an effort to confront head-on the problem of developing community in mass society.

II. A Proposed Model for Education in Community

Because we believe that efforts at reform have generally failed to consider the fundamental importance of *contexts* in which education is pursued, we begin by conceptualizing alternative modes of, and environments for, learning.[5] Imagine a hypothetical community in which learning is pursued in three quite different contexts: the "school" context, the "laboratory-action-work" context, and the "community seminar" context. Subjects or

---

[5] A critique of current efforts at educational reform appears in Newmann and Oliver (1967).

problems for study and also student-teacher relations would be construed quite differently in each context.[6]

A. The School Context

Systematic instruction is clearly needed in basic communication skills, math, health and hygiene, etc. Learning of this sort is preplanned, programmed, and formalized. The teacher has clear outcomes, objectives, or "terminal behaviors" in mind as the products of instruction, and he hopes to assess the extent to which instruction results in the performance of the predetermined skills or competencies. Most activity in today's schools falls into this category. This is not to suggest that school-based learning should continue to follow traditional subject matter lines, nor that instruction be didactic and rote. On the contrary, school learning should be problem-centered and exciting and should constantly consider reorganizing basic content to make it lead toward more powerful insights and understandings; for example, coordinate and symbol systems used in graphs, charts, and maps might be combined with linguistic analysis and musical notation in teaching a course in symbolics. Technology has thrust upon us rich possibilities for more effective instruction through greater opportunity for self-instruction, availability of multi-media approaches, and more accurate assessment of student needs and progress. Teaching within a school context may take many forms: tutorial between teacher and student, student with computer or programmed instruction, students in small groups, or large groups watching films. The distinguishing feature of the school context is that it concerns itself only with those aspects of education involving systematic, planned instruction. We see this kind of learning as only *one* among three critical types.

B. Laboratory-Action-Work Context

In the laboratory context, the major objective is not formal instruction, but completing a significant task — solving problems that the learner wants to attack, regardless of educational by-products that dealing with the problem might bring. The physical location of the laboratory context might be a factory, art studio, hospital, library, science, or industrial laboratory, political party headquarters, or government agency. The activity of participants would be governed, not by a skill or a product that is programmed for students to learn, but only by the developing nature of the problem-task itself. Such problems might include painting a picture, rebuilding an auto, writing an essay, promoting a concert, organizing a protest demonstration, lobbying for legislation, selling insurance, programming a computer, acting in a play, nursing in a hospital, competing in a sport, participating in con-

---

[6] These "three contexts" are discussed in a mimeographed document, "Walden III," by Joseph C. Grannis and Donald W. Oliver, presented to a seminar at the Harvard Graduate School of Education, 1965. Similar ideas are also contained in an earlier paper by Grannis (1964).

servation and wildlife management, caring for children, planning and participating in a church service, broadcasting on radio and television, making a dress, printing a newspaper, making physical and chemical experiments, serving as a United Nations guide, organizing a raffle to raise money, or even creating instructional materials for use in a school context. Laboratories are contexts for learning in the midst of action; learning occurs not because it is planned, but only as an inevitable by-product of genuine participation in problem- and task-oriented activities. The laboratory is not seen primarily as apprenticeship or vocational training for breadwinning, but rather as the opportunity to satisfy broader humanistic and aesthetic goals. At present many adults are engaged in laboratory contexts — their jobs — that are not recognized or supported for their educational value. Young people are not deemed "ready" to participate until they first spend twelve to sixteen years in school. We believe the laboratory offers important educational benefits at all ages; it should not be restricted to adults.

C. Community Seminar Context

The purpose of the seminar is the reflective exploration of community issues. The seminar would provide an opportunity for heterogeneous or homogeneous groups to gather, for youth and/or adults to examine and discuss issues of mutual concern. Seminars might begin by focusing on problems specific to group members (e.g., the meaning of productive work for people unemployed, retired, or dissatisfied with their jobs). Discussion might be stimulated by outside provocateurs who present new ways to see economic, ethical, or aesthetic questions. Seminars could have at their service a qualified resource staff that would gather information (readings, films, television programs) and arrange such experiences as field trips to observe unfamiliar ways of life, technological innovations, or social problems in action. In addition to relatively specific problems (What kinds of working conditions are we entitled to?) and general public policy questions (How should the community be zoned?), we would hope that the seminars would concern themselves with the broadest questions raised in planning for education in community. Other possible topics include: understanding various conflicts between youth and adults, the functions of the family in modern society, attitudes toward nonconformity and deviance in the community, prejudice and pluralism among ethnic groups, changing mores in sex and religion, various approaches to child-rearing, using increased leisure, population control, consumer protection, moral implications of advances in biology (e.g., selective breeding), reconstructing the political and legal system, evaluating current programs sponsored by government and private agencies, creating new professions, and problems of vocational retraining. As in radio and television talk shows, in coffee houses, and church seminars, the major thrust is reflection and deliberation, although the questions discussed would be highly relevant to the laboratory "action" contexts. Learning in the seminar would not be preplanned, nor would there be specific tasks or problems to solve. Questions would be raised, investigated, and discussed. Regardless of numerous and unpredictable possible outcomes, this process is of high educational value. For the most part, both youth and adults are denied the kind of learning afforded by this context; school monopolizes the time of youth, jobs or "laboratories" monopolize adult time.

D. Points of Clarification

These contexts represent three critical facets of education: systematic instruction, action, and reflection. The facets are not listed in order of importance nor chronologically. All three should occur concurrently at all stages of life. A child learning to read in a school context can participate in a laboratory project of building a model airplane (using the symbolic skills acquired in "school"); he can also discuss with children and adults in a seminar what to do about noise control for the local airport. An adult interested in politics might study government systematically in school; he might participate in the "laboratory" of a political campaign; and in the community seminar, he might lead discussions on political organization appropriate for the modern community. Although some communities may choose to place most young children in the school context and allocate much adult education to the seminar, we see no logical reason for this particular arrangement. People of different ages can learn together in common contexts (adolescents teaching children how to read; adults and children in a beginners' ski class). The analytic distinctions between the three contexts is not meant to imply physical or experiential segregation. That is, all three contexts could conceivably be located in a school building, a city hall, a factory, or a home. The contexts should not be fragmented in the learner's mind as separate phases to pass through, although a thorough attack on most problems would require participation in each. Finally, we should not imply that the three contexts constitute a complete or exhaustive concept of education. We assume, for example, that significant learning and growth occurs in situations allowing for individual privacy, carefree play, and intimate interpersonal relations—situations where it makes little sense to construe experience as instruction, laboratory-action, or community reflection.

Who would fill the leadership roles in such an educational scheme? If formal school comprises only one-third of the educational program, would professional educators be put out of work? Possibly, but not necessarily. Those most qualified to carry on instruction may well be teachers and educators currently working in schools. Thus many teachers and administrators would stay in schools (although advances in technology suggest radical changes in their roles and jobs even if they do stay there). Because learning in school would occupy only a small portion of the student's day — perhaps three hours — one might expect school staffs to dwindle. If, however, adults also used the school for instruction, then the school's "student" population would increase, even though any given student spent only a small amount of time there. The demand for professional educators would remain high.

Leaders in the laboratory contexts would be persons with diverse experience and skills (engineers, lawyers, mechanics, poets, politicians, community organizers, journalists, athletes, secretaries) who would be given released time to take on educational responsibility for youth and adults interested in laboratory activity. It is possible that professional educators can be converted into laboratory leaders: for example, an English teacher could take on apprentices in writing poetry, but in his laboratory role, he would be interested primarily in creating and analyzing artistic works, not in teaching. The laboratory context would rely primarily upon private enterprise, government, the arts, labor, etc., to provide creative practitioners willing to assume on-the-job educational responsibility. If we are willing to recognize as teachers the vast number of talented practitioners in such fields, we shall approach a dramatic solution to the manpower problem of finding enough intelligent "teachers." By taking advantage of the educational value of the on-the-job activities, we may begin to break the stranglehold by which the education profession has restricted our conception of education.

Community seminars could be run by professional educators, businessmen, politicians, parents, laborers, policemen, boy scouts, gang leaders, criminals, musicians, or journalists. The community seminar, perhaps more than the school or laboratory, raises the issue of incentive. What would induce people to participate in such activities? The success of such programs depends upon the willingness of various organizations to provide released time for leaders and participants. Financial arrangements must ensure that such activities do not economically penalize participants. It would be reasonable to offer stipends for participation. Paying people to undergo training is already done on a large scale (neighborhood youth corps, Job Corps, scholarships and fellowships, prizes and rewards for high grades, training programs of businesses, etc.), and is quite consistent with the idea of making an investment in developing human resources. We would assume that, given the time and money, the tasks and issues explored in these contexts could be sufficiently exciting to attract wide participation.

A community concerned with implementing some of these general ideas would require coordinating several resources, including such private voluntary agencies as churches, businesses, museums, libraries, political parties, economic and political pressure groups, and social service organizations. It would require flexibility and attention to individual differences; yet, to avoid fragmentation or specialization, it would have to facilitate participation in common experiences through which members could relate across economic, racial, political, ethnic, or occupational lines.

Implementing a program along these lines seems at first glance an administrator's nightmare, involving coordinating disparate agencies and cooperating with conflicting vested interests. Will colleges recognize the value of laboratory and seminar experience in their admissions policies? Would the education establishment be willing to relinquish much of its control over the learning of youth? Would business accept for employment people with varying, rather than standardized educational bacgrounds? Who would have the power to accredit educational programs, and what new criteria would be needed? What if the three contexts evolved into an educational bureaucracy as rigid as the present one, with tight scheduling and compartmentalization equal to, or worse than, the current system?

At the moment we have no solutions to these problems and are well aware of the difficulties they raise. Moreover, we hesitate to suggest specific plans or models, because we feel these should arise from the basic concerns of particular communities. We envision no national model that could be replicated across the land. Instead, a plurality of structures and programs should develop. Jencks (1966) has suggested ways in which private groups could compete with each other and with the public education establishment by offering qualitatively different types of education, sensitive to community needs. In a single community, schools, laboratories, and seminars might be run by businesses, parents' groups, teachers, and churches — each competing with each other for students. It should be possible to fund competing enterprises without allowing a single centralized bureaucracy to gain total control. In some communities, literacy training may be a major problem (e.g., an urban slum); in others technical retraining (e.g., an area with a rapidly growing electronics industry); other areas may have particularly acute problems in human relations, or even in using leisure time.

Basing education on the needs of particular communities does not imply that students (youths and adults) are being trained for life within that community only. On the contrary, with communication and transportation breakthroughs likely to continue, all communities are becoming more dependent upon each other; their problems are therefore increasingly generalizable. Producing a television program to publicize the plight of migrant workers involves the same considerations as producing a program to plead for better equipment for the local football team. Organizing tenants to protest against landlords involves processes similar to organizing real estate brokers to protest to Congress. Painting a picture of harvest time is in many ways similar to painting a scene of industrial smokestacks. Discussing the boring process of cotton picking may be helpful in a later discussion on the meaning of work in an assembly-line. We see no reason to be alarmed that a community's education be focused on critical contemporary issues.

E. The Search for Examples

Communities interested in pursuing "tri-school" experiments would benefit from examining current and previous projects consistent with the model. Unfortunately, we have not been able to locate many exemplary efforts. Some worthwhile ventures have attacked parts of the problem, however. Using "para-professionals" has broadened somewhat our conception of who is qualified to teach. That is, to solve school staffing problems, we are now turning to the elderly, the disadvantaged, the suburban housewife, the "noncertified" Peace Corps volunteers. There are some efforts to decentralize school administration and allow education to become the concern of citizens in the immediate locale served by a school (e.g., the community control controversy in New York). For community service or vocational exploration some high schools have placed students in apprentice roles in hospitals, schools, day care centers, and businesses. A few teachers and principals have allowed students to venture out of school to attend community meetings, interview public officials, conduct opinion surveys related to public issues. Businesses, civic, and religious groups and neighborhood and community centers have offered interesting programs and workshops beyond the school walls for adults and children. Private schools in the progressive tradition, and recently modeled after Summerhill or the Leicestershire Infant Schools, have allowed students to learn freely according to intrinsic interests. These scattered but valuable efforts confront aspects of the larger problem. But we are unaware of any community-wide attempt to shift significantly the emphasis in public education from formal instruction (however ungraded, team-taught, or modularly scheduled) to a multicontext approach that focuses not merely on training youth, but on broader issues in building community.[7]

III. Applying Education and Community Model to Study of Public Issues[8]

Given our observations on education and community, what would be an appropriate format for studying public issues? Clarifying public controversy in a classroom can become as sterile and irrelevant as more traditional curriculum if it is not related to the student's role as a citizen facing dilemmas in and obstacles to his exercise of power in the community.

[7] A project worthy of attention is Philadelphia's Parkway Program, which disperses students into the community for their total ninth through twelfth grade curriculum, and claims not even to have a central school building or classrooms. Contact Parkway Program, 1801 Market Street, Philadelphia, Pennsylvania 19103.

[8] Most of this section is quoted and adapted from Newmann (1968).

A. Critique of
   Current
   Curriculum

1. Misleading
   Conceptions
   of Political
   Process

The part of school instruction relevant to the political process (courses in history and government, student government activity, etc.) emphasizes a formal, legalistic view of public affairs based on the Constitution (representation, separation of powers, checks and balances), local and state government organization, and the procedures by which a bill becomes a law or a case goes to court. In such instruction, a patriotic acceptance and admiration of American institutions minimizes persistent, divisive value conflicts and problems of social injustice. The effects of administrative bureaucracies, big business, labor, the mass media, the church, popular protest movements, or pressure groups on political process are largely neglected, except for passing references to "lobbyists" and "interest groups." The significance of personal ambitions, motives, and passions in forming public policy is ignored. Newer courses reflecting behavioristic interests in political science (despite their use of "case studies") emphasize abstract models or methods of inquiry rather than the interplay of concrete human choices in political life. Teachers stress learning facts or explaining phenomena, rather than taking a stand and justifying one's position. Finally, contemporary explosive issues — civil rights or Vietnam — are given only the most superficial "coverage" in once-a-week current events classes.

Outside school we may learn "the way it is" through more realistic portrayals in the media, occasional personal encounters, or active political involvement. Many become disillusioned with the education that misled them and cynical toward the society that sponsored it. Those who accept the large dose of misinformation may never know how powerless they are. Others conclude that politics is either too dirty or too complicated and thus make a conscious personal decision not to become involved. A small minority (for various reasons) does take the plunge and learns about politics in the heat of action, often at considerable risks to their educational credentials, vocational advancement, and family life.

2. Neglect of
   Action

By teaching that the American constitutional system guarantees a benevolent government serving the needs of all, the schools have fostered massive public apathy. Whereas the Protestant ethic calls for engagement (to survive economically one must *earn* his living), the political creed breeds passivity. One need not struggle for political rights, but only maintain a vague level of vigilance, obey the laws, make careful choices in elections, perform a few duties (taxes, military service), and his political welfare is assured.

Yet rebellions in the cities and universities and the Vietnam protest movement indicate that important segments of the population are awakening to demand a voice in the formation of policy, both as a value unto itself and as requisite to attaining other values: equal economic opportunity, academic freedom, freedom of conscience, or international peace. Although widespread affluence satisfies many, and those in secure positions of power have few complaints, such abuses as invasion of privacy, inadequate standards for consumer health and safety, substandard housing, crime, and destruction of property illustrate dire consequences for individuals who, instead of aggressively acting to wield power, trust and wait for the system to guard their rights and serve their needs.

Because young people are considered not sufficiently mature or responsible, and because education is assumed to result primarily from detached reflection rather than committed action, schools and other institutions deter the young from political engagement. Teachers who do discuss controversial issues are known to pride themselves on a posture of neutrality or "objectivity." So as not to "indoctrinate" students they deliberately restrain themselves from indulging in opinions and arguments characteristic of impassioned political involvement. Yet this stance itself constitutes indoctrination — attributing evil, danger, or at least intellectual irresponsibility to personal commitment and action. Though schools do support nonacademic "action" — sports, music, hobby clubs, and student government — it occurs under paternalistic adult supervision that denies students reponsibility and that is limited to safe, noncontroversial enterprises. What schools would be willing to give "credit" for participating in a civil rights campaign, leading a movement to gain more elective courses in the curriculum, helping pass a resolution in the local Republican committee, or trying to persuade the police department to launch an antinarcotics campaign?

Adults too are limited in opportunities for activism because of the constraints of a job, raising a family, and social mores that frown upon "politics." Neither the schools, the business and labor communities, the professions, nor the churches (though this may be changing) offer significant opportunities or incentives for involvement. Ironically, the democratic rhetoric calls for a politically active citizenry, but its institutions perpetuate apathy.

B. Proposals

Mindful that agencies other than schools must also assume leaderhip in education for activism, we propose the following first steps that might be taken by secondary schools and colleges.[9]

1. Reality-Oriented Courses in School

New courses should be developed on uses of political power in various contexts: legislatures, courts, bureaucracies, voluntary associations, neighborhoods, churches. Instructional materials and strategies must be designed to aid studying tactical and moral dilemmas in the exercise of power. The formal, legalistic, and abstract picture of government that now dominates

---

[9] The proposals assume issues and activities more relevant to adolescents and adults than to children, though elementary education has an obligation to offer instruction at least not inconsistent with the goal of maximizing the individual's ability to wield political power.

curriculum should be balanced (if not replaced) by emphasizing the influence of personal motives and ambitions, emotions (envy, hate, love, pride), political debts, accidents, and even honest mistakes in the formation of public policy. In this regard, using such artistic media as novels, feature films, plays, or television documentaries would help to offer more holistic and human conceptions of politics than the Constitution or textbooks provide. Academic disciplines, particularly social sciences, should be searched for findings and theories relevant to personal decisions in the use of power; these would be included, not as means for teaching disciplines or inquiry, but as tools for more effective political action. By closely examining concrete personal consequences, reality-oriented courses could bring local, national, and international issues to life in the classroom. Such courses, while presenting introductory material for understanding political life, would at the same time stimulate students to participate in action projects beyond the classroom.

2. Action Experiences in the Field

If developing positions on public issues is to be meaningful, it must be related to experiences that improve the citizen's ability to exercise power in the political system, not only within such obvious political contexts as parties, legislatures, or city halls, but in and upon all institutions — hospitals, universities, businesses, the military, social service bureaucracies, courts — that influence his life. An individual may wish to learn techniques for functioning more effectively within established institutions (e.g., knowing how to identify and persuade the most powerful person in an agency dealing with a given grievance) or for fundamentally changing the institutions themselves (i.e., the more revolutionary methods aimed at social change: civil disobedience, strikes, "subversion"). In either case, learning would be directed toward helping the individual gain more direct control over public decisions that affect him.

This is not to suggest that students unwilling, apathetic, or apolitical should be required to become passionately committed activists. The intention is only to provide more meaningful opportunities than are now available for those who wish to engage in different types of action. It is difficult to know whether those to benefit most would be deprived minorities (Negroes and the poor), disenfranchised majorities (consumers, students), or what. One might predict, however, that increased leisure, combined with the expanding role of the public sector in meeting human services, might transform heretofore dormant topics (hair length or auto insurance) into live political issues about which the average citizen will be seriously concerned.

Willing students should receive educational credit for participation in causes of their choice, and the school must arrange enough flexibly allocated time to make this effective. So as not to imply a conception of activism denoted exclusively by more spectacular, quasi-anarchic forms of group protest (draft resistance, student strikes, mass civil disobedience), this proposal recognizes significant educational value in the following "causes": efforts to redress grievances of individuals against bureaucracies (unreasonable treatment by registries of motor vehicles, draft boards, schools, employers, welfare departments); community improvement projects (recreation facilities, pollution control, interfaith cooperation, housing rehabilitation, curriculum reform); and even promoting parochial "personal fulfillment" interests of individuals and associations (drama, music, and sports clubs struggling for finances and facilities, organizing a neighborhood day care center, or entrepreneurs starting in business). Depending upon the constraints of the situation and the student's interest, his involvement could range from detached study and observation in the field to apprenticeship to leadership. It will be necessary to learn to use conventional lines of influence: election campaigning, behind-the-scenes lobbying, testifying, letter-writing, publicity campaigns, and canvassing, as well as more subtle and dramatic techniques. Whatever the project, the purpose for including it in an educational program is to help the individual operate more effectively within the political system, not to provide charity or service to the community, though individuals should be free to choose that sort of project if they wish. Programs established along these lines must be sensitive to the fact that individuals have differing needs and contexts within which activism becomes relevant: a middle-class student may want to work to change university policy, while the working-class ghetto dweller may wish to focus on urban renewal housing policy.

For these experiences to be meaningful, the school would have to share supervisory responsibility with such agencies as political parties, ad hoc protest committees, churches, student organizations, or various pressure groups. School administrators must recognize the educational legitimacy of student action that attacks (or supports) school policy itself (protest over cafeteria food, dress codes, disciplines, curriculum, recruiting policy, etc.). A community resource specialist could be hired to seek out action possibilities in the community, inform students of opportunities, and work with action groups and agencies to assess the educational merit of student involvement. Action in the field would bring continuing controversy into the school: Should schools give credit for participation in fund-raising projects for the local heart association, but deny it to a group advocating draft resistance? Allowing such disputes to flourish, with student and community participation to establish procedures and criteria for "approving" projects, would in itself be worthwhile education in the use of power.

3. Counseling for Action

As opportunities for serious personal involvement become available, students are likely to face difficult choices, bringing high levels of anxiety that call for assistance from sympathetic professional counselors. The professional should himself be schooled in the realities of political action, clinically trained to deal with crises and choices of students, and he should have access to information on long-term vocational or "career" possibilities appropriate for the youthful activist. Questions discussed between student and counselor could include: Am I being pushed into something I don't believe in just to go along with my friends? How can I handle conflict in my family that my political involvement causes? Should I flee to Canada to avoid the draft, work on draft resistance here, or obey the law and work within the system to change it? The counselor would be a source of confidential and reasonably objective discussion of alternative actions and their consequences in the light of an individual's interests, abilities, personality, and unique place in the social world. Such counseling, *not* conceived as therapy for patients who need continuing treatment, might be useful for activists at large, unaffiliated with any school program.

4. Community Seminars

Students (and nonstudents) engaged in diverse action projects should have the chance to: (1) reflect upon questions of feasibility, prudence, morality, etc., relevant to their current commitments or projects; and (2) meet with activists of different (but not necessarily antagonistic) interests to gain information and perspective on other causes and contexts for action. Both the in-group (1) and the heterogeneous (2) seminars would be intended as brief retreats from the action front for the purpose of assessing more carefully the appropriate direction and meaning of one's involvement.

C. Implementation

Implementation will involve several problems: locating the talent to restructure and teach new courses; creating the new professional roles of community resource specialist and action counselor; administering action projects and community seminars; and persuading colleges or employers to accept the educational value of action projects on a par with other extracurricular activities. Nevertheless a case can be made for the feasibility of these innovations. Considerable difficulties will be avoided by the provision that such programs are not intended as mandatory for all students, though an introductory course on political process and public issues could reasonably be required. The voluntary nature of the program not only alleviates scheduling problems, but also eliminates the danger of forcing students into projects irrelevant to their vital interests. Although the community resource office would try to offer the widest range of possibilities, there would be no obligation to create artificial causes simply to involve students. Colleges in the past have admitted students with unconventional secondary school preparation (the Eight Year study of progressive education in the thirties) and they do so at present.

A problem far more serious than the obvious ones suggested above is the possibility that programs will be administered in such a way as to reduce conflict (allowing the heart fund, but not Black Panthers) and to encourage activism just for the sake of playing the game (by setting up rigid standards of supervision, propagating a school "party line," or other subtle forms of paternalism). To the extent that students choose action experiences to please school authorities or enhance their dossiers rather than out of genuine need to protect and advance intrinsic interests, activism becomes a farce.

To sense the feasibility of these proposals, even in a relatively traditional school, consider the following imaginary situation:

Disturbed about student complaints of "irrelevant education" in history and social studies courses, Mr. Brown, principal of Downtown High, invited some of his concerned teachers, along with an activist educator from a nearby university and several people in the community, to collect materials for a new course in politics along lines recommended here. They reviewed novels like *The Last Hurrah* and excerpts from television programs such as "Public Broadcasting Laboratory" and "Slattery's People," and asked local activists to write about and tape-record experiences in Downtown's affairs. Within a year they had assembled a library of realistic cases and made suggestions for a new course which they began to teach experimentally to seniors.

Mr. Jackson, a teacher interested in community issues, was given released time to investigate possibilities for student involvement in the community. First he interviewed students, and after learning their interests, contacted businessmen, politicians, bureaucrats, and clergymen, many of whom expressed a desire to participate. College admission officers told Jackson that community action projects on students' records would not jeopardize their chances for higher education.

Brown appointed a committee that represented students, teachers, and diverse community interests. Chaired by Mr. Jackson, the committee evaluated proposals of five seniors who had applied. Jones wanted to organize a group to press for a city-built drag strip and he knew some businessmen who would help. Burton wanted to work on the campaign for alderman and had received a go-ahead from Mr. Greene, his chosen candidate, to organize student canvassing. Wicker, with the support of an English teacher, proposed founding a civil rights organization in the school. Kaplan, interested in procedures for handling juvenile delinquents, had persuaded a local judge to accept him as an "apprentice." These projects were approved. One was rejected: Johnson wanted to organize a community protest to fire a teacher who he charged was a racist. The committee said Johnson failed to produce enough evidence to support the charge.

Mr. Jackson, in conference with his committee and each student, established guidelines for the projects. The school board required parents to release school authorities from legal responsibilities when students were off premises. Because the school had begun flexible scheduling these students could take major instruction early in the day. By excusing them from study halls, much of the afternoon was free so the students were released (as were athletes and participants in other extracurricular activities). The project students could also be excused for a few full days if situations required more sustained continuous involvement (assuming they made up work in their major subjects). Conferences were to be held periodically with Mr. Jackson, and the committee if necessary, to evaluate progress.

During the election campaign, Mr. Brown received a call from Henry Tierney, the candidate for alderman opposing Mr. Greene. Tierney complained that by supporting Burton's action project the school was endorsing a candidate for office and using students to exert political influence. "Schools should be impartial," Tierney charged. "As a public institution you have no right to take partisan sides in elections. Why should I pay tax money for the education of students who are trying to defeat my bid for public office? This nonsense better stop or I'll see to it that school board members supporting it have a rough time when *they* come up for election." In conference over this issue, Mr. Jackson, members of the school board, and Mr. Brown decided not to withdraw support from Burton's project. They felt it had legitimate educational value and did not represent the school's endorsement of a candidate. In his reply to Mr. Tierney, Brown pointed out that students who wished to work on his behalf would be given equal opportunity to do so.

As students reported their experiences, and as the politics course stirred excitement, twenty-four other seniors (in a class of four hundred) submitted action proposals. Mr. Jackson requested professional assistance—an action counselor to discuss students' personal problems and choices so that Jackson would be free to handle administrative matters. Adults began to question teachers, students, and community people about the program. In response, Jackson's committee organized a community seminar in which concerned citizens were invited to discuss the program's merit and prospects for the future. School officials were seriously concerned that the program might be expanding too rapidly. They hoped that through the community seminar they could establish communication among various sectors, and thereby gain support for continuing their efforts to improve political education.

It is problematic whether the general three-context model for education in community or this specific hypothetical account represents likely directions for educational reform. Critics raise troublesome questions: How much time would students spend in school? Would the rest of their time be completely free or planned and supervised in some way? Who would pay for extracurricular activities? How could adults be released from their jobs to take responsibility for community education? How would legal authority be allocated among community agencies? Would state departments of education change their requirements? Would colleges accept students with this sort of education? Would the students perform better on standard tests and attain standards of "excellence" comparable, for example, to European education? Can we demonstrate that education organized around these ideas would have any real pay-off in later life?

To deal directly with such questions at this point would be inappropriate. Until people in a community have argued about and accepted some premises of this book and are vitally concerned with implementation for their particular situation, it would be foolhardy for armchair professors to prescribe programs. Providing blueprints in the abstract, not tied to a specific situation, would be inconsistent with our premise that education should arise from real needs and issues within community, not from the drawing boards of distant national planners.

We may be chastized for evading the issue of practicality, as critics despair at our "unrealistic," "unfeasible" ideas. This criticism and preceding questions reflect a commitment by critics to the present system, a reluctance to search for fundamental deficiencies in the status quo. The major issue from our point of view is not our inability to give blueprints and specific answers to such questions. Financial, logistic, and administrative problems of diverse educational contexts should not detain us at the outset. The immediate issue is whether or not we can find people willing to begin serious discussion on premises and ideas rather than only on blueprints and programs. The next step lies not in a more concrete plan, but in a *search for a group of people,* some "missing community," with the courage and energy to reexamine how education, most broadly conceived as the interaction between reflection and action, can invigorate the lives of all its citizens. Clarifying public issues in the conventional classroom, however faithful to jurisprudential reasoning, rational dialogue, use of case studies, and serious consideration of students' views will risk a lack of relevance that can be corrected only by a community's willingness to test the potential of new educational models.

BIBLIOGRAPHY

Almond, Gabriel A. *The American People and Foreign Policy.* New York: Praeger, 1960.

Archibald, David. "Certain Aspects of the Validity of a Content Analysis System for the Evaluation of Public Controversy." Unpublished doctoral dissertation, Harvard Graduate School of Education, 1965.

Ardrey, Robert. *Territorial Imperative: A Personal Inquiry into the Animal Origins of Property and Nations.* New York: Atheneum, 1966.

Baier, Kurt. *The Moral Point of View: A Rational Basis of Ethics.* New York: Random House, 1965.

Bailyn, B. *Education in the Forming of American Society: Needs and Opportunities for Study.* New York: Vintage, 1960.

Benn, S. I., and R. S. Peters. *The Principles of Political Thought.* New York: Free Press, 1965.

Berelson, Bernard, and Gary A. Steiner. *Human Behavior: An Inventory of Scientific Findings.* New York: Harcourt, Brace & World, 1964.

Berelson, Bernard, P. F. Lazarsfeld, and W. N. McPhee. *Voting: A Study of Opinion Formation in a Presidential Campaign.* Chicago: Univ. Chicago Press, 1954.

Berlak, Harold. "The Construct Validity of a Content Analysis System for the Evaluation of Critical Thinking in Political Controversy." Unpublished doctoral dissertation, Harvard Graduate School of Education, 1963.

———. "The Teaching of Thinking." *School Review,* 73 (1965): 1–13.

Blanshard, Brand. "Morality and Politics." In *Ethics and Society: Original Essays on Contemporary Moral Problems,* edited by Richard T. De George. New York: Anchor, 1966.

Bolster, Arthur Stanley. "History, Historians, and the Secondary School Curriculum." *Harvard Educational Review,* 32 (1962): 39–65.

Brandt, Richard B., ed. *Social Justice.* Englewood Cliffs, N.J.: Prentice-Hall, 1962.

Brown, B. F. *The Nongraded High School.* Englewood Cliffs, N.J.: Prentice-Hall, 1963.

Bruner, Jerome S. *The Process of Education.* New York: Vintage, 1960.

———. *Toward a Theory of Instruction.* Cambridge, Mass.: Harvard University Press, 1966.

Burdick, E., and A. J. Brodbeck, eds. *American Voting Behavior.* Glencoe, Ill.: Free Press, 1959.

Cahn, Edmond. *The Predicament of Democratic Man.* New York: Macmillan, 1961.

Callahan, R. E. *Education and the Cult of Efficiency: A Study of the Social Forces that have Shaped the Administration of the Public Schools.* Chicago: Univ. Chicago Press, 1962.

Campbell, Angus, Gerald Gurin, and W. E. Miller. *The Voter Decides.* Evanston, Ill.: Row, Peterson, 1954.

Conant, J. B. *The American High School Today.* New York: McGraw-Hill, 1959.

———. *The Education of American Teachers.* New York: McGraw-Hill, 1963.

———. *Shaping Educational Policy.* New York: McGraw-Hill, 1964.

Cremin, Lawrence A. *The Transformation of the School: Progressivism in American Education, 1876–1957.* New York: Vintage, 1964.

Dewey, John. *The Child and the Curriculum.* Chicago: Univ. Chicago Press, 1902.

———. *The School and Society.* Chicago: Univ. Chicago Press, 1900.

———. *How We Think.* Boston: Heath, 1933.

Domhoff, G. William. *Who Rules America?* Englewood Cliffs, N.J.: Prentice-Hall, 1967.

Edel, Abraham. *Ethical Judgment: The Use of Science in Ethics.* New York: Free Press, 1955.

Ellis, A. B. "Multivariate Analyses and Computer Techniques Applied to the Evaluation of Critical Thinking." Unpublished doctoral dissertation, Harvard Graduate School of Education, 1963.

Elkins, Stanley. *Slavery: A Problem in American Institutional and Intellectual Life.* Chicago: Univ. Chicago Press, 1959.

Encyclopedia of Philosophy. Edited by Paul Edwards. New York: Macmillan, 1967.

Ennis, Robert H. "A Concept of Critical Thinking." *Harvard Educational Review,* 32 (1962): 81–111.

———. *Logic in Teaching,* Englewood Cliffs, N.J.: Prentice-Hall, 1969.

Erikson, Erik H. *Identity: Youth and Crisis.* New York: Norton, 1968.

———. "Youth: Fidelity and Diversity." *Daedalus,* 91 (1962): 5–27.

Fletcher, Joseph. *Situation Ethics: The New Morality.* Philadelphia: Westminster, 1966.

Frankena, William K. *Ethics.* Englewood Cliffs, N.J.: Prentice-Hall, 1963.

Fuller, Lon. *The Morality of Law.* New Haven: Yale Univ. Press, 1964.

Galbraith, John Kenneth. *The New Industrial State.* Boston: Houghton Mifflin, 1967.

Grannis, J. C. "Team Teaching and the Curriculum." In *Team Teaching,* edited by J. T. Shaplin and H. F. Olds. New York: Harper & Row, 1964.

Green, Thomas F. "Education and Pluralism: Ideal and Reality." J. Richard Street Lecture, School of Education, Syracuse University, 1966.

———. "Schools and Communities: A Look Forward." *Harvard Educational Review,* 39 (1969): 221–252.

Gross, Bertram M., ed. *A Great Society?* New York: Basic Books, 1966.

Harris, Errol E. "Respect for Persons." In *Ethics and Society: Original Essays on Contemporary Moral Problems,* edited by Richard T. De George. New York: Anchor, 1966.

Hero, A. O. *Americans in World Affairs: Studies in Citizen Participation in International Relations,* vol. 1. Boston: World Peace Foundation, 1959.

Hofstadter, Albert. "The Career Open to Personality: the Meaning of Equality of Opportunity for an Ethics of Our Time." In *Aspects of Human Equality,* edited by L. Bryson, C. H. Faust, L. Finkelstein, and R. M. MacIver. 15th Symposium of Conference on Science, Philosophy and Religion. New York: Harper, 1956.

Hullfish, H. Gordon, and Philip G. Smith. *Reflective Thinking: The Method of Education.* New York: Dodd, Mead, 1961.

Hunt, Maurice P., and Lawrence Metcalf. *Teaching High School Social Studies.* New York: Harper & Row, 1968.

Inkeles, Alex. *What is Sociology: An Introduction to the Discipline and Profession.* Englewood Cliffs, N.J.: Prentice-Hall, 1964.

International Encyclopedia of Social Science. Edited by David Sills. New York: Macmillan, 1968.

Jencks, Christopher. "Is the Public School Obsolete?" *Public Interest,* Winter 1966, 18–27.

Kallen, H. M. "Democracy and the Melting Pot." In *Immigration: An American Dilemma,* edited by B. M. Ziegler. Boston: Heath, 1953.

Kaplan, Abraham. *The Conduct of Inquiry: Methodology for Behavioral Science.* San Francisco: Chandler, 1964.

Kelly, George. *The Psychology of Personal Constructs.* Vol. 1. New York: Norton, 1955.

Kimball, S. T., and J. E. McClellan. *Education and the New America.* New York: Random House, 1962.

Klein, Herbert S. *Slavery in the Americas: A Comparative Study of Cuba and Virginia.* Chicago: Univ. Chicago Press, 1967.

Kohlberg, Lawrence. "The Child as a Moral Philosopher." *Psychology Today,* 2 (1968): 24–30.

Kolko, Gabriel. *Wealth and Power in America: An Analysis of Social Class and Income Distribution.* New York: Praeger, 1962.

Lane, Robert E. *Political Ideology: Why the Common Man Believes What He Does.* New York; Free Press, 1962.

Lee, Irving. *How Do You Talk About People?* New York: Anti-Defamation League of B'nai B'rith, 1956.

Levi, Edward H. *An Introduction to Legal Reasoning.* Chicago: Univ. Chicago Press, 1948.

Levin, Malcolm. "Some Criteria for Evaluating Dialogues About Controversial Issues." Unpublished doctoral dissertation, Harvard Graduate School of Education, 1968.

———, Fred M. Newmann, and Donald W. Oliver. *A Law and Social Science Curriculum Based on the Analysis of Public Issues.* Report to U.S. Office of Education, Bureau of Research, 1969. Available through English ERIC, U.S. Office of Education.

Lichtman, Richard. "Toward Community: A Criticism of Contemporary Capitalism." An occasional paper. Santa Barbara, Calif.: Center for the Study of Democratic Institutions, 1966.

Lindsay, A. D. *The Modern Democratic State.* London: Oxford Univ. Press, 1943.

Lorenz, Conrad. *On Aggression*. New York: Harcourt, Brace & World, 1966.

Lundberg, Ferdinand. *The Rich and the Super-Rich*. New York: Bantam, 1968.

Mills, C. Wright. *The Power Elite*. New York: Oxford Univ. Press, 1956.

Mink, Louis O. "The Autonomy of Historical Understanding." *History and Theory*. 5 (1965): 24–47.

Myrdal, Gunnar. *An American Dilemma: The Negro Problem in Modern Democracy*, New York: Harper & Row, 1944.

Newmann, Fred M. "Consent of the Governed and Citizenship Education in Modern America." *School Review*, 71 (1963): 404–424.

———. "Discussion on Political Socialization." *Harvard Educational Review*, 38 (1968): 536–545.

———. "Questioning the Place of Social Science Disciplines in Education." *Teachers College Record*, 69 (1967): 69–74.

———, and Donald W. Oliver. "Education and Community." *Harvard Educational Review*, 37 (1967): 61–106.

Nisbet, Robert A. *Community and Power*. New York: Oxford Univ. Press, 1962.

Olafson, Frederick A., ed. *Justice and Social Policy*. Englewood Cliffs, N.J.: Prentice-Hall, 1961.

Oliver, Donald W. "The Selection of Content in the Social Studies." *Harvard Educational Review*, 27 (1957): 271–300.

Oliver, Donald W., and James P. Shaver. *Teaching Public Issues in the High School*. Boston: Houghton Mifflin, 1966.

Piaget, Jean. *The Moral Judgment of the Child*. New York: Collier, 1962.

Plamenatz, John P. "Equality of Opportunity." In *Aspects of Human Equality*, edited by L. Bryson, C. H. Faust, L. Finkelstein, and R. M. MacIver. 15th Symposium of the Conference on Science, Philosophy and Religion. New York. Harper, 1956.

———. *Consent, Freedom and Political Obligation*. London: Oxford Univ. Press, 1968.

Rickover, H. G. *Education and Freedom*. New York: Dutton, 1960.

Robinson, James Harvey. Quoted in Earnest Beaglehole. *Property: A Study in Social Psychology*. London: George Allen & Unwin Ltd., 1932, p. 7.

Roszak, Theodore, ed. *The Dissenting Academy*. New York: Pantheon, 1968.

Schwab, Joseph J. *College Curriculum and Student Protest*. Chicago: Univ. Chicago Press, 1969.

———. "Problems, Topics, and Issues." In *Education and the Structure of Knowledge*, edited by Stanley Elam. Chicago: Rand McNally, 1964.

Scriven, Michael. *Primary Philosophy*. New York: McGraw-Hill, 1966, Chap. 7.

Shaver, James P. "A Curriculum Focused on Thinking Reflectively About Public Issues." Interim report to U.S. Office of Education, Bureau of Research, September 1968. Contact James P. Shaver, Bureau of Educational Research, Utah State University, Logan, Utah 84321.

———, and Harold Berlak, eds. *Democracy, Pluralism and the Social Studies: Readings and Commentary*. Boston: Houghton Mifflin, 1968.

Smith, B. O. "Report on Critical Thinking Project." Mimeographed. Urbana, Ill.: School of Education, University of Illinois, undated. See especially Chap. III, "Critical Thinking Abilities: Their Scope and Sequence."

Smith, M. Brewster, Jerome S. Bruner, and Robert H. White. *Opinions and Personality*. New York: Wiley, 1956.

Stone, Julius. *Human Law and Justice*. London: Stevens & Sons, 1965.

Thelen, Herbert A. *Education and the Human Quest*. New York: Harper & Row, 1960.

Williams, Bernard. "The Idea of Equality." In *Philosophy, Politics and Society*, edited by Peter Laslett and W. G. Runceman. New York: Barnes & Noble, 1962.

Zelermyer, William. *The Process of Legal Reasoning*. Englewood Cliffs, N.J.: Prentice-Hall, 1960.

INDEX

abolitionists, see Fugitive Slave Law

accommodation (of conflicting interests), 86

action, vs belief, 162; counseling for, 341–342; in education, 332–333, 338–345; vs inaction in responsibility, 114–115

ad hominem, in discussion, 76–77

adults, need for education, 316, 332–334

advocate, teacher as, 294

age, discrimination by, 133

Almond, Gabriel A., 193

American Creed, 11–19

American Education Publications (AEP), 28, 86, 116n, 123n, 141n, 170n, 177n, 197n, 202n, 204n, 222n, 229n, 237–240, 243–245, 250–254, 256, 263, 287, 288

American Indians, case on, 229–230

Amish, case on, 202–204

analogy, exercises on, 276–277; to explore consistency, 46, 47; illustrated use of, 46–47, 78, 265, 267–270, 280–281, 302–303; function in argument, 264–270; problems of relevance, 77–78; use in outlines, 271–273

analytic thinking, vs discussion performance, 312; exercises for, 287–293; two-level thinking in discussion, 71

anthropology, 87

Archibald, David, 283

Ardrey, Robert, 216

atheists, case on, 204–206

authorities, see source and authority

authority, as source of evidence, 59

autonomy, see freedom of choice

Baier, Kurt, 90

Bailyn, B., 314

belief systems, 66–68

beliefs, discrimination by, 134

beneficence, basis for moral judgment, 96

Benn, S. I., 131

Berelson, Bernard, 68, 193

Berlak, Harold, 10, 68, 283

bias, and neutrality in classroom, 32–33, 293–296; in organization of content, 249–250

birth, discrimination by, 133–134; and inheritance as basis for ownership, 212

Black nationalism, 66

Black separatism, discussion question, 152

blame, and responsibility, 109–115

Blanshard, Brand, 90

Bolster, Arthur Stanley, 70

bootstrap, approach to poverty, 219

Brandt, Richard B., 90

Brodbeck, A. J., 193

Brown, B. F., 317

Brown v. Board of Education, Topeka et al., 145

Bruner, Jerome S., 67, 314, 316

Burdick, E., 193

bureaucracy, as threat to consent, 21

Cahn, Edmond, 114

Callahan, R. E., 324

Campbell, Angus, 193

cases: Black Boy, 116–122; Businessmen: the NRA, 222–227; Can Separate Be Equal, 143–145; The Case of Homer Plessy, 141–143; The Case of Sharon Garber, 202–204; The Case of William Murray, 204–206; The Case of the Woodville Barber, 274; Facing the Mob in Little Rock, 146–151; The Fugitive Slave Law; 197–200; Halberg Goes Nazi, 123–127; Mrs. Webster's Rooming House, 264; The Mutiny Act, 36–41; Oppenheimer: Scientist Accused, 177–182; The Pullman Strike, 170–175; A Tale of the Tuscarora, 229–230

cases, types, 238–239

causation, as determinism, 107

cause, in determining responsibility, 91–92, 107–108